The Glory of the Great Goddess in
LALITHĀ SAHASRANĀMAM

Thanks to Sringeri Vidya Bharati Foundation, North (*svbfnorth.org*), Detroit, MI, USA for the opportunity to participate in

the **"Vande Vidya Shankaram - Lecture Series."**

Subi Subramanian

ISBN 979-8-89544-894-6

The Viswa Roopam (Cosmic Form) of the Great Mother
Goddess Sri Sivakāmasundari, also known as Gnaneshwari.
Cover page includes Her Portrait.

Sri Bhuvaneshwari

Sri Lalithāmbal

Sri Bhāskararāya carrying Devi on his shoulder

The Author's Revered Gurus.
Sri Sānthananda Swamigal & Sri Kanchi Mahāperiyavā

Sri Kāmākshi

Sri Tripurasundari

The Lotus Feet of Devi

Shiva creates Bhandasura

Sri Bhavani at Kolhapur

Sri Durgā Devi

Shiva Shakti Aikyam

Ardhanāreeswara

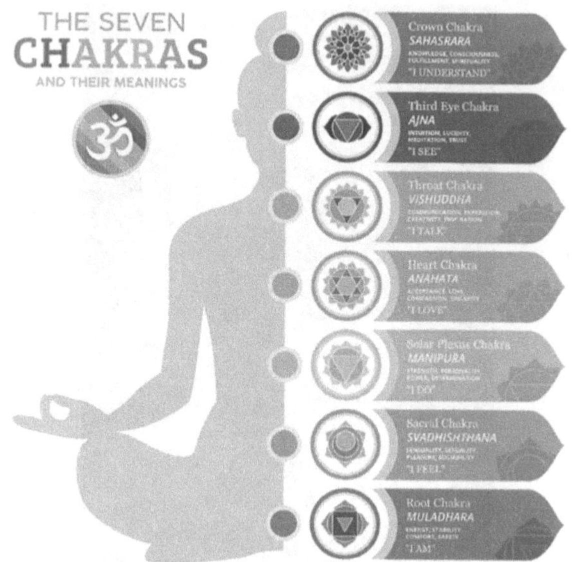

Energy Centers in the Human Body

Sri Chakram

Sringeri Sri Sharadamba

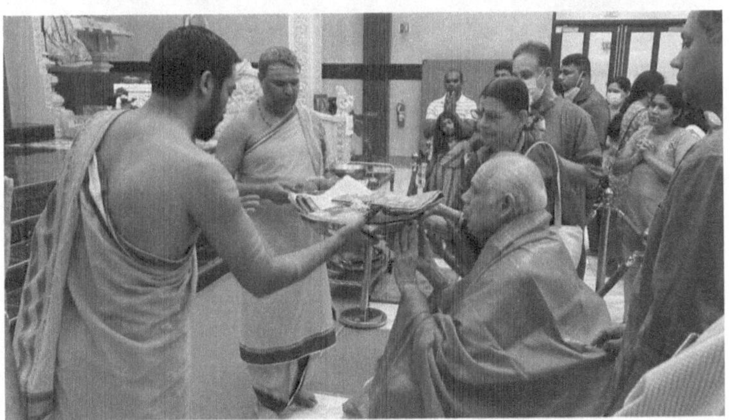

The priests at SVBF North Temple in MI,
USA honoring the author.

About the Book

Lalithā Sahasranāmam is a sacred Hindu scripture in Sanskrit that describes the thousand names of Sri Lalitha Devi, the Great Mother Goddess. There are many books on Lalithā Sahasranāmam but this book is unique and includes the following special features:

It provides an insight into the divine significance of each name of Lalitha Devi based on Sri Bhāskararāya's most outstanding work *'Sowbhagya Bhaskaram'* which is a detailed commentary on Lalithā Sahasranāmam. Sri Bhāskararāya (1690-1785) was a Sanskrit scholar and a Srividya Upāsaka (an eminent worshipper of Mother Goddess) and well-known as an authority on the worship of the Mother Goddess in the Shākta tradition of Hinduism.

1. This book is compiled from a series of online lectures delivered by the author under the *'Vande Vidya Shankaram'* program of the Sringeri Vidya Bharati Foundation (SVBF, North), MI, USA. The videos of the complete lecture series are available on the website svbfnorth.org or on the author's YouTube channel.

2. In this book, each verse of Lalithā Sahasranāmam is provided in Sanskrit followed by transliteration in English. Many intricate Sanskrit words are explained in detail with meanings and examples. So, this book will

immensely benefit those readers who are not familiar with Sanskrit language and the Devanagari script.

3. To explain some complex concepts, the author has included practical examples from his own long experience.

The special features of this book will provide an enjoyable reading experience. They will also help the readers to develop a strong sense of devotion and hidden inner strength.

About the Author

 Subi Subramanian is an accomplished energy and environmental professional with an impressive array of international experiences in multinational corporations and U.S. Government agencies. His experience is backed by brilliant academic qualifications in engineering and management.

With ancestral roots from Maharajapuram in South India, Subi Subramanian learnt Sanskrit and Scriptures at a young age as a school student in Pune, India. Inspired by his Gurus and partly by his ancestry, the author developed a deep interest in Sanatana Dharma. He was driven by a passion to teach some of the Sanskrit scriptures. So, he began teaching *Sri Rudram* with meanings to a group of people in his Chicago home. Later, he launched innovative global online learning programs that included *'Easy Sanskrit"* for adults and kids, *'SanGita'* (Sanskrit plus Bhagavad Gita), *Introduction to the Upanishads, The Glory of Vishnu Sahasranamam, Aditya Hrudayam, Vidura Neeti* and many more. Many of his videos are shared on YouTube. Currently, the author's YouTube channel (@subi654) has over 24,500 subscribers with over one million views. He received many encouraging reviews on YouTube partly shared here:

Samples of Feedback

"Nice explanation easily understandable. Good for generations born and brought up in West and east of India."

–K. Raman, Santa Clara, USA

"Great content, thank you guruji"

–Sidharth M. Patil

"Excellent explanation and thank you Sir"

–Gomathy Krishnamoorthy

"I liked this session very much. Your explanation helped understand the meaning of Aditya Hrudayam Stotram in a simple language. Thank you."

–Brajadulal Patnaik

"I have just found your channel Sir and I'm so happy that I found someone who has in-depth knowledge of things, I feel lucky. My obeisance to you sir. Looking forward to learning more from you"

–Sarika Trivedi

"Glad to hear that you are doing well and happy to hear about your upcoming book.. Our prayers and wishes for your efforts. Thanks & Regards,"

–(Dr.) Jambunathan Ramanathan,
SVBF North Working Committee

The author can be reached at gurujisubi@gmail.com

Author's Preface

Om Sri Mhātre Namaha.
Om Sri Gurubyo Namaha.

Namaste to all readers! The inspiration to write this book came to me from three main sources:

1. It was my revered Guru Sri Shāntananda Avaduta Satguru Swamigal of Bhuvaneswari temple in Pudukottai who had initiated me into the worship of the great Mother Goddess (called Ambāl or Devi in this book). He taught me many things on how the Grace of Ambāl could help me to effectively meet challenges in my life. He was a source of constant guidance to me and encouraged me to always remember Ambāl and recite the stotras.

2. Another great guiding force and a fountain of inspiration to me was His Holiness Jagadguru Shri Chandrasekharendra Saraswati Swamiji, the 68th Sankaracharya of the Kānchi Kāmakoti Peetam popularly known as 'Kānchi Mahaperiyava.' It was my good fortune to receive Him once with Purnakumbam. I have read many of his interesting discourses in the Tamil book "Deivathin Kural." Kānchi Mahaperiyava inspired me even more to continue my worship of Ambāl with passion and determination. Based on his lectures, I had compiled a book on Ambāl titled, 'Kāmakshi.'

3. The Sringeri Vidya Bharati Foundation in Detroit, MI
    (SVBF North, USA) provided me with a great opportunity
    to deliver a series of monthly online lectures on Lalithā
    Sahasranāmam for its *'Vande Vidya Shankaram'* program.
    This lecture series, spread over two years (2021-23),
    served as a key motivation for me to write this book.

I offer my humble namaskārams to the great Gurus. I am
extremely grateful to the SVBF team for recording my online
lectures and honoring me at the Sri Sharadambal Temple in
Detroit, MI, USA.

Lalithā Sahasranāmam is an ancient sacred scripture that
teaches about the Supreme Mother Goddess. It occurs in the
ancient scripture of Brahmānda Purana as a conversation
between Hayagreeva and Sage Agasthya.

On a specific request from Sage Agasthya, Hayagreeva,
the horse-headed incarnation of Bhagavan Vishnu, preaches
to him the 1000 names (sahasra namas) of Lalitha Devi, the
Mother Goddess. The Sahasranāmam is said to have been
composed by the eight Vaak Devis upon the command of the
Mother Goddess Lalithā Herself.

Reciting and listening to Lalithā Sahasranāmam with
perfect intonation is indeed a pleasure. My wife Vidya and I
had the golden opportunity to recite it at many public places
including the Ambāl temple in Bhaskararājapuram and at the
Lalithambika Temple in Thirumeeyachur in South India. Like
many other devotees, we too have experienced the Grace of
Ambāl in our lives.

Among the many *'bhāshyams'* (commentaries) on Lalithā
Sahasranāmam, *"Sowbhāgya Bhāskaram"* written by the

Author's Preface

great Devi Upāsaka and Sanskrit Scholar Sri Bhāskararāya is considered the most significant. Bhāskararāya lived in the village of Bhaskarājapuram adjacent to my ancestral village of Maharājapuram, near Kumbakonam in India. In his bhāshyam, Bhāskararāya quotes several of his predecessors, puranas, Saundarya Lahari, and several other scriptures. This book includes many valuable comments made by Bhāskararāya in 'Sowbhagya Bhaskaram' (translated into English by Sri. Ananthakrishna Sāstry). The videos of my online lectures for SVBF were recorded and may be accessed on the SVBF website 'svbfnorth.org' or from my YouTube channel (@ Subi654).

There are numerous Sanskrit words used in this book. So, a knowledge of Sanskrit is most helpful in following the contents of this book.

To assist readers who are not familiar with the Devanagari script of Sanskrit language, I have used The International Alphabet of Sanskrit Transliteration (IAST) in most places.

One of the formidable challenges I found in my work was in translating Sanskrit terms into English. There are no exact equivalent English words that express the true meanings of many of the Sanskrit terms like *ātmā, brahman, dharmā, pāpam, punyam* and other words. I apologize for the possible confusion arising from linguistic appropriation and distortion.

Lalithā Sahasranāmam consists of powerful hymns in praise of the Mother Goddess. It describes Lalithā's origin, Her complete form, Her Divine names, Her Leelas (divine plays), Her power, Yogā, Sri Chakra, Advaita (non-dualism) and much more.

Reciting the Lalithā Sahasranāmam with devotion can fulfill many spiritual and material aspirations. It is believed to yield several other benefits, including:

- Purifying the mind from clutter
- Effectively meeting challenges in life
- Protecting from dangers
- Relaxing the nervous system
- Improving the 'Gunas' (qualities) within us
- Gaining the ability to see and appreciate beauty
- Leading to a contented and rewarding life

Understanding the meaning and regular chanting of Lalithā Sahasranāmam is said to give inner peace, clarity of thoughts and eventually enlightenment.

I offer my prayers to Sri Lalithambika, the Great Mother Goddess, and seek Her blessings. It is my pious desire that the younger generation takes up the study of Lalithā Sahasranāmam and reap the benefits of Ambāl's Grace. I hope this book serves as an effective tool for this purpose.

Subi Subramanian
Chicago

About Bhāskararāya (1690-1785)

Bhāskararāya was a great Srividya Upāsaka (worshipper of Devi) and a writer known for his contributions to the Shakta tradition of Hinduism. He was born in Thanuja, a village close to Bhaga in Maharashtra, to the learned Gambhira and his wife Konambika. He started learning the Rig Veda at the young age of five and later went to Benares (now Varanasi) where he learnt all the eighteen Vidyas from Guru Nrisimha.

Following initiation into the Srividya Upāsana by Shivadatta Shukla in Gujarat, he travelled widely in various regions of India. He initiated many kings of his time into Srividya worship and built many temples. He married and lived for some time at Benares with his wife Anandi, where he defeated many other Pandits in debating assemblies.

Later, King Serfoji II of Bhonsle dynasty who was the ruler at Thanjavur at that time, invited him to South India. He accepted the king's invitation and settled in the village Baskararajapuram, near Kumbakonam on the banks of River Cauvery.

Bhāskararāya authored more than 40 writings that range from

Vedanta to poems of devotion, from Indian logic and Sanskrit grammar to the studies of Tantra. Several of his texts are notable to the Shaktism tradition, particularly the following books focused on the Mother Goddess.

- Bhāsyam (Commentary) on Devi Māhatmiyam, titled *Guptavati.*

- *Varivasya Rahasya*, a commentary on Sri Vidya mantra and worship.

- *Sowbhāgya Bhāskaram*, Bhāsyam on Lalithā Sahasranāmam.

Readers may view more details on Bhāskararāya in the author's YouTube video titled *"Bhāskararāya Parichaya: An Introduction to Bhāskararāya."*

Contents

Chapter 1

Introduction and Dhyanam

Origin and Background

Lalithā Sahasranāmam is a Sanskrit text from the *Brahmānda Purana*. 'Brahmānda' means universal or cosmic egg. It is believed that in the beginning there was a universal Uni-Cell known as the Brahmānda, that split into two, one part of which appeared as the Cosmic Man and another part the Cosmic Woman. Some call these parts 'Shiva and Shakti.'

Brahmānda Purana is an ancient Sanskrit text authored by Veda Vyasa. Brahmānda Purana covers:

- A detailed description of the creation of cosmos, time as a dimension and details of Kalpa and Yuga. (long before scientists discovered cosmos)

- Lalitopakhyana, an explanation that highlights the theology of Lalitha, the mother goddess and her central importance

The text of Lalithā Sahasranāmam appears in a dialogue between Hayagreeva and the sage Agasthya.

Who was Hayagreeva? The name Hayagreeva consists of two words viz. 'Haya' meaning 'horse' and 'Greeva' meaning 'neck'. Therefore, it literally means 'one whose neck is that of a horse'. And refers to the avatāra (incarnation) of Lord

Vishnu where he adorned the face of a horse. The story of Lord Hayagreeva appears in the Mahabharata and many other Puranas. I will tell you the story as it appears in Devi Bhagavadam. Once an extremely tired Lord Vishnu fell asleep resting his head on a bow. Wanting to awaken him, Brahma, Rudra and others induced some ants to bite the bow string. It was done but the bow string took off the head of Lord Vishnu. They could not find the head and worshipped Tripurasundari who directed them to join the head of a horse to the body. Why a horse? Because horse represents power – we still use the word horsepower to indicate the power of a car engine or a motor. Thus, a head transplant took place, and Vishnu was transformed into Hayagreeva.

Who was Agastya? Agastya derives his name from the Sanskrit word 'Aga', a mountain, and 'Stya' to fix.

There are many stories about Agastya. Agastya is one of the seven sages in the famous "Saptarishi" constellation.

He is the son of Pulastya, one of the ten *"Manasika Putras"* (born out of the mind) of Brahma.

He appears in numerous Itihasas and Puranas (Hindu historical stories and regional epics) including the Ramayana and Mahabharata. Agastya Rishi is credited to composing the powerful "Aditya Hridayam" (in praise of Sun god) as Upadesam (advice) to Lord Sri Ram when he struggled to fight against Ravana and felt depressed. Sri Ram was inspired by this stotram and defeated Ravana.

Agastya Rishi is known in many of the Southeast Asian countries. He was a unique sage, known to be short and heavy in build. A story goes that once the mountain Vindhya (central India) started growing upward in gigantic proportion due to its ego. The sage Agastya decided to subdue the pride of Vindhya. For this purpose, he came from North India and fixed its ego, stopped its growth to balance the weight of Himalayas and Vindhyas. A short humble man could conquer the big mountain and suppress its ego. It shows humility can conquer the mighty. Thereafter, Agastya is believed to have settled down in South India. Distressed by the evil trends in Kali Yuga, he was unable to bear the burden of the grief and performed severe penance meditating on Lord Vishnu. Vishnu appeared to the sage in the form of Hayagreeva. The sage asked Haygreeva to narrate the story of Para Shakti. It was then that the Hayagreeva-Agastya Samvādham (dialogue) took place. Vādam means an argument. Samvādam is a dialogue for good purpose. Hayagreeva tells the *"Lalitopakhyana"* to Agastya. (Lalitha + Upakhyana) means "The Great Narrative of Lalitha."

Hayagreeva tells the story of Lalitha in detail to Agastya Maharishi. He describes the Sripura (Sri Chakra) in all its glory, the greatness of 15-syllabled Panchadasi, the unity of the Sree Yantra etc.

However, Hayagreeva did not tell him about Lalithā Sahasranāmam. So, Agastya Maharishi asked: "You did not tell me Lalithā Sahasranāmam. So, my doubt is – Have you forgotten it or knowingly neglected it, or do you think I am unworthy to listen? Please tell me the reason."

Hayagreeva replied:

"Lopamudra's husband Agastya, please listen to me carefully. I will tell you the reason why I did not instruct you the Sahasranāmam. I thought it was a secret and not for any other reason. *'Guhyati Guyham' -Rahasya Nama Sahasra*, Secret evokes interest. Since you have asked me again with Bhakti, I will now tell you. It should not be taught to anyone without Bhakti."

Hayagreeva then preached the Lalithā Sahasranāmam to Agastya Maharishi.

The Purana says that Lalitha Devi Herself commanded the eight *Vaak Devis* literally meaning Goddesses of Speech to compose the Sahasranāmam in praise of Her. These eight Vaak devis are Vasini, Kameshwari, Aruna, Vimala, Jayinee, Modhinee, Sarveshwari, Koulini.

Worshippers of the Goddess Lalita Devi look upon Her as the Divine Mother in the form of Shakti.

How did Lalitha Devi originate? There is an interesting story behind it.

Lord Shiva married Sathi, the daughter of Daksha. As she was born to Daksha, Sathi was also called Dakshayani. Daksha and son-in-law Shiva did not get along well and consequently Daksha did not invite shiva for one of the great 'Yajyams' fire sacrifices that he conducted. However, Sathi went to attend that event despite shiva's warning not to do so. Daksha did not even welcome his daughter and in fact insulted Shiva. Sati felt shattered!

In Srimad Bhagavadam, Sati addresses her father Daksha in the following verse:

यद्द्व्यक्षरं नाम गिरेरितं नृणां सकृत्प्रसङ्गादघमाशु हन्ति तत्
पवित्रकीर्तिं तमलङ्घ्यशासनं भवानहो द्वेष्टि शिवं शिवेतरः

yad dvy-akṣaraṁ nama gireritaṁ nṛṇaṁ, sakṛt prasaṅgad agham aśu hanti tat

pavitra -kīrttim alaṅghya-śāsanam, bhavan aho dveṣṭi śivam śivetara

Meaning: *Respected father, the two-lettered name of 'Shi- va' even if uttered just once instantly frees one from sin. His order is never neglected. Lord Shiva is always pure, no one else but you alone hate him.*

Unable to bear the humiliation, in sheer disgust and disappointment, Sati jumped into the holy fire and ended her life. On hearing this Shiva got furious. He ordered his *Bhutaganas* (Shiva's fighting tribe) to kill Daksha and destroy the yajna. There are several versions of this story but what is important is that Shiva later entered deep meditation.

Later, Sati reincarnated as Parvati, daughter of Himavat, king of the mountains. Parvati sought and received Shiva as her husband.

At that time, the devas faced an enemy in *Tarakasura* - a fierce demon who had a boon that he could be killed only by a son of Shiva and Parvati. So, to rouse Shiva from his deep meditation, the devas deputed Manmatha, the God of love who shot his flower arrows at Shiva to arouse him from his meditation. In his anger at being disturbed, Shiva opened his third eye which reduced Manmatha to ashes. Ambāl took Manmatha's sugarcane bow and arrows and looked at Easwara, with eyes filled with love and affection. With a bow and arrow in her hands, love and affection in her vision, she assumed the form of "*Kāmākshi*". Here, Kāma – means love and affection, Akshi – means Eyes.

The Devas and Rathi Devi, the wife of Manmatha requested Paramashiva to give life to Manmatha. Heeding their request Paramashiva looked at the ashes of Manmatha. From the ashes arose an Asura -a demon called Bhandasura, who started troubling the devas and made them feel miserable.

So, a new problem came up. How to get rid of this demon Bhandasura?

The devas under the leadership of Indra then sought the advice of Sage Narada who advised them to conduct a great Yagna – a fire sacrifice and seek the help of Para Shakti. As Lalithā Sahasranāmam says,

चिदग्नि- कुण्ड- सम्भूता देवकार्य- समुद्यता

Chitagni-Kunda-Sambhuta-Devakarya-Samudyata

                The Glory of Lalithā Sahasranāmam

From this holy fire called *Chitagni* (fire of consciousness), Lalitha Devi arose to fulfill the task for the Devas.

'Sat' is Easwaran, and *'Chit'* is Ambāl. This knowledge or awareness gives happiness. That happiness is called 'Ānandam'. So, Easwarān and Ambāl - Kameswara and Kāmeswari together are *Sat Chit Ānandam or Sachidānandam.*

Agnikunda means a fire altar, in which fire sacrifices are done. Sambhutha means born. In Sanatana Dharma, everything of significance in people's lives is around fire. Without fire, there is no worship, no marriage, no yajnyam, or even cooking.

Next line in the verse says:

चम्पकाशोक-पुन्नाग-सौगन्धिक-लसत्कचा

Champakashoka-Punnaga-Sowgandhika-Lasatkacha

From the holy fire, Lalitha Devi emerged as an extremely beautiful woman, having dark thick long hair with the fragrance of Champaka, Asoka and Punnaga flowers.

The Lalithā Sahasranāmam describes Devi's beauty, and attributes in detail. Vaakdevis sing the Glory of Lalitha Devi; Devi eventually kills Bhandasura as the story is included in the first 84 names of the first 34 shlokas of Lalithā Sahasranāmam.

Contents of Lalithā Sahasranāmam

Bhāskararāya's 'Sowbhagya Bhaskaram' defines the meaning of Lalitha as "one who plays."

The Padmapurana says: "Having passed beyond the worlds She plays; Hence she is called "Lalitha." What does play mean? Have you seen a mother and baby playing with each other? The baby looks at the mother's face and smiles. The mother responds with a hug and kiss to the baby and tickles the baby with her fingers. The baby laughs beautifully. That's the kind of play – both Mother and baby enjoying themselves together. It's an exclusive world for them. The baby feels safe and protected by the mother. It will not trust strangers. Likewise, animals too display very strong maternal instincts. That's the kind of unique relationship a devotee will develop with Devi through chanting Lalithā Sahasranāmam with devotion.

Ambāl's Play includes punishment too. We complain about it. Yashoda tied Krishna with a rope – that's why Krishna is called Damodara. When a mother punishes a child, the child may think, what sort of a mother is she. She is brutal and has no mercy at all. I don't like her at all. The child cannot think why the mother is punishing him – to correct him, to make him realize his mistakes and put him on the correct path. To some extent we are like this child, however old we are. We are unable to bear Her punishment for our past misdeeds. We are just blaming the mother who tied our hands to prevent us from committing the same misdeeds, Ambāl has tied our hands with a cloth called problems or challenges to teach us lessons. Don't we call prisons as 'correctional facilities?' Ambāl offers opportunities for correcting us. So, when we experience hardships, it is to alert and awaken us to reality. However, when someone refuses to be corrected, Ambāl destroys the incorrigible evil demons.

Ambāl is described as *Graha Anugraha Dayini*. In the larger context, Her play includes creation, sustenance, dissolution of the universe. So also helping devotees to get out of Samsara -the cycle of births and deaths.

Lalithā Sahasranāmam has three parts. It contains 320 shlokas (verses) in three chapters in the second part of Brahmānda Purana.

1. Poorva Bhaga (51 verses)
2. Stotra (182 verses)
3. Uttara Bhaga (87 verses)

The poorva bhaga talks about the origin of the shloka. Stotra contains the 1000 names of Lalitha Devi and Uttara Bhaga gives details on the benefits (phalashruti) of reciting this shloka. There are 182 shlokas in this Sahasranāmam. It is set Anushtup Chandas (Meter), 32 letters divided into quarters of 8 letters each. The Stotras include a variety of topics such as: A description of the physical form of Lalitha Devi, (*Kesadi Paada Varnana-Head to Foot description*), *Srinagara Varnana* (abode of Ambāl), *Bhandasura Vadam, Mantra Rupam, Bhakta Anugraham, Nirguna Upasana, Saguna Upasana, Panchabrahma Swarupam, Khestra Rupam, Angadevatha Peetams*, Stotrams ending with *ShivaShaktya Aiykyam* on the oneness of Kameshwari and Kameshwara.

Worship of Lalitha Devi is of two kinds: *Nirguna* (without a physical form) and *Saguna* (with form). Nirguna is hard, beyond imagination. Lalithā Sahasranāmam offers both -Nirguna & Saguna Upasana of Lalitha Devi.

She is Parāshakti-the superpower ruling the universe.

The thousand names are like thousand Mantras. What is a Mantra? A Sanskrit adage is *"Manana Trayete iti Mantraha"* –

meaning that which protects you by chanting in mind. In management language it is panacea for ills - the word Mantra is included in English too.

It can be chanted in stotra form, or namavali form. The names must be pronounced correctly. You need to practice it. I have seen some people struggle to pronounce the names due to ignorance of the Devanagari script.

For example, take the word श्रीमहाराज्ञी in the very first line of Lalithā Sahasranāmam. It is pronounced as mahārājñī, - ज्ञ -ज्ञा like in ज्ञानं jñāna (wisdom), yajña (sacrificial worship). Some people have trouble pronouncing the consonant jña ज्ञ, so, they recite the word as Maharāngee. It is incorrect. The rule is to chant correctly with devotion, dedication and belief, and complete surrender to Sri Lalithambikā Devi. To get beneficial results, the right pronunciation is extremely important. Mantras are not merely a combination of sounds but a subtle form of the Devata Herself.

There are four levels of speech – para, pashyanti, madhyama, vaikari. Generally, most of us speak only the fourth level of vaikari. Vaikari is that speech that operates in the mouth alone, via the physical tongue; madhyama meaning medium emerges into the world through the nose, via the breath; pashyanti means "seeing"-it is spoken with the eyes; para is telepathic, you may call it as intuition, or sixth sense materializing directly from the faculty of awareness.

Volumes can be spoken without words, merely by looking at the eyes. You can't lie with your eyes. Lovers look into their eyes to communicate their feelings.

It shows the importance given to our eyes. While it might not seem so at first glance, animals are able to communicate simply through looks! In domesticated animals, such as dogs, eye contact is an important part of their communication with humans. They understand. A speaker's true intentions may often be detected behind those eye transmissions. It is said that a fish keeps her roving eyes on the eggs until they hatch.

Ambāl has other names such as Kāmākshi, Meenākshi, Visālākshi, etc. In these names, *'Akshi'* means eyes. These names extoll Devi in all her attributes, achievements, powers, and forms.

What's in a name? Most traditional Hindu names relate to divine meanings-like Aditya, Chandramouli, Gowrishankar, Hariharan, Natarajan, Sambamurthy, Venugopal and so on.

There is something special about female names in Hinduism. Most of them end either in A or E. For example, Lalitha, Aparna, Ambika, Vidya, Rekha, Radha and so on. Ending with e are: Meenakshi, Kamakshi, Saraswathi, Vishali, Bhavani, Ranjani, Kumari and so on.

In Lalithā Sahasranāmam, the names are organized in the form of hymns (*stotras*). A specialty of this Sahasranamam is that no names are repeated!

In most stotras, the deities are described from their feet upwards. In Lalithā Sahasranāmam, Ambāl's description is *Kesadipada* (meaning from head to feet).

The Beauty of Lalithā Sahasranāmam

Lalithā Sahasranāmam contains the most beautiful poetical verses in Sanskrit. Take the following verses as examples:

भवानी भावनागम्या भवारण्य-कुठारिका।

भद्रप्रिया भद्रमूर्तिर् भक्त-सौभाग्यदायिनी॥४१॥

भक्तिप्रिया भक्तिगम्या भक्तिवश्या भयापहा।

Bhavani Bhavanagamya Bhavaranya Kutarika

Bhadrapriya Bhadramurtir Bhakta Sowbhagyadayini

Bhaktipriya Bhaktigamya Bhaktivashya Bhayapaha. (41)

Every word starts with '*Bha*' throughout this verse.

Another example:

शाम्भवी शारदाराध्या शर्वाणी शर्मदायिनी॥४२॥

Shambavi Sharadaradya Sharvani Sharmadayini. (42)

In this line every word starts with '*Sha*'

There are hundreds of such beautiful verses. Lalithā Sahasranāmam is like the *Sahasradala Padmam*- the thousand petalled lotus. Each petal is beautiful. The eyes of Ambāl are compared to this petal – like *Pankajakshi, Ambujakshi*. Lotus is a beautiful flower that grows in muddy waters. Likewise, the Lalithā Sahasranāmam is a beautiful gift to humanity that is mired in the muddy waters of stress and strains of modern life.

There is another important aspect of Lalithā Sahasranāmam – that is "*Alankara*" referring to the exquisite beauty of verses.

In Vishnu Sahasranamam, many words are three-syllabled. In contrast, Lalithā Sahasranāmam has many sixteen-syllabled and eight syllabled and four syllabled word.

Lalithā Sahasranāmam does not use conjunctions like '*cha*' '*tu*' '*api*' in Sanskrit. It is a unique enumeration of the 1000 holy names of the goddess by maintaining a perfect metrical, poetical and mystic requirement of the sahasranāmam.

Starting with Devi's Avataram, Lalithā Sahasranāmam describes Devi's exploits, encounter and killing of many demons and ends with *Shiva Shakti Ikyam*- the divine union of Shiva and Shakti. It includes many references to Yoga and ritualistic worship like Sri Chakra Puja. Known for its phonetic excellence, chanting the Sahasranāmam improves clarity of speech and memory. As you chant with correct pronunciation, your tongue starts rolling and your speaking skill will gradually improve. Regular chanting improves emotional strength remarkably, halts the wandering mind. It helps to concentrate and focus your energy. In short, it presents the simplest approach to elevating your quality of living and unleashing the power hidden within you.

Lalitha Devi as Supreme Mother

The very first word of Lalithā Sahasranāmam begins with ॐ श्रीमाता श्रीमहाराज्ञी श्रीमत् सिंहासनेश्वरी – *Om SriMatha Sri Maharajni Srimat Simhaneswari*. Lalitha Devi is seen as the Supreme Mother. 'Para' is superlative in Sanskrit.

Mother is given the greatest importance in Sanatana Dharma. *Maatru Devo Bhava, Pitru Devo Bhava, Acharya Devo Bhava .... Says Taittriya Upanishad.*

You call Nature as Mother nature, country as Motherland, India as Bharat Mātha. Lalithā Sahasranāmam is meant to create an intimate relationship like what exists between an adorable mother and child. To illustrate this unique relationship, I would like to share my experience here –

Many years ago, I was at the Madras central station to board a night train. The station was crowded and extremely noisy with the porters moving carts shouting to make way, loud announcements, and people talking loudly.

As I was waiting for my coach to arrive, I took a walk on the platform and found many people sleeping on the platform unmindful of the noise around. You know how it is – chaotic. I saw a mother and her baby sleeping peacefully. Suddenly, the baby cried, and the mother woke up. She fed the child and again went back to sleep. What surprised me was that the mother slept well with all that loud noise around, but she could hear the shrill cry of her baby as if there was a telepathic connection. For her, waking up was automatic, materializing directly from the faculty of motherly awareness. This is the kind of unique relationship that is possible with the Supreme Mother who is conscious of all her children.

Another verse reads- *'Manorupekshu Kodanda Panchatanmatra Sayaka'*-

Lalithambā holds five arrows made of long-stemmed flowers, a bow made of sugarcane, a noose (Paasam), and Angusham a goad. The arrows are our five senses and the bow with which they're dispatched is our mind. When our senses are offered to the Goddess and our thoughts are directed to the Divine, our life becomes sweet and fragrant. But when we get distracted by one thing or another, and stray away, Lalita gently prods us along with her angusam. If we resist her, and continue the wrong path, like a mother, she pulls us with her noose and drags us, like a mother pulls misbehaving children, back to her lap. Paasam is the rope that helps us to get rid of desires, unwanted relationships and draws towards Ambāl. Whenever feelings of discrimination come up, it in turn stirs anger in our mind, Angusham will bring this under control.

Lalithā Sahasranāmam claims in the following verse, *"raga swarupa pāsadya.... Krodhānkara kushothvala"*, meaning pasam representing desire, Angusa represents the discriminating mind, which will be controlled by Ambāl.

Thus, Ambāl carrying the four weapons in Her hands comes from the colorless Brahmam. Ambāl emerges in bright red color, the color of Kumkum.

Her bright red complexion is like the rising sun, or pomegranate red or like the saffron color or like Hibiscus flower. The moment we approach Her, She manifests Herself in brilliance. Brahma, Vishnu, and Shiva represent Parashakthi's Rajo Guna.

Devi is described as *"Pancha krtya parayana"* -the doer of five functions.

सृष्टिकर्त्री ब्रह्मरूपा गोप्त्री गोविन्दरूपिणी ॥६३॥

संहारिणी रुद्ररूपा तिरोधान-करीश्वरी।

सदाशिवाऽनुग्रहदा पञ्चकृत्य-परायणा ॥६४॥

"Shristi Kartri Brahmarupa, Gophtri Govindarupini (63)

Samharini Rudrarupa, Tirodaana Kareeshwari

Sadashiva anu-grahada Pancha-kritya-paraayana." (64)

Devi is described as the creator (*Shrishtikarthri and brahmarupa*), the preserver (*gopthri, govindarupini*) and destroyer (*samharini, rudrarupini*).

Devi is therefore described as an aspect of Brahma while creating (*Srishti*) an aspect of Govinda (Vishnu) while sustaining (*Sthiti)*, an aspect of Rudra (Shiva) during dissolution (*samhara*), an aspect of Maaya while concealing (*thirodana)*, and an aspect of Sadashiva while blessing (*anugraha*).

These five entities (Brahma, Vishnu, Rudra, Isvara and Sadashiva) are known as *"pancha-brahma."* The goddess is described as "pancha-brahma swarupini" (she whose form is composed of the five Brahmas)

The power of the *Brahmam* is called *Brahmapatni,* also as Kameshwari.

The Three-fold Aspects

Lalitha Devi symbolizes many three-fold aspects – we may call them Triads.

Lalithā Sahasranāmam provides many examples to illustrate the three-fold aspects. For example, a verse says she is in *Mantra, Tantra and Yantra*:

महातन्त्रा महामन्त्रा महायन्त्रा महासना।

महायाग-क्रमाराध्या महाभैरव-पूजिता॥५६॥

Mahatantra Mahamantra Mahayantra Mahasana

Mahayaga Kramaradhya Mahabhairava Pujita... (56)

The first line of this verse indicates that Devi is in the triad of:

- Maha Tantra – A mystical technique or practice

- Maha Mantra – That which protects by recitation

- Maha Yantra – A device, the mystical diagram Sri Chakra

Another example of a triad is in the name of Ambāl as Tripura-Sundari. Tripura refers to three Cities- built of gold, silver, and iron, in the sky, air, and earth, by Maya for the Asuras, and destroyed by Shiva.

- Three Shaktis: *Iccha, Jnana, Kriya*

  It refers to the three fundamental energies of Devi in the manifestation: iccha shakti – the energy of will, jnana shakti – the energy of knowledge, and kriya shakti – the energy of action

- Three Functions: *Shristi, Sthiti, Laya*

  Srishti or creation would be performed by Brahma, Sthithi (sustenance) by Vishnu, and Laya(destruction) by Rudra.

- Three Gunas: *Sat, Rajas, and Tamas*

There are three gunas (qualities), according to this worldview, that have always been and continue to be present in all things and beings in the world. These three gunas are called: sattva (goodness, calmness, harmonious), rajas (passion, activity, movement), and tamas (ignorance, inertia, laziness). The three gunas along with Ahamkara are present in all beings. The aim is to control Ahamkara and focus on the positive effects of Sattva, Rajas, and Tamas.

निर्लेपा निर्मला नित्या निराकारा निराकुला।

निर्गुणा निष्कला शान्ता निष्कामा निरुपप्लवा॥४४॥

Nirlepa Nirmala Nitya Nirakara Nirakula

Nirguna Nishkala Shanta Nishkama Nirupaplava ... (44)

She who is free from all impurities, She who is eternal, She who is without form, She who is 'Cool' without agitation. निर्गुणा -She who is beyond all three gunas of nature, namely sattva, rajas and tamas.

- Three States: *Jagrat, Swapna, Sushupti*

  Mind has got three *Avasthas* or States, viz., Jagrat (waking state), Svapna (dreaming state) and Sushupti (deep sleep state). She is the sovereign of the 3 realms in all three areas and resides in all states.

Dhyanam

Dhyanam means to focus your mind on the deity. It is a form of meditation. The mind is like a monkey. It has the inherent tendency to jump here and there like a monkey. Hold the monkey with a tight leash and train your mind to be steady. Without such focus, all the prayers offered become a waste. Sri Lalithā Sahasranāmam should be recited after the dhyana shlokam with devotion and sincerity, visualizing the Divine Mother in all her

The Glory of Lalithā Sahasranāmam

glory. All those who chant Sri Lalithā Sahasranāmam, should try to picturize (meditate) her in this form in their mind, and then start chanting the namams. Sri Lalithambikā's beautiful presence can be described in infinite ways.

Let us see some highlights of this Dhyana Shlokam.

1. In this dhyana shloka, Ambāl is described beautifully to stir your imagination and meditate upon her in specific rupams (appearances).

2. This dhyana itself shows us that Lalithambā is a combination of all these 3 devis (Parvathi Lakshmi Saraswathi).

3. Nowhere in this dhyana shlokam, the name of Lalithambā is mentioned.

Before reciting Lalithā Sahasranāmam, the dhyana shlokam should be chanted first and later the same dhyana shlokam should be recited again on completion. If it is an archana, we can stop with naamas itself and no need to recite dhyana again.

Dhyana Shlokam

सिन्दूरारुण विग्रहां त्रिनयनां माणिक्यमौलि स्फुरत्

तारा नायक शेखरां स्मितमुखी मापीन वक्षोरुहाम्।

पाणिभ्यामलिपूर्ण रत्न चषकं रक्तोत्पलं बिभ्रतीं

सौम्यां रत्न घटस्थ रक्तचरणां ध्यायेत् परामम्बिकाम्॥

sindūrāruṇa vigrahaṁ trinayanaṁ māṇikyamauli sphurat

tārā nāyaka śekharāṁ smitamukhī māpīna vakṣoruhām|

pāṇibhyāmalipūrṇa ratna caṣakaṁ raktotpalaṁ bibhratīṁ

saumyāṁ ratna ghaṭastha raktacaraṇāṁ dhyāyet parāmambikām||

अरुणां करुणा तरङ्गिताक्षीं

धृत पाशाङ्कुश पुष्प बाणचापाम्।

अणिमादिभि रावृतां मयूखै-

रहमित्येव विभावये भवानीम्॥

aruṇāṁ karuṇā taraṅgitākṣīṁ

dhṛta pāśāṅkuśa puṣpa bāṇacāpām|

aṇimādibhi rāvṛtāṁ mayūkhai-

rahamityeva vibhāvaye bhavānīm||

ध्यायेत् पद्मासनस्थां विकसितवदनां पद्मपत्रायताक्षीं

हेमाभां पीतवस्त्रां करकलितलसद्धेमपद्मां वराङ्गीम्।

सर्वालङ्कार युक्तां सतत मभयदां भक्तनम्रां भवानीं

श्रीविद्यां शान्त मूर्तिं सकल सुरनुतां सर्व सम्पत्प्रदात्रीम्॥

dhyāyet   padmāsanasthāṁ   vikasitavadanāṁ padmapatrāyatākṣīṁ

hemābhāṁ pītavastrāṁ karakalitalasaddhemapadmāṁ varāṅgīm|

sarvālaṅkāra yuktāṁ satata mabhayadāṁ bhaktanamrāṁ bhavānīṁ

śrīvidyāṁ śānta mūrtiṁ sakala suranutāṁ sarva sampatpradātrīm||

सकुङ्कुम विलेपनामलिकचुम्बि कस्तूरिकां
समन्द हसितेक्षणां सशर चाप पाशाङ्कुशाम्।
अशेषजन मोहिनीं अरुण माल्य भूषाम्बरां
जपाकुसुम भासुरां जपविधौ स्मरे दम्बिकाम्॥

sakuṅkuma vilepanāmalikacumbi kastūrikāṁ

samanda hasitekṣaṇāṁ saśara cāpa pāśāṅkuśām|

aśeṣajana mohinīṁ aruṇa mālya bhūṣāmbarāṁ

japākusuma bhāsurāṁ japavidhau smare dambikām||

Let us see the meaning of these verses.

sindūrāruṇa vigrahāṁ

Red has over 400 different shades. You have blood red, scarlet, crimson, burgundy, wine-red, rust-red and so on.

Here Ambāl's color is described as सिन्दूरारुण. It is vermilion, an orange red like what you see in Aruna, the rising sun. Red symbolizes energy, action, confidence, courage, and vitality. Devi's color is described thus as orange red.

Vigraham means form. *Trinayanam* means three-eyed. Who has three eyes? Shiva. But Shiva and kameshwari, are always together. There is a temple for Ardhanareeswara (Shiva and Shakti together) in Tiruchengode near Erode.

māṇikyamauli sphurat

Manickam is Rubies. Mauli refers to forehead or crown. Chandramouli. In this case, Ambāl wears a crown studded with Rubies. Only Royalty wears a crown. Kohinoor diamond is on the British Royalty crown.

tārā nāyaka śekharāṁ

tārā means stars. Nayaka is chief referring to the moon. śekharāṁ means crown or crest -like Chandrashekar. Ambāl wears a crescent moon on her crown, like Shiva too. Moon and mind are connected. The word 'Lunar' is adjective for moon from which comes the word Lunatic. By holding the moon on her crown, Ambāl controls your mind.

Smitamukhī- Ambāl has a smiling face

māpīna vakṣoruhām

A splendid bust. A source of nutrition to all living beings. All mothers feed their young ones through breast milk, which is the purest form of food without any harmful ingredients.

pāṇibhyāmalipūrṇa ratna caṣakaṁ

Pāni – means hand like in kothandapāni, chakrapāni etc. Ambāl holds in one hand a jewel-cup brimming with nectar- a beverage of fermented honey with water.

raktotpalaṁ bibhratīṁ- In another hand she holds a red-colored flower, a lotus.

          The Glory of Lalithā Sahasranāmam

*saumyāṁ   ratna   ghaṭastha   raktacaraṇāṁ   dhyāyet
parāmambikām:*

*Ratna -rubies Ghatam is pot. Ambāl is keeping her foot on a
precious pot containing rare gems. I meditate on this super
Ambikā.*

Gist: The Divine mother is to be meditated upon as shining
in a vermilion-red body, with triple eyes, sporting a crown
of rubies studded with the crescent moon, a smiling pleasant
face, a splendid bust, one hand holding a jewel-cup brimming
with nectar, and the other twirling a red lotus, with her foot on
a pot containing gems.

aruṇāṁ- who shines like rising sun karuṇā is merciful

taraṅgitākṣīṁ- waves of mercy

dhṛta pāśāṅkuśa puṣpa bāṇacāpām- holding the noose and
the goad and the flower arrows

*aṇimādibhi   rāvṛtāṁ   mayūkhai-rahamityeva   vibhāvaye
bhavānīm*

Surrounded by siddhis who shine like streaks of ray, I
meditate on that Bhavani.

Gist: I meditate on Devi Bhavani, who shines red like rising
sun, whose eyes emit eternal waves of mercy. Who holds
pāsa and *angusa* in her hands to bind and control souls (every
living non-living entity). Who holds bows of sugarcane and
arrows of flowers.

dhyāyet padmāsanasthāṁ

I meditate on that Divine Mother who is seated in the
padmasana (lotus pose). It also means that She is seated within
a padmā (lotus). Lotus and Lakshmi are closely associated.

vikasita-vadanāṃ- She possesses a charming face which also is the cause for our upliftment/ growth (*vikasa*).

padma-patrāyatākṣīṃ- Her eyes are elongated like the lotus petals (lotus-eyed). Even a side glance (*Kataksham*) will do.

hemābhāṃ pītavastrāṃ- Hema means gold; bha means light. She wears yellow color clothes (*pita vastram*), is of golden complexion and is glowing like a golden light.

kara-kalita-lasaddhema padmām varāngīm

With a beautiful body that is of medium gait, neither too fat nor too thin and with a golden lotus held in Her hand, She attracts everyone.

This golden lotus which cannot wither away causes the lotus within us to glow.

sarvālaṃkāra-yuktāṃ- She has adorned herself with all types of decorations (sarva alamkara) such as jewels, flowers etc. *Aabaranam* (jewellery) makes a woman more beautiful.

satatamabhayadāṃ- She displays Abhaya mudra (fear not) of protection towards all beings.

bhakta-namrām bhavānīṃ- I am bowing down to the Divine Mother Bhavani (wife of Bhava or Shiva) in complete reverence.

śrividyāṃ- She is an embodiment of the entire knowledge of Srividyā.

śāntamūrtiṃ- She is of a peaceful form.

sakala-sura-nutāṃ- Worshipped with reverence by all the Suras (Devatas).

sarva saṃpat pradātrīm- She bestows every form of prosperity (*sarva sampat*). Here prosperity means knowledge (vidya/ jnana) and yogā.

Gist: The Divine Goddess is to be meditated upon as seated on the lotus with petal eyes. She is golden hued and has lotus flowers in Her hand.

She dispels fear of the devotees who bow before Her. She is the embodiment of peace, knowledge (vidya), is praised by gods and grants every kind of wealth wished for

Sakuṃkuma-vilepanāṃ- She is anointed with kumkum. In our Dharma, Kumkum is very auspicious. Ambāl is pleased with Kumkum offered to her.

alika-chumbi-kastūrikāṃ- She wears a kasturi (generally refers to deer musk) pottu (bindi) enhancing her beauty. The bees are drawn by the fragrance of this Kasturi, encircle Her.

samanda-hasitekṣaṇām- Her laugh is gentle, lovable, wholehearted, and beautiful. She looks upon Her devotees with such a benevolent smile. Her laugh is visible in Her smiling eyes.

saśara-cāpa-pāśāṅkuśa- She holds all her weapons- the bow and arrows, (sugar cane as bow and flowers as arrows), the goad and the noose.

aśeṣa-jana-mohinī- She has the power of universal attraction. Irrespective of whether a person believes in Her or not, he/she will find it impossible to avoid Her and instead will be attracted towards Her.

aruṇa-mālya-bhūṣāṃbarāṃ- The red (*aruna*) garland (*māla*) She wears it jewellery that is exquisite.

japā-kusuma-bhāsurām- She is glowing like the red hibiscus flower and wears it (*japakusuma*).

japavidhau smaredambikām

One must meditate on this form of Divine Mother Ambika during japa (i.e., during recitation of this Sahasranāma).

I meditate on the Mother, whose eyes are smiling, who holds the arrow, bow, noose and the goad in Her hand. She is glittering with red garlands and ornaments. She has kumkum on her forehead that is red and tender like the japa flower.

Chapter 2

Start of Stotrams

The first three shlokams (verses) deal with *Devi's Avatāram (incarnation)*. Both the words Ambāl and Devi used in this book refer to Lalithambika.

श्रीमाता श्रीमहाराज्ञी श्रीमत्सिंहासनेश्वरी।

चिदग्निकुण्डसम्भूता देवकार्यसमुद्यता॥ १ ॥

śrī mātā, śrī mahārājñī, śrīmat-siṃhāsanēśvarī |

chidagni kuṇḍasambhūtā, dēvakāryasamudyatā ॥ 1 ॥

The first three Namas denote the three great actions (shrishti-creation, sthithi-sustenance and samharam-destruction) performed by the Mother as seen from the following explanation.

1. śrī mātā:

The very first nāma in Lalithā Sahasranāmam refers to the Holy Mother. She is the source of all creation. The names of great people, things and places have the honorific word Sri prefixed to them. - Srividya, Srichakra, Srisaila, Srinagar, Srirangam etc.

In Sanskrit, there is an amazing wealth of words for a single object.

single object.

Take water for instance. जलं, वारि, सलिलं, उदकं, तोयं, पानीयं, आपः, नीरं, कीलालं, *(Jalam, Vaari, Salilam,*

Udakam, Toyam, Paaniyam, Aapa, Neeram, Keelalam) there are many such Sanskrit words for water.

So, the word 'Sri' in Sanskrit has several meanings. One meaning is -Sri refers to Lakshmi. The name Srikant refers to Vishnu. 'Sri' also means snake. Srikantan referring to Shiva who wears a snake around his neck. Sri also means wealth and prosperity. In this verse, Sri means auspicious, and Sri Mata means auspicious universal mother of all.

The historical background to worshipping Devi as Mother Goddess starts from the time of Adi Sankara. Sri Adi Shankara -an avataram of Lord Shiva Himself, established six paths of worship named *Shaivam, Vaishnavam, Shauram, Sāktham, Gānapatyam and Kaumāram.*

Of these, Sāktham is the only path related to the worship of a feminine deity called Shakti- the Mother Goddess. Interestingly, of the six, this is the only mode of worship reverentially referred to as Srividya to with the attribute `Sri'.

Goddess Lalitha Devi is extolled as the universal mother, the energizing principle of every creature in this universe. Lalithā Sahasranāmam says *'Aabrahma Keeta Janani'* - She created many beings -right from Brahma to even the tiniest worm.

It is said that she created the ten avatars of Lord Vishnu! Sahasranāma Sthothra describes, *"Karanguli nakhothpanna Narayana dasakrthi"*. So, the action referred to here is Creation.

She is unique. What is the uniqueness of Mother? Every creature is born from a mother. She is the personification of supreme self-sacrifice! A mother goes through a variety of sacrifices right from conception to delivery of a child. She nourishes the child with her own blood, bears it for a length of time despite work inconveniences, endures the pain during delivery, and even after delivery tends the child. Is it not sacrifice? Mother provides an overwhelming share of childcare-physically and emotionally. Lalithambā is the supreme mother of all creations. She exists in a perpetual state of perfect harmony, ever benevolent, full of compassion for all beings. Such is the greatness of Lalithambā.

The name for mother in different languages is almost similar. Sanskrit – Mātha, English-Mother, German-Mutter, Latin - Mater, Russian-Mama, Spanish- Madre, Hindi-Maa, and so on. Bhāskararāya says that the Ma in Mātha signifies measure – like Maap in Hindi – She is considered as limitless, beyond measure, meaning eventually salvation for devotees!

2. **śrī mahārājñī:**

श्रीमहाराज्ञी The Supreme Empress. राज्ञी means Queen. She is महाराज्ञी- the great queen. One who controls the created universe. She is called 'Parāshakti' – the supreme power. The one who rules and maintains the universe. The action here is Sthithi – Preservation.

3. **śrīmat-siṃhāsanēśvarī:**

The One with a Lion Seat. Royal thrones are generally seen with golden figures of lions placed at either end.

Bhattatri Narayana says the prefix Sri denotes Devi's Simhāsana (throne) is surrounded by many Lakshmis.

As you all know, Devi's vāhanam (vehicle) is a Lion. Lion alludes to might, valor and destruction.

Bhāskararāya mentions that *Simha* also means pain. Grammarians say: the word *Simha* came from the root *'Himsa'* meaning pain. He adds that the two words Himsa and Simha might have been formed by reversing the letters like the word 'Pashyaka' (seer, one who sees) to 'Kashyapa'. Like Madurai city is spoken sometimes as *Marudai or* Kudarai (horse) *as Kurudai* in Tamil. So, Himsai is 'That into which creatures enter at their death" So, Simhāsaneswari can be taken as Himsaneshwari. The action here is Samhaara – Destruction.

Thus, inferring by the above three names, Devi is seen in the three aspects of creator, preserver and destroyer.

4. chidagni kuṇḍasambhūtā

The One who was born from the alter of the Fire of Consciousness. Chit is pure Brahman, which is the altar of fire. It dispels darkness of ignorance. Devi came out of the fire of Pure knowledge and consciousness to promote the cause of divine forces (devas). You hear the word Sat-Chit-Anandam, the bliss that comes out of the combination of satyam and Chit -consciousness.

5. dēvakāryasamudyatā

Markandeya Purana says that Devi is eternal, but She manifested Herself for fulfilling the objects of the Devas. On seeing the Devi appearing from the fire, Indra and the Devas were filled with ecstasy as She came to slay the Asuras -Bhandasura and Mahishasura who were enemies

The Glory of Lalithā Sahasranāmam

of the Devas. The key intent of Devi's appearance was to enhance the welfare of the whole universe.

उद्यद्भानुसहस्राभा चतुर्बाहुसमन्विता।

रागस्वरूपपाशाढ्या क्रोधाकाराङ्कुशोज्ज्वला॥२॥

udyadbhānu sahasrābhā, chaturbāhu samanvitā |

rāgasvarūpa pāśāḍhyā, krōdhākārāṅkuśōjjvalā ||2||

6. udyadbhānu sahasrābhā

During sunrise, we can see the splendor of red color in different shades.

What magnificent splendor it would be to visualize 1000 rising suns! This Nāma refers to the great radiance of the Divine Mother by comparing it to the splendor of 1000 rising suns. Ambāl emerges in bright red color, the color of Kumkum. Her bright red complexion is like what you see in the rising sun, pomegranate red or like the saffron color or like Hibiscus flower. Also, it alludes to the fact that during Creation (Udyad-rising), the energy equivalence is extremely high. There are three forms of Devi - the physical (Sthula), the subtle (Sukshma) and the Supreme (para). The physical form has limbs like hands feet while the subtle form consists of mantra and the Supreme is the 'vāsana' means ideal or mental. The physical form is described in the next mantra.

7. chaturbāhu samanvitā

Endowed with four arms. Each arm has a tool or weapon. These are not weapons like guns that kill people. These are meant to do good for devotees as you will learn later. Four is a key number – there are four yugas Krita, Threta, Dwapara and Kali. There are four stages in human activities – Dharma-Artha, Kaama, Moksha. Devi's four arms bless us in many ways which we shall see how.

After mentioning Devi's arms, the weapons are described. There is a popular shlokam in Sanskrit that says:

Paasangusa Varadbhaya hastadhaarim,

Peetambarim kanaka mouthika Bhushitanngam.

The weapons held by Ambāl are of three kinds. *Paasam (Noose), Angusam (Goad-spiked iron stick), and a bow with arrows.*

The Yoginihrdaya, a Hindu tantric text dating back to the tenth or eleventh century says, "The noose is Ichashakti, the goad Jnanashakti, and the bow and arrows Kriyashakti."

8. rāgasvarūpa pāśāḍhyā

Raga has several meanings: Desire (Icha), Attachment, Anger. In this verse, Devi is holding the noose (a rope) of desire. Desire is what causes bondage or Paasam. It is an essential feature for all creatures to survive. We have seen the bond between a mother and a child, between friends, with pets, and others. Noose is the gross form that she holds in her left lower hand that appears on top left. It is a tool that creates bondage.

9. krōdhākārāṅkuśōjjvalā

Krodha is hatred. Also anger. Some say it also means knowledge. Shining with the Angusam - the goad, a sharp iron stick used to manage an errant elephant. It is a control

     The Glory of Lalithā Sahasranāmam

instrument. Ujwala -She shines holding in her lower right hand the goad -the elephant hook to control hatred and worldly knowledge. So, on one hand, she holds the noose (rope) of desire and the other the goad to control hatred.

The concepts used in physics are attraction and repulsion, in the same way we get tangled by desires and discriminating attitudes. To help control the desire and relieve us from the tangled knots of bondage in our mundane life, Ambāl holds the Pāsam and Angusam in Her two hands. Pāsam represents desire, Angusa represents the discriminating mind, which will be controlled by Ambāl. Whenever feelings of discrimination come up, it stirs anger in our mind, Angusham will bring this under control.

मनोरूपेक्षुकोदण्डा पञ्चतन्मात्रसायका।

निजारुणप्रभापूरमज्जद्ब्रह्माण्डमण्डला ॥ ३ ॥

manōrūpēkṣukōdaṇḍā, pañchatanmātra sāyakā |

nijāruṇa prabhāpūra majjad-brahmāṇḍamaṇḍalā ॥3 ॥

In the other two hands, Devi holds a sugarcane bow and five flower arrows. The next line describes them.

10. manōrūpēkṣukōdaṇḍā

Ambāl has a sweet heart, influences our mind by this sugary bow (*ikshu* -sugar cane, *kodanda* -bow).

Kanchi Mahaperiva explains, "The bow she holds is made up of sugarcane. Arrows are made of flowers. Usually, a bow is made of hard iron metal. On the contrary, She has a bow made of the sweet sugarcane in Her hand. Instead of sharp piercing arrows, She holds floral arrows. Sugarcane bow represents the heart. Having a sweet heart, Ambāl influences our mind by this bow and controls our senses with five floral arrows." More on the five flowers in the next mantra.

11. pañchatanmātra sāyakā

Holding the arrows of the five subtle elements. (Sayaka means arrow-in this case the flower arrows). The five subtle elements are the five senses- sound, touch, smell, taste, and sight. These are called 'Jnanedriyams' - the intellectual ones - five sense organs, referred to as ears, eyes, nose, tongue and skin. Intelligent use of these five senses is what leads to success in life.

By a gift of God, they perceive senses naturally and provide inputs for us to act through five karmendriyams -the ones that act like - hands, legs, tongue for speech, the excretory and reproductive organs. Those five floral arrows will grab our senses and control them or inactivate them.

(Readers may like to refer to the author's book titled "Kamakshi'" – a compilation of Kanchi Mahaperiva's lectures on Ambāl. Both English and Tamil versions are available on the website easyhinduism.com)

12. nijāruṇa prabhāpūra - majjad-brahmāṇḍamaṇḍalā

Devi is already compared to thousand rising suns. She spreads her red effulgence 'Nija Aruna' throughout the whole universe majjad-brahmāṇḍamaṇḍalā.

The word Brahmāndam here refers to the Universe. Long before modern scientists discovered about the elliptical

The Glory of Lalithā Sahasranāmam

galaxies, our ancient scriptures including the Vedas talk about 'Brahmāndam' - the big cosmic egg!

चम्पकाशोकपुन्नागसौगन्धिकलसत्कचा।

कुरुविन्दमणिश्रेणीकनत्कोटीरमण्डिता॥४॥

champakāśōka punnāga saugandhika lasatkachā

kuruvinda maṇiśrēṇī kanatkōṭīra maṇḍitā ॥4॥

13. champakāśōka punnāga saugandhika lasatkachā

The physical description of Devi starts from this verse. You will find it exquisite, and many exotic comparisons made like poets generally do.

It starts from the head. In this stotram, Ambāl's beautiful locks of hairs and crown on her head are praised. Lasat means play or appear. kachā means hair.

Devi's hair is adorned with Champaka, Asoka, Punnaga, Sowgandhika – all exotic flowers. Normally flowers give fragrance to hair but in Ambāl's case, her shining locks of hair give fragrance to the flowers.

14. kuruvinda maṇiśrēṇī kanatkōṭīra maṇḍitā

Kreetam is a common word for crown. Devi's crown is special called Kotiram, not hiding the beauty of hair tresses. It is filled with rows of kuruvinda mani (gems). Kuruvindamani, also called Padmaraga or rubies. Mandita means decorated. The crown is decorated with rare gems obtained from mines and riverbeds. They confer love, prosperity and devotion. Bhāskararāya says, if one meditates on Devi wearing these gems, his or her devotion will increase.

अष्टमीचन्द्रविभ्राजदलिकस्थलशोभिता।

मुखचन्द्रकलङ्काभमृगनाभिविशेषका॥५॥

aṣṭamī chandra vibhrāja daḻikasthala śōbhitā।

mukhachandra kaḻankābha mṛganābhi viśēṣaka ॥5॥

15. aṣṭamī chandra vibhrāja daḻikasthala śōbhitā

After hair, comes the description of the forehead. In this verse, Devi's beautiful forehead is described. Devi's forehead is bright as the aṣṭamī chandra -moon on the Ashtami eighth lunar day. It is exactly halfway to the full moon. *Alika sthala shobita* means the place where the hair tress adds beauty to the forehead.

16. mukhachandra kaḻankābha mṛganābhi viśēṣakā:

Kasturi is Musk - a fragrant material obtained from a deer (*mruga*). The Kasturi Tilaka adorns Devi's moonlike face, like the kaḻankābha -a spot in the moon. Moon has a dark spot that looks like a rabbit. Shasi means rabbit.

वदनस्मरमाङ्गल्यगृहतोरणचिल्लिका।

वक्त्रलक्ष्मीपरीवाहचलन्मीनाभलोचना॥६॥

vadanasmara māngalya gṛhatōraṇa chillikā।

vaktralakṣmī parīvāha chalanmīnābha lōchanā ॥6॥

17. vadanasmara māngalya gṛhatōraṇa chillikā

Going further down to the face (*vadana*), the beauty of Devi's eyes and eyebrows are described.

Smaran is the name of Manmathan, the lord of love, cupid. Since he emerged from mind (*manas*), he is called Manmathan. The house of Manmathan is called

'*Mangalya Gruha*'. It is the most beautiful house, adorned with *Thoranams*, the floral decorations typical of any festivity.

Devi's face has eyebrows that resemble archways leading to that abode of the auspicious home of *Kaama* (Cupid).

18. vaktralakṣmī parīvāha chalanmīnābha lōchanā

Devi is called Meenalochani, Meenakshi– one with eyes shaped like a fish. The fish always keep moving in the water and lays eggs. The fish does not sit over them but hovers round the eggs, looking at them intently and the eggs hatch. The very sight of mother fish makes the eggs hatch and later nurtures the babies. It is called Matsya Deekshai. Parivaha is a flood of water. Like the fish playing in flowing water, Devi has Her eyes play in the streams of beauty flowing from Her face.

नवचम्पकपुष्पाभनासादण्डविराजिता।

ताराकान्तितिरस्करिनासाभरणभासुरा ॥७॥

navachampaka puṣpābha nāsādaṇḍa virājitā |

tārākānti tiraskāri nāsābharaṇa bhāsurā ॥7॥

19. navachampaka puṣpābha nāsādaṇḍa virājitā

The nose and the ornament worn on the nose of Devi are described in this Stotram. In India, traditional Hindu families, especially in South India, attach much importance to nose piercing and wearing of diamond nose rings by women.

It is believed to enhance the beauty of women. Devi's shapely nose is like a *Navachampaka pushpa* – freshly

bloomed Champaka flower bud. *Nāsadanda*- a nasal
ornament, *virajita* means beautiful. The ornament makes
Devi's nose look more beautiful. How does this ornament
look? Next line explains.

20. tārākānti tiraskāri nāsābharaṇa bhāsurā

Tiraskari means causes to disappear. Bhasura means light
or splendour. (e.g. Bhaskar) The ornament is so beautiful
that it offsets the luster of a bright star (tarakanti).

कदम्बमञ्जरीक्लृप्तकर्णपूरमनोहरा।

ताटङ्कयुगलीभूततपनोडुपमण्डला॥८॥

kadamba mañjarīklupta karṇapūra manōharā।

tāṭaṅka yugalībhūta tapanōḍupa maṇḍalā ॥8॥

21. kadamba mañjarīklupta karṇapūra manōharā

Beauty of Devi's ears are described here. Devi is radiant
and charming with a bunch of Kadamba flowers filling
her ears.

22. tāṭaṅka yugalībhūta tapanōḍupa maṇḍalā

Tāṭaṅka is ear pendants (Thodu in Tamil), Yugali means a
pair. The beauty of Tātanga is coupled with great power in
them to protect the husband. In Saundarya Lahari, verse
28 reads:

करालं यत् क्ष्वेलं कबलितवतः कालकलना।

न शम्भोस्तन्मूलं तव जननि ताटङ्क महिमा॥

karAlaM yatkShvelaM kabalitavataH kAlakalanA

na shambhostanmUlaM tava janani tATaNkamahimA
॥ 28॥

करालं means most dangerous क्ष्वेलं is poison कबलितवत: swallowed शम्भो: Shiva कालकलना no end or death तन्मूलम् the reason for it is तव your ताटङ्ग महिमा, the glory of your ear pendants. Lord Shiva, even after consuming poison, survived due to the power of Ambāl's Tātangam - ear pendants. Such is the power of ear pendants that were once so simple that they were made from the leaves of palm tree (panai olai in Tamil). Even today, during Varalakshmi Puja, many homes decorate the face of Lakshmi with maroon *'Panai Olai'* ear pendants.

tapanōḍupa maṇḍalā

Tapan refers to Sun. Udupa is Moon. Mandala is a circle. Devi is wearing the Sun and Moon as Her ear ornaments.

पद्मरागशिलादर्शपरिभाविकपोलभू:।

नवविद्रुमबिम्बश्रीन्यक्कारिरदनच्छदा॥९॥

padmarāga śilādarśa paribhāvi kapōlabhūḥ।

navavidruma bimbaśrīḥ nyakkāri radanachChadā ॥9॥

23. **padmarāga śilādarśa paribhāvi kapōlabhūḥ:**

Padmaraga is a gem. It is clear ruby red in color. Kapolam means cheeks. Devi's cheeks outshine the beauty of Padmaraga.

24. **navavidruma bimbaśrīḥ nyakkāri radanachChadā**

This line describes the beauty of Devi's lips and teeth. There is a beautiful comparison here related to the color of Devi's lips. Nava vidruma refers to fresh coral. Coral is a marine gem, and it is found in intense red color.

Red Coral Praval or gemstone imparts courage and helps in overcoming fear and nervousness). The color of lips is also compared to bimbasri – a fruit that is bright red in color. It's called *'Kovaipazham'* in Tamil. (Tindora, Tondli is a common Hindi/marathi name). People cook raw green fruit and eat it.

The bright red color of Devi's lips is natural, and it puts the color of coral and bimbasri to shame.

शुद्धविद्याङ्कुराकारद्विजपङ्क्तिद्वयोज्ज्वला।

कर्पूरवीटिकामोदसमाकर्षिदिगन्तरा॥१०॥

śuddha vidyāṅkurākāra dvijapaṅkti dvayōjjvalā।

karpūravīṭi kāmōda samākarṣaddigantarā॥10॥

25. śuddha vidyāṅkurākāra dvijapaṅkti dvayōjjvalā

Suddha -pure Vidya -Knowledge Ankurakaara -fresh buds. Dvija is a term used for twice born-a brahmin. Upanayanam is considered another birth for brahmins and hence they are called Dwija. Likewise, even birds are first born as eggs and then hatch into little birdlings. Hence, called dwijā. The first set of teeth that we cut when young usually fall off and we get a second set of fresh bright teeth and hence these are termed as Dwijā.

Dwijā also has another meaning as explained by Bhāskararāya.

Vidya begins with Vedas by Brahmins. In turn, Vidya gets spread by Brahmins who are the buds of Vidya. Devi shines with her two rows of teeth in the form of the bud of pure knowledge. Bhāskararāya adds - There are

The Glory of Lalithā Sahasranāmam

thirty-two Dikshas or initiations laid down in the Tantras. These are called the two rows of Brahmins - like two rows of teeth. Suddhavidya - ankura beginning is a certain initiation to be begun before going into 32 Dikshas. Devi can be attained by those great men who go through 32 Dikshas.

26. karpūravīṭi kāmōda samākarṣaddigantarā

Karpura Vitika Moda refers to the fragrance of chewing camphor embedded Tamboolam – Betel leaves or Paan. Devi is described as 'Tamboola Purita Mukhi' Generally, in India, people consume betel leaf containing various ingredients after meals. It is not only a digestive but also a kind of deodorant.

Sama Akarshi Digantara – the fragrance pulls or spreads in all the 'Dishas' meaning directions. The Sanskrit word 'Dig' means directions like east west etc.

निजसल्लापमाधुर्यविनिर्भर्त्सितकच्छपी।

मन्दस्मितप्रभापूरमज्जत्कामेशमानसा॥ ११ ॥

nijasallāpa mādhurya vinirbhatsita kachChapī|

mandasmita prabhāpūra majjat-kāmēśa mānasā || 11 ||

27. nijasallāpa mādhurya vinirbhatsita kachChapī

This line describes the about the words coming from Devi's mouth. *Kacchapi* is the name of Saraswathi's Veena. Veena is a unique musical instrument having strings that produce beautiful melody. Saraswathi's Veena produces a super melody. *Sallapam* means conversation. Madhuryam also madhuram is sweetness. The sweet melody of Devi's speech puts to shame even the Veena of Saraswathi.

In short, Devi's speech is more melodious than Sarasvati's veena.

28. mandasmita prabhāpūra majjat-kāmēśa mānasā

Mandasmita means gentle smile. Prabhapura – fullness of glory. Majat -drowned.

The mind of Kamesa is drowned in the fullness of the glory of Devi's sweet smile. When it is said that the mind is drowned, it means that Devi's glory is unlimited. This verse also exemplifies the unity of Kamesa Kameshwari. Or Shiva Shakti Aykyam (Unity).

अनाकलितसादृश्यचुबुकश्रीविराजिता।

कामेशबद्धमाङ्गल्यसूत्रशोभितकन्धरा॥१२॥

anākalita sādṛśya chubuka śrī virājitā।

kāmēśabaddha māṅgalya sūtraśōbhita kantharā॥12॥

29. anākalita sādṛśya chubuka śrī virājitā

Next verse comes to describe Devi's Chin and Neck. Chubukam means Chin. Illuminated by the beauty (Virajita – spoken earlier) of Devi's chin the equal of which is not seen (Adrushya). Devi's chin is beyond comparison because of its unparallel beauty.

30. kāmēśabaddha māṅgalya sūtraśōbhita kantharā

Kamessa badda – Tied by kamesha. Mangalya Sutra – mangal Sutra, the holy marriage thread, Thaali. Shobita Kantara – Beautifully Adorned with the thali (Mangal Sutra) tied by kamesha around her neck.

कनकाङ्गदकेयूरकमनीयभुजान्विता।

रत्नग्रैवेयचिन्ताकलोलमुक्ताफलान्विता॥१३॥

kanakāṅgada kēyūra kamanīya bhujānvitā |

ratnagraivēya chintāka lōlamuktā phalānvitā || 13 ||

31. kanakāṅgada kēyūra kamanīya bhujānvitā

Going further, this verse describes Devi's arms. Kanaka means gold. You may know the famous *Kanakadharā stotram* composed by Adi Sankara as a brahmachari to help a poor woman.

Keyura means 'Armlet.' It is a decorative band, usually of gold, sometimes featuring precious gems, worn as an ornament around the upper arm. Armlets have been worn since ancient times.

You may see pictures of Kings wearing it. Kamaniya is pretty or beautiful. Bhuja refers to arm. Devi's arms are beautifully adorned with golden armlets.

32. ratnagraivēya chintāka lōlamuktā phalānvitā

This line says Devi's neck is adorned with a gem-studded necklace and a locket made of pearl hanging from it (lola). Graieva, refers to Neck-like in Hayagrieva-having horse's neck. Chintaka refers to meditation.

Bhāskararāya interprets - Ratnagraivēya chintaka -are those who meditate on the gem-studded neck. They worship her externally but not in their heart. They are kind of middle-class worshippers. The pearl hanging (lola) refers to those who are bound by earthly desires.

Agni Purana says, "Lola means change and desire". There are certain kinds of worshippers who belong to this type. They are the lowest class of worshippers. Muktas are the highest class of worshippers.

कामेश्वरप्रेमरत्नमणिप्रतिपणस्तनी।

नाभ्यालवालरोमालिलताफलकुचद्वयी॥१४॥

kāmēśvara prēmaratna maṇi pratipaṇastanī।

nābhyālavāla rōmāḻi latāphala kuchadvayī॥14॥

33. kāmēśvara prēmaratna maṇi pratipaṇastanī

Devi's bosom is described here. Her two breasts are the prize offered in return for that priceless gem- the love of Kameswara.

34. nābhyālavāla rōmāḻi latāphala kuchadvayī-

Those two breasts seem like the two fruits grown on the creeper-like hair that springs from Her navel.

लक्ष्यरोमलताधारतासमुन्नेयमध्यमा।

स्तनभारदलन्मध्यपट्टबन्धवलित्रया॥१५॥

lakṣyarōmalatā dhāratā samunnēya madhyamā।

stanabhāra daḻan-madhya paṭṭabandha vaḻitrayā॥15॥

35. lakṣyarōmalatā dhāratā samunnēya madhyamā-

Devi's waist is so thin that it is to be inferred only from the creeper-like hair.

36. stanabhāra daḻan-madhya paṭṭabandha vaḻitrayā

Her golden belt (pattabandha-odyanam) supports her waist that bends under the weight of the breasts (sthanabara) and makes visible the three folds of the skin below the bosom (valitraya).

अरुणारुणकौसुम्भवस्त्रभास्वत्कटीतटी।

रत्नकिङ्किणिकारम्यरशनादामभूषिता॥१६॥

arunāruna kausumbha vastra bhāsvat-katītatī |

ratnakiṅkiṇi kāramya raśanādāma bhūṣitā ‖ 16 ‖

37. aruṇāruṇa kausumbha vastra bhāsvat-katītatī-

Her waist is bright with an intense red (aruna-runa) garment.

38. ratnakiṅkiṇi kāramya raśanādāma bhūṣitā

It is decked in a belt (*odyanam*) beautified with jeweled bells (causing 'kinkini' sound). The odyanam is an ornament worn like a belt in the midriff part by traditional women in India mostly on occasions like wedding or festivals.

कामेशज्ञातसौभाग्यमार्दवोरुद्वयान्विता।

माणिक्यमुकुटाकारजानुद्वयविराजिता ॥१७॥

kāmēśa jñāta saubhāgya mārdavōru dvayānvitā |

māṇikya mukuṭākāra jānudvaya virājitā ‖ 17 ‖

39. kāmēśa jñāta saubhāgya mārdavōru dvayānvitā

The verse goes to describe Ambāl's legs. Ooru refers to the thigh. The symmetry and smoothness of her thighs are known only to Kamesha.

40. māṇikya mukuṭākāra jānudvaya virājitā

Her two knees (janu dwaya) shine like jeweled crowns (manikya mukuta)-refers to the kneecaps. In Latin, knee is termed Jenu. Some similarity with Janu.

इन्द्रगोपपरिक्षिप्तस्मरतूणाभजङ्घिका।

गूढगुल्फा कूर्मपृष्ठजयिष्णुप्रपदान्विता ॥१८॥

indragōpa parikṣipta smara tūṇābha jaṅghikā |

gūḍhagulbhā kūrmapṛṣṭha jayiṣṇu prapadānvita ‖ 18 ‖

41. indragōpa parikṣipta smara tūṇābha jaṅghikā

Janghika refers to calves – the portion below the knees and the ankle. Also called Shank. Thuni means the quiver – a circular case for the arrows. You can see it in the pictures of Rama and Lakshmana carrying the quiver on their backs. Parishipta means surrounded or overlaid. Devi's calves are like the sapphire-studded quiver of Manmatha- the god of love. The arrows point downwards in the quiver. In this case, it may mean that Devi's toenails may be considered as the arrow ends.

42. gūḍhagulbhā- Gulfa or Gulbha refers to Ankle bone. Gudhagulbha is hidden ankle bone.

43. kūrmapṛṣṭha jayiṣṇu prapadānvitā- Koormaprishta – Koorma is tortoise, Prishta is the backside. The hidden ankles have the instep arched like the back of a tortoise.

नखदीधितिसञ्छन्ननमज्जनतमोगुणा।

पदद्वयप्रभाजालपराकृतसरोरुहा॥ १९॥

nakhadīdhiti sañChanna namajjana tamōguṇā।

padadvaya prabhājāla parākṛta sarōruhā ॥ 19 ॥

44. nakhadīdhiti sañChanna namajjana tamōguṇā

Nakha Deethiti sanchanna- Nakha -Nails. The bright rays from her nails dispel the darkness (tamo guna) of her worshippers (namajjana). The worshippers include Brahma and Vishnu and others.

45. padadvaya prabhājāla parākṛta sarōruhā

Padadwaya: The two paadams- feet, prabhajala: by their beauty, parakrta saroruha: Shame the lotus Lotus (saroja). The soles of her feet by their beauty shame the lotus.

Meditation on her feet dispels ignorance. Feet are always respected in Sanatana Dharma. Hindus worship Padukas. Bharatan took Rama's Padukas and kept them on the Simhasana.

Glory of Devi's Lotus feet described in various scriptures. One example is श्रीपादसप्ततिः *Sripadasaptati* that contains 70 Exquisite Verses in Sanskrit in praise of Devi's Holy Feet. Composed by Sri Narayana Bhattatri of 'Narayaneeyam' fame at Mukthiṣṭhala (near Guruvayur).

On Ambāl's feet, my Guru used to narrate an interesting dialogue between two great scholars Appaya Deekshitar and Neelakanta Deekshitar.

Appaya asked: आपदि किं करणीयं? '*Aapadi kim karaneeyam?* -In calamity what should one do? Neelakanta answered: स्मरणीयं चरणयुगलम्बायाः। *Smaraneeyam Charana Yugalaambayaaha*-Remember the Lotus Feet of Devi Appaya continued: तत्स्मरणं किं कुरुते? *Tat smaranam kim kurute?* What will that remembrance do? Neelakanta replied: ब्रह्मादीनपि किङ्करीकुरुते *Brahmadeenapi Kimkari Kurute.* - All deities including Brahma will do anything for you.

Bhāskararāya adds an interesting story from Matsya and Padma Puranas. It is about Narada's comments after interpreting the *samudrika lakshanam* of Pārvati to her mother Mena. "A husband is not yet born for her. She will be devoid of good bodily marks. And her feet will err by their own shadow." Himawan got annoyed by this remark, but Narada clarified. " You are annoyed because you did not understand my comments. When I said A husband is not born for her, it meant someone who is not created."

Shiva does not belong to the group of created beings. I will explain what I meant by saying her feet will err by their own shadow. Her feet are like lotuses, shining with bright nails. When the Devas and Asuras prostrate before her, the colors of their crowns reflected will drive away the rays of her nail entering their hearts and dispel their Tamas guna.

Devi's feet are thus given the highest importance in Hindu scriptures.

शिञ्जान मणिमञ्जीरमण्डितश्रीपदाम्बुजा।

मरालीमन्दगमना महालावण्यशेवधिः ॥२०॥

śiñjāna maṇimañjīra maṇḍita śrī padāmbujā।

marāḷī mandagamanā, mahālāvaṇya śēvadhiḥ ॥20॥

46. śiñjāna maṇimañjīra maṇḍita śrī padāmbujā

Her lotus feet are adorned with jeweled anklets (*golusu* in Tamil) that tinkle.

47. marāḷī mandagamanā Marali- is a female swan (Hamsa). You know how a swan moves in an elegant and gentle manner. Devi's gait is slow and gentle that of the swan.

48. mahālāvaṇya śēvadhiḥ It is a treasure house of great beauty

सर्वारुणाऽनवद्याङ्गी सर्वाभरणभूषिता।

शिवकामेश्वराङ्कस्था शिवा स्वाधीनवल्लभा॥२१॥

sarvāruṇānavadyāṅgī sarvābharaṇa bhūṣitā|

śivakāmeśvarāṅkasthā, śivā, svādhīna vallabhā ||21||

49. **sarvāruṇāna Sarvaruna-** RosyRed-hued all over, Her garments, limbs, ornaments etc.

50. **navadyāṅgī** Having faultless limbs

51. **sarvābharaṇa bhūṣitā** Adorned with all types of ornaments. It is said there are at least 40 ornaments from head to toe.

52. **śivakāmeśvarāṅkasthā** Sitting on the lap of Sivakameshwara.

    With this verse, the description of Devi's physical form ends.

53. **Siva- the beneficial, the auspicious.** Devi does good, hence called Siva. Also, as Samkari. She possesses excellent qualities like Siva. She is identical with Siva.

54. **Svādhīna vallabhā -** She has won over Her Lord. Without her, Siva is powerless as the very first verse of Soundarya Lahari says:

Shivah shakthya yukto yadi bhavati shaktah prabhavitum

Na chedevam devo na khalu kusalah spanditumapi;

Atas tvam aradhyam Hari-Hara-Virinchadibhir api

Pranantum stotum vaa katham akrta-punyah prabhavati

Lord Shiva becomes able to do creation in this world only with Shakthi with him. Without her, he cannot move even an inch. And so how can, one who does not do good deeds, or one who does not praise you, become competent to worship you Oh, goddess Who is worshipped by the trinity.

Chapter 3

The Killing of Bhandasura

From the shlokam number 22, the description of Ambāl's abode continues until nāma 63.

सुमेरुमध्यशृङ्गस्था श्रीमन्नगरनायिका।

चिन्तामणिगृहान्तस्था पञ्चब्रह्मासनस्थिता॥२२॥

sumēru madhyaśṛṅgasthā, śrīmannagara nāyikā।

chintāmaṇi gṛhāntasthā, pañchabrahmāsanasthitā ॥22॥

55. sumēru madhyaśṛṅgasthā

After the description of Devi's physical form from head to foot earlier, this verse starts the description of Srinagaram, Ambāl's place of living or abode

Ambāl is Omnipresent. Vishnu means All Pervasive. So, what does abode mean? Lord Shiva's abode is seen as Mount Kailash in the Himalayas; This abode helps us to visualize Shiva with a background of the big mountain Himalayas. Vishnu's abode is Vaikuntam where he is seen on the middle of *Khsheera Sagaram*- milky ocean reclining on the bed of Adisheshan. Likewise, Ambāl too has an abode to help us visualize. It is described here in this verse. Devi dwells in the mid-peak of Mount Meru; and, in the Bindu, the central circle of bliss in Sri Chakra.

What does 'sumēru madhyaśṛṅgasthā' mean? It means Ambāl lives on the beautiful middle peak of Mount Sumeru. Mount Meru is a mystical and sacred five-peaked mountain which is referenced in many Hindu texts. It is thought to be the center of all spiritual universe. Mount Meru is invisible to the normal eyes.

In Sanskrit, the prefix su-, adds an adjective like 'excellent or wonderful to the word -like you say 'Swagatam and Suswagatham" (Welcome, Sweet welcome) "prabhatam, suprabhatam, Priya and Supriya. Praja and Supraja. Su- makes the noun beautiful. So, Sumeru means beautiful Meru. Madhya is middle, sringam refers to the peak of a mountain (It also means horns of animals).

As a great Devi Upaska and a Sanskrit scholar Bhāskararāya gives different perspectives of slokas.

Bhāskararāya quotes from *Lalitaa Stava Ratna*, a book authored by the great sage Durvaasa. He quotes the following verses 2 to 4 (in AryA dvishatI) describing Lalitha Devi's abode and his worship of it.

Verse 2:

स जयति सुवर्णशैलः सकल जगच्चक्र सङ्घटितमूर्तिः।

काञ्चन निकुञ्जवाटी कन्दलदमरीप्रपञ्च सङ्गीतः॥२॥

sa jayati suvarNashailaH sakalajagachchakrasaNghaTitam UrtiH|

kAnchana nikunjavATI kandaladamarIprapancha saNgItaH||2||

स जयति सुवर्णशैलः Let the gold mountain be victorious. सकलजगच्चक्रसङ्घटितमूर्तिः whose body is made up of the whole universe, कन्दलदमरीप्रपञ्च सङ्गीतः filled by the music of the divine women काञ्चन निकुञ्जवाटी living the golden creepers of mountain peak;

"Let the gold mountain be victorious, whose body is made up of the whole universe, filled by the music of the divine ladies living in the golden creeper-bowers of mountain peak."

Verse 3:

हरिहयनैरृतमारुतहरितामन्तेष्ववस्थितं तस्य।

विनुमः सानुत्रितयं विधिहरिगौरीशविष्टपाधारम्॥३॥

harihayanairRitamArutaharitAmanteShvavasthitaM tasya|

vinumaH sAnutritayaM vidhiharigaurIshaviShTapAdh Aram||3||

Meaning: We salute the three peaks of it which are the seats of Brahma, Vishnu and Siva, expanding to the four quarters of the globe.

Verse 4:

मध्ये पुनर्मनोहररत्नरुचिस्तबक रञ्जितदिगन्तम्।

उपरि चतुः शतयोजनमुत्तङ्ग शृङ्गम्पुङ्गवमुपासे॥४॥

madhye punarmanohararatnaruchistabaka ranjitadigantam|

upari chatuH shatayojanamuttaNga shRiNgampuNgavamup Ase|| 4||

 The Glory of Lalithā Sahasranāmam

Meaning: In the middle of them, there is another peak, four hundred yojanas in height beautifying the place by the golden rays of flowers and I worship it.

56. śrīmannagara nāyikā

It means Ambāl is the ruler of this beautiful city of Srinagar. We have seen the different meanings of the prefix 'Sri' in our last session. Here Sri means 'wealth.' Nagara refers to a city. Naayika – Ruler. There are different interpretations to this city.

Bhāskararāya says: The cities are of two kinds. One is on the middle peak of Mount Meru. It is believed to be constructed by Devas. The second city is the one beyond universe in an island called "Ratna Dweepam."

Bhāskararāya quotes another text in Vidyaratnahbasya. It says, "There is also another city in the midst of the Ocean of milk. The second city of Srinagar is outside and beyond all the worlds, in the island of gems (Ratnadveepa), in the middle of the Ocean of Nectar."

Srinagar city has 25 outer corridors. Each one is built with different metals such as iron, brass, silver, gold, panchaloham (five metal alloy), and, gems of different kinds like pearls, emeralds, sapphire, topaz, ruby and so on. The city also has several abodes for deities like shyamala devi, vaarahi, yoginis, mahavishnu, esanan, digpalakas, taradevi, vaaruni, kurukulla devi and others. At the center is the Chintamanigruham, referred to in the next line.

In Vidyratna bhashsya, this beautiful city is explained as Sri Chakra. It says, "Chakra means city, house, town and abode;" meaning Nagara and Chakra are one and the same. Devi devotees are familiar with Sri Chakram, also called Sri Yantra – a device, the mystical sacred diagram having a complex geometry of circles, squares and triangles, used in Shakti worship.

There are various interpretations and many figures that represent the Sri Chakra. Chakra is in three main types, single-dimensional plane, pyramidal and spherical. The worship of Devi in a diagrammatic form, is regarded as the highest form of Devi worship. The Chakra is formed by nine interlocking triangles that radiate from the center. It represents the goddess Tripura Sundari and Shiva-Shakti Aykyam, the union of Shiva and Shakti, the central focus in Lalithā Sahasranāmam.

Adi Shankaracharya installed Sri Chakra in many important temples in India. Sri Chakra is an important aspect of Shakti worship. There is a beautiful song that begins *"SriChakra Raja Simhaneswari, Sri Lalithambike Bhuvaneswari."* It has Sanskrit and Tamil verses.

57. chintāmaṇi gṛhāntasthā

It means residing in a house built of Chintamani. Chintamani is a jewel stone which yields all the objects desired by a devotee. If a single stone gives what all you want, just imagine Ambāl residing in a house built of Chintamani stones. Living in the city of wealth and in a house of generous Chintamani stones, Devi grants anything that you ask. Reciting Lalithā Sahasranāmam serves as a *Kalpaka Vraksham* – a tree that grants your desires for ever.

58. Pañchabrahmāsanasthitā

Sitting upon a seat formed by five Brahmas. Who are the five Brahmas? On a beautiful couch, the mattress is Sadasiva; the four supports of the couch are Brahma, Hari, Rudra and Eesana; The supreme Lalitha Devi is seen seated majestically over these five Brahmas, representing Panchakrityas – the five activities.

महापद्माटवीसंस्था कदम्बवनवासिनी।

सुधासागरमध्यस्था कामाक्षी कामदायिनी॥२३॥

mahāpadmāṭavī saṃsthā, kadamba vanavāsinī।

sudhāsāgara madhyasthā, kāmākṣī kāmadāyinī॥23॥

59. mahāpadmāṭavī saṃsthā

Residing in the great forest full of big lotuses. In general, in Hinduism, lotus flower represents spiritual enlightenment, growth, purity.

In Sanskrit, one object can be defined by many words. So, the lotus has many names like:

सरोजा, पद्मा, नीरजा, पंकजा, कमला, अंबुजा (Saroja, Padma, Neeraja, Pankaja, Kamala, Ambuja) and so on.

Here the lotus is called mahāpadmāṭavī. 'Mahapadmam' is no ordinary lotus, it means a giant lotus, the thousand petalled lotus, Sahasradalapadmam. It is extremely beautiful.

The most important thing about the lotus is that even after growing in murky waters, it is untouched by the impurity of water and remains beautiful. The lotus is symbolic of the fact that a human being struggling in the dirty waters of 'Samsara' can still emerge from it into a superior being like a lotus.

Puranas say that the lotus emerged from the navel of Lord Vishnu. Lotus is the symbol of Lakshmi and prosperity.

Muthuswamy Deekshitar sings on Ambāl as 'Kanchadalayadakshi Kamakshi Kamala manohari' One who has eyes ("akshi") like lotus ("kancha") petals ("dalaya") in Kamalamanohari Ragam.

Another shloka reads, *"Sahasra dhala padhmastha Sarva varnopi shobitha"* She who sits on thousand petalled lotus; She who shines in all colors.

Sahasrara सहस्रार, is a word used in Yoga which also means "thousand-petalled." In yogic tradition, it is the seventh chakra located near the crown of the head and represents a thousand-petaled lotus flower.

Let me clarify here about a common misunderstanding about Yoga as we see hundreds of Yoga centers sprouting everywhere. Yoga is not just a system confined to a set of physical exercises. It is much more than that.

The mightiest power in humans is the power of thought. Yoga has a big impact on the mind. Yoga means "union"- arising from the verb 'Yuj' -to join. The union of the Jeevatma with Paramatma. Patanjali, the author of Yoga Sastra talks a lot about its significance to controlling and harnessing the power of mind to achieve bliss like a true Yogi. Physical exercises like Asanas are a small part of Yoga Sastra.

The human body has many Chakras or energy centers through which the Cosmic energy flows. Through Yoga it is possible to awaken these inner dormant energy centers and achieve peace, harmony and happiness. It is said that Kundalini Shakti lies dormant, coiled up like a serpent at the base of the human body.

Through rigorous yogic practices, this shakti can be awakened and sent up through the main nerves of the body Sushumna nadi (central path) through other chakras until it reaches the highest of chakras at the top of the head, Sahasrara or crown chakra.

This unique and most difficult process is believed to achieve different levels of awakening and a mystical experience producing an extremely profound transformation of consciousness.

60. kadamba vanavāsinī

Devi lives in a grove of trees called Kadamba Vanam. So, she is described as 'Kadmaba Vana Vasini.' In that forest, there are many lotus blooms.

61. sudhāsāgara madhyasthā – Residing in the center of the ocean of nectar

62. kāmākṣī

63. kāmadāyinī

She who has beautiful eyes, who grants all wishes.

Is it true that Devi really grants wishes? Many people including me and some of my friends have really experienced it. History shows that many devotees received Ambāl's blessings. I will give you some examples.

1. The great poet Kalidasa (5th Century) who was just a shepherd became an instant Kavi by the blessings of Devi. He composed the first poem – a beautiful verse called 'Shyamala Dandakam' in praise of Devi starting with the lines:

माणिक्यवीणामुपलालयन्तीं, मदालासां मञ्जुलवाग्विलासाम्।

माहेन्द्रनीलद्युतिकोमलाङ्गीं, मातंगकन्यां मनसा स्मरामि॥१॥

चतुर्भुजे चन्द्रकलावतंसे, कुचोन्नते कुङ्कुमरागशोणे।

पुण्ड्रेक्षुपाशाङ्कुशपुष्पबाण-हस्ते नमस्ते जगदेकमातः॥२॥

mANikyavINAmupalAlayantIM

madAlasAM manjulavAgvilAsAm|

mAhendranIladyutikomalANgIM

mAta~NgakanyAM manasA smarAmi||1||

chaturbhuje chandrakalAvata.nse

kuchonnate kuNkumarAgashoNe|

puNDrekShupAshANkushapuShpabANa-

haste namaste jagadekamAtaH||2||

He authored two mahākāvyas, Kumārasambhava (Kumāra meaning Kartikeya, and sambhava an incident – a birth. Kumārasambhava thus means the birth of a Kartikeya) and Raghuvaṃśa ("Dynasty of Raghu").

2. **Bhāskararāya** (1690–1785) was another mahaan who lived barely 300 years ago (during the reign of King Serfoji of Thanjavur). He lived in the village next to my ancestral

village of Maharajapuram gifted by the king. Still, there are some lands in his name. He is considered an authority on Devi worship and wrote over 40 works including the Bhasyam on Lalithā Sahasranāmam. It is said that these meanings were revealed to Bhāskararāya by the Goddess Herself. He has performed many miracles. A temple of 'Baskareshwar' and a Mantap (memorial hall) is built in his honor at this village.

3. **Ramakrishna Paramahamsa** (1836-1886) was a Priest at Dakshineswar Kali Temple near Kolkata. Ramakrishna developed intense devotion to Mother Kali and spent hours in loving adoration of her image, forgetting priestly duties. Sri Ramakrishna did not write any books, nor did he deliver public lectures. Instead, he chose to speak in a simple language using parables and metaphors by way of illustration. His disciple was the famous Swami Vivekananda who visited Chicago in 1893 and spoke brilliantly at the World's Parliament of Religions. He founded the well-known organization called Ramakrishna Mission that operates worldwide.

4. **Abirami Battar** was another person who received Devi's instant blessings. He lived around the same time as **Bhāskararāya** in a town called Tirukadaiyur in Tamil Nadu. His original name was Subramaniya Iyer. He served as a priest at the local shiva temple where Abhirami is the Goddess. Lord Shiva in the temple is known as Amrithagateswarar. Legend goes that the Devas kept a pot of Amritha(nectar) in Thirukadaiyur. This pot became one with the land and became the Shiva linga. At this

temple, it is believed, that the Sage Markandeya prayed Lord Shiva and avoided death forever. People worship at this temple for long life and perform *Sadabhishekam*. Abhirami means "She who is always attractive". This goddess is believed to fulfil the wishes of all her devotees. Subramanya was not only a priest but a great devotee who never used to think of any other thing except Devi. This made him look like a mad man. One day King Serfoji, the Mahratta king who was ruling over Thanjavur region visited the temple. The king asked Abhirama Bhattar the "Thithi" meaning the phase of the moon. Abhirama Bhattar, who was at the time seeing the Goddess in his reverie answered that it was Pournami (Full moon). But it was really an Amavasya (No moon) day. The king was annoyed by his wrong reply and ordered that Subramanya be executed if the moon failed to light the sky that night. Subramanya later realized his mistake. He instantly composed a divine song called "Abirami Anthaadi" in Tamil praising the glory of Goddess Abirami. Anthaadi is a compound word made up of 2 words: Antham (last) and Aadi (first). In this style of poetry, the last word of the previous stanza must be the same as the first word of the next stanza. It has one hundred and one verses. The beauty of this Anthaadi is the story behind it. Subramanya had completed 78 verses when dusk set in, while his own future was still in darkness. At the 79th verse, the Goddess Abirami appeared in person and flung her diamond earring into the sky. It shone brilliantly like the full moon for all to see! The King too saw it. Thus, inspired by the full

The Glory of Lalithā Sahasranāmam

moon, Subramanya sang 22 more verses. The King felt sorry and honoured him.

From that day Subramanya became the famous Abirami Bhattar. Each stanza of the poem Abhirami Anthaadi is a gem of poetry.

Above all, Adi Sankara himself was a great devotee of Ambāl and his *Soundaryalahari* is an outstanding work on Devi.

Next verses 24 to 33 describe many divine activities of Devi including the slaying the demon Bhandasura, creation of the ten avataras and revival of manmadan, the god of love.

In Lalithā Sahasranāmam and in Devi Bhagavadam, Devi fights with many asuras. Why is Devi shown with weapons and described as fighting demons? One must understand a few basic things to better appreciate why Devi holds weapons.

Throughout history, good and evil always existed. There are good guys and bad guys. Even today, in schools and communities, the strong bodied boys harass the puny ones. There is always a fight between them. In Hinduism, we believe there were four yugas and legends show that in every yuga there were fights between the good and the evil.

In Satya or Krita Yuga, the fight was between Devas and Asuras. Almost all the Devas vs Asuras battles were held in Satyayuga. The Puranas say that the Vedas were stolen from Brahma by an Asura Hayagriva and hidden underneath the ocean. Lord Vishnu took Matsyavataram (incarnation as a fish) to retrieve them. In Varaha Avatara, he destroyed the demon 'Hiranyaksha' who hid Bhooma Devi - Mother Earth in the ocean. In Narasamiha Avatara, he killed Hiranyakshipu and protected Prahlada.

In Treta Yuga, the fight was between good and bad humans; between Parashuram and Kshatriyas; between Rama and Ravana.

In Dwapara Yuga, the fight was between the members of one family -the Kuru Vamsa. Between cousins -the Kauravas and Pandavas. Despite the best efforts by Lord Krishna to patch up differences, war was inevitable. Krishna justifies it in the Bhagavad Gita.

In Kali Yuga, the fight is within the minds of human beings-full of conflicts and sinful thoughts, the pulls of evil desires, greed, jealousy and so on tearing up human lives. These emotional pulls within one's mind get shaped into violent and destructive acts like fights, rapes, shootings and killings around the world. In the previous Yugas, the bad guys or Asuras like Bhandasura were openly seen as aggressive. The good people either moved away from them or prayed Bhagavan to kill the Asuras and protect them. In the current Kali Yuga, the Asuras are in the minds of people. So, it is difficult to identify them because they are not visible or aggressive but look as though they are good and get us carried away.

Don't we hear of shootings and killings at public places done by persons who are least known to be violent or suspected?

What's the reason? It is because their minds are restive and turn aggressive due to a variety of critical social issues such as single moms, depression and sufferings in childhood. How do you address such issues? Law alone is not adequate. Our wise ancestors recommended a four-step approach to avoid conflicts and war situations. It is called "Saama-Dhana-Bheda-Danda."

1. Sama- the first step, is to talk and reach an agreement.

2. Dana- the second, means to give gifts or compensation.

3. Bheda- refers to usage of Logic or comparisons to influence the mind.

4. Danda- literally meaning stick, to apply force or armaments. wage a war.

So, weapons and war are required as a last step to win over evil. If you face a hungry lion in a forest, can you say "Look Lion, I am a pure vegetarian. I have never harmed any animal. please don't kill me." Do you expect the lion will listen to you? Here the four-step approach won't work. You must either kill the lion or get killed. No options. Ahimsa does not work here.

Look at the situation in a forest. There are millions of animals, stronger ones killing weaker ones for food. The lion kills a deer; The vulture kills a racoon; The python strangles a goat; The alligator kills a big fish and so on. Does this stop any activity? Animals continue to procreate and live there. So, it is all a part of nature.

The lesson is - we need to live with nature and at the same time protect ourselves from enemies and aggression. That's why we need police and the army.

There are aggressive elements all round the world. Every country must defend itself. Those who cause terror and harass innocent people are inherently not interested in ethics and morality.

History shows many leaders who were arrogant with power and did not respect righteous behavior and social order. Stories of Mahabharata and Ramayana tell us of such leaders like Duryodhana and Ravana. Following any peaceful means or ethics with such people is impossible. So, in such a situation, war is the only solution.

Lalithā Sahasranāmam and Devi Māhatmyam show us reality. Devi's killing the asuras must be viewed in the right perspective of killing the bad guys for the sake of protecting the good guys.

"Dharma Samstapa Narthaya, Sambavami Yuge Yuge" – To establish Dharma, I shall appear in every Yuga- says Bhagavan in Vishnu Sahasranamam.

The unpredictable human mind is the main cause for creating many problems in present day world. Devi helps us kill the Asuras or evil thoughts in our minds in very simple ways. Lalithā Sahasranāmam is one of the key instruments. As I mentioned before, every naama in LalithaSahasranamam is a mantra. What is mantra? *'Manana trayate iti mantra:* By repeated chanting, there is less conflict and more peace in the mind. Don't we say, Om Shanti, Shanti, Shantihi! -Peace, Peace, Peace! at the end of reciting shlokams.

देवर्षिगणसङ्घातस्तूयमानात्मवैभवा।

भण्डासुरवधोद्युक्तशक्तिसेनासमन्विता॥२४॥

dēvarṣi gaṇasaṅghāta stūyamānātma vaibhavā।

bhaṇḍāsura vadhōdyukta śaktisēnā samanvitā॥24॥

64. dēvarṣi gaṇa saṅghāta, stūyamānātma vaibhavā

dēvarṣi (DevaRishi) gaṇa (groups) saṅghāta (assemblies)

Devi's power is praised by the assemblies of multitudes of Devas and Rishis. Bhāskararāya gives more interpretation. Samghata (literally. much destruction) is one of the names of hell—to be saved from this hell. Or, Sam, entirely ghata, slaying, namely Bhandasura.

stūyamānātma vaibhavā She is the soul or Atma and Power in devotees.The deeper meaning of 'stuyammanatma vaibhava' is explained by Bhāskararāya. It is described in Shaiva scriptures that Atman alone is praised by Devas. The universal form Lalita is declared to be the very Self; as she is inseparable from the Self, her Vaibava (power) is all-pervading.

65. bhaṇḍāsura vadhōdyukta śaktisēnā samanvitā

Devi was endowed with an army of various Shakties (energetic forces) for the sake of slaying Bhandasura.

Now, let's first see who is this Bhandasura and why should Devi kill him? There is a story about Bhandasura.

Earlier, I had mentioned that Shiva burnt Manmatha to ashes. There are different versions of Bhandasura on how he emerged from the ashes of Manmatha. Bhāskararāya quotes *Lalitopakhyina* and explains: The fighting between Devi and Bhandasura is fully described in the Lalitopakhyina. Concerning the burning of Manmatha, it is said in the same book, "Ganesa, the skillful worker, seeing the ashes of Manmatha, the god of Love, made from them a beautifully formed idol of a man. Don't we see kids playing with clay, unmindful of the dirt?

When Shiva looked at it, the idol became alive. Brahma on seeing this action, said, "well done. Well done" (Bhanda, Bhanda), hence, in the world he is called Bhandasura." When he emerged Bhanda was a good person. He worshipped Shiva.

Shiva is *Asutosh* meaning He gets pleased very quickly and showers boons. Being pleased with Bhanda's faith and perseverance, Shiva told him to ask for boons. Bhanda desired that half the strength of his foes during battle should be transferred to himself and that none of the weapons of his foes should have any effect on him. Siva granted the boons and gave him power to rule all kingdoms and gave him many celestial weapons too. Then how did the good Bhandasura turn into a bad guy? Let's see further.

Asura: Asu, life; Ra: to take away; Asura: he who takes away life. The fierce quality (asuratva) of Bhandasura is explained in the same scripture "As the powerful Bhanda sprang from the fire of Rudra's anger, his nature was terrible (Raudra), hence he became the terrible one (dhanava).

He became very powerful and most invincible. Bhanda also means 'bondage' that causes ignorance out of desires. Bhandasura was mindless and ignorant.

In addition To Bhanda, thousands of Rakshasas emerged out of the ash of Manmatha. All of them became followers of Bhandasura. They formed a strong army. Shukracharya became Bhandasura's Guru and initiated him with many mantras of mysterious power. As advised by Shukracharya, Bhandasura engaged himself in those mantras, and became very powerful. Power corrupts and absolute power corrupts absolutely.

Bhandasura became arrogant with power and started harassing the Devas including Indra. Nobody dared to fight him because of the boons he had received from Lord Shiva. On the advice of Sage Narada, Indra and Devas performed Tapas to Parashakti Devi for necessary help to vanquish Bhandasura.

We saw earlier that Indra and his devas built the homa gunda and performed a great Yagna. We learnt that out of this kunda's Fire, Devi emerged magnificently to fulfill the wishes of Devas as said in *Deva karya Samudyata*. The lesson of Bhandasura is that even good people can turn bad if they get corrupted by power or wealth.

In the next verse, Devi's army and its strengths are described. In every country, organization or community, there is always a hierarchy. If you take a country, there is a president or prime minister who is the chief or CEO. He has many ministers, and each minister is endowed with some power. A company has a CEO supported by COO, CFO and so on. Even in the flat management structure, there is an informal hierarchy where someone calls the shots.

In defense, the line of command is most important to ensure discipline. If orders by a superior officer are not followed, there could be a court martial. So, the defense of a country has a very clear hierarchy - is controlled by a defense minister and a Chief of Armed forces, supported by Army, Navy and Airforce.

In each of these divisions, there is a clear hierarchy. In the army, starting from a second lieutenant it goes up to the General. Likewise in the Airforce, starting from a pilot officer, the ranking goes right up to Air Marshal. An army consists of many divisions like infantry, corps of engineers, tank brigades and so on.

In ancient days, the defense forces consisted mainly of what is called- *Ratha, Gaja, Turuka, Patati* - like in chess, an army had chariots, elephants, horses, and soldiers. They too had a hierarchy. While Devi served as the commander-in-chief there were several other sub-commanders serving her.

The Brahmānda Purana describes the powerful military commanders who accompanied Devi, all amazing shaktis, demi-goddesses eager to fight and free the world from evil.

This section of the scripture is somewhat yogic: the shaktis are the innate energies of the subtle body, and their chariots are the yantras or sacred mandalas in which these energies embody themselves when yogis worship their yantras with reverence. Some of the army commanders are named and described here in the following verse.

सम्पत्करीसमारूढसिन्धुरव्रजसेविता।

अश्वारूढाधिष्ठिताश्वकोटिकोटिभिरावृता ॥२५॥

sampatkarī samārūḍha sindhura vrajasēvitā |

aśvārūḍhādhiṣṭhitāśva kōṭikōṭi bhirāvṛtā ||25 ||

66. sampatkarī samārūḍha

Attended by herds of elephants conducted by Sampatkari.

Sampatkari is the chief leading the elephants. She is deity about whom the Svatantra Tantra says, "There is a certain Vidya called Sampatkari of unimaginable power. This goddess is described in the Lalitopikhyana as the head of the elephants belonging to Devi. Sampatkari sprang from the 'angusa' elephant-goad of the Supreme Lalita. You need the angusam -the spear shaped goad to control elephants.

Sampatkari herself rode upon the elephant named *'Rana kolihala'* (delighting in war). Thousands of the finest elephants followed her.

sindhura vrajasēvitā- Sindhura means elephants. There are many kinds of elephants, i.e., Bhadra, Mandra, Mrga, etc.

67. aśvārūḍhā dhiṣṭhitāśhva kōṭikōṭi bhirāvṛtā - Lalita Devi is surrounded by (kotikoti) crores (a crore is ten million) of horses led by Asvarudha.

Aruda in Sanskrit means seated on – a rider. Asvaa-is a female horse. Asvaarudha is a goddess, and she is the mistress of the horses of Devi.

The Brahmānda Purana says, "Asvaruda sprang from the noose (paasam) of Lalita Devi and rode in front with great speed on a horse called aparajita, and crores of swift horses followed her."

Horse denotes power. The rook in the game of chess is very powerful as it can jump over other players. (Chess or Chaturang was invented in India). Even now, the power of an engine or a motor is denoted by the letters H.P. indicating Horsepower. How is a horse controlled? By the reins – long narrow straps that are attached to the horse's mouth. It seems logical that Asvaruda emerged from Devi's rope of Paasam.

Bhāskararāya adds a philosophical meaning to it. Senses are also called horses. Don't experience our senses running fast like horses?

For example, you go into a restaurant; the sense of taste runs high. We can't decide what to order. When we see a horrific scene in the TV like people getting killed, our sense of fear runs high.

Every day, we experience senses of joy and sorrow. Aruda is a rider considered as the controller of the senses, that is mind. Senses are compared to horses as they run faster and without control, if let loose. Mind is the jockey of the horse as mind alone can control the senses. Devi is seated as a jockey in the mind. So, Devi directs endless sense-impressions in

The Glory of Lalithā Sahasranāmam

many minds simultaneously. How can we harness the power of mind? Through Mantra-shakti.

We have now seen that the powerful elephant and horse brigades have emerged from the two hands of Devi. They are ready to fight against Bhandasura.

The next verse describes more on other strengths of Devi's army.

चक्रराजरथारूढसर्वायुधपरिष्कृता।

गेयचक्ररथारूढमन्त्रिणीपरिसेविता॥२६॥

chakrarāja rathārūḍha sarvāyudha pariṣkṛtā |

gēyachakra rathārūḍha mantriṇī parisēvitā ||26||

68. chakrarāja rathārūḍha, sarvāyudha pariṣkṛtā

Seated in the chariot named Chakraraja, Devi is armed with all the weapons.

The LalitopAkyAna describes several types of chariots used in the devi's army. These include three main types, Chakraraja geyachakra and kirichakra; chakrarAja is the foremost amongst them. Chakra itself means wheels.

Chakraraja is described as: "The best of chariots, Chakraraja which belongs to the great queen, is ten Yojanas in height and four in circumference with the Ananda flag on top of it."

Bhāskararāya adds: Chakraraja may also be taken to mean SriChakra.

Chakrarajaratha may be taken as one word meaning the Siddhi called Chakre satva, or power of controlling the Chakras.

Arudha: capable of conferring; to be contemplated upon. (Arudam in Tamil mens forecasting) Sarvayudha: all the weapons. Isn't Devi described as SriChakra Raja Simhaneswari?

69. Geyachakra ratharūḍha mantriṇī parisēvitā

Geyachakra is the next best chariot, with huge wheels and driven by a deity called Mantrini. Geya means to be praised or important.

Mantrini is another name for Shyamala Devi -the dusk-colored deity. Mantrini with her army worships Devi.

किरिचक्ररथारूढदण्डनाथापुरस्कृता।

ज्वालामालिनिकाक्षिप्तवहिनप्राकारमध्यगा॥२७॥

kirichakra ratharūḍha daṇḍanāthā puraskṛtā |

jvālāmālini kākṣipta vahniprākāra madhyagā ॥27॥

70. kirichakra ratharūḍha daṇḍanāthā puraskṛtā

She is preceded by Dandanatha who rides her chariot Kirichakra. Kiri means a boar. The chariot called Kirichakra is of the form of a boar. It may also mean that it is drawn by boars. Dandanatha is the goddess, Varahi.

She is called Dandanatha because she always carries a rod (Danda) in her hand.

Kirichakra which is considered one of the best chariots was also there. Where the chariot Chakraraja was, Geyachakra was also there, and where the Geya chariot stood, there the Kirichakra was also seen. These three chariots are the equivalent to modern armoured tanks. They seemed like the three animated worlds.

71. jvālāmālini kākṣipta vahniprākāra madhyagā

She resides in the center of the fortress of fire constructed by Jvalamalini.

Jvalamalini is the Nitya deity of Chaturdasi, on the fourteenth day of the lunar month. Jvala, fire; Mala, garland; Aksipta, destroying; Vahniprakara, sparks of fire; Madhyaya, she who is seated in the midst. In battles, fire is often used to scare and ward off enemies and protect one's own commanders from enemies' attacks.

In the Brahmānda Purana, it is said that Devi asked Jvalamalini to protect the great army by constructing a fortress of Fire which shall cover the earth and extend over a hundred Yojanas in circumference, and thirty Yojanas in height. So, Jvalamalini followed Devi's instructions and is performing the role of protecting Devi who resides right at the center of the fort of fire.

Bhāskararāya gives a philosophical interpretation:

There are two states or conditions (Avasthas), action and energy. Action perishes, while the other is imperishable. Effort directed towards action may be stopped: when that effort ceases, the ignorant man thinks, that he is himself asleep. But his inner self never sleeps, though others may, for want of perception in themselves, believe it to be asleep.

Though action manifested in the form of sparks, flame, etc., perishes, the wise man who is in the fire of consciousness, who is the brightness of the fire and who is brightness itself, never perishes.

भण्डसैन्यवधोद्युक्तशक्तिविक्रमहर्षिता।

नित्यापराक्रमाटोपनिरीक्षणसमुत्सुका॥२८॥

bhaṇḍasainya vadhōdyukta śakti vikramaharṣitā|

nityā parākramāṭōpa nirīkṣaṇa samutsukā ||28||

72. bhaṇḍasainya vadhōdyukta śakti vikramaharṣitā

She is delighted at the activity of the Shaktis that are prepared to destroy the army of Bhanda. Shaktis here refer to Nakuli and other goddesses.

73. nityā parākramāṭōpa nirīkṣaṇa samutsukā

She rejoices at beholding the rising valor of the Nityas.

Who are Nityas? The Moon is considered as a Devata in Sanatana Dharma. It is a planet in Astrology.

Purusha Suktam says:

चन्द्रमा मनसो जात: श्चक्षोः सूर्यो अजायत।

मुखादिन्द्रश्चाग्निश्चं प्राणाद्वायुरंजायत॥२८॥

candramA manaso jAtaH| caksho sUryo ajAyata|

mukhAdindraScAgniSca| prANAt vAyurajAyata||14||

Moon emerged from the mind of the great Purusha. So, the Moon has power over the mind and is responsible for the soundness of the mind. Mind and moon are closely connected.

We feel very happy on full moon days – in fact, it is romantic. The moon rules the mind and our emotions. Amavasai (no moon day) is dark, and moods are down. The name lunatic meaning a mad man comes from lunar.

Hindu sastras believe in the spiritual and cosmic significance of the phases of the moon.

Moon waxes and wanes. There are 15 Days between Poornima and Amavasya. Each lunar phase called a *Thithi* is ruled by a Nitya. (By the way, Athithi- meaning a guest is opposite to Thithi, which means a guest who can come any time without notice. Beautiful Sanskrit!).

Nityas are Kameswari, Bhagamalini, Nityaklinna, Bherunda, Vanhivasini, Maha Vajreswari, Shivadooti and so on. who preside over the fifteen days of the lunar month.

The worship of the Nitya Devis connected with the phases of the moon is an important aspect of Tantrik worship. Each Nitya has her own mantra, yantra and tantra and ritual applications. Nityas also denote Kala Chakra or the wheel of time. In the Sri Chakra these 15 nityas are present in the innermost circle and the Devi is in the central Bindu. These 15 Nityas rule the famous 15 letters Devi mantra known as Panchadasakshari Mantra. This is a very powerful Mantra. It should be got directly from a Guru.

A commander is always happy if the morale of his soldiers is high. Likewise, Devi rejoices (samutsuka) at the rising parakramam -valor of the Nityas.

भण्डपुत्रवधोद्युक्तबालाविक्रमनन्दिता।

मन्त्रिण्यम्बाविरचितविषङ्गवधतोषिता॥२९॥

bhaṇḍaputra vadhōdyukta bālāvikrama nanditā।

mantriṇyambā virachita viṣaṅga vadhatōṣitā ॥29॥

74. bhaṇḍaputra vadhōdyukta bālāvikrama nanditā

She rejoices in the valor of Bala who was ready to slay the sons of Bhanda.

Who is Bala? In Sanskrit, Bala means a child. Here, according to Brahmānda Purana, it means a child of Lalitha Devi. She is always shown as a nine-year old daughter of Devi. See picture. Bala is a child version of Devi Herself.

On hearing about the fight against Bhandasura, Bala showed interest in it.

The young girl, like most children are, was overcome by curiosity. She requested Devi for permission to fight. On observing her firm mind, Lalita Devi was very happy at the courage displayed by Bala. She granted her permission. She gave Bala one of her armors and some weapons and sent her off.

The sons of Bhanda were thirty in number – from Chaturbaahu, to Upamaaya. Bala killed all the thirty sons of Bhandasura.

75. mantriṇyambā virachita viṣaṅga vadhatōṣitā

Devi is delighted at the destruction of Visanga effected by mother Mantrini.

Mantrini is Shaymalamba. Visanga and Visukra are the two brothers of Bhanda. The Brahmānda Purana says:

"Once Bhandasura, the head of the Asuras, desired to create different kinds of Asuras. From his right shoulder he created Visukra, who was able to protect the company of the Daityas and who was equal to Sukra (the Guru of Asuras

The Glory of Lalithā Sahasranāmam

in the matter of counselling), and from his left shoulder, he created Visanga."

Vi-shanga, means no attachments (is opposed to, Sanga, attachments, or the craving for worldly objects.) Or Visha is poison; ya, to go; Vishanga – perceiving sensuous objects with a poisoned view.

विशुक्रप्राणहरणवाराहीवीर्यनन्दिता।

कामेश्वरमुखालोककल्पितश्रीगणेश्वरा॥३०॥

viśukra prāṇaharaṇa vārāhī vīryananditā ।

kāmēśvara mukhālōka kalpita śrī gaṇēśvarā ॥30॥

76. viśukra prāṇaharaṇa vārāhī vīryananditā

Rejoicing in the strength of Varahi, the taker of the life of Visukra. (another brother of Bhandasura)

77. kāmēśvara mukhālōka kalpita śrī gaṇēśvarā

Sri Ganesvara was formed by Devi's glances at Kamesvara.

Brahmānda Purana says: Devi Lalita looking at the face of her Lord, smiled, and from the rays of that smile a certain god arose. Thus, Ganesvara was born out of a mere glance of Lalitha at Kameshwara.

Bhāskararāya again quotes Brahmānda Purana. "Seeing the devas fettered by magical figures set up by daityas, Devi by merely looking at her husband, gave birth to the great Ganapathy whose mantra is of 28 syllables, by which the fettering influence of the magical figures were destroyed, and the devas released"

How did the Devas get fettered? And what are those magical figures? In warfare strategy is important. In fact, in early days, the term "strategy" was primarily used only in war and politics, not business. Now it is used in business as business is also like a war nowadays with severe competition.

Witnessing the destruction of his army, Bhandasura thinks of a strategy. He set up a yantra by name 'jaya vignam' (obstruction to victory - by magical figures of eight angles and eight tridents) in the midst of Devi's army. When this yantra was kept, the army of Lalitha started losing their self-confidence. It broke the morale of Devi's army. This yantra had to be removed to restore the confidence of Devi's army. How can this yantra be removed?

It can be removed by one who has won over purya ashtakam – a knowledge which has eight components. Ganeswara was required for this purpose. Why Ganeswara?

Ganesvara-split into Gana and Easwara- Gana the city formed of eight things of Puryastakam consisting of (1) Five karmendriyas 2) Five Jnanendriyas 3) Four Manas etc 4) Five Pranas. 5) Five Bhutas 6) Kama 7) Karma 8) Avidya. And Eswara -the Lord. Puryastakam is a knowledge attained by ascertaining the true nature of his own self, then as there are no other qualities that need to be qualified. Ganeswara was one such God.

The total components of puryashtakam are 27 and with this, the attributes of Shiva if added takes the total to 28. The moola mantra of Maha Ganapathi is also 28. Thus, Ganeswara could remove the 'Jaya Vignam' set up by Bhandasura. So, by the formation ganeswara, the obstacle of fetters was removed, and the confidence of Devi's army restored.

Lesson here: Life is full of obstacles. Winning over them requires human effort backed by intelligence. This effort builds up growth of knowledge.

Science helps us in this regard. For example, Hunger is an obstacle. You overcome it by finding food.

Food is made with various ingredients that are grown and produced through various means beginning with fertile soil, ploughing, planting, guarding from pests, harvesting, transportation – all in the supply chain. Thus, serving humanity. It pleases Devi if all are fed well. That's why Anna Dhānam is specially highlighted in our sastras.

महागणेशनिर्भिन्नविघ्नयन्त्रप्रहर्षिता।

भण्डासुरेन्द्रनिर्मुक्तशस्त्रप्रत्यस्त्रवर्षिणी॥३१॥

mahāgaṇēśa nirbhinna vighnayantra praharṣitā।

bhaṇḍāsurēndra nirmukta śastra pratyastra varṣiṇī॥31॥

78. mahāgaṇēśa nirbhinna vighnayantra praharṣitā- Devi is delighted at Mahaganesha breaking the obstacle of 'Yantra' (set up by Bhandasura)

79. bhaṇḍāsurēndra nirmukta śastra pratyastra varṣiṇī

Devi is showering missiles in response to the weapons thrown by Bhandasura.

According to Dhanurveda, the difference between Shastra and Astra is Shastra is that with which one strikes his enemies. It is always held in hand. Astra is that which is thrown out. or discharged by the hand, as the arrow of a bow.

कराङ्गुलिनखोत्पन्ननारायणदशाकृतिः।

महापाशुपतास्त्राग्निनिर्दग्धासुरसैनिका ॥३२॥

karāṅguḷi nakhōtpanna nārāyaṇa daśākṛtiḥ।

mahāpāśupatāstrāgni nirdagdhāsura sainikā ॥32॥

80. karāṅguḷi nakhōtpanna nārāyaṇa daśākṛtiḥ

From the nails of her (ten) fingers sprang the ten forms of Narayana.

Ten forms (Das'a+Akrtih) of Narayana refer to the ten incarnations of Vishnu, Matsya Kurma Varaha Narasimha Vamana, Parasurama, Rama, Balarama, Krishna and Kalki. It also supports the theory of evolution, closely synchronizing with Darwin's theory of evolution. From fish to human, progressing through various stages.

Bhāskararāya explains - The Daityas sprung into existence from the missile called Sarva asura Astra, which was aimed by Bhandasura.

The Asuras included Somaka and Ravana. Bali, Hiranyaksa and others who were known to have fought several battles, who had their origins thus.

To destroy these Daityas, Devi created from her finger ends the ten main incarnations of Vishnu in regular order from her right thumb to the left small finger.

Lalitopakhyina describes: "From the right thumb nail of the great Queen there sprang the divine, all-pervading Narayana in ten forms.... The ten Avataras (incarnations) having performed their respective onerous tasks stood with folded hands before Mother Lalitha saluting her."

81. mahāpāśupatāstrāgni nirdagdhāsura sainikā

She burnt up the army of Daityas (sons of Dhiti) with the fire
of the astra called *Maha PaasuPata*

कामेश्वरास्त्रनिर्दग्धसभण्डासुरशून्यका।

ब्रह्मोपेन्द्रमहेन्द्रादिदेवसंस्तुतवैभवा॥३३॥

kāmēśvarāstra nirdagdha sabhaṇḍāsura śūnyakā।

brahmōpēndra mahēndrādi dēvasaṃstuta vaibhavā॥33॥

82. kāmēśvarāstra nirdagdha sabhaṇḍāsura śūnyakā

Bhandasura with his army was burned up by the fire of the
(weapon of) Kamesvara.

The Brahmānda Purana says, "The supreme Mother, Lalita
blazing with anger, and throwing the whole universe into
confusion, suddenly rendered lifeless, with the great weapon
of Kamesa shining like the sun, the mighty

Asura, the fierce and wicked Bhanda who was left alone,
all his relations killed.

By flames discharged from that weapon his city called
Shunyaka, (emptiness) with the women, children, cattle, and
wealth, was suddenly burnt up and the site alone remained: thus,
the city became empty and its name Shunyaka was justified."

83. brahmōpēndra mahēndrādi dēvasaṃstuta vaibhavā

Her supreme power is praised by Brahma, Vishnu, Mahendra
and others (deities).

All the deities including Devendran rejoiced Devi's victory,
for which they prayed to Her. (Devakarya Samudyata).

Thus ends the Bhandasura Vadam (The killing of
Bhandasura) by Devi.

Chapter 4

The Revival of Manmatha

We begin this chapter with Shlokam 34. The very first line of this shlokam relates to the revival of manmatha-the god of love or cupid who was burnt by Lord Shiva. Man refers to mind and Matha is agitation or madness. One who causes agitation in mind is called Manmathan. He tried his cupid tricks on Shiva and was burnt.

हरनेत्राग्निसन्दग्धकामसञ्जीवनौषधिः।

श्रीमद्वाग्भवकूटैकस्वरूपमुखपङ्कजा॥३४॥

haranētrāgni sandagdha kāma sañjīvanauṣadhiḥ।

śrīmadvāgbhava kūṭaika svarūpa mukhapaṅkajā॥34॥

84. haranētrāgni sandagdha kāma sañjīvanauṣadhiḥ

She became the life-giving medicine for kAmadeva (Manmatha - Cupid) who was burned to ashes by the Agni (fire) from shiva's (third) eye.

Hara- Shiva, Netra -Eye (Third), Agni-fire, Kama-manmathan, Sanjiva-life giving, Aushadihi-Medicine. Ambāl gave life to Manmatha who was burnt to ashes by the fire from Shiva's third eye. How did Devi become the life-giving medicine for Manmatha? There is a story behind it.

There was a time when ferocious asuras like Tharakasura and Surapadma, were creating total anarchy in all the worlds. They had done much tapasya and obtained such boons of unlimited power, that they were assured that only Parameswara's own Son only could kill them. But then, Parameswara had no son at that time. He was totally engaged in meditation as Dakshina Murthy. Some of you must have seen the idol or picture of Dakshinamurthy. He is seen sitting still, holding a japamalai, totally inert and actionless. At the Shiva temple in *Suchindram,* Shiva is seen still and called Sthānumurthy. 'Sthānu' means still -like a dead tree. The Devas were really concerned about how to get Eswara involved in procreating a son.

Harassed by the Asuras, the Devas could only think of one way. If Manmatha (Cupid-the God of Love) responsible for inducing Kaama, could divert the attention of Parameswara towards Parvathy, then the birth of a Son to Siva - Parvathy was possible. So, they engaged Manmatha to show his prowess on Parameswara.

Manmatha, bloated by arrogance and pride, thought that he could easily make Parameswara enamored of Parvathy, by his antics! He directed the flower arrows on Parameswara.

When Parameswara felt some movement on him, He slightly opened the third eye. Fire emitted from the eye and in a fraction of a second, Manmatha was burnt and reduced to ashes.

Even now, Kāma Dahanam is a ritual performed in some of the South Indian states -AP, Telangana, Karnataka and TN around the time of Holi festival. They make an effigy of sticks, dried cow dung, and grass and burn it as a symbol of Kama. The sacred ash is given to the villagers. Kāman Pandigai is a festival celebrated in Tamil Nadu and Kāmuni Panduga in Andhra Pradesh.

Manmatha had pride that he was too beautiful and too good to resist. The incident proved that bodily beauty cannot stand before the fire of Knowledge. From being 'sarva anga sundaran' that is 'all body beautiful', he became, 'ananga' that is, 'without a body' or a nobody!

On seeing her husband's loss, Manmatha's wife Rathi was distressed. She cried before Ambāl. She appealed to Her for reviving Manmatha.

Parvathi gave her 'Anugraha' that, 'Ananga' will continue to function as a Devata with duties as usual but be visible to Rathi's eyes only. Devi told Manmatha, "I am the one who gave you the Sugarcane bow and Flower arrows. I am giving them back to you. Your job is to involve all the life forms in the act of procreation. Otherwise, all of them would have remained celibate. Only when they take life again and again can they progressively get across the ocean of repeated births and deaths. Otherwise, there would have been stagnation and chaos. So, you have been given certain powers."

Thus, Devi became *Sanjiva Aushadi* -the life-giving medicine for kAmadeva (Manmatha Cupid) who was burnt to ashes by the Agni (fire) from shiva's (third) eye.

Let's now see the second line of this verse:

85. śrīmadvāgbhava kūṭaika svarūpa mukhapaṅkajā

Earlier, we learnt descriptions of Devi's 'Sthula' or physical form and her divine activities. Now, starting with the second line, we will learn about the 'Sukshma' the unseen form or

The Glory of Lalithā Sahasranāmam

swarupam of Ambāl. It has a lot of philosophy, and some may find it difficult to understand.

Sukshma is a Sanskrit word meaning "subtle" or "dormant." The presence of sukshma is felt, but not seen. Sukshma Swarupam is inseparable from Her Physical form.

This subtle form has three divisions, subtle, subtler and subtlest: the first representing the fifteen syllabled Mantra (Panchadasi), the second Kamakala. and the third one is Kundalini. The first part of panchadasi is described under three names:

śrīmadvāgbhava - Srimad (divine) having power of conferring Wisdom and other exalted powers. It is the seat of 'Jnana' shakti. Vagbhava, that by which a person attains the power of speech. The Vagbhavakuta is a divine group of five syllables in the Panchadashi. Devi's (mukha pankaja) lotus face represents the divine Vagbhava group of syllables in the panchadashi.

Now, what is Panchadashi? It is the most powerful mantra for the upasana of Sri Lalita Maha Tripurasundari consisting of fifteen syllables called "Panchadasakshari". The sixteenth syllable must be provided by the Guru.

Muthuswamy Deekshitar's composition *panchAshat pITha rUpiNi mAm pAhi shrI rAja rAjEshvari, panchdashAkSari pANDyakumAri padmanAbha sahOdari shaNkari- in Devagandhari Ragam*

The main mantra of Lalithambika is Panchadasi - containing fifteen bijas or roots. It has three groups-each called a kuta. (Tamil-Koottam). The three kutas are known as Vaghbhava Kuta, Madhya Kuta and Sakti Kuta. Vaghbhava

Kuta represents Devi's lotus face, Madhyam Kuta the portion between Her neck and hip, and Sakti kuta - below the hip. The entire form of Devi is made up of these three kutas.

Vak, Speech is of four forms – Paraa, Pasyanti,Madhyama and Vaikhari. Paraa means the highest, is eternal form, pasyanti is when seers "see" it, madhyama is when it translates as sound-form, anahata, and vaikhari are in spoken form.

The general perception is that when we speak, sound comes from the throat. But what happens actually is when we have the urge or the thought to speak, our life force in the form of vaayu, starts from the root chakra and brings Paraa, the subtle sound, then travels up to the navel, heart chakras as Pasyanti and Madhyamaa respectively, then comes to the throat, mouth, teeth and tongue as Vaikhari to come out as speech or sound at the gross level. When pandits recite Veda mantras, the sound comes from the mid region of the body. Just as Samkalpa – a pure thought, must pass through several stages before it manifests as concrete creative force, the sabda also must pass through several stages before it is fully audible at the gross level.

These four stages are termed as *Paraa, Pasyanti, Madhyamaa and Vaikhari.*

Let's see the next verse

कण्ठाधःकटिपर्यन्तमध्यकूटस्वरूपिणी।

शक्तिकूटैकतापन्ननकट्यधोभागधारिणी ॥ ३५॥

kaṇṭhādhaḥ kaṭiparyanta madhyakūṭa svarūpiṇī।

śaktikūṭaika tāpanna kaṭyathōbhāga dhāriṇī॥ 35॥

86. kaṇṭhādhaḥ kaṭiparyanta madhyakūṭa svarūpiṇī

Kantam means neck (like in Neelakantan). Kati is waist. kaṇṭhādhaḥ kaṭiparyanta means from the neck to the waist, she represents the Madhyakuta-a group of six syllables. Madhya literally means the middle one.

Madhya kuta or the middle group of Panchadasi mantra refers to that portion between Devi's neck and the hip. It is also called Kamarajakuta. Because Kama (to create the universe) resides in Her Heart (i.e., second part of Her Subtle body) it is called Kamarajakuta

The previous nama of vagbhava represents jnana shakthi, this nama is iccha shakthi and the next nama of Saktikuta is kriya shakthi.

87. śaktikūṭaika tāpanna kaṭyathōbhāga dhāriṇī

From the waist downwards she represents Saktikuta. This is a group of four syllables

मूलमन्त्रात्मिका मूलकूटत्रयकलेबरा।

कुलामृतैकरसिका कुलसङ्केतपालिनी ॥ ३६ ॥

mūlamantrātmikā, mūlakūṭa traya kaḷēbarā।

kuḷāmṛtaika rasikā, kuḷasaṅkēta pālinī ॥ 36 ॥

88. mūla mantrātmikā-

She is the root Mantra itself. Mula is root, this is the fifteen syllabled mantra, Pancadasi, it is the root of the four objects of life set out for us (Purusharthas: Dharma, Artha, Kama, Moksham).

Mantra, man repetition; tra-protection—it protects those who repeat it. It is declared "Mantra is said to be that, with increasing repetition (Manana) of which, with full reflection. Of 'I-ness,' destroys one's transmigratory life (Samsara), and protects (tra) him."

Sri Lalitha Devi is *"Maha Tantra, Maha Mantra, Maha Yantra Mahasana."* She is the greatest Tantra, Mantra and Yantra!

89. mūlakūṭa traya kal̲ēbarā -

The three divisions of the root (Mantra) form her body. We talked about the three Kutas earlier. The outer form of Ambāl has three Kutas.

90. kul̲āmr̥taika rasikā -

She has the special taste of the nectar of kula.

What is Kula Amritam? Now, this requires a detailed explanation as we are going to see more nāmas relevant to Devi's Shuksma roopam.

Lalithā Sahasranāmam now proceeds to describe Devi's subtlest form called Kundalini and its impact on the human body.

The human body has seven Chakras or energy centers. (see slide).

Chakra means wheel. The chakras are centers of force shaped like a wheel located within the inner bodies. They are situated along the spinal cord from the base to the cranial chamber.

They are in the brain (Sahasrara), medulla oblongata (Ajna), and the 5 spinal centers—cervical (Visuddha), dorsal (Anahata), lumbar (Manipura), sacral (Svadhisthana), and coccygeal (Muladhara). The lowest chakra at the base is

                    The Glory of Lalithā Sahasranāmam

called *Mooladharam or Kulam,* and the topmost is Sahasrara or crown chakra, also called Akulam.

Kundalini Shakti is the divine power within every human being.

It is an astonishing energy said to lay dormant and coiled like a serpent at the base of the spine. It is not a material force, it lies dormant or sleeping in the Muladhara Chakra, the centre of the body. This serpent energy can be woken up from its slumber by the practice of certain yogic postures, breathing exercises and mantras. When aroused by yogis, the kundalini shakti surges upwards through an invisible network of nerves piercing through the six lotus-like cakras in the body as well as the three knots, called Brahman, Vishnu and Rudra granthis, and proceeds to the Sahasrara on top of the head, releasing a wave of ecstasy.

Through rigorous yogic practices, this shakti can be awakened and sent up through the Sushumna nadi (central path) through other chakras until it reaches the highest of chakras at the top of the head, Sahasrara or crown chakra. This unique and most difficult process is believed to achieve different levels of awakening and a mystical experience producing an extremely profound transformation of consciousness. When the kula shakti meets with Akulam on the top it produces a feeling of total bliss as if amrutam is flowing. That is called *kulamrutam.* Kula is the shakti. 'Akulam' is Shiva. The nectar flowing from the Sahasrara is called Kulamrta; Devi enjoys the flow of Kulamrtam. So, she is *kulāmṛtaika rasikā*

Saundarya Lahari also supports Kulamrutam in the following verse. 10.

सुधाधारासारै-श्चरणयुगलान्त-विगलितैः

प्रपञ्चं सिन्ञ्न्ती पुनरपि रसाम्नाय-महसः।

अवाप्य स्वां भूमिं भुजगनिभ-मध्युष्ट-वलयं

स्वमात्मानं कृत्वा स्वपिषि कुलकुण्डे कुहरिणि।।

Sudha-dhaara-saarais charana-yugalanta virgalitaih:

Prapancham sinchanti punarapi rasaamanya-mahasah;

Avaapya svaam bhumim bhujaga-nibha madhyusta-valayam

Svam atmanam krtva svapishi kulakunde kuharini

Sudha-dhaara-saarais charana means streaks of nectar streaming from between your twin feet, *Prapancham sinchanti* sprinkling blessings over the worlds, *punarapi rasaamanya-mahasah* and again from that point of high intelligible values, *Avaapya svaam bhumim* reaching back to your place, *bhujaga-nibha madhyusta-valayam* and coiling like a serpent having three and half coils, *Svam atmanam krtva svapishi kulakunde kuharini* -you sleep in the hollow of the *Kulakunda* with a hole in the middle.

So, Kundalini Shakti is Devi Herself in dormant form sleeping like a serpent. It is a divine power in every human being. Our ancient belief is that there is tremendous power within us that can be unleashed through mantras and rigorous spiritual processes. There were ordinary people who were mortals but have emerged as great saints. To name a few – Ramana Maharishi, Seshadri Swamigal, Shirdi Sai Baba, Kanchi Mahaperiva, and so on…

The human brain is an amazing creation of God. It has more latent power than any computer. In a jiffy, you can recollect what happened some 50 years ago. It can store more information than an encyclopedia Brittanica. Yet, we are using only a very small percentage of its power. You can unleash brain power by Pranayamam, and regular chanting of Lalithā Sahasranāmam.

The kundalini awakening can of course unleash a tremendous power.

91. ku_lasaṅkēta pālinī

Sanketa -secret. Devi safeguards the secret of kula. She is the protector of the secrets of the Kula. Kula has different meanings like country, house, family, a collection of things belonging to the same species, tribe, body and conduct. The thousand petalled red lotus is also called Kula. Kula here refers to right conduct. Devi never allows the revealing of the secret of the scripture and right conduct to the ignorant.

कुलाङ्गना कुलान्तस्था कौलिनी कुलयोगिनी।

अकुला समयान्तस्था समयाचारतत्परा॥३७॥

kulāṅganā, kulāntaḥsthā, kaulinī, kulayōginī|

akulā, samayāntaḥsthā, samayāchāra tatparā ||37||

In this verse, the word Kula appears several times. As I mentioned before, Kula in Sanskrit has many meanings –race, family, house, flock, herd, camp, body, including the nervous system. It is difficult to translate it correctly in English. Philosophically the term is said to represent a unifying connectedness, processes and living entities of this world. There are thirty-two lotuses (in the body) some facing upwards, and some downwards. Amongst these, the lowest one is called akula. and the other lotuses which are above it are called Kulas.

So, the meaning must be interpreted relevant to the context.

92. kulāṅganā

Kula the chaste family with good conduct. Angana means a beautiful woman. Aren't we proud of our lineage and respected family? Devi is a part of such a family. Women are always respected in Sanatana Dharma.

93. kulāntaḥsthā- Residing in the Kula. One who is established in the Kula. Kula also means scriptures. She is in the midst of sacred scriptures.

The Glory of Lalithā Sahasranāmam

94. kauḷinī

Belonging to Kula. Because she is worshipped in every house, in every place, in everybody, and in every family; Kula here means country, house. She is called Kaulini, the core of the Kaula form of worship. Kaulācāra ("the Kaula conduct") is a religious tradition in Tantric Shaktism and Shaivism. She is the Deity of the Kaulas. She belongs to all those who worship her.

According to the Tantras "Kula means Shakti, akula refers to Shiva, and union of Kula with Akula is called Kaula." Kaula means the essence common to both Shiva and Shakti, hence Devi is called Kaulini.

95. kuḷayōginī - Kaula means offering worship to a cakra mentally inscribed in ether. She is called Kulayogini because she relates to the chakra through Yoga.

96. Akula- is the opposite of Kula – meaning No Kula.

97. samayāntaḥsthā- Living in the Samaya.

What is Samaya? Samaya is commonly explained as offering worship, to a cakra in the ether of the heart. That (worship) is unanimously decided by all the yogins as the supreme, hence it is called Samaya.

98. Samayachara tatpara

Devoted to the conduct of Samaya. She is the reality of the Samaya tradition of worship.

There are two ways of worshipping Devi. One follows the Kula Acharam or Tradition – also called Kaulacharam. Acaharam is given great importance in our Dharma. Vishnu Sahasranamam says

'Sarvagamana Achara Pratomo Parikalpitaha,

Achara Prabhuvo Dharma, Dharmasya Prabhur Achyutaha.'

Apart from Kula Acharam, the other is Akulacharam or Samayacharam. Samaya is also Devi's name.

Sama means equality. One who attains, both- Shiva and Devi. She is the center of the Samaya doctrine in which the worship is done internally through meditation, and which holds Siva-Sakti as of equal importance (Samam-equal) in all respects.

मूलाधारैकनिलया ब्रह्मग्रन्थिविभेदिनी।

मणिपूरान्तरुदिता विष्णुग्रन्थिविभेदिनी॥३८॥

mūlādhāraika nilayā, brahmagranthi vibhēdinī।

maṇipūrānta ruditā, viṣṇugranthi vibhēdinī॥38॥

99. mūlādhāraika nilayā-

Devi resides in Mooladhaara. Devi is believed to reside inside the Mulaadhaara Chakra as Kundalini.

100. brahmagranthi vibhēdinī

Severing the knot is called Brahmagranthi. Of the six chakras, each has two knots on both sides. The Svadhisthina chakra has three including Brahmagranthi

Devi in Her ascent from the Mooladhaara breaks through the Brahma-grandhi (the Barrier of Brahma to the subtle dimension) and then emerges in the Manipura – chakra, then breaks through the Vishnu – granthi (the barrier to still subtler dimensions).

The Glory of Lalithā Sahasranāmam

She penetrates through the Brahma Grandhi or the barrier of Brahma and enables her devotees practicing Yoga to be conscious while awake.

With this, we complete the first 100 Naamas in Lalithā Sahasranāmam.

We now start with the 101st Naama

101.maṇipūrānta ruditā

Manipura chakra is in the navel and there is a ten petalled lotus; in that while engaged in the act of Samaya worship Devi appears decked with gems (mani). Hence this cakra is called Manipura.

Then a devotee is facilitated to have vision of Devi in Manipura while in a condition of stupor; further a devotee must pierce through the Vishnu Grandhi or the Vishnu knot when the Yogi becomes unconscious, and his body and thoughts are felt irrelevant.

102. viṣṇugranthi vibhēdinī

Severing the knot called Vishnugranthi.

Above the Manipura is the knot called Vishnugranthi; (Vibhedini): Vi—completely and Bhed'ém', breaking. As Vishnu resides in Manipura, this knot is called Vishnugranthi. Similarly, the Brahma and Rudragranthis are so called, because Brahma and Rudra reside in these centers respectively.

आज्ञाचक्रान्तरालस्था रुद्रग्रन्थिविभेदिनी।

सहस्राराम्बुजारूढा सुधासाराभिवर्षिणी ॥३९॥

ājñā chakrāntarālasthā, rudragranthi vibhēdinī।

sahasrārāmbujā rūḍhā, sudhāsārābhi varṣiṇī ॥39॥

103. ājñā chakrāntarālasthā

Residing in the centre of the Ajnachakra.

Between the eyebrows there is a two-petalled lotus; it is called *"Ajnachakra"*, because in it is the Guru, who instructs (Ajna) resides. Jnana is knowledge, knowledge arises first in Guru and mentally attains the conquest of that chakra. Therefore, it is called Ajna.

104. rudragranthi vibhēdinī

Severing the knot is called Rudragranthi. Severing means here penetrating.

Bhāskararāya comments:

The chakras really signify the roots or origins of the universe as said in the fourth chapter of the Dattatreya-Samhita.

"Muladara and the other five (Chakras are together called Kula; there are three knots among them, these three are called Devi-chakras. The earth (and water) cakras are indicated by the Brahmagranthi. The next two powerful and shining chakras are fire and sun; these two are indicated by the Vishungranti; this shining one confers all the siddhis. The next two chakras in the form of air and other are indicated by the Rudragranthi, the seat of mighty benefits."

105. sahasrārāmbujā rūḍhā- Having ascended the thousand — petalled lotus.

106. sudhāsārābhi varṣiṇī

Showering down torrents of ambrosia or nectar. This ambrosia comes from the moon of the pericarp of the lotus.

तडिल्लतासमरुचिः षट्चक्रोपरिसंस्थिता।
महासक्तिः कुण्डलिनी बिसतन्तुतनीयसी ॥४०॥

taṭillatā samaruchiḥ, ṣaṭ-chakrōpari saṃsthitā |

mahāśaktiḥ, kuṇḍalinī, bisatantu tanīyasī || 40 ||

107. taṭillatā samaruchiḥ

Devi is Brilliant as the lightning flash.

108. ṣaṭ-chakrōpari saṃsthitā

Devi is Residing above the six chakras.

Sam, permanently, sthita', residing in the six chakras, *Muladhara, Svadhisthina, Manipura, Anahata, Visuddhi and Ajna.*

109. mahāśaktiḥ

Greatly attached to festivals. Festival-union of Shiva and Shakti.

110. kuṇḍalinī

Kundala means coiled, hence Kundalini what is coiled. Its own form is like a coiled serpent.

The Tantraraja says, "The shining (Tejas) vital energy (Sivasakti), which is the manifestation of life (Prana), is called Kundalini, which resides in the center of the flames of fire of Muladhara. She is sleeping like a serpent, having three (and half) coils, radiant, she is ever hissing in the centre of susumna where she resides, in the head of Maya.

111. bisatantu tanīyasī- Fine as the fiber of the lotus stalk. The Shakti, called Kundalini in the form of a serpent, beautiful, fine as lotus, fiber, resides in the Muladhara.

भवानी भावनागम्या भवारण्यकुठारिका।

भद्रप्रिया भद्रमूर्तिर्भक्तसौभाग्यदायिनी ॥४१॥

bhavānī, bhāvanāgamyā, bhavāraṇya kuṭhārikā |

bhadrapriyā, bhadramūrti, rbhaktasaubhāgya dāyinī

112. bhavānī

Bhava refers to Mahadeva. As His consort, Devi is called Bhavani.

Vayu Purana says: Because all beings came from Mahadeva and subsist in water, as he is the origin and supporter of all beings, he is called Bhava. She is Bhavani because she is the giver of life Bhava, water.

Saundarya Lahari says:

भवानि त्वं दासे मयि वितर दृष्टिं सकरुणां

इति स्तोतुं वाञ्छन् कथयति भवानि त्वमिति यः।

तदैव त्वं तस्मै दिशसि निजसायुज्य-पदवीं

मुकुन्द-ब्रम्हेन्द्र स्फुट मकुट नीराजितपदाम् .... Verse 22

Bhavani means Ambāl. Lord Shiva has eight different names, one among them is "Bhavān." Bhavān's spouse is "Bhavānī". *Bhavani Thwam* – meaning "Bhavani, I am yours". Now, when the devotee utters Bhavanithwam, Ambāl blesses the devotee with the high status of Bhavānithwam, meaning "the status of becoming Bhavāni."

We normally use *"Dheerga Sumangali Bhava"* meaning live long as a Sumangali (a Married women). Here in this phrase is a verb "Bhava" means "to be". And Bhavani means "becomes". So now, *Bhavanithwam* means "I become like Bhavāni." The devotee is blessed with the higher state of consciousness – Unity Consciousness.

 The Glory of Lalithā Sahasranāmam

If one prays to Ambāl with this verse, starting the prayer as "Bhavani, I am yours, so kindly grace with your divine vision for a moment".

The moment we utter these words, Ambāl will intercept with a blessing that means "You and I are not different, both are one and the same (Advaitham)." So, *Bhavanithwam,* can be interpreted in two different ways. That is, "Mother, I am your devotee, and you are my mother."

In another way, we can interpret it as "Mother, you and I are one and same." At the end, devotee gets the Parāshakthi's divine grace and becomes Bhavani.The beauty of this verse is that even before devotee has completed the full prayer, Ambāl simply grants the sAyujya-status 'then and there.' This is the implication of the words 'tadA-eva' in the beginning of the third line of the stanza

Oh. Bhavani, please bestow on me, who is your Daasa slave [of your divine power], your divine vision full of kindness. Thus, whomsoever desirous of praying you, chants the two words- "Bhavani you!", then immediately, you, who has the divine lotus feet, being worshipped with neerajanam by the great Gods, Vishnu, Brahma, Indra and others by the brilliant rays flowing from their divine crown will bestow him saayuja padavi-the highest position.

There is the famous Tulja Bhavani temple in Tuljapur in Maharashtra. Tuljapur is about 45 km from Solapur. Historically this temple was built in the 12th century. It is the family deity of the Bhosale royal family and one of the 51 Shakti Peethas.

113. bhāvanāgamyā

She is to be attained by meditation. Bhavana. Bhāvana is a combination of intense deep feelings, and mental perceptions. This feeling has an emotional quality to it. There is a Sanskrit saying- *'yat bhavam tat bhavati' meaning* you become what you think. There are two kinds of meditation, one on the words themselves (Shabda) and the other on the meanings (Artha); words mean here sacred words which are to be meditated upon intensely keeping in mind the meanings so that gradually you start visualizing it and merge into it.

114. bhavāraṇya kuṭhārikā

The woodcutter of the forest- of earth existence.

Kutarika means axe. In Tamil, it is called Kodali. In Marathi, it is called Kuṟhāḍa.

Ambāl axes away the 'Aranya' forest called bhava (bondages that entrap the being in continuous cycle of births and deaths, samsara).

115. bhadrapriyā-

Delighting in auspiciousness. She who loves auspiciousness is Bhadra-priyā.

116. bhadramūrti-

Of auspicious appearance. She is a personification of auspiciousness (bhadra).

117. bhaktasaubhāgya dāyinī

Conferring prosperity on the devotees. Bhaga means "fortune, desire, magnanimity, strength. effort, sun, and fame." Subhaga, Lalita herself. Saubhagyas are her qualities. Bhagya is luck, She makes her devotees fortunate.

From here onwards, the description is on how Devi responds to Bhakti or devotion.

भक्तिप्रिया भक्तिगम्या भक्तिवश्या भयापहा।

शाम्भवी शारदाराध्या शर्वाणी शर्मदायिनी॥४२॥

bhaktipriyā, bhaktigamyā, bhaktivaśyā, bhayāpahā।

śāmbhavī, śāradārādhyā, sarvāṇī, śarmadāyinī॥42॥

See "Alankara" – Exquisite beauty of verses; does not use any conjunctions like 'cha' 'tu' 'api' etc. As we go along, we will learn more about this beauty.

118. bhaktipriyā

Delighting in Bhakti or devotion.

What is Bhakti? The word bhakti comes from the root bhaj, which means to serve unconditionally. Sincere devotion. In the Shrimad Bhagavad Mahapurana (VII.5:23-24) Prahlada tells his father, Hiranyakashipu, about the nine forms of Vishnu- bhakti which he learnt from his preceptor. These are *shravana, kirtana, smarana, pada-sevana, archana, vandana, dasya, sakhya and atma-nivedana.* So, there are many kinds of Bhakti like the above which should be known. All these are included in the word Bhakti.

119. bhaktigamyā

Ambāl is to be approached with devotion.

Bhagavad-Gita. (XI, 54) says

भक्त्या त्वनन्यया शक्यमहमेवंविधोऽर्जुन।

ज्ञातुं द्रष्टुं च तत्त्वेन प्रवेष्टुं च परंतप॥11.54॥

bhaktyā tv ananyayā śhakya aham evaṁ-vidho Arjuna

jñātuṁ draṣhṭuṁ cha tattvena praveṣhṭuṁ cha parantapa

By total devotion, I may thus be perceived, Arjuna, and known and seen and entered in essence,0 Parantapa."

120. bhaktivaśyā

Controlled by devotion. It is said, "O Shiva, though independent, has become subservient to Devi by devotion."

121. bhayāpahā

Remover of fear.

The Vayu Purana also says, "In the forest, and other places, in water, on earth, in the presence of a tiger, and before wild beasts, and robbers, and especially in all difficulties and diseases, the names of Devi should be repeated."

122. śāmbhavī- The wife of Shambu.

123. śāradārādhyā- Sharada Aradya, Worshipped by Sharada, Saraswathi. (Main deity at Sringeri Temple)

124. Sarvani- Shiva is called Sarva – all in his earth form; His spouse is called Sarvani

125. Sharmadayani- Bestower of Happiness. She makes her devotees happy.

शाङ्करी श्रीकरी साध्वी शरच्चन्द्रनिभानना।

शातोदरी शान्तिमती निराधारा निरञ्जना॥४३॥

śaṅkarī, śrīkarī, sādhvī, śarachchandranibhānanā |

śātōdarī, śāntimatī, nirādhārā, nirañjanā ॥43 ॥

126. śaṅkarī

Sankara has two words- Sam, happiness and Kara doer. One who does good. Samkari is the wife of Sankara. She also does good.

Deekshitar sings beautifully- *Samkari, Samkuru Chandramukhi, Akhilandeswari Sambhavi - in Saveri Ragam*

127. śrīkarī- producing success.

128. sādhvī- Chaste. Pativrata. The Devi Bhagavada Purana says," You are praised as sadhvi (the virtuous one) an account of unequalled fidelity (to thy Lord)."

129. Śarachchandranibhānanā- Having a face like the spring moon.

Chandramukhi. Abirami Bhattar saw the face of Devi as full moon. So, when the King asked him the Thithi, he replied Pouramani even though it was Amawasya day.

130. śātōdarī - Slender-waisted. Udari refers to waist.

131. śāntimatī - Very peaceful always. Also bestows peace on other

132. nirādhārā - Without dependence. She is independent

133. nirañjanā - stainless. Free from any kind of stain. Anjana - refers to the black paste that women use to beautify the eye.

The next verse describes some of the gunas or attributes of Ambāl

निर्लेपा निर्मला नित्या निराकारा निराकुला।

निर्गुणा निष्कला शान्ता निष्कामा निरुपप्लवा॥४४॥

nirlēpā, nirmalā, nityā, nirākārā, nirākulā।

nirguṇā, niṣkalā, śāntā, niṣkāmā, nirupaplavā ॥44॥

134. Nirlepa- Lepa means polish or impurity. She who is free from all impurities, Lepa, the impurity arising from action (Karman). By the knowledge of Devi, the devotee becomes free from impurity.

135. nirmalā- without spot of blemish. Malam is dirt.

136. nityā, - She who is eternal

137. nirākāra - She who is without form

138. nirākulā - She who is 'Cool' without agitation

139. nirguṇā -Without quality. She is beyond all three gunas of nature, namely sattva, rajas and tamas.

This is explained in the Matsya and Padma Puranas where Narada says to Himavan: "As I have said, Devi is devoid of attributes, listen well, to the explanation of the meaning of this saying: attributes (Laksana) are the marks of Devas, and qualities (guna) depend upon body; this Devi is without qualities and cannot be distinguished by attributes

140. niṣkalā, -without parts

141. śāntā, -tranquil, ever peaceful -Ambāl is described as Santhakumari.

142. niṣkāmā- without any desire

143. nirupaplavā- indestructible; none of the asuras could win over and destroy her.

Durga also means the same as a fort is built indestructible.

नित्यमुक्ता निर्विकारा निष्प्रपञ्चा निराश्रया।

नित्यशुद्धा नित्यबुद्धा निरवद्या निरन्तरा॥४५॥

nityamuktā, nirvikārā, niṣprapañchā, nirāśrayā।

nityaśuddhā, nityabuddhā, niravadyā, nirantarā॥45॥

144. nityamuktā -Ever free. Her devotees too become ever free

145. nirvikārā -unchanging

146. niṣprapañchā -without extension/ Prapancha means accumulation, extension, expansion.

147. Nirāśrayā- without body

148. nityaśuddhā - ever pure

149. nityabuddhā - ever wise

150. niravadyā - Avadya, blame. (avadhuru). She is without blame. Blameless

151. nirantarā- compact

Chapter 5

Attributes of Ambāl

The following verses continue to describe Ambāl's *"Sukshma"* swarupam (the unseen form) that describes Devi's hidden qualities. Most of these Sanskrit words are simple to understand and easy to follow. You will find many of them starting with *Ni* which really means 'without.'

निष्कारणा निष्कलङ्का निरुपाधिर्निरीश्वरा।

नीरागा रागमथनी निर्मदा मदनाशिनी॥४६॥

niṣkāraṇā, niṣkalaṅkā, nirupādhi, rnirīśvarā।

nīrāgā, rāgamathanī, nirmadā, madanāśinī॥46॥

152. niṣkāraṇā, -

Karana is cause. Niskarana is Without cause. Since she is the cause of everything she is without a cause. She does not need a cause.

153. niṣkalaṅkā-

Kalanka is fault. Niskalanka is Without Fault. She does not have blemishes. She is pure, untouched by sin.

154. Nirupādhi

Without Limitation. Upa, near, + adhi, gives. If you place a red flower near a crystal, it will transfer the color and reflect it in all directions. It is the upadhi.

Similarly, ignorance in our lives is the upadhi which causes the appearance of plurality in our consciousness (cith). Devi is without upadhi.

155. Nirīśvarā- Iswara is the superior. Nirisvara is Without a superior. She who does not have anyone controlling her Because she is the ruler of all, she herself has no superior. She is the boss.

156. nīrāgā, Without Raga, desire. Ambāl is without any desire. Bhāskararāya gives one more meaning. Nir, water. and aga, mountain, both being her forms.

157. Rāgamathanī - Destroying desire by not endowing devotees with passion. By Raga is meant here, "Desire, aversion and ardent attachment to life" as described in the Yoga-Sutra (II, 3). She who removes desires from us.

158. nirmadā, Without pride. The true devotee of Devi who recites regularly will slowly start suppressing pride.

159. madanāśinī- Destroying pride.

निश्चिन्ता निरहङ्कारा निर्मोहा मोहनाशिनी।

निर्ममा ममताहन्त्री निष्पापा पापनाशिनी ॥४७॥

niśchintā, nirahaṅkārā, nirmōhā, mōhanāśinī।

nirmamā, mamatāhantrī, niṣpāpā, pāpanāśinī ॥47॥

160. niśchintā

Without care. *Bhāskararāya* says: Chinta means recollection generally; here it means recollection of painful topics.

It is said, "Anxiety should be known as (resembling) a funeral pile called Chita, the only difference is the additional N sound in chinta, but as the pile (chita) burns the corpse, so anxiety

     The Glory of Lalithā Sahasranāmam

burns the living man"; or chinta also means delusion also—
she is without delusion.

161. nirahaṅkāra -Without egoism. It is sad, "Ahankara is of
three kinds, Vaikarika, Taijasa, and Bhutadi (according to the
Sattva, Rajas and Tamas, respectively.)

162. nirmōhā- Moha, is confusion of thought, distraction of
the mind. a feeling of being perplexed and confused. Moha
causes bewilderment. Ambāl is without bewilderment; Ambāl
is without Moha.

163. Mōhanāśinī

Destroying bewilderment. Not only she is without Moha but
also, She destroys the Moha of her devotees by imparting the
idea of unity. Bhāskararāya quotes the shruti (Isa Upanishad.,
7), "To him who perceives unity what bewilderment and what
sorrow can there be?"

164. nirmamā- mama means 'Me'. Nirmama is without
me meaning Without self-interest. Self-interest necessarily
implies separateness and as she is without separateness, she is
said to be without self interest

165. mamatāhantrī- The destroyer of self-interest.

166. niṣpāpā- Papa means Sin. Devi is without sin.

167. pāpanāśinī

Destroyer of Sins.

How does she destroy sins?

By the repetition of (her) mantra. etc., she destroys the sins
of devotees. "Chandokya Upanishad V, 24, 3 says, "Like the
point of a reed in the fire, so all his sins are burned up."

The Vasistha Smrithi says, "The Brahmana who is devoted to learning and penance and who continually repeats (mantras), even if he is always committing sinful actions, he is not afflicted thereby. Sin never resides in those who repeat (mantras), or offer oblations, or meditate, or make pilgrimages, or who perform Shirovrata (the rite of carrying fire on the head).""

The Padma Purana, in its Puskarakhanda, says, "The mass of sins though as great as Mount Meru is instantly destroyed by approaching Katyayani. He who is devoted to Durga, is not stained even by committing heinous crimes, in the same manner as the lotus leaf which is not affected by water."

The Devi Bhagavadam also speaks to the same effect. The Brahmānda Purana. says, "The sinful actions of those who are devoid of Varna and Asrama, and the wretched, by mere meditation on Devi, become virtuous."

Such is the great power of Devi in Mantras (47).

निष्क्रोधा क्रोधशमनी निर्लोभा लोभनाशिनी।

निःसंशया संशयघ्नी निर्भवा भवनाशिनी॥४८॥

niṣkrōdhā, krōdhaśamanī, nirlōbhā, lōbhanāśinī।

niḥsamśayā, samśayaghnī, nirbhavā, bhavanāśinī॥48॥

168. niṣkrōdhā

Krodha means anger. Ni means No or Without. Devi is Without anger

Because she has no object of hatred. The Bhagavad Gita says (9-29), " There is none hateful to me nor dear."

Someone can ask a question. How is it that Devi is without anger? In Bengal, Kali is portrayed as a ferocious Devi with bulging eyes, red tongue sticking out, armed with all kinds of weapons and seen as very angry. True. How do we deal with criminals? You must make them fear the police or punishment. Creating fear is the key thing. So, Devi creates fear by looks and weapons. Is it because of real anger? No, it is fake anger. Inside she is cool. When Krishna played mischief, Yashoda faked anger and tied him with a rope. Was she really angry?

Ambāl always keeps her cool but strikes fear in the minds of evil people. The Vishnu Durga in my village is in "Sowmya Roopam" – ever cool.

In Devi Mahatmyam, Ambāl is not only cool and humble but displays a sense of humor to the Asuras. In Chapter 5, Verses 118-121, of Sri Durgā Saptashati, Devi says to the Dhoota (messenger) of Shumba and Nishumba who are asking Devi to marry either of them:

॥ श्रीदुर्गासप्तशती - पञ्चमोऽध्यायः॥

देवी दूत संवादः देव्युवाच॥117॥ Devi says.

सत्यमुक्तं त्वया नात्र मिथ्या किञ्चित्त्वयोदितम्।

त्रैलोक्याधिपतिः शुम्भो निशुम्भश्चापि तादृशः॥118॥

devyuvAcha||5\.117||

satyamuktaM tvayA nAtra mithyA kinchittvayoditam|

trailokyAdhipatiH shumbho nishumbhashchApi tAdR^ishaH||5\.118||

What you say is true. Shumba and Nishumba are emperors of the three worlds.

किं त्वत्र यत्प्रतिज्ञातं मिथ्या तत्क्रियते कथम्।,

श्रूयतामल्पबुद्धित्वात्प्रतिज्ञा या कृता पुरा॥119॥

kiM tvatra yatpratijnAtaM mithyA tatkriyate katham|

shrUyatAmalpabuddhitvAtpratijnA yA kR^itA purA||
5\.119||

But what to do. I made a promise long ago due to my
(alpabuddhi) ignorance.

यो मां जयति संग्रामे यो मे दर्पं व्यपोहति।,

यो मे प्रतिबलो लोके स मे भर्ता भविष्यति॥120॥

yo mAM jayati saNgrAme yo me darpaM vyapohati|

yo me pratibalo loke sa me bhartA bhaviShyati||5\.120|

The one who wins against me in a battle and is stronger than
me shall be my husband.

तदागच्छतु शुम्भोऽत्र निशुम्भो वा महासुरः।

मां जित्वा किं चिरेणात्र पाणिं गृह्णातु मे लघु॥121॥

tadAgachChatu shumbho.atra nishumbho vA
mahAbalaH|

mAM jitvA kiM chireNAtra pANiM gR^ihNAtu me
laghu||5.121||

So, please go and tell shumba and nishumba to fight me, win
and take my hands easily.

Even in a provoking situation, Ambāl displays such
coolness and humor without the slightest anger. Eventually,
Ambāl kills both Shumba and Nishumba.

169. krōdhaśamanī - Destroyer of anger.

Anger is one of the six enemies; so Apastamba says, "He who sacrifices, offers oblation, or worships while angry, is deprived of all (benefit therefrom) like water in a vessel of unbaked clay."

170. nirlōbhā- Without Lobha - greed or miserliness. Ambāl is exceedingly liberal. She is not miserly.

171. lōbhanāśinī

Destroying greed. removes miserliness

It is said, "Greed destroys all good qualities." The Tantraraja on the characteristics of the guru says, "He is the guru who is without doubt, the remover of doubt and expects nothing."

172. niḥsaṃśayā- Without doubt. The word *Samsayam* is also used in Malayalam.

173. saṃśayaghnī - Destroying doubt.

174. nirbhavā- Without origin. The Bhagavad Gita (13-12) says, "The Supreme Brahman is Without origin".

175. bhavanāśinī - Destroying samsara. helps us not have another birth

निर्विकल्पा निराबाधा निर्भेदा भेदनाशिनी।

निर्नाशा मृत्युमथनी निष्क्रिया निष्परिग्रहा॥४९॥

nirvikalpā, nirābādhā, nirbhēdā, bhēdanāśinī।

nirnāśā, mṛtyumathanī, niṣkriyā, niṣparigrahā॥49॥

176. nirvikalpā

Without False Imagination.

What is Vikalpa? The Yoga-Sutra (I, 9) says, "Vikalpa (fancy) is a notion conveyed by mere words, but of which there is no object corresponding to reality." "One that is not real which is created in the mind." Devi is in the form of unconditioned eternal knowledge.

177. niraabhaada- Undisturbed. Calm and ever peaceful

178. nirbhēdā- Without difference.

179. bhēdanāśinī- Destroyer of difference; Bheda the dual knowledge: she causes its destruction by the knowledge of reality. Promotes oneness.

180. nirnāśā- Imperishable. - Nasa means destruction or the end. The Shruti, (Taittriya Up., III) "Brahman is Truth, Knowledge, and Infinity"

181. mṛtyumathanī- Destroying death. Devi removes fear of death.

Bhāskararāya adds:

The Tripura Upanishad says, "Why it is said, because from mortality he obtains immortality, he attains imperishable state; attains the eternal existence."

182. niṣkriyā- Without action; The Shruti, (Chandogya Upanishad 8, 12, 1) says "Only one who has no body is unaffected by likes or dislikes."

183. niṣparigrahā- Receiving nothing. She who does not seek help from others

The cluster of 17 nāmās from 156 Niraga, Ragamadhani to Nishkriya 183. Nishparigraha when recited with concentration & devotion, removes the 17 dōṣas (weaknesses) present within us.

All these words contain the 'Ni' Upasarga which means without, or no.

The 17 dōṣas present within us are:

1. rāgā – Attachment, 2. mada – Haughtiness, 3. cinta – Worry, 4. ahaṅkāra – Ego, 5 mōha – Delusion, 6 mamata – Affection, 7 pāpa – Sin 8 krōdha – Anger, 9 lōbha – Greed, 10 śamśāya – Doubt, 11 bhava – Existence; Cycle of births & deaths;, 12 vikalpa – Wavering mind, 13 bādha – Transformation, 14 bhēda – Differences; with others & within oneself,15 nāśā – Destruction, 16 kriya – Action, 17 parigraha – Acceptance

निस्तुला नीलचिकुरा निरपाया निरत्यया।

दुर्लभा दुर्गमा दुर्गा दुःखहन्त्री सुखप्रदा॥५०॥

nistulā, nīlachikurā, nirapāyā, niratyayā।

durlabhā, durgamā, durgā, duḥkhahantrī, sukhapradā॥50॥

184. nistulā- Incomparable. Tula means weighing balance. In Hindi, we say 'Tolna' to weigh. When you add 'nis' to 'tula', it means you cannot weigh to compare.

185. nīla chikurā- blue-haired.

186. nirapāyā - imperishable

187. niratyayā - Without transgression; Atyaya means, transgression - an offense. Punishment, obstruction.

188. durlabhā- Difficult to attain

189. durgamā- Difficult to approach; or durgama is the name of a Daitya Whom Devi caused to be slain

190. durgā – Durg means fort. It is built impenetrable to protect from enemies. The Sanskrit word Durga means undefeatable. Bhāskararāya adds: The word Durga is explained in the Devi Purana: "Indra, and other Devas were delivered from mental and physical fear, in difficulty and in battle. hence (Devi) is called Durga (120., deliverer)."

191. duḥkhahantrī- Destroyer of pain.

Dukha, pain, caused by Samsara. The Gautama-Sutra (I, 22) says, "Salvation is the complete release from that (pain)."

192. sukhapradā- Conferring happiness. Sukam is happiness.

दुष्टदूरा दुराचारशमनी दोषवर्जिता।

सर्वज्ञा सान्द्रकरुणा समानाधिकवर्जिता॥५१॥

duṣṭadūrā, durāchāra śamanī, dōṣavarjitā।

sarvajñā, sāndrakaruṇā, samānādhikavarjitā ॥51॥

193. duṣṭadūrā- Unattainable by Sinners.

Dusta means sinners - bad guys. Dura- distance. Keep your distance from bad people.

194. durāchāra śamanī- Putting an end to evil customs; Evil customs are contrary to the Scriptures. Vishnu Sahasranama says, *"Sarvagamana Acharam Pratamam Parikalpate."*

Before everything, Acharam or Customs came first. *"Achara Prabhavo Dharma, Dharmasya Prabur Achutah:"* Achara led to Dharma and Dharma's Prabhu is Achuta."

195. dōṣavarjitā- Devoid of faults; Dosha means hatred, passion – bad qualities.

196. sarvajñā- Omniscient. possessed of universal or complete knowledge. As she knows everything, she is called sarvajñā or Omniscient.

197. sāndrakaruṇā- Intense compassion. Devi shows intense compassion to her devotees.

198. samānādhikavarjitā- Having neither 'Samam' -equal, nor 'Adhika' -Superior

सर्वशक्तिमयी सर्वमङ्गला सद्गतिप्रदा।

सर्वेश्वरी सर्वमयी सर्वमन्त्रस्वरूपिणी॥५२॥

sarvaśaktimayī, sarvamaṅgalā, sadgatipradā।

sarvēśvarī, sarvamayī, sarvamantra svarūpiṇī॥52॥

199. sarvaśaktimayī

Possessing all Shaktis or powers. The text now sets forth her qualified forms (Saguna). She is not to be separated from any of the Shaktis such as Bale, Bagala etc. She is the aggregate of all the divine powers.

200. sarvamaṅgalā

The source of all good fortune.

She gives all the good fortune (longed for) in the heart, all desired good objects, hence she is called Sarvamangala. Thus ends the second hundred shlokam. Now, we start with the third hundred.

201. sadgatiprada- Leading into the right path. Sadgati includes all stages from Svarga to Moksa. -or, sat, Brahman, gati, knowledge; or, sat, of wise, gati.-goal.

202. sarvēśvarī- Ruler of all. Because she is the ruler of all, she leads into the right path

203. sarvamayī- She is All. Sarva includes all the Tattvas from Earth to Shiva.

204. sarvamantra svarūpiṇī- She is the very essence of all mantras.

Mantras include seven crores of mantras. The Sundari—Tapaniya Upanishad. says, "Many mantras are arranged on either side of the Vidya (the fifteen syllabled mantra-Panchadasakshari).

This and the next two following names together express the previous name Sarvamayi.

सर्वयन्त्रात्मिका सर्वतन्त्ररूपा मनोन्मनी।

माहेश्वरी महादेवी महालक्ष्मीर्मृडप्रिया॥५३॥

sarvayantrātmikā, sarvatantrarūpā, manōnmanī|

māhēśvarī, mahādēvī, mahālakṣmī, rmṛḍapriyā ॥53॥

205. sarvayantrātmikā

She is the soul of all Yantras. Yantra, means "instrument," "apparatus" or "machines." It is derived from the root word, yam, meaning "to support" or "to sustain the essence of an object/concept." Yantras here it refers to devices or tools of

     The Glory of Lalithā Sahasranāmam

worship. It is a mystical diagram used for worship. SriChakra is the most powerful Yantra.

206. sarvatantrarūpā

She is the spirit of all Tantras. In Sanskrit, the word tantra means woven together. Mantra, Yantra and Tantra are all Sanskrit words each defining an element of worship. Mantra refers to a combination of words that is chanted in a particular order. It is believed that on chanting these mantras, the desired results can be achieved.

For example, the 'Gāyatri Mantra' is regarded as one of the most important Sanskrit Mantras. It is believed that chanting this Mantra can lead to immense happiness. This Mantra is composed of a meter that consists of 24 syllables.

Yantra refers to devices that are used for balancing of mind and achieving peace. They are typically used as symbols or geometric figures. Yantra uses geometric patterns that can comprise squares, circles, triangles and floral patterns. All these geometric patterns represent some cosmic power. The Sri Chakra is a great Yantra. There are various symbols that are used in yantras. Some are in 2D and some in 3D like a pyramid. Sri Chakra worship should be done after initiation and guidance by a competent Guru. We already talked about Chakras in the human body in our last session.

The word "tantra" is a Sanskrit literally meaning 'strategy, groundwork, doctrine', from tan 'stretch'. Tantra is often associated with black magic, but the followers of Tantra believe that it as the application of cosmic science. *'Atharva Veda'* is one of the prime scriptures related to Tantra.

It refers to powerful spiritual acts that are used to let ourselves free from problems and for the enlightenment of the soul. Tantra defines rituals and meditation acts that can be used to get the freedom from uncontrollably recurring problems. Tantropasana procedures have the highest complexity and most difficult in Kaliyuga. Devotees should therefore take the highest precautions in practicing Tantras.

207. manōnmanī

Manonmani is a spot between the eyebrows. This is called the Shakti of Shiva; in it there is neither subject nor object, spotless.

In Yoga sastra, it is a kind of mudra. By this process the eyes neither close nor open, by which breath is neither inhaled nor exhaled and the mind is a blank neither speculating nor doubting, it is directed to that Manonmani. By Concentration (Dharana) of your attention you increase your mental power. Devi is Manonmani.

208. māhēśvarī

The Spouse of Maheshvara; The Shruti says, "Maheshvara as transcending the three gunas."

The Linga Purana says, "In his dark quality (Tamas) he is called Rudra, the destroyer; in his passionate quality (Rajas) the one born from the golden egg (Brahma); in his pure quality (Sattva) he is the all-pervading Vishnu; devoid of the three qualities (Nirguna) he is Maheshvara. He is Mahesvhara whose emblem (the Linga) is worshipped.

Shlokas 54 to 57 speak of the greatness of Ambāl. So, it has many words containing 'Maha' meaning great -like Mahadeva, Mahalakshmi.

209. mahādēvī

The great Devi: Great, whose body is immeasurable. The Devi Purana says, "Her body is immense and cannot be computed by any measurements, the root Maha. means worship; hence she is termed. Mahadevi."

210. mahālakṣmī

Markendaya Purana says Mahalakshmi is the origin of everything manifested as the three gunas. Mahalakshmi is also the presiding deity at the Karavira -Kolhapur.

211. mṛḍapriyā- Beloved of Mrda. Shiva in his saatvic qualities is called Mrda meaning Happy.

महारूपा महापूज्या महापातकनाशिनी।

महामाया महासत्त्वा महाशक्तिर्महारतिः ॥५४॥

mahārūpā, mahāpūjyā, mahāpātaka nāśinī।

mahāmāyā, mahāsattvā, mahāśakti rmahāratiḥ ॥54॥

212. mahārūpā- Great shape.

213. mahāpūjyā

Mighty object of worship. That is worshipped even by Siva and others. Devi Bhagavadam says Devi is worshipped by Siva, Brahma, Vishnu, Kubera, Visvedevas, Vaayu, Vasu, Varuna, Agni, Surya, Soma, Grahas (planets), and several others.

214. mahāpātaka nāśinī- Destroying great sins.

Brahmanada Purana says, "The highest expiation of all sins whether committed knowingly or unknowingly is brought about by the remembrance of the feet of the supreme Shakti

215. mahāmāyā

The great illusion

That divine Devi, Mahamaya, forcibly draws away the minds of even the sages and leads (them) into confusion."

The very first Shlokam of Durga Saptasloki says –

ज्ञानिनामपि चेतांसि देवि भगवती हि सा।

बलादाकृष्य मोहाय महामाया प्रयच्छति॥१॥

Jnyaaninaam-Api Chetaamsi Devi Bhagavadii Hi Saa|

Balaad-Aakrshya Mohaaya Mahaa-Maayaa Prayacchati||1||

Devi Bhagavadi, with the power of Maha Maaya, attracts even Jnanis towards 'Moha' (delusion).

Also, She is described *as 'srishti kartri brahma rupa, gophtri govinda rupini,*

samhaarini rudra rupa, tirodhanakarishvari, sadashivanugrahada pancha kritya paraayana'

216. mahāsattvā- The great reality.

Sattva means reality, existence, strength, quality of friends and being.

217. mahāśaktir – The Great Energy. Parashakti. The Super Shakti.

Visnu Purana says, "Just as the brightness of a fire is spread abroad, so the energy of the supreme Brahman (spreads throughout) the whole world; just as the brightness is greater or less according to the distance (of the fire) so it is with this energy

218. mahāratiḥ- The great delight.

महाभोगा महैश्वर्या महावीर्या महाबला।

महाबुद्धिर्महासिद्धिर्महायोगेश्वरेश्वरी॥५५॥

mahābhōgā, mahaiśvaryā, mahāvīryā, mahābalā।

mahābuddhi, rmahāsiddhi, rmahāyōgēśvarēśvarī॥55॥

219. mahābhōgā- Bhāskararāya says it means the great extension of the earth. Bhoga also means joy, wealth, etc. Direct interpretation of the Nāma would mean Devi is a great enjoyer. The mere thought of Almighty Devi gives immense happiness to devotees.

220. mahaiśvaryā- is made of two words Maha+Aishwarya. Aishwarya generally means prosperity, but Bhāskararāya has given the meaning of "Great Sovereignty." So, it means great sovereignty.

221. mahāvīryā- Virya means strength. Mahāvirya means great strength. Devi represents the greatest strength, and she makes devotees strong.

222. mahābalā- The great might. Like in Balarama, Mahābali.

223. mahābuddhi

The great intelligence. All of us are endowed with Buddhi. How we use it is up to each person. When the intelligence is directed towards her nothing remains to be known. Devi has the greatest intelligence to guide us.

224. mahāsiddhi- Siddhis are the well-known superhuman powers, like anima Mahima, Lagima siddhis. Other Siddhis are also explained in the Skanda Purana. Mahasiddhi here means the greatest attainment.

225. mahāyōgēśvarēśvarī- The ruler of the great rulers. Another interpretation is Devi is sought after by great Yogis.

महातन्त्रा महामन्त्रा महायन्त्रा महासना।

महायागक्रमाराध्या महाभैरवपूजिता॥५६॥

mahātantrā, mahāmantrā, mahāyantrā, mahāsanā।

mahāyāga kramārādhyā, mahābhairava pūjitā॥56॥

226. mahātantrā- The great Tantra. It is great because they confer many results. Tantrās include Kulaarnava, Jnananarvava and others.

227. mahāmantrā- The great Mantra.

228. mahāyantrā- The great Yantra. We talked about yantras earlier. The magical figures Pujachakra, Padmachakra etc.

229. mahāsanā- The great seat - the seat is the thirty-six tatvās beginning with the earth.

230. mahāyāga kramārādhyā - Worshipped by Mahāyaaga called as Mahāyāgakrama Aradhyā. It is the worship by sixty-four yoginis from Akshobya. Krama means arrangement.

231. mahābhairava pūjitā- Worshipped by Mahābhairava. Mahābhairava is Paramsivan-the accomplisher of creation, preservation and destruction.

Bha refers to creation, Ra preservation, and va-destruction.

महेश्वरमहाकल्पमहाताण्डवसाक्षिणी।

महाकामेशमहिषी महात्रिपुरसुन्दरी॥५७॥

maheśvara mahākalpa mahātāṇḍava sākṣiṇī।

mahākāmeśa mahiṣī, mahātripura sundarī॥57॥

232. mahēśvara mahākalpa mahātāṇḍava sākṣiṇī- The witness to the great dance of maheswara in the great cycle. From the small hand-held drum of Maheswara came the 14 Maheswara Sutrani. Mahākalpa, the great dissolution (Pralaya): mahātāṇḍava - Great dance is caused by the fact that the Self alone remains and having become bliss after the universe has been drawn into it: as, at that time, there was no one else besides herself. sākṣiṇī -Devi was the witness.

233. mahākāmēśa mahiṣī- The wife of Mahakamesvara

234. mahātripura sundarī- The great Tripurasundari.

Tripura, three cities were constructed by the great Asura architect Mayasura. They were great cities of prosperity, power and dominance over the world, but due to their impious nature, Maya's cities were destroyed by Tripurantaka, an aspect of Shiva. "Tripura Sundari", which means beautiful lady of three cities.

चतुःषष्ट्युपचाराढ्या चतुःषष्टिकलामयी।
महाचतुःषष्टिकोटियोगिनीगणसेविता ॥५८॥

chatuḥṣaṣṭyupachārāḍhyā, chatuṣṣaṣṭi kalāmayī|

mahā chatuṣṣaṣṭi kōṭi yōginī gaṇasēvitā ॥58॥

235. chatuḥṣaṣṭyupachārāḍhyā

Chatushasti is sixty-four. Upachārams are ceremonies. Aradhya is worship. What is Upachāram? It means 'Welcoming, making one comfortable, showing hospitality, saying things that are agreeable, offering that are close to one's heart'

Ambāl is worshipped with sixty-four Upachārams or offerings.

In daily worship, one usually offers sixteen upachāras to the principal deity.

The sixty-four upachāras are offered throughout the day in many temples. They include right from waking the deity with vedic verses and instrumental music, followed by various Upachāras like *svagatam, abhishekam, alankaram* offering her scents, flowers, garlands, bangles, jewels, fanning, food and tambulam.

236. chatuṣṣaṣṭi kalāmayī

She embodies sixty-four forms of fine arts. It includes (1) The knowledge of the eighteen letters (Lipi), (2) and (3) the power of writing and reading these quickly, (4) knowledge of different languages, (5) composing verses in them, (6) gambling, (7) to (14) the four Vedas and the four auxiliary Vedas, (15) to (26) the twice six auxiliary sciences, (27) Tantra, (28) Purana. (29) Smrti, (30) poetry, (31) rhetoric, (32) drama, (58) dancing, (59) singing, (60) alchemy, (61) knowledge of gems, and so on.

237. mahā chatuṣṣaṣṭi kōṭi yōginī gaṇasēvitā

Attended by the great sixty-four crores of bands of yoginis. The Brahmi and other seven divinities each have eight Shaktis who are parts of them. Thus, eight multiplied by eight becomes sixty-four. Each has a crore of bands. Yogini gana are demigoddesses. Devi is worshipped by these sixty-four crores (640 million) deities.

Here is an interesting story about Bhāskararāya. When he was living in the holy city of Kashi (now Varanasi), some

The Glory of Lalithā Sahasranāmam

scholars who were jealous challenged him in public. They wanted to tarnish his image. They asked him to recite the names of all the 640 million Yoginis. He agreed and asked them to write down the names as he was speaking.

The challengers were ready with palm leaves and stylus. He kept on giving names one after another with minute descriptions. They got tired of writing and realized his greatness before long and fell at his feet.

An enlightened soul in the crowd, Kumkumananda Swami, had warned all the challengers not to test him. The reason was that he could see the goddess herself sitting on his shoulder telling the 640 million names.

(Readers may like to see my YouTube video titled "Bhāskararāya Parichayaha: An Introduction to Bhāskararāya.")

मनुविद्या चन्द्रविद्या चन्द्रमण्डलमध्यगा।

चारुरूपा चारुहासा चारुचन्द्रकलाधरा॥५९॥

manuvidyā, chandravidyā, chandramaṇḍalamadhyagā।

chārurūpā, chāruhāsā, chāruchandra kalādharā॥59॥

238. manuvidyā

Devi is the personification of Manuvidya. Srividya comprises twelve kinds according to 12 devotees: Manu, Chandra, Kubera, Lopamudra, Manmatha, Agastya, Agni, Surya, Indra, Skanda, Shiva and Durvasa. These are great devotees of Ambāl. Manuvidhyaa refers to worship by Manu while Chandravidhyaa refers to worship by Chandra (Moon).

239. chandravidyā- She is also the personification of Chandravidya (the same Srividya as practiced by Chandra, one of the twelve authorities).

240. chandramaṇḍalamadhyagā- Devi residing in the center of Chandra Mandala. In Shiva Purana, Lord Shiva says to Devi "I am residing in the head of fire, you are residing in the head of the Moon, thus the world consisting of fire and moon is upheld by us". The secret meaning is the moon's disc is the Srichakra itself.

241. chārurūpā- Charu means beautiful. Devi's form is exquisite, and She is beauty incarnate.

242. chāruhāsā

With a beautiful smile. Devi has a charming smile. Her smile is compared to the Moon.

Moon and mind are closely linked. Lunar is the adjective for moon. Lunatic is a mad person. Moods vary according to the phases of the moon.

All the above naamas refer to the Moon. The full moon represents supreme consciousness. (Raakendu vadana-She who has a face like the full moon)

If Devi is worshipped on full moon night, devotees will attain Manthra Siddhi. If the Full Moon combines with Friday, performance of Lalithā Sahasranamā *archanai* during twilight time will yield multiple results.

243. chāruchandra kalādharā- Wearing a beautiful crescent moon. Devi wearing a beautiful crescent moon, in her crown.

Chapter 6

The Supreme Goddess

We begin this chapter with verse 60. In this chapter, there are poetical descriptions of Ambāl's supremacy in different forms and activities.

चराचरजगन्नाथा चक्रराजनिकेतना।

पार्वती पद्मनयना पद्मरागसमप्रभा॥६०॥

charāchara jagannāthā, chakrarāja nikētanā।

pārvatī, padmanayanā, padmarāga samaprabhā॥60॥

244. charāchara jagannāthā.

Charam + Achāram. Charam -that which moves. Achāram- that which does not move. Jagannatha -Ruler of both animate and inanimate worlds. Devi is the supreme ruler of the entire world.

245. chakrarāja nikētanā- Abiding in the SriChakra.

246. pārvatī.

Parvata (पर्वत) is one of the Sanskrit words for "mountain"; "Parvati" derives her name from being incarnated as the daughter of the mountain king called Himavan. The word Himalayas is derived from Himavan.

247. padmanayanā

Lotus-eyed, Padmam is lotus, nayana is eyes. The lotus is a symbol of purity and perfect beauty. Lotus is often used often in describing divine eyes. Devi has Lotus petal-like eyes. Another example is *Neerajadalanayana*.

248. padmarāga samaprabhā- Shining like the Ruby. Padma-Lotus, Raga-Red, Prabha-color.

पञ्चप्रेतासनासीना पञ्चब्रह्मस्वरूपिणी।

चिन्मयी परमानन्दा विज्ञानघनरूपिणी॥६१॥

pañchaprētāsanāsīnā, pañchabrahma svarūpiṇī |

chinmayī, paramānandā, vijñāna ghanarūpiṇī ||61 ||

249. pañchaprētāsanāsīnā

Pancha is five and Preta is corpse. Devi is seated on five corpses.

Brahma, Vishnu, Rudra, lsvara and Sadasiva, are motionless without shakti and hence deemed five corpses. Devi reclines on the cot, whose four legs are Brahma (the Creator), Vishnu (the Protector), Shiva (the Destroyer) and Ishwara (Disappearance) and whose top surface is Sadasiva (grace).

Brahma looks after creation, Vishnu looks after sustenance, Rudra is the destroyer (causing death), Mahadeva holds the dissolved universe (thirodhanam) and Sadashiva again re-creates the universe (anugraham). It is said that these five divinities cannot function without Shakthi. So Great is the unifying principle of Shakthi.

Adi Sankara's Soundarya Lahiri's very first shlokam says-

शिवः शक्त्या युक्तो यदि भवति शक्तः प्रभवितुं

न चेदेवं देवो न खलु कुशलः स्पन्दितुमपि।

अतस्त्वामाराध्यां हरिहरविरिञ्चादिभिरपि

प्रणन्तुं स्तोतुं वा कथमकृतपुण्यः प्रभवति॥

shivaH shaktyA yukto yadi bhavati shaktaH prabhavituM

na chedevaM devo na khalu kushalaH spanditumapi|

atastvAmArAdhyAM hariharavirinchAdibhirapi

praNantuM stotuM vA kathamakR^itapuNyaH

prabhavati||1||

Meaning: Shiva becomes inert without Shaktī. He is incapable of doing anything without Shakti.

When Shiva is not united with Shakti, He is powerless. Sri Lalita's 5-Deity seat demonstrates and emphasizes the fact that there is no Deity who is superior to Lalita. Lalita's supremacy is unquestionable. That's why she is called ParaShakti.

Bhāskararāya gives another explanation. In tantric literature Brahma, Vishnu, Rudra, Iswara, SadaShiva are considered 'pancha bootha' or five elements

Brahma – Prithvi (on which all living things get created) – earth

Vishnu – aapu - water.

Rudra – Agni- fire

Iswara – Vayu -air

sadashiva – Akasha - sky

Each of these five elements reside in the different sense organs of embodied beings. So, in another way Lalita Devi sitting on the Pancha Brahmas implies that she is the master of all these senses and ruler of those.

250. pañchabrahma svarūpiṇī

The five Brahmans are her form. As we saw before, the five begin with Brahma and end with Sadasiva. Bhāskararāya adds more:

These are included under Brahman, because the Tripurisiddhanta says. "The unconditioned Brahman by the play of the Maya becomes, Brahma, Vishnu, Rudra, Isvara, and Sadasiva. Thus, by name only Brahman is in five forms." Or, the five Brahmas are Isana, Tatpurusa, Aghora, Vamadeva and Sadyojaata. The Linga Purana says, "Jiva, Prakrti, Buddhi, Ahamkara, and manas; the five senses, viz" ear, skin, eyes, tongue, and nose; and the subtle elements are the forms of the five Brahman."

It is described in the same book that the above (five subtle elements) are the causes creating the five gross elements. These are her forms.

251. chinmayī- Consciousness itself

252. paramānandā- Supreme bliss. Param is superlative.

253. vijñāna ghanarūpiṇī- Vijnana here means Chaitanya, ghana one strong essence, one essence of consciousness.

ध्यानध्यातृध्येयरूपा धर्माधर्मविवर्जिता।

विश्वरूपा जागरिणी स्वपन्ती तैजसात्मिका॥६२॥

dhyanadhyātṛ dhyeyarūpā, dharmādharma vivarjitā।

viśvarūpā, jāgariṇī, svapantī, taijasātmikā॥62॥

254. dhyānadhyātṛ dhyēyarūpā- The root 'Dhyai' means to think. Dhyanam comes from this root meaning meditation. Ambāl is meditation, meditator, and the object of meditation.

255. dharmādharma vivarjitā.

Dharma comes from the root Dhr to bear and ma, in greatness, so, as it bears and as it is a great one. it is called Dharma." Thus, the word Dharma is explained. "That which leads to a desirable result, and taught by teachers as Dharma, and Adharma is the opposite of this. Ambāl is Devoid of virtue and vice. Dharma is what is prescribed in scriptures. Devi is free from these two because the Scriptures are meant only for the common people who are ignorant.

From the next nāma 256 to 263, the eight nāmas describe the different stages of consciousness in which Ambāl exists. These are more philosophical and are discussed in detail in Mandukya Upanishad.

From the fully conscious state to the alert (jagrat), dreaming (svapna), deep sleep (susupti), ecstasy (turya) and beyond.

256. viśvarūpā. Omnipresent. the meaning is that her form is the Universe Itself.

257. jāgariṇī, The waking state. Jagrat -jagratai…alert.

258. svapantī. The dreaming state. Svapnam.

259. taijasātmikā

She is Taijasa itself. What is Taijasa?

Taijasa literally means 'one who is bright'. The individual soul jīva has three states of consciousness. They are:

Jāgrat - waking state

Svapna - dream state

Suṣupti - deep-sleep state

When Jīva gets associated with these three states it is called viśva, taijasa and prājña respectively.

To explain further, the three stages of consciousness in Jiva are:

Vishva - the waking stage, engaging the gross, sthula-sharira physical body

Taijasa - the dream stage, engaging the subtle body or suksma-sharira

Prajna - the deep sleep stage, engaging the bliss body, the ultimate experience of Brahman.

Taijasa is the second aspect where the sphere of activity is the dream state. The self is given a name, taijasa, the luminous one. In this state the self builds its own world of dreams. The dream objects give delight to the self for sometimes. In this sense, the self is liberated from the empirical world. In the second state of consciousness, namely the dream state, awareness is experienced consisting of mere impressions that are subtle. Hence the enjoyment of them too becomes subtle. While the first state is the waking life of outward moving, external consciousness, the second state is the dream life of inward-looking consciousness.

सुप्ता प्राज्ञात्मिका तुर्या सर्वावस्थाविवर्जिता।

सृष्टिकर्त्री ब्रह्मरूपा गोप्त्री गोविन्दरूपिणी ॥६३॥

suptā, prājñātmikā, turyā, sarvāvasthā vivarjitā।

sṛṣṭikartrī, brahmarūpā, gōptrī, gōvindarūpiṇī॥63॥

260. suptā

State of sleep. Bhāskararāya says, the description of it is given in the Siva-Sutra "The state of sleep is incapacity of discrimination, viz" illusion." One says, "I slept happily, I know nothing," thus one says from recollection.

By this saying, three modifications of Avidya are indicated; viz "ignorance, egoism, and happiness; sound sleep is that state in which these three exist.

261. prājñātmikā- Prajna Himself; Prajna, lsvara who is the collective form of the jivas above described in 260.

262. turyā

It means a State of ecstasy. Turiya state is the state in which the experience called Shuddhavidya is acquired and the result of discrimination of these (lower) three states and enjoyers thereof.

The Shiva-Sutra (I, 7) also says, "Though there are different states, Jagrat, Swapna and Susupti vie-z, waking, dreaming, and sleeping, (real) enjoyment exists only in the fourth one. Ecstasy in the fourth state should be allowed like oil to permeate the other three." Devi is known by the name Turiya

263. sarvāvasthā vivarjitā

It means Transcending all the states. There is a fifth state of Jivas but as it has no special name and as it is beyond the Turiya state, it is simply called, 'beyond Turiya'; this name indicates the fifth state; all the states. Vivarjita means transcending: Vi, entirely, that is one does not return to the other states. This state also has two aspects, the individual and the collective. This fifth state arises from firmness in the fourth one (Turiya).

After the description of the five divisions of Jiva's consciousness in which Ambāl exists, Lalitha Sahasranam proceeds to describe the five main functions of Ambāl.

264. sṛṣṭikartrī- Ambāl is the Creator.

265. brahmarūpā- In the form of Brahma.

266. gōptrī- Protector. Sustaining the universe

267. gōvindarūpiṇī- In the form of Govinda

संहारिणी रुद्ररूपा तिरोधानकरीश्वरी।

सदाशिवाऽनुग्रहदा पञ्चकृत्यपरायणा॥६४॥

saṃhāriṇī, rudrarūpā, tirōdhānakarīśvarī |

sadāśivānugrahadā, pañchakṛtya parāyaṇā ||64||

268. saṃhāriṇī- Destroyer: Samhāra, Sam-Hara means reducing the universe into atoms. Devi is also the destroyer.

269. rudrarūpā- In the form of Rudra.Ru, means pain, or the cause of pain, he who drives this out, (dra), Shiva, the supreme cause, is called Rudra. Ambāl is in the form of Rudra, who drives away sorrow.

270. tirōdhānakari- Causing the Disappearance. Creating Māya or illusion.

271. īśvarī- The Ruler.

272. sadāśivā- Devi is called Sadashiva when the superlative Sattva quality. Predominates

273. Anugrahadā- Conferrer of blessing. Tirodhana and Anugraha, mean respectively bondage and release.

274. pañchakṛtya parāyaṇā

Panchakritya means five functions. Parāyana, means, fond of, devoted to, and dependent. Devoted to the five functions.

The Devi Bhagavada Purana IV, says, "She creates the universe, she protects, she destroys what she protects at the end of the cycle; She is who in her Three forms bewilders the universe.

Brahma united with her to create the universe, Vishnu united with Her protects, Rudra united with Her destroys. She binds the whole universe and holds it bewildered by the noose of illusion.

भानुमण्डलमध्यस्था भैरवी भगमालिनी।

पद्मासना भगवती पद्मनाभसहोदरी॥६५॥

bhānumaṇḍala madhyasthā, bhairavī, bhagamālinī |

padmāsanā, Bhagavadī, padmanābha sahōdarī ॥65 ॥

275. bhānumaṇḍala madhyasthā- Bhanu is sun. Ambāl is abiding amid the sun's disc.

276. bhairavī- Wife of Bhairava, or Paramashiva

277. bhagamālinī

Bhaga means six parts -The full supremacy, righteousness, fame, prosperity, wisdom, and discrimination.

Devi is also called Bhagavadi in Kerala. Malini is one who wears a garland. Bhagamalini means Wearing the garland of prosperity.

278. padmāsanā- Seated on the lotus.

279. Bhagavadī

Bhaga has many meanings. It means supremacy, magnanimity, wisdom, dispassion, fame, power, righteousness, prosperity, and worldly concerns"; these are in Devi. So, she is called Bhagavadi just as Bhagavan.

Saktirahasya says, "The word Bhaga is derived from the root Bhaj to worship; she who is worshipped by all Devas and she blesses them, hence she is called Bhagavadi."

280. padmanābha sahōdarī

Sister of Padmanabha or Vishnu.

The one Brahman assumed two forms. male and female, the male is Vishnu who is the material cause of the whole universe; the female became the spouse of Paramsiva. The secret of the Saiva theory is that these three in combination become the one indivisible Brahman. Vishnu in the male form is said to be NarayaNa and in the female form it is thought of as NarayaNi or Parvathy.

Thus, NarayaNa and NarayaNi are considered as brother and sister.

They also look, dress and decorate alike with similar character qualities! Vishnu and Parvathi are said to be siblings. Likewise, Brahma & Lakshmi and Shiva & Saraswathi are siblings.

उन्मेषनिमिषोत्पन्नविपन्नभुवनावली।

सहस्रशीर्षवदना सहस्राक्षी सहस्रपात्॥६६॥

unmēṣa nimiṣōtpanna vipanna bhuvanāvaliḥ।

sahasraśīrṣavadanā, sahasrākṣī, sahasrapāt ॥66॥

      The Glory of Lalithā Sahasranāmam

281. unmēṣa nimiṣōtpanna vipanna bhuvanāvaliḥ

The series of worlds arise and disappear with the opening and shutting of Her eyes.

The creation of the supreme is simply the expression of His Wish. Bhāskararāya quotes Kalidas: "The universe consisting of the seer, the seen 'and the seeing, with all its parts, existed in you before you thought (of creation). At the manifestation of the universe at your will, your eyes open, at the destruction of the universe (at your will) your eyes shut."

282. sahasraśīrṣavadanā

Thousand headed and thousand faced. Cosmic being. Purusasuktam from Rig Veda begins with

सहस्रशीर्षा पुरुषः। सहस्राक्षः सहस्रपात्।

स भूमिं विश्वतो वृत्वा। अत्यतिष्ठद्दशाङ्गुलम्...

Sahasrasheersha Purushaha, Sahasraksha Sahasrapaad,

sa bhumim viswatho vrtva, atyathistadasangulam

— the unit of measurement was known then as *angulam*.

"Purusha is thousand headed, thousand eyed and thousand footed."

283. sahasrākṣī- Thousand eyed

284. sahasrapāt- With Thousand feet

The Devi Bhagavada Purana (Book III) says, "Devi, having thousands of eyes, thousands of hands, thousands of heads and feet, vividly shines forth."

आब्रहमकीटजननी वरणाश्रमवधिायिनी।

नजिाज्ञारूपनगिमा पुण्यापुण्यफलप्रदा॥६७॥

ābrahma kīṭajananī, varṇāśrama vidhāyinī |

nijājñārūpanigamā, puṇyāpuṇya phalapradā || 67 ||

285. ābrahma kīṭajananī

Mother of all from Brahma to a worm.

Let me narrate a true story. Kanchi Mahaperiyava was camping in Calcutta in 1935 as part of His All-India Vijaya Yatra. It was Navarathri time and there was a grand celebration at Periyava's camp. Everyday there was a 'Navā Varna Pooja', Sumangali Pooja, Kanya Pooja & many more. There was a devoted lady who never missed it out. She was Chellamma Mami who had settled in Calcutta. She was also a regular visitor to Sri Rabindranath Tagore's ashram. After visiting Periyava's camp, she went to Tagore's ashram. Tagore was a 'Sri Vidya Upāsaka' but he had some modern thoughts.

Tagore's command of literature is known well. Mami had visited Tagore after a short break. When Tagore enquired her why she had been missing for some days, she explained that Mahaperiyava had come & there were several Pujas like Navāvarna pooja, Sumangali pooja, Kanya pooja, etc.

Tagore understood that Mahaperiyava was also a Devi Upāsaka. Tagore, "Does Swamiji do Kanya Pooja with any child or only with Brahmin child?"

Mami, "No! Periyava never deviates from the tradition. He does Kanya Pooja only with a Brahmin child". Tagore, being one of the world's highly respected scholars (Nobel prize winner), quoted one of the namas from the Sri Lalitha Sahasra Namam *"Aabrahma keeda Janani"* and said "He

   The Glory of Lalithā Sahasranāmam

is a great Devi Upasaka, won't he know the meaning of it? It means SHE is the source of everything, from tiny worms all the way to Brahma (who creates the world). Still, is he is thinking having only a Brahmin child for Kanya Pooja?"

Mami was very upset to hear someone like Tagore taking a dig at Mahaperiyava. When she met Mahaperiyava the next day, Periva asked, "Why Didn't you come to puja yesterday?" Mami said "I went to meet Tagore."

Periyava understood and asked, "Did he say anything about me?" She couldn't withhold her tears and narrated what Tagore had said. Periyava smiled & said, "What he quoted is true but there are three more askharams that follow. They are वर्णाश्रमविधायिनी – *Varna Ashrama Vidayini* -ask him to include them also while reading". Later, Mami went back to Tagore & said what Periyava said. Tagore Repeated "आब्रह्मकीटजननी वर्णाश्रमविधायिनी। निजाज्ञारूपनिगमा पुण्यापुण्यफलप्रदा a few times. "Aha! Aha! This is the way to understand Devi's Sahasranamā. I never knew it. Swamiji has replied to my very own question." Tagore told her with a bit of excitement, "Swamiji is a Mahaan! Oh! What I told was a mistake."

Immediately, he found out the next step and told her "I must have his darshan."

286. varṇāśrama vidhāyinī

She established the castes and orders of life.

The Vedas are divided into two parts, the Karmakanda and the Brahmakanda; Karmakanda is that part of the Sruti or Vedic writings which relates to ceremonial acts and sacrificial rites. The devas and lower animals have no share in the Karmakanda.

The (divine) Mother established righteousness (Dharma) through Karmakanda after dividing men into four castes and four orders.

The system of four varnas (Brahmana, Kshatriya, Vaisya and Sudra) as ordained in the Vedas was based on mutual support and service. The brahmanas serve the eyes and mouth of society. They provide a spiritual vision for society and teach people accordingly. Just as the arms are raised to defend the body, the kshatriya's main duty is to protect society.

The vaishya's main duty is material nourishment, and the shudra supports all sections of society. In olden days, the Kings supported the brahmins and provided protection to them. My native village of Maharajapuram was gifted by the Maharaja to a group of Brahmin scholars; so also, Baskararajapuram was gifted by the King to Bhāskararāya. There are many such villages that were gifted by the Mahratta Kings.

Even today, many Veda pātashalas (Vedic schools) are run with the help of Vaishyas or business communities. Temples with amazing architecture were built by skilled artisans of the fourth varna. Even today, some communities who work on a hereditary basis, like weavers, potters, goldsmiths, sculptors are doing well in their respective professions and preserving their time-honored skills, winning appreciation from people around the world. History shows the four varnas cooperated well with each other for hundreds of years and lived happily as pointed out by many historians. However, after the British came and adopted the 'divide and rule' policy, and later with

 The Glory of Lalithā Sahasranāmam

different government policies, things changed. Today, one might ask, where is varnashrama? It may still be there but in a decayed condition. The Vedas are unchanged. Even recently some 100 years ago, people were mostly driven by their duty and simple satisfaction.

In fact, Mahaperiva said that Varna Ashrama kept communities together and perpetuated respective skills generation after generation.

287. nijājñā rūpa nigamā

The Vedas are the expression of Her command.

Aajna, command, is ascertained by the knowers of the Vedas through reflection on the words (of the Vedas) what set forth the object to be attained, the means and the practical directions, by giving out the real meaning, meditation and praise; these three belong to the Karmakanda part of the Vedas. Veda-s prescribe the actions to be done.

Nigama (निगम) is another name for Vedas. Whereas Āgama (आगम) is the name for other sacred scriptures which are closely aligned with the Vedas but have their own distinct language, structure and philosophy.

Grammatically, both Nigama and Āgama signify something passed down through a lineage. The prefix "ni" (nishcayena āgatah) has more of a sense of fixed and arranged. The prefix "ā" (āsamantāt āgatah) has more of a sense of coming from many sources. Hence, we see that the Vedas are well-defined and have remained a closed, unchanged for thousands of years. Whereas the Āgama literature has been more fluid and accumulated over the centuries. Devi represents Nigama – the Vedas.

288. puṇyāpuṇya phalapradā

Giver of results, good and bad.

Puṇyāpuṇya consist of two words puṇya + a-puṇya. Puṇya means the good or right, virtue, purity, good work, meritorious act, moral or religious merit, and a-puṇya means the illusionary puṇya. "You reap what you sow" is an adage. Results arising out of such actions are transferred to one's karmic account.

The result of karmic account is rebirths and its associated pains and sufferings. Such results accrue at Her command as She is the Lord of karma-s. Brahma Sūtra (III.ii.7) confirms this. It says, "फलमत् उपपते: (phalamat upapateḥ)" which means "The fruit of action is from Him, this being the logical position." Mother gives the good and bad results arising from ordained and prohibited actions respectively.

श्रुतिसीमन्तसिन्दूरीकृतपादाब्जधूलिका।

सकलागमसन्दोहशुक्तिसम्पुटमौक्तिका ॥६८॥

śruti sīmanta sindhūrīkṛta pādābjadhūḷikā।

sakalāgama sandōha śuktisampuṭa mauktikā ॥68॥

289. śruti sīmanta sindhūrīkṛta pādābjadhūḷikā

After describing the Karmakanda devoted to rites (sarificers and other performances), the scripture now proceeds to explain Brahmakanda also i.e., Brahman is Siddhavastu (through the mother's command alone).

Shruti -Vedas, Seemantha-Seema and Antha -border, end, parting of the hair on the head sindooree-kr'tha-where the sindoor is applied = the essence of the vedas = upanishads,paada abja-lotus feet, dhoolikaa-dust

The dust of Her lotus feet forms the vermilion mark on the parting of the hair on the head of the Vedas. also means the dust of whose feet is the essence of the Upanishads.

Seemantham, a ritual performed to a woman during pregnancy, literally means the hair parting just above the eyebrow. It is said that Ambāl resides in that parting. This is why the practice of applying Kumkum on the parting, as a manner of propitiating Devi and bless the woman as Sumangali. To this day, many Bengali Hindu women follow this practice of applying Kumkum on the hair parting. SEP

290. sakalāgama sandōha śuktisampuṭa mauktikā

Āgama-s are traditional shastras that lay down guidelines for various rituals in temples. It is a highly complex subject, and provides information on temple building codes, image making, and religious procedures.

Bhāskararāya explains that Ambal's pearl (in the nose ring) is enclosed in a shell having all the collected scriptures. Pearl expression indicates her attributes (Dharma) of creation, etc. The Scriptures describe only her nose pearl and other jewels and not her real nature.

पुरुषार्थप्रदा पूर्णा भोगिनी भुवनेश्वरी।

अम्बिकाऽनादिनिधना हरिब्रह्मेन्द्रसेविता॥६९॥

puruṣārthapradā, pūrṇā, bhōginī, bhuvanēśvarī।

ambikā,'nādi nidhanā, haribrahmēndra sēvitā॥69॥

291. puruṣārthapradā

Granting the objects of men. The four puruṣārthas (goals for human living) are Dharma (righteousness, moral values), Artha (prosperity, economic values), Kama (pleasure, love, psychological values) and Moksha (liberation, spiritual values)

292. pūrṇā

The fullness.

Shanti Mantram says,

ॐ पूर्णमदः पूर्णमिदं पूर्णात्पूर्णमुदच्यते।

पूर्णस्य पूर्णमादाय पूर्णमेवावशिष्यते॥

oṃ pūrṇamadaḥ pūrṇamidam pūrṇātpurṇamudacyate

pūrṇaśya pūrṇamādāya pūrṇamevāvaśiṣyate॥

The outer and inner worlds are full of divine consciousness. From Purna is manifested Purna. Taking Purna from Purna, Purna indeed remains (Because Divine Consciousness is Non-Dual and Infinite).

The concept of zero was born out of this. 0+0=0. 0-0=0. Devi is free from the limitations of time, place and circumstance.

Purna is also the name of a river in Kerala.

293. bhōginī- The enjoyer.

294. bhuvanēśvarī

Ruler of the universe.

Bhuvana fourteen worlds, or water. Or Bhuvanesvari is the deity, indicated by the syllable Hrim, or she is in the mantra form of Hreem. There is a famous Bhuvaneswari temple

in Pudukottai that was built by my Guru Sri Shanthananda
Swamigal.

295. ambikā- The mother. Amba, Amma, SriMatha, all refer
to the great mother goddess. She is the mother of the Universe.

296. Anādi nidhanā- Having neither beginning nor end.

297. haribrahmēndra sēvitā

Worshipped by Hari, Brahma and Indra.

Bhāskararāya explains: "In the Srichakra (Nagara), in the
center between the seventeenth and the eighteenth walls, is
the seat of Vishnu; between the sixteenth and the seventeenth,
is of Brahma; between the fourteenth and the fifteenth, is of
Indra and other Lokapalas (protectors of the world).

All these reside (in their respective places) for the sake of
worshipping Devi."

The Devi Bhagavadam Purana says, "Brahma, Vishnu,
Shiva, Indra, Varuna, Yama, Vayu, Agni, Kubera, Pusan,
Asvins, Bhaga, Adityas, Vasus, Rudras, Visvedevas,
Marudganas, all these meditate on Devi, the cause of creation,
preservation, and destruction."

नारायणी नादरूपा नामरूपविवर्जिता।

ह्रीङ्कारी ह्रीमती हृद्या हेयोपादेयवर्जिता॥७०॥

nārāyaṇī, nādarūpā, nāmarūpa vivarjitā |

hrīṅkārī, hrīmatī, hṛdyā, hēyōpādēya varjitā ॥ 70 ॥

298. nārāyaṇī

The sister of Vishnu is called Narayani. SankaraNarayanan
is a deity where Shiva and Vishnu are in one form. It is in

Sankaran Kovil where the vigraham (idol) has Vishnu to the left of Shiva.

Ambāl is also on the left side of Shiva in Ardhanareeswara. So, Ambāl is Narayani. In Durga Saptasloki, we *say Sarvamangala Mangalye Shive Sarvartha Sadhike, Charnaye trayambake Gowri, Narayani Namosthute.*

Bhāskararāya adds:

The explanation of the word Narayana is given in Manu Smriti (I, 10): "The water is called Nara, because it emanated from Nara (Brahman): that is his first abode (ayana). hence, he is named Narayana." The Devi Puranam says, "Because she has her abode in the water, or she has her seat in the ocean, hence she is called Narayani, the creator of Nara (men) and women."

299. nādarūpā

In the form of sound. There are eight notes (varnas) above the bindu of the syllable Hrim, such as, Ardhcandra, Rodhini, Nada, Nadanta, Shakti, Vyapika' Samana, and Unmani which are subtle, more subtle, and most subtle;' of these the third is Nada. Nada is simply sound.

300. nāmarūpa vivarjitā

Transcending name and form. There are five forms of the universe which appear inextricably intertwined in the knot of spirit and matter. These are as analyzed by great men as "existence, knowledge, bliss, name and form."

The first three belong to Brahman, and the other two belong to the world. As the latter two, name and form are illusory, she transcends them.

We conclude this chapter with the three hundredth nāma.

In his commentary *Saubhagyabhaskara*, Bhāskararāya has divided the Lalithā Sahasranāmam into twelve kalās or sections. In chapter 6, we have covered the fourth Kala called *Marichi*.

Chapter 7

The Adorable Ambāl

We will start with nāma 301 that appears in the second line of verse 70.

नारायणी नादरूपा नामरूपविवर्जिता।

ह्रीङ्कारी ह्रीमती हृद्या हेयोपादेयवर्जिता॥७०॥

nārāyaṇī, nādarūpā, nāmarūpa vivarjitā।

(completed 300 nāmas)

hrīṅkārī, hrīmatī, hṛdyā, hēyōpādēya varjitā ॥70॥

The second line - hrīṅkārī, hrīmatī, hṛdyā, hēyōpādēya varjitā- is related to Devi mantras.

301. hrīmkārī

The syllable *'Hreem'* is Bhuvaneswari Beeja Mantram. It is a key mantra for Adi Shakti. This beeja mantra is also known as Shakti Beeja. Bhuvanesari is seen as *'Ekakshari.'* It means she is seen to be single *aksharam* (syllable) *r*eferring to Hreem.

Hrimkari is also the one who makes the sound Hrim. Bhāskararāya says that the meaning of Hrim given in the Svatantra-Tantra by a Vyākula Akhsara verse as "The Vyoman (Ha) indicates the manifestation, Vahni (Ra) as involution, ee as perfection, and the dot (m) controlling the three." The meaning is Hrim corresponds to creation. preservation and destruction; Kari is the doer.

What is this Vyākulāksara verse? Bhāskararāya explains. It is a verse wherein the most secret meaning of certain mantras is given out in a perplexing manner, with a key also in another verse in the same way in order that it may not be understood by the uninitiated. Such verses are called Vyākulāksara verses.

302. Hrimati

Hri has many meanings as the Shruti says, "shyness, mind, satisfaction, desire, nourishment." Here, we can say Hri is shyness or bashfulness. Hrimati means Possessor of Hri. We have this shlokam in Devi Māhatmyam that says *'Yaa Devi Sarva Bhuteshu Lajja Rupena Samstita'* describing the natural shyness of Devi.

303. hṛdyā- Refers to Devi Abiding in the heart. That is in the heart of ascetics. Or Hrdya, also means delightful.

304. hēyōpādēya varjitā- *Heyam* means discarding something because there is no desire. *Upadeyam* means accepting something because there is a desire. Ambāl has no desires and hence has nothing to regret nor to accept.

राजराजार्चिता राज्ञी रम्या राजीवलोचना।

रञ्जनी रमणी रस्या रणत्किङ्किणिमेखला॥७१॥

rājarājārchitā, rājñī, ramyā, rājīvalōchanā |

rañjanī, ramaṇī, rasyā, raṇatkiṅkiṇi mēkhalā ||71 ||

Again, Lalithā Sahasranāmam describes the attributes of Ambāl.

305. rājarājārchitā

Worshipped by Rajaraja (Kings). Who are these Rajarajas? Bhāskararāya says they are Manu and Kubera. Manu is considered as the king of human beings. Manusmriti or "reflections of Manu" is an ancient text that served as a code of conduct for human society. Kubera is the king of Navanidhi, nine kinds of wealth. Hence, they are Rajarajas.

306. rājñī- राज्ञी Queen. Because she is the queen of Rajarajesvara (Shiva).

307. ramyā- The beautiful one.

308. rājīvalōchanā- Rajiva has many meanings like - "deer, fish, lotus, a dependent of a king." Depending on the context. In this case it means - With eyes like those of a deer or lotus.

309. rañjanī- Delightful to her devotees. It also means colorful. By her presence, the rosy-tinted Devi colors the pure Paramashiva as the red flower colors the crystal.

310. ramaṇī- Makes devotees glad by "Laughing, playing and rejoicing."-like a child, so easy, innocent, freely. Devi provides a delightful experience for devotees.

311. rasyā- One who must be experienced or worshipped.

312. raṇatkiṅkiṇi mēkhalā

Kinkini refers to the melodious sound produced by bells. In our dharma, the sound of the bell is considered auspicious. It welcomes divinity and dispels evil.

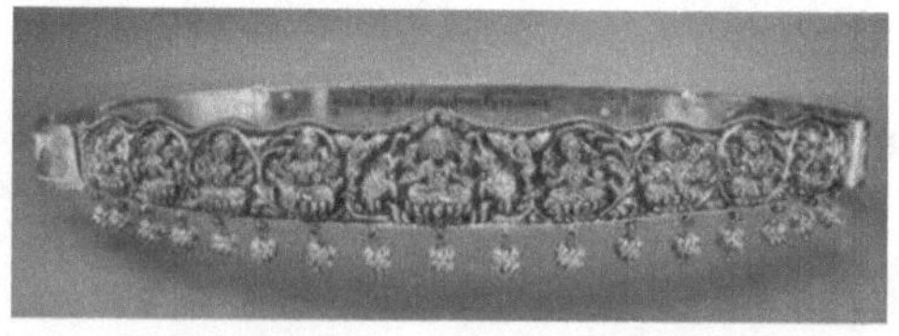

Mekhala is an *"Abharana"* a jewel which is a type of hip ornament like *'odyanam'* as they say in Tamil. It is a waist

          The Glory of Lalithā Sahasranāmam

band worn by women. It has tiny bells attached that make lilting *kinkini* sound during movement. Ranatkinkini mekhala means Ambāl wears a waist band fitted with tinkling bells.

In Soundaryalahari, Sloka 7 begins with क्वणत्काञ्चीदामा *kwanatkanchidaama,* that means 'the bells in the waist band making lilting sounds.' The description is for Kanchi Kamakshi. She is the only deity who has all the physical description of Lalitha Tripurasundari. In fact, the name Kanchi refers to the midriff portion just above the belly button. When Ambāl walks, it is not only her anklets that make the 'jaljal' or 'kinkini' sound but also her odyanam (waistband).

Talking about 'kinkini' sound, there is a nice song composed by Oothukaadu Venkatasubbaiyer on Mannargudi Rajagopala set in Neelambari Ragam. It begins with '*Maninupuradhaari Rajagopala Maninupuradhaari Kankana Kinkini kana.*' He describes the sound coming from the tiny bells in the anklet worn by the Rajagopala Swami.

There is another interesting story about the kinkini sound from anklet. Adi Shankara won the debate with Mandanamishra and blessed him with the title of Sureshvaracharya. Soon after, Mandanamishra and his patni (spouse) Sarasawani (an avatara of Saraswathi) agreed to follow Adi Sankara. Sarasawani said, "I will follow you. But you should not turn back to see me. If you do so, I will stay then and there." Adi Sankara agreed to her condition and the three started their journey towards the South. Adi Sankara knew that Saraswani was following behind as he could hear the soft kinkini sound coming from the tiny bells in Saraswani's anklets. While coming near the river Thungabathra, Adi Sankara was impressed with an extremely beautiful and scenic spot. At the same time, the 'kinkini' sound from Sarasawani's anklets had stopped. Shankara turned back to check and Sarasawani stopped there. It is said that place became Sringeri- the abode of Goddess Sharadha Devi.

रमा राकेन्दुवदना रतिरूपा रतिप्रिया।

रक्षाकरी राक्षसघ्नी रामा रमणलम्पटा॥७२॥

ramā, rākēnduvadanā, ratirūpā, ratipriyā|

rakṣākarī, rākṣasaghnī, rāmā, ramaṇalampaṭā ‖72‖

313. ramā- In the form of Lakshmi.

314. rākēnduvadanā- Indu means moon; *vadanā* is face. Ambāl has a face like the full moon. Remember the story of Abirami Bhattar that I narrated earlier. He saw Ambāl's face as full moon on Amavasya Day!

315. ratirūpā- In the beautiful form of Rati, the wife of Manmatha. Ambāl assumes different names, and this is one such name.

316. Ratipriya- Beloved of Rati. Ambāl made Manmatha visible to the eyes of Rati alone out of compassion for Rati.

317. rakṣākarī- Raksha is protection and kari is the doer. Devi is the Protector of devotees

318. rākṣasaghnī- Slayer of Raakshaas. Agni is fire. She destroys Asuras like fire. Devi Mahatmyam explains how Devi kills many asuras.

319. rāmā- Raamaa means A woman. Bhāskararāya quotes the BrahmaVaivarta Purana that says, "Whatever in the three worlds appear in female form all that O Devi, is thy form; thus, is declared in the scriptures."

Our dharma asks to view all women as a form of Devi.

The Brahma Parasara Smriti says, "As women are pleased or displeased, so the Gods also are pleased or displeased. If they are pleased the family increases; if they are displeased the family is spoilt."

In Sanatana Dharma, women are given the highest importance. Woman is a divine helpmate of the man, in all his rituals. The wife gives the fire with which a homa should start.

Any ritual at the household level and higher should be done by the couple together. Happy women in the family keeps all others always happy.

320. ramaṇalampaṭā- Devoted to her husband. Husband is the primary and most intimate relative of a woman. In Sanatana Dharma, single pointed devotion is considered essential between husband and wife.

काम्या कामकलारूपा कदम्बकुसुमप्रिया।

कल्याणी जगतीकन्दा करुणारससागरा॥७३॥

kāmyā, kāmakalārūpā, kadamba kusumapriyā ‖

kalyāṇī, jagatīkandā, karuṇārasa sāgarā ‖73‖

321. kāmyā- To be desired. Those who desire liberation to obtain Her by knowledge. Ambāl is one who fulfills all the desires of devotees.

322. kāmakalārūpā- In the form of Kamakala. she is the manifestation of all (Kala) arts of desire (Kama).

323. kadamba kusumapriyā

Fond of Kadamba flowers. In fact, Ambāl is said to reside in the forest of Kadamba.

Muthuswami Deekshitar, one of the Carnatic Music trinities sang: *"Meenakshi Memudam"* in which he has referred to Kadamba Vanam. Composed in raga Purvikalyani, it has only one request to the Goddess – *O' Meenakshi, Me Mudam Dehi* – Give me eternal bliss. Deekshitar really attained bliss while singing *Meena Lochani Pasha Mochani.* He breathed his last. It is interesting to note that in Madurai Meenakshi Sundareswara Temple, the Sthala Vruksham (The temple tree) is a Kadamba tree.

The Kadamba tree has immense medicinal values besides being a beautiful ornamental tree with scented golden ball like floral heads.

Later, in one of the verses, we will hear the words paśupāśa vimōchanī.

324. kalyāṇī- kalya, good words, ana, to speak. She is beneficent, offers auspiciousness and hence worshipped as Kalyani.

325. jagatīkandā- Devi is the Root of the world. kanda refers to roots.

326. karuṇārasa sāgarā- Karunarasa is compassion. Sagara is an ocean. Devi is the ocean of compassion.

कलावती कलालापा कान्ता कादम्बरीप्रिया।

वरदा वामनयना वारुणीमदविह्वला॥७४॥

kalāvatī, kalālāpā, kāntā, kādambarīpriyā।

varadā, vāmanayanā, vāruṇīmadavihvalā॥74॥

327. kalāvatī- Devi is the seat of the 64 kalas or sciences.

328. kalālāpā- Kala means sweetly sounding-alapa is speech. Kalai itself means something nice and beautiful. Ambāl's ordinary conversation itself is sweet.

329. kāntā- Beautiful

330. kādambarīpriyā- Fond of mead. Mead is a beverage created by fermenting honey with water, sometimes with various fruits, spices, grains, or hops.

331.varadā- Ambāl is a giver of boons.

To Brahma, Vishnu and other devotees. This is said by Narada in the Matsya and Padma Puranas. "What I told you of this (Devi) about (her) ever-uplifted hand; for this uplifted hand of Devi ever confers boons. She will become the giver of boons to all Devas, Daityas and ascetics."

As in the world the hand is the instrument of giving, here the hand (of Devi) is said to confer boons.

The expression means simply to fulfil the desire of the gods.

The Devi Bhagavadam Purana also says "She fulfils the desires of the Devas who seek boons. From the root *vr* to choose, she is called Varada, conferrer of boons - giver of the thing chosen."

332. vāmanayanā- Vāma, fair and nayanā eyes. Ambāl has beautiful eyes.

She is also described as padmanayanā. Lotus-eyed, Padmam is lotus, nayanā is eyes. The lotus is a symbol of purity and perfect beauty.

333. vāruṇīmadavihvalā- Vāruni: the juice extracted from dates, called Vāruni, because the god Varuna is fond of it.

The expression means forgetting external objects and simply enjoying. Ambāl is always in such a happy disposition.

विश्वाधिका वेदवेद्या विन्ध्याचलनिवासिनी।

विधात्री वेदजननी विष्णुमाया विलासिनी॥७५॥

viśvādhikā, vēdavēdyā, vindhyāchala nivāsinī।

vidhātrī, vēdajananī, viṣṇumāyā, vilāsinī॥75॥

334. viśvādhikā- Visvā means Universe. Visvādhika means Transcending the Universe

335. vēdavēdyā

The word Veda comes from the root vid to know. Vedavedyā means -To be known through the Vedas. There are four gates to Ambāl's abode -the Chintamani palace; these are the four Vedas; as the deity cannot be seen unless the gates are entered, hence it is said she is to be known, through the Vedas alone. The great quarter, the east is said to be of the Rig; the endless southern quarter, they say, is that of the Yajus; the west of the Adharvan; and the great northern quarter is that of Sāman."

The meaning is that Devi should be known through the four goddesses, who are the deities of the four Vedas.

336. vindhyāchala nivāsinī

One who resides in the Vindhyā Mountain. There is a Vindhyavasini temple located at Vindhyāchal, 8 km away from Mirzapur on the banks of river Ganges, in Uttar Pradesh. Legend says it is the place Devi chose as her abode after she escaped from the hands of kamsā as Yoga Maya Devi, when Kamsā tried to kill her as she was presumed born as the eighth child of Devaki and Vasudeva.

337. vidhātrī- Dhatri is known as the mother, because she bears. Vidhātri means nourisher or supporter of universe.

338. vēdajananī- Mother of the Vedas.

The Devi Purana says, "Because there arose from the Kundalini, which is triangular in form, the vowels and consonants; hence she is the mother of the Vedas."

339. viṣṇumāyā

Vishnu, all-pervading, unlimited by place, time. Māyā, conditions of illusion belonging to Vishnu.

The Bhagavad Gita (7-14) says

दैवी ह्येषा गुणमयी मम माया दुरत्यया।

मामेव ये प्रपद्यन्ते मायामेतां तरन्ति ते॥14॥

daivī hyeṣhā guṇa-mayī, mama māyā duratyayā

mām eva ye prapadyante, māyām etāṁ taranti te

My divine energy Maya, consisting of the three modes of nature, is very difficult to overcome. But those who surrender unto me cross over it easily.

340. vilāsinī- means Playful

क्षेत्रस्वरूपा क्षेत्रेशी क्षेत्रक्षेत्रज्ञपालिनी।

क्षयवृद्धिविनिर्मुक्ता क्षेत्रपालसमर्चिता॥७६॥

kṣētrasvarūpā, kṣētrēśī, kṣētra kṣētrajña pālinī।

kṣayavṛddhi vinirmuktā, kṣētrapāla samarchitā ॥76॥

341. kṣētrasvarūpā

Bhāskararāya defines Kshetra as matter. Earth, Land, Field and Body are all matter. Ambāl's body is matter. Kshetra,

Kamarupa and other abodes, or thirty-six categories from earth to Shiva, form her body.

The Linga Purana says, "Devi, the wife of the destroyer of the three-cities (Shiva) becomes Kshetra (matter). Ambāl is in the form of Kshetras or places. Names of many cities in India are believed to be derived from Devi's name.

It is believed that the name Kolkata is derived from Kalighat; Chandigarh from Chandika; and Shimla from Shyamala.

342. kṣētrēśī- The wife of the ruler of matter.

343. kṣētra kṣētrajña pālinī

The protector of matter and of the knower of matter.

Kshetrajna, is the Jiva. The Vishnu Smriti. says, "This body is called Kshetra; one who knows this is called Kshetrajna. Baskraraya quotes Bhagavad Gita (BG) in which Krishna says the same in Chapter 13 verses 1 and 2.

अर्जुन उवाच।

प्रकृतिं पुरुषं चैव क्षेत्रं क्षेत्रज्ञमेव च।

एतद्वेदितुमिच्छामि ज्ञानं ज्ञेयं च केशव।।1।।

prakṛitiṁ puruṣhaṁ chaiva kṣhetraṁ kṣhetra-jñam eva cha

etad veditum ichchhāmi jñānaṁ jñeyaṁ cha keśhava

13.1 Arjuna said, "O Keshav, I wish to understand what are prakṛiti and puruṣh, and what are kṣhetra and kṣhetrajña? I also wish to know what is true knowledge, and what is the goal of this knowledge?

श्रीभगवानुवाच।

इदं शरीरं कौन्तेय क्षेत्रमित्यभिधीयते।

एतद्यो वेत्ति तं प्राहुः क्षेत्रज्ञ इति तद्विदः॥2॥

idaṁ śharīraṁ kaunteya kṣhetram ity abhidhīyate

etad yo vetti taṁ prāhuḥ kṣhetra-jña iti tad-vidaḥ

BG 13.2: The Supreme Divine Lord said: O Arjun, this body is termed as kṣhetra (the field of activities), and the one who knows this body is called kṣhetrajña (the knower of the field) by the sages who discern the truth about both.

In modern science, we have terms like "field of energy." A magnet has a magnetic field around it, which creates electricity on rapid movement. An electric charge has a force field around it. Here, the body is the receptacle for the activities of the individual.

Hence, it is termed as kṣhetra (the field of activities).

The soul is distinct from the body-mind-intellect mechanism, but forgetful of its divine nature, it identifies with these material entities. Yet, because it has knowledge of the body, it is called kṣhetrajña (the knower of the field of the body).

This terminology has been given by the self-realized sages, who were transcendentally situated at the platform of the soul, and perceived their distinct identity separate from the body.

344. kṣayavṛddhi vinirmuktā

Khsayam means decay. Tuberculosis is called *Kshayarogam* as it causes decay of the body. Vriddhi means growth.

Vinirmukta means free from. Devi is Free from decay and growth. Growth and decay belong to Kshetra and change. Though She controls them, she is free from them.

Again, Bhāskararāya quotes Bhagavad Gita chapter 2 verse 23 which says

नैनं छिन्दन्ति शस्त्राणि नैनं दहति पावक:।

न चैनं क्लेदयन्त्यापो न शोषयति मारुत:॥23॥

nainaṁ chhindanti śhastrāṇi nainaṁ dahati pāvakaḥ

na chainaṁ kledayantyāpo na śhoṣhayati mārutaḥ

BG 2.23: Weapons cannot shred the soul, nor can fire burn it. Water cannot wet it, nor can the wind dry it.

Likewise, Devi is free from decay and destruction.

345. kṣētrapāla samarchitā

Worshipped by Kshetrapala. There is a story behind this n nāma. Kali was created by Shiva to slay the Daitya, Daruka asuras. Even after killing him the fire of Kali's wrath was not appeased. To dispel her anger Shiva assumed the form of a crying infant. Kali saw the baby and suckled the child who drank up the fire of her anger with milk. This child, which is an incarnation of Shiva, is called Kshetrapala. This story occurs in the Linga and other Puranas. The literal meaning is Kshetra, the area of the sacrificial ceremony, and Pala, the protector.

विजया विमला वन्द्या वन्दारुजनवत्सला।

वाग्वादिनी वामकेशी वह्निमण्डलवासिनी ॥७७॥

vijayā, vimalā, vandyā, vandāru janavatsalā।

vāgvādinī, vāmakēśī, vahnimaṇḍala vāsinī ॥77॥

                    The Glory of Lalithā Sahasranāmam

346. vijayā

A very common name among Hindus. It means Ever victorious.

Bhāskararāya adds many explanations: According to the Devi Purana she is the deity of Kasmira which is one of the sixty-eight Sacred places. As regards the meaning of Vijaya, the same book says: "After conquering the very powerful king of the Daityas named Padma, Devi is known in the three worlds by the epithet Vijaya (ever victorious) and unconquerable (Aparājita)."

According to the Chintamani, Vijaya is an auspicious time or Muhurtam; "In the month Ashvina (Tamil month Purattasi), in the tenth day of the bright fortnight (Shukla Paksha), when the stars appear, that time is known as Vijaya, giving success to undertakings."

In the Ratnakosha, we read, " The time, just after the twilight (sandhya) when the stars begin to shine, is called Vijaya favorable to all undertakings. The eleventh Muhurtha (eight hours and forty-eight minutes after midday) is named Vijaya. A journey should be begun at that time by all who desire success."

347. vimalā

Malā means impurity. Vimalā is just the opposite meaning unsullied. Devi is Absolutely pure.

Bhāskararāya adds: Also, Vimala is a kind of house. The Visvakarma-Sastra enumerates the following houses. "Dhruva, Dhanya, Jaya, Kanta, Vipula. Vijaya, Sumukha, Vimala, Nanda, Nidhana and Manorama."

348. vandyā- Adorable. One who is worshipped.

349. vandāru janavatsalā- Vandaru Jana means- worshippers. Vatsala means fond of. affectionate. Devi is always fond of worshippers.

350. vāgvādinī- The speaker of the world.

The Tripura-Siddhanta says: "As she always abides in the form of speech on the tongue of all her devotees, she is known in the world as Vagvadini."

Worshipping Devi improves speaking skills.

351. vāmakēśī- Having beautiful hair. Vamakesa is one (of the twenty-eight) Tantras promulgated by Shiva; as she is treated of in that work, she is Vamakesi.

352. vahnimaṇḍala vāsinī- Residing in the circle of fire.

Vaahimandala, is that in the Mulādhara, or that in the supreme ether (Paramaa AKasa).

Or Vahni means three, hence three mandalas, thus she resides in the three circles of the moon, the sun and the fire.

भक्तिमत्कल्पलतिका पशुपाशविमोचिनी।

संहृताशेषपाषण्डा सदाचारप्रवर्तिका॥७८॥

bhaktimat-kalpalatikā, paśupāśa vimōchanī।

saṃhṛtāśēṣa pāṣaṇḍā, sadāchāra pravartikā॥78॥

353. bhaktimat-kalpalatikā

The Kalpa creeper of the devotees. The Kalpa is a creeper that yields everything desired. Devi is like The Kalpa Latha (Wish-Granting) Creeper to Her devotees.

Baskararaya adds: Kalpa means imperfect, 'i.e., she makes perfect even her imperfect devotees. This is mentioned in the Shakti Rahasya: "He who worships Bhavani irregularly or with imperfect devotion, in the next birth becomes possessed of regular and perfect devotion."

354. paśupāśa vimōchanī

Pasu means literally cattle. Shiva is known as Pasupati.

Pāsa means bondage. Pasa (bondage) has two words: pa, thirst, As'a, hunger. The ignorant people are called Pasus because they possess the desire of eating and drinking only. This (hunger and thirst) belongs only to the ignorant, and Devi, as Vimochani releases them from ignorance.

Bhāskararāya offers a very extensive commentary to this nāma. I am sharing with you an essential part of it that explains Pāsas.

There are fivefold afflictions or Pāsas. viz nescience, egoism, desire, anger, ardent attachment (to life).

1. Nescience is the absence of discrimination between the Self and the non-self. In other words, lack of knowledge; ignorance.

2. Egoism is the assumption that body and materials which are not Self are Self.

3. Desire is the craving for flowers, scents, etc., which are the means of bodily enjoyment.

4. Anger is aversion to whatever obstructs their attainment of them.

5. Ardent attachment is not renouncing a thing even though one knows it is not beneficial.

These fivefold afflictions are 'Pāsas' There are different kinds of these fivefold afflictions- said to be fifty-two in all.

Pāsa Vimochani means remover of these afflictions.

355. saṃhṛtāśeṣa pāṣaṇḍā- Devi is destroyer of all heretics (heratiks). Heretic is one who differs in opinion from an accepted belief or doctrine: In short, it means here a nonconformist to Vedas and Dharmic scriptures.

Bhāskararāya explains further with quotes.

The Linga Purana describes the nature of the heretics thus: "Observers of vows not enjoined in the Ve\das and those who are excluded from the ceremonies enjoined by the Shruti and Smrtis are called heretics.

Pāshanda refers to those that are imagined by men beyond the Vedas. The Brahma-Vaivarta Purana also says "If you take the (1) Puranas, (2) Nyaya, (3) Mimamsa, (4) Dharma-Sastras, (5) Six Vedaangas (Shiksa to Jyotisha), and (6) the four Vedas which are the source of knowledge, they totally make up fourteen. These fourteen are the seat of righteousness (Dharmasthana). Taking these fourteen as true, what is beyond these imagined by men is called hearsay or Pāshanda.

Samhruta means destruction. Ambāl destroys all those Pāshanda that are not true. The very next nāma says Ambāl nurtures righteous dharmic actions.

356. sadāchāra pravartikā

Sad Achara - Right Action; Pravartika means one who inspires. Because Devi destroys the wicked, and she inspires to right action.

Bhāskararāya quotes the Kurma Purana in which Devi herself proclaims:

"The eighteen Puranas were promulgated by Vyasa, by the command of Brahman: in them Dharma is established. The other supplementary (upa) Puranas were promulgated by his pupils. In every age (yuga) he, Vyasa the knower of the science of righteousness, is the promulgator of all puranas Shiksha, Kalpa, Grammar, Nirukta, Chandas, and Jyotisa, and Logic etc., (four) and the four Vedas, thus the fourteen (scriptures) are the sources of knowledge. Dharma is not to be found elsewhere. Thus, the supreme Dharma, which has come down from the grandsire, Manu, Vyasa and others, by my command, is established till the dissolution of the universe."

So, 'sada, chara, pravrtika' means Devi always moves into right action.

तापत्रयाग्निसन्तप्तसमाह्लादनचन्द्रिका।

तरुणी तापसाराध्या तनुमध्या तमोऽपहा ॥७९॥

tāpatrayāgni santapta samāhlādana chandrikā।

taruṇī, tāpasārādhyā, tanumadhyā, tamō'pahā ॥79॥

357. tāpatrayāgni santapta samāhlādana chandrikā

It is one long word. Tāpa means misery or anguish. Tāpa trayāgni means the triple fire of misery. The three miseries are, that belong to body, to elements, and to deities.

Miseries are of three types: People are constantly having to endure the threefold miseries of life:

1. **Adhidaivikā:** miseries caused by nature like storms, typhoons, extreme heat or cold, old age, death. You have no control over it as they are caused by Daivika -nature. They are all 'acts of nature' as they specify in insurance contracts.

2. **Adhyātmikā:** Atmikā is self. Adhyātmikā are miseries caused by one's own mind or body. For example, drinking alcohol is a choice. You can choose a discipline in your life. You can choose not to worry unnecessarily. A study conducted revealed 90 percent of what people worry about never occurs.

Mark Twain said "I 've had a lot of worries in my life, most of which never happened." Such miseries are within your control.

3. **Adhibhautikā:** Bhautikā refers to elements. Adibhautikā refers to miseries caused by other living entities. We may be bitten by mosquitoes, animals or fall sick due to a virus. Sometimes, we may be intentionally hurt by other human beings. You have limited control over such miseries. Like you can use a cream or a net to ward off mosquitoes. Take a vaccine to protect from virus.

We say Om Shānti Shānti Shāntihi – 3 times to appease the cause of these three miseries.

The word chandrika means moon. So, this nāma means Devi is like the moonlight delighting those who suffer by the triple fire of misery. She brings solace to the people who suffer from these afflictions.

358. taruṇī- Always young. The Tamil word *'Tarunam'* meaning a moment seems derived from it. The time refers to present time which is young.

359. tāpasārādhyā

Tapasvi means ascetics, saints. Aradhya is worship. Ambāl is worshipped by ascetics.

Bhāskararāya adds: Tāpa. Samsāra -the father of misery, Sāra is essence. A is deep, dhyā is meditation, -i.e., Devi is the essential object of meditation amidst the earthly misery. In other words, she is worshipped by deep meditation of ascetics.

360.tanumadhyā- Slender-waisted.

Tanumadhyā is a deity worshipped in Bileswara temple located on the banks of river Neeva in Andhra Pradesh.

Tanumadhyā is also the name of a certain metre in Sanskrit.

361. tamō'pahā

Tamo here refers to Tamas, ignorance. Devi is the remover of ignorance.

There are people who do not know that they do not know. They are ignorant. It happens even with many educated people. Devi Upāsana removes ignorance. By listening to lectures of knowledgeable Gurus we learn many things that we did not know earlier. Devi shows the way to remove your ignorance!

चितिस्तत्पदलक्ष्यार्था चिदेकरसरूपिणी।

स्वात्मानन्दलवीभूतब्रह्मादयानन्दसन्ततिः ॥८०॥

chiti, statpada lakṣyārthā, chidēka rasarūpiṇī।

svātmānanda lavībhūta brahmādyānanda santatiḥ ॥80॥

362. chiti- Chith is intelligence. It is wisdom as opposed to avidya. The Mahavasistha, "Devi is called *chiti,* because she is the life of those who desire life"; She is Chaitanya.

363. statpada lakṣyārthā.

'Tat' means that. What is that? It denotes Brahman endowed with the work of creation of the Universe. The same word 'Tat' also indicates (indirectly Lakshya) unconditioned Brahman who is without attributes. The relation between the two Brahmans (unconditioned and conditioned) is the sameness. Devi represents "tat"

364. chidēka rasarūpiṇī – Chideka is *'Chit Eka'* meaning the one Intelligence. Rasarupini, appears as the essence.

Devi is never separated from the chit. Though the two appear as different (by attributes) yet at the same time they are one.

365. svātmānanda lavībhūta brahmādyānanda santatiḥ

Long word - to be split up as 'Svātma, Ananda, Lava, Bhuta, Brahāmadya, Ananda Santatih. Annada is bliss. Lava means a particle. It means the totality of the bliss of Brahma and others is but a minute portion of Devi's own bliss.

परा प्रत्यक्चितीरूपा पश्यन्ती परदेवता।

मध्यमा वैखरीरूपा भक्तमानसहंसिका॥८१॥

parā, pratyakchitī rūpā, paśyantī, paradēvatā |

madhyamā, vaikharīrūpā, bhaktamānasa haṃsikā ॥ 81 ॥

366. parā.

Bhāskararāya offers a detailed explanation of this word.

It may sound a bit difficult to understand as he quotes many ancient scriptures to trace the origin of the word 'parā.'

He starts by saying words which are the physical forms of speech (Vaikhari) only express the physical form of Brahman and do not correspond to the pure (unconditioned) Brahman. He divides speech into four forms and offers the background to it.

During Pralaya, the big deluge when the actions of beings are about to be manifested but not yet ripe, the Brahman, bound my Māya and by those actions is called Ghanibhuta (the congealed one). Congealed means coagulated. At the moment of ripeness, when the modification of Māya appears, Brahman, endowed with Māya. in the form of ripened actions, is called Avyakta (unmanifested). That (Avyakta) is the sprouting root of the universe. It is termed as the Karanabindu (the cause dot). From this Karanabindu proceeds the Karyabindu (effect dot). From the Karyabindu came Nāda (sound); thence the Bija; thus, the three came into being.

These (three) Bindu, Nāda and Bija are also called by the words (the supreme), subtle (Suksma) and physical (Sthula).

In the bodily aspects (Adhyatmā), the Karanabindu resides in the Mulādhāra and is known as Shakti, Pinda (mono-syllabled mantra), Kundalini, etc.

When it sprouts to create the three, (Kāryabindu, etc.), then the unmanifested sound called Shabda brahman (Brahman-word) arises in it. This sound, since it is one with the Kāranabindu and is therefore all-pervading, first appears in the Mulādhāra of persons by the power of air acted upon by the effort of manifestation. That air acted upon by the effort of a person desiring to speak, produces the all-pervading Shabda brahman."

That Shabdabrahman which is in the Kāranabindu, when it is manifested, remaining motionless (nispanda) in its own place, is called Para speech.

The same (Shabdabrahman), produced by the same air proceeding as far as the navel, joined with the reasoning intellect, (Manas) possessing the nature of the manifested

Kāryabindu is named Pashyanti speech. Next the same Shabdabrahman, produced by the same air proceeding as far as the heart, joined with the determining understanding (Buddhi), in the manifested Nāda, endowed with special motion (Vishesaspanda) is called Madhyama speech. Next the same (Shabdabrahman), produced by the same air, proceeding as far as the mouth, developed in the throat in the form of articulation, capable of being heard by the ears of others' possessing the nature of the manifested Bija, with the universal motion (Spastatara) is called Vaikhari speech.

Acharyas explain further: "That (sound) which first arises in the Mulādhāra is called Para; next the Pashyanti; next when it goes as far as the heart and is joined to the understanding (Buddhi) it is called Madhyama; and the full manifestation is Vaikhari; Thus, articulated sound is produced by air."

Thus, though there are four kinds of speech, gross minded men who do not understand the first-three, think speech to be Vaikhari alone. Rig-Veda 1, 164, 45, also says: "Four are the definite grades of the speech; those Brahmanas who are wise know them: three deposited, are in secret and motionless; men speak the fourth grade of speech."

Para also means highest- like Parmeswaran. Devi is the supreme source of grace, she is Para. Sambhavi is called Para.

367. pratyakchitī rūpā- It means Inner consciousness. Pratyak, inwardly, one who approaches the Self, the unmanifested Brahman, as her form.

368. paśyantī- Saubhagya-Sudhodaya says, "As she sees all in herself, and as she rises (Uttirna) above the path of action, hence this Mother is called Pas'yanti, and Uttirna."

369. paradēvatā- Supreme deity. Para is superlative. Nothing above. That's why she is called Parashakti.

370. madhyamā- Because she abides in the midst.

It is said: "She is neither like Pashyanti, nor does she proceed outwards like Vaikhari, with articulation fully developed; but she is in the middle between these two."

371. vaikharīrūpā- According to the saying of the Yoga-Shastra, "She is called Vaikhari because she was produced by the Prana called Vikhara"

372. bhaktamānasa haṃsikā- Hamsika means Swan. Bhaktamanasa is in the minds of devotees. Devi is like the swan in the minds of the devotees. As the mythical swans live in the celestial lake called Manasa (Manasrover) so she lives in the minds (Manasa) of her devotees. Manasarover is a high-altitude freshwater lake fed by the Kailash Glaciers. "Mānas" means "mind", "sarovara" means "a lake or a large pond deep enough for a lotus.

Chapter 8

Devi's Glory

In this chapter, the glory of Devi is described in many ways.

कामेश्वरप्राणनाडी कृतज्ञा कामपूजिता।

शृङ्गाररससम्पूर्णा जया जालन्धरस्थिता॥८२॥

kāmēśvara prāṇanāḍī, kṛtajñā, kāmapūjitā ‖

śṛṅgāra rasasampūrṇā, jayā, jālandharasthitā ‖82‖

373. kāmēśvara prāṇanāḍī

Prāna is the life force or energy that animates every aspect of life within creation. The conscious control of this prana (life force) is known as prānayāma. *(Readers may view the author's video titled 'Easy Prānayāma' over YouTube)* Nādis are the energy pathways or channels that move prāna. Kāmeswara prānanādi means Ambāl is the vital force or energy of Kāmeswara. Lalitha Devi and Kāmeswara are inseparable. They live like a body and prāna in one unit. To reinforce this concept, Saundarya Lahari shlokam 28, says-

सुधा मप्यास्वाद्य प्रतिभय जरामृत्यु हरिणीं -

sudhāmapyāsvādya pratibhaya jarāmṛtyu hariṇīṁ

विपद्यन्ते विश्वे विधि शत मखाद्या दिविषदः।

vipadyante viśve vidhiśatamakhādyā diviṣadaḥ|

कराலं यत्क्ष्वेलं कबलितवतः कालकलना

karālaṁ yatkṣvelaṁ kabalitavataḥ kālakalanā

न शंभोस्तन्मूलं तव जननि ताटङ्कमहिमा॥

na śaṁbhostanmūlaṁ tava janani tāṭaṅkamahimā

AsvAdya api: Even after having consumed; sudhAm: the nectar; prati-bhaya-jarA-mRtyu-hariNIM: (which) eradicates the dreadful old age and death; vishve divishhadaH: all the divines; vidhi-shatamakhAkhyAH: like BrahmA, Indra and others; vipadyante: meet their end (at the time of pralaya). Yat: (But) the fact that; shambhoH: for Lord Shiva; kabalitavataH: who had consumed; karALaM kshhvelaM: the terrible poison (of KalakuTa) kAla-kalanA: there is no submission to Time; tan-mUlaM: has its reason (in); janani: Oh Mother; tava tATangka-mahimA: the Glory of Your ear-ornament.

During Amrita Manthana, the churning of the ocean to get nectar, Shiva consumed the deadly poison coming from the snake Vasuki. Pārvathi held his neck to hold the poison. His neck became blue and so, Shiva is called Neelakanta, Neelagriva, Visahkanta.

The last line in this verse says,

"When Shiva drank the virulant poison, his days did not end owing, 0 mother, due to the power of your 'Tātangam'-ear ornaments." '

Brahma, Indra and crores of Devas had the fortune of consuming Amrit the Nectar which confers immunity from frightful old age and death, but they also perish at the time of pralaya -the cosmic dissolution.

O Mahādevi, Shiva will not perish by time, despite having swallowed the dreadful poison because of "Tātanka Mahima, the greatness, the power of your ear ornaments, Tātanka Mahima. What is important here is to know the greatness and power of Devi's Tātanka, the ear ornaments. Even the poison consumed by Shiva had no effect and he became *Mrutyunjaya*- one who has won over death. So, Ambāl is Parmeshwara's 'Prānanādi' -life giving force

There is Akhilandeswari at the Jambukeswar temple- one of the five pancha bhoota sthalams, in Tiruvanaikaval near Tiruchi in Tamil Nadu. It is believed that the Devi in the temple was once a *'Ugra Devatha'* -in deep anger. So, during Adi Sankara's visit to the temple, he installed a pair of Sri Chakra *tātankas* (earrings) and the idols of Ganesha and Muruga to appease her. You can imagine how old the temple is if Adi Sankara visited it.

In the olden days when our ancestors led a life of simplicity, a woman's tātanka-earring, and the mangala sutra's padakam- -sacred pendant on her neck--her important symbols, of *saumangalya (refers to married women)* were both made of *'Tāli'*, that is, the palm leaf (*olai* in Tamil). In 'shyāmala navaratna mālā' Ambikā herself is described as ताली पलाश ताटंकाम -"tāli palāsha tātankām (verse 6)" wearing only a cut palm leaf for her tāli and a rolled one for her tātanka. Many Hindus use such a tātankam for decorating Varalakshmi during Varalakshmi Puja.

Thus, in Sanatana Dharma, ornaments have spiritual significance. For example, a Mangal sutra is a symbol of marriage, and the wife is meant to wear it all her life indicating

     The Glory of Lalithā Sahasranāmam

the love and commitment the husband and wife have towards each other. It is a tradition to wear bangles after marriage, symbolizing health, luck, and prosperity.

374. kṛtajñā

Kru is the root that means to do. Krta refers to actions. The Sun, the moon, the god of death, time, and the five elements, these nine are the witnesses of good and bad actions. Ambāl is not separated from these actions and hence she is called Kritajna. She who knows all.

Bhāskararāya adds: Krta, the actions done, jna is she rewards the devotees by (imparting) knowledge.

375. kāmapūjitā

Worshipped by Kāma, Manmatha. When did Kāma or Manmatha worship Ambāl? There is a story behind this.

Manmatha (cupid) was reduced to ashes by Shiva when he shot his arrow at him. Shocked at the sudden demise of Manmatha, his wife Rathi cried and prayed to Ambāl to revive him. Ambāl was compassionate to revive him but told Rathi that only she could see him in physical form and nobody else.

Then, Ambāl took Manmatha's sugar cane bow and floral arrows in Her Own Hands and looked at Shiva overwhelmingly with love and compassion. Thus, She acquired the name Kāmakshi (Kāma – love and Akshi – Eye). Kāmakshi is one whose eyes are filled with love and compassion. Parameshvara, who was in rigorous penance, got enamored of Pārvati and married Her, So, Subrahmanya was born. Kāmakshi is still holding the sugarcane bow, which is symbolized as our mind (*mano roopekshu kothanda panchatan matra sayaka*). Manmatha, who was revived by Ambāl for the sake of his wife Rathi wanted to get due recognition for his role.

For this, the only course available to him was to pray at the Feet of Ambāl. So, he goes to Kanchipuram and starts his rigorous penance. That's the history of *Kāma Pujitha*. Kamakshi was pleased with his penance and appeared before him. Manmatha, looking at Ambāl says, "Amma! After burning me to ashes, Parameshvara became enamoured of you. It is You who had appointed me as the Head of Love and lust for the whole Universe. Therefore, whoever falls in love, the credit should come only to me. In this case too, Parameshvara falling in love with you is only because of my efforts. Therefore, its credit should accrue to me alone". Mother then takes pity on Manmatha. So, She withdraws all Her powers from Kailasa and in all Shiva temples and moves them into the Kanchipuram.

Following this, the life-force of Ambāl goes missing from Kailasa. Similarly, on earth too, all Ambāl statues became lifeless. Parameshvara felt depressed.

Looking at Shiva, Brahma came forward in support of Him and appealed to Ambāl for restoration. Ambāl told Brahma, "Only for the sake of Manmatha I have withdrawn my power, so that the role of Manmatha is known to all. Now, the entire world knows Manmatha's heroism." Saying so, Ambāl restored Her power everywhere. Thus, Shiva was relieved of His solitude and all the temples were restored with the sanctity of Her life force.

 The Glory of Lalithā Sahasranāmam

This story has been excellently narrated in "Kamakshi Vilasam (Glory of Kamakshi)". There are also stone inscriptions that stand as evidence of this incident.

Many stone inscriptions reveal that Ambāl Shrines in various Shiva Temples are called "Kāmakottam". To give credit to Kāma, Ambāl did two things.

One is that no other Shiva temple in Kanchipuram (other than Kāmakottam) will have a sanctum sanctorum of Ambāl; (In the Shiva temples in Kanchipuram, there is no separate Ambāl sannadhi).

Second, Kanchipuram is to be given a new name as *"Shivajit Kshetram"* as a mark of Manmatha's victory over Shiva. By doing so, people coming to Kanchipuram temples will come to know of this Purana by which Manmatha's victory will come to limelight. So, Kāma's Pujai or Penance ultimately gave him what he wanted.

Kanchi Mahaperiyava has spoken extensively on this subject of Ambāl being an essential part of Shiva. He explains the meaning of a verse in Sri Rudram in a very interesting perspective.

In Krishna Yajur Veda, the 2nd mantram of the 10th anuvAkam says:

या ते रुद्र शिवा तनूः शिवा विश्वाह भेषजी।

शिवा रुद्रस्य भेषजी तया ना मृड जीवसे॥१०-२॥

"yate Rudra Śivā tanuhu Śivā Vishvaha Bheshaji ॥

Śivā Rudrasya Bheshaji taya no Rudra mrudaya Jeevase"

Mahaperiyava interprets this as "Oh Rudra! You have a form which includes the most auspicious form of parāshakti, which is a cure for the entire universe, and which is in total unison with your form, let that bless us to live a full life." In other words, it says there are two bodies for the Lord; when it shows up as Rudra it is frightening ("ghora"). When it shows up as Shiva it is "auspicious", because He has also this other body which is the one in unison with Shiva (ambā).

For the above mantra in the Vidyāranya Bhāshyam, the root word 'jIvase', means, "By that Shakti" Just as there are medicines for diseases, for this 'ghora' frightful events of life, there is a medicine of 'shivam'!

But even that does not cure the illness totally. We get hungry and we eat to satisfy the hunger. But hunger is not for ever satisfied! Again, we get hungry and again we must eat! So also, the 'ghora' part of life comes again and again and the shivam part gives us the medicine every time. That medicine is called 'Shivā.' It is the 'extended shivā', namely 'SHIVAA' the feminine word.

376. śṛṅgāra rasasampūrṇā

Sringara rasam means the essence of love. Sampurna means filled with. The most common meaning is Filled with the essence of love. There is no life without Sringara rasam.

Bhāskararāya gives more interpretations: *Shringa,* two horns, *Ara,* petal, *Rasa* six, so Sringararasa means, the centre called Anahata which has twice six petals. *Sum,* frequently, *purna* remains, i.e., she frequently remains in that center between Jalandhara and Odhyana centres.

Or *Sringa* chief, *arara,* covering, the *Avidya.* which veils: Sa, with *sampurna* Brahman (perfect), i.e., she is both the conditioned and unconditioned Brahman.

377. jayā- Victorious. The one who manifests as victory in the devotee. *Satyameva Jeyate* – Truth alone wins is a popular slogan.

378. jālandharasthitā

Remaining in Jalandhara. Jal means water and dhara to hold. Jalandhara refers to the throat region.

Yogashastra states that Jalandhara is the Vishuddhi chakra in the throat region in human body. Jalandhara bandha is one of the energetic locks used in a Hatha yoga practice.

This powerful energy lock is said to compress and stimulate the sinuses.

The Divine Mother resides there as the embodiment of Brahma-as-sound. According to the Padma Purana, Jalandhara is a place where she is worshipped under the name of *Vishnumukti.*

ओड्याणपीठनिलया बिन्दुमण्डलवासिनी।

रहोयागक्रमाराध्या रहस्तर्पणतर्पिता॥८३॥

ōḍyāṇa pīṭhanilayā, bindumaṇḍala vāsinī।

rahōyāga kramārādhyā, rahastarpaṇa tarpitā ॥83॥

379. ōḍyāṇa pīṭhanilayā

Abiding in the centre called Odhyana. The human body has many chakras as we learnt in one of the earlier sessions. One of the abodes of The Divine Mother is known as Odhyana. Odhyana is the name for one of the six chakras in the human body. Odhyana means the forehead center or ajna chakra. In Hatha Yoga, there is a mudhra named Odhyana. When the kundalini, the dormant energy coiled up like a serpent in the mooladhara crosses ajna chakra, it reaches the bindu, the region of absolute bliss.

380. bindumaṇḍala vāsinī

Dwelling in the center of Bindu. She resides in Bindu-Mandala, which is the innermost point in Sri Chakra, representing Anandamaya.

In the human body, of the seven body chakras, "Sahasrara" is at the crown in top of our head. That is also called Bramandha or Bindumandala. The Kundalini moves up from Muladhara to reach the Sahasrara in the crown. The Divine Mother is in chit form in Bindumandala. Yogashastra points out the presence of this primordial energy Kundalini within the human body. In one of our earlier sessions, we talked about Kundalini in detail.

Ramakrishna Paramahamsa gives a simple example. A wealthy man has many houses but has only one of these as a favorite house. Likewise, Bindu Mandala is a favorite home of Ambāl.

381. rahōyāga kramārādhyā

To be worshipped in secret by sacrificial rites. Bhāskararāya explains- Raho, in the secret (in the Sahasrara), yaga, the sacrifice of the eight oblations of good actions, etc. in the fire of chit supported by the golden Kundalini: kramaradhya, worship in a particular order.

Shāktam has different modes of worship. Shakti may be awakened by Dhyana, Bhava, Japa and Mantra Shakti. The traditions include Samayacharam, Dakshinacharam, Kaulaacharam and Vamacharam. The Samayacharam mode involves the secret of the kundalini awakening through several powerful mantras. She is in the Muladhara Chakra in our bodies.

She vitalizes the body through the Chakras. Each Chakra has its own seed mantra.

Constant repetition of these mantras, recited with concentration on the energy centre, slowly awakens the Kundalini. This process is the secret yaga or rahoyaga. It's an arduous task and cannot happen overnight, for a normal person at least.

When the kundalini finally reaches and stays at the Sahasrara Chakra, the devotee enjoys supreme happiness (paramananda).

When the chords of a musical instrument are struck harmoniously, fine music is produced. Likewise, when the chords of the mantras are struck in their order, the Mother who moves in the six Chakras awakens Herself.

Thus, the devotee attains Siddhi easily when She is roused. It is difficult to say when and how She shows Herself and to whom.

Bhāskararāya adds -Rahoyaga means the meeting (of Shiva and Shakti) in a lonely place (in the Sahasrara); Krama, stepping into (that place); aradya is to be attained.

Saundarya Lahari Shlokam 8 says: "In the Sahasrara lotus, in the secret place, you sport with your husband."

सुधा सिन्धोर्मध्ये सुरविटपि वाटीपरिवृते
मणिद्वीपे नीपो पवनवति चिन्तामणिगृहे।

शिवाकारे मञ्चे परमशिव पर्यङ्कनिलयां

भजन्ति त्वां धन्याः कतिचन चिदानन्द लहरीम्॥8॥

The identity between Shakti and Cit is referred to in the word 'cidAnandalaharI' in this verse. भजन्ति त्वां धन्याः कतिचन चिदानन्द लहरीम् *"bhajanti tvAm dhanyAH katicana cidAnanda-laharIm",* meaning, 'Only the most fortunate few (recognize you and) worship you as the flood of knowledge-bliss (cidAnanda)'.

382. rahastarpaṇa tarpitā

Gratified by the Secret Tarpanas or oblations.

What is Rahastarpana? Rahas is secret -just as in *Rahasyam* in Tamil.

Tarpanam itself means 'Satisfying.' It is a secret tarpana. A Mantra describes it thus: "Holding in both hands, representing brightness and darkness (Prakasa and Vimarsa) the sacrificial ladle of *Unmani* (it is a Yogic state), pouring out the ghee of dharma (righteousness) and adharma (unrighteousness) and the senses (Kalas) in the fire of consciousness, I sacrifice."

Bhāskararāya adds another description - "I sacrifice the Universe from Earth to Shiva in the fire of samwit, ever burning without fuel, and ever-increasing, dispelling the darkness of illusion, the center from which ever emanates beautiful rays."

According to the method of devotion to Srividya one should only adopt the path after having recognized the higher self. The Divine Mother is happy with secret Tarpana, as the soul merges back to its original source Brahman.

 The Glory of Lalithā Sahasranāmam

सद्यःप्रसादिनी विश्वसाक्षिणी साक्षिवर्जिता।

षडङ्गदेवतायुक्ता षाड्गुण्यपरिपूरिता॥८४॥

sadyaḥ prasādinī, viśvasākṣiṇī, sākṣivarjitā।

ṣaḍaṅgadēvatā yuktā, ṣāḍguṇya paripūritā ॥84॥

383. sadyaḥ prasādinī

Sadyah is immediately; prasadini means conferring. Conferring immediate grace. She is immediately gratified by the sacrifice and oblation mentioned above.

Shiva is called 'Ashutosh' -one who is satisfied immediately. In Bengal, this name Asutosh is common. Devi's grace is immediate like Shiva.

384. viśvasākṣiṇī- Witness of the universe. The Divine Mother is witnessing all the universal actions, as they happen in real time.

385. sākṣivarjitā- She Herself is unwitnessed. There is no witness to the one who is the witness of all things.

386. ṣaḍaṅgadēvatā yuktā

Shad Angas are six limbs. What are they? They are the most essential to be guarded when someone goes to war. The Angas (limbs) are hridayam-heart, shiras-head, shikai-tuft of hair, netram-eyes, kavacham-armour and astram-weapons. Devata Yukta means accompanied by the Shaktis belonging to these limbs.

Sadangas also refer to the six Vedangas- Siksha or phonetics, Kalpam-ceremonies, Vyakarana of Panini or grammar, Nirukta or philology, Chandas or the metre dealing with prosody, and Jyotisha or astronomy and astrology. Surrounded by the deities of these six, means that the Vedas are Devi's form. Vedas are called Vedamātha.

387. ṣāḍguṇya paripūritā

Possessing the six qualities. The six gunās or qualities are essential for a king before going to war. It is a lesson on the management of warfare. According to the Kaamandaka (ethical code), these are: peace, war, marching, sitting encamped, dividing forces and allies. First attempt is to reach peace by sending a messenger (Examples: Hanuman to Ravana, Krishna from Pandavas to Duryodhana), if it fails, then war, march with soldiers, set up war camps, strategic deployment of forces. Devi Mahatmyam describes the shadgunyam in detail. When Ambāl goes to kill Bandasura, she is an example of Shadgunya Paripurita.

Bhāskararāya adds - The Puranas describe Rajagunas as, "Prosperity, righteousness, fame, wealth, wisdom and dispassion." Ambāl confers such qualities to Her devotees.

नित्यक्लिन्ना निरुपमा निर्वाणसुखदायिनी।

नित्याषोडशिकारूपा श्रीकण्ठार्धशरीरिणी॥८५॥

nityaklinnā, nirupamā, nirvāṇa sukhadāyinī ॥

nityā, ṣoḍaśikārūpā, śrīkaṇṭhārdha śarīriṇī ॥85॥

388. nityaklinnā

Ever compassionate. Klinna means wettened. A hard heart is also said to be a stone heart that is totally dry. In Tamil they call *'Eeramilla Nenjam"* meaning a hard heart without any compassion. On the other hand, Ambāl's heart is dripping with compassion for Her devotees.

Devi Māhatmiyam says:

या देवी सर्वभुतेषु दयारूपेण संस्थिता।

नमस्तस्यै नमस्तस्यै नमस्तस्यै नमो नमः॥२३॥

To that Devi Who in All Beings is Abiding in the Form of Kindness, our namaskarams.

Bhāskararāya adds- Nityaklinna is the deity of the third day of the lunar fortnight (*moonram pirai* in Tamil is a lovely crest moon). This deity has been described in the Garuda Purana beginning with the verse, "Next I describe Nityaklinna... she is Tripura herself giving happiness and salvation."

389. nirupamā- Upama is equal or comparable. Nirupama means without an equal. Devi is incomparable.

390. nirvāṇa sukhadāyinī

Conferring the bliss of Nirvana. Nir, freed; Vana (or Bana) body. So here Nirvana means without body, 'i.e., indescribable bliss. In Buddhism also Nirvana is the goal that means ultimate bliss.

391. nityā ṣōḍaśikārūpā

In the form of sixteen eternal deities.

The sixteen deities are from Kameshvari to Tripurasundari.

The names of the fifteen Nitya deities are as follows:

1) Kameshvari, (2) Bhagamalini, (3) Nityaklinna. (4) Bherunda, (5) Vahnivisini. (6) Mahavajres'vari, (7) S'ivaduti, (8) Tvarita, (9) Kulasundari, (10) Nitya, (11) Nilapatakini. 12) Vijaya, 18) Sarvamangala, (14) Jvaalamalini, (15) Chitra and (16) Tripurasundari.

The Tantrarāja says, "The fifteen deities are the limbs of Lalithā who is the first (of the sixteen); as she is endowed with these limbs, she is the body, of which they are parts."

Shodashi also refers to the sixteen syllable mantra, which consists of the fifteen syllable *panchadasakshari* mantra plus a final seed syllable.

392. śrīkaṇṭhārdha śarīriṇī

Srikanthasya Ardha Sharinini. Possessing half the body of Srikanta.

She forms one body with Shiva. Hence the Brihadaranyaka Upanishad (1, 4, 1 to 8) says, "In the beginning Self was alone... He then divided himself into two, and thence arose the couple of husband and wife."

Srikanta: Sri, Poison or Snake, Kanta throat, as the Snake or poison is in his throat, Shiva is called Srikantan – a popular name in Karnataka. Sri also has another meaning referring to Mahalakshmi. Srikāntan is Mahavishnu.

It is well-known that Shiva gave half of his body to Ambāl. Hence, He is known as *Ardhānareeswara* -meaning Eswara with half body of a woman. There is a beautiful temple of Ardhanāreeswara on top of a hill in Tiruchengodu, near Erode in South India. Here the deity is dressed half in male form and the other half in female form.

प्रभावती प्रभारूपा प्रसिद्धा परमेश्वरी।

मूलप्रकृतिरव्यक्ता व्यक्ताव्यक्तस्वरूपिणी॥८६॥

prabhāvatī, prabhārūpā, prasiddhā, parameśvarī।

mūlaprakṛti ravyaktā, vyaktā'vyakta svarūpiṇī॥86॥

393. prabhāvatī- Luminous. Prabha, the surrounding Avarana Devatas namely Anima because there is a saying, "(Devi) is surrounded by Anima. and other luminaries." In Mumbai, there is an area called Prabhadevi.

394. prabhārūpā- In the form of brightness. This indicates the identity of the quality and the possessor of it.

395. prasiddha

Well-known. Celebrated. Devi Bhagavadam Canto 01, Chap. 15 says, सरव खलविदमवाह नानयदसति सनातनम॥ *Sarva Kala vidamavaha naanayadasathi sanatanam*; All that is seen is Myself; there is nothing other than eternal.

396. parameśvarī- spouse of Parameswara. Param is Supreme. Easwari is Ruler. Supreme ruler

397. mūlaprakṛti

Mula means root and Prakriti means "that which is put or made before," i.e., "Primary substance." Devi as supreme mother has got the name Mulaprakriti or Primordial Nature or the original principle. She is the root nature of all manifestation. To give you a simple analogy, iron ore is the raw or root substance from which iron and steel products are made in different shapes and sizes. Rice is the primary substance to make a variety of dishes.

Bhāskararāya provides extensive comments on this word. Of the Pancha Bhutam, five elements from ether to earth, each is the Prakrti (origin) of succeeding one; The successive evolution will show that Brahman is infinite, the śruti (Taittriya Upanishad II, 1) describes as follows:

तस्मादृा एतस्मादात्मन आकाशः संभूतः।

आकाशाद्वायुः। वायोरग्निः। अग्नेरापः।

अद्भ्यः पृथिवी। पृथिव्या ओषधयः।

ओषधीभ्योऽन्नम्। अन्नात् पुरुषः॥३॥

tasmādvā etasmād ātmana ākāśaḥ sambhūtaḥ|

ākāśādvāyuḥ| vāyoragniḥ| agnerāpaḥ|

adbhyaḥ pṛthivī| pṛthivyā oṣadhayaḥ|

oṣadhībhyo'nnam| annāt puruṣaḥ||3||

From That, verily, —from This Self—is ākāśa (ether) born; from ākāśa, the air; from the air, fire; from fire, water; from water, earth; from earth, plants; from plants, food: from food, man. The Shruti (Taittriya Upanishad II, 1) says, "From the Self arose ether." That Brahman has no Prakrti. So, he is the root (Mula), the first cause.

In the Pancaratra Agama, Shiva says, "There is one mother of the Universe, the mother of the Scriptures, Sarasvati, who has no origin; hence she is called Mulaprakrti."

It is said in the Samkhya saptati "That is the Avyakta, which is subtle, without characteristics. inanimate, without beginning or end, capable of production, without parts, one and universal."

398. avyaktā

Undeveloped. Inanimate. Avyakta is the manifestation of Maya. There are different definitions.

It is said in the Samkhya saptati "That is the Avyakta, which is subtle, without characteristics. inanimate, without beginning or end, capable of production, without parts, one and universal.

Or Avyakta means Brahman for in the place (Ved. 811. III, 2-23) it is said, "That (Brahman) is Avyakta for the scriptures say so."

Or Avyakta means Vishnu. The Linga Purana says,

"The names of Vishnu, who is ever capable of creation, are Pradhana, Avyaya, Yoni (origin), Avyakta, Prakrti and Tamas."

399. vyaktā'vyakta svarūpiṇī

Devi is in the form of manifested and unmanifested. In simple words, vyaktam is the lokam--world that is seen; avyaktam is the unseen paramAtmA--supreme soul, is the general meaning. Here Devi is described as both- what is seen and what is unseen. When a tumbler full of water is pervaded by sugar dissolved in it, that sugar only remains avyaktam--unseen, right?

But, if you drink the water, then you can experience the taste of sugar in it. It is seen in the taste. So, sugar becomes both vyakta and avyakta. Again, there are different descriptions of what they are.

Bhagavad Gita Chapter 8, verse 18 says

अव्यक्ताद्व्यक्तय: सर्वा: प्रभवन्त्यहरागमे|

रात्र्यागमे प्रलीयन्ते तत्रैवाव्यक्तसञ्ज्ञके||18||

avyaktād vyaktayaḥ sarvāḥ prabhavantyahar-āgame

rātryāgame pralīyante tatraivāvyakta-sanjñake

At the advent of Brahma's Day, all living beings emanate from the unmanifest source. And at the fall of his night, all embodied beings again merge into their unmanifest source.

Bhāskararāya adds -The Linga Purana says, "Vyakta is called Sat (existence), as it is the second modification of the elements; Avyakta is called Asat because it is devoid of that (modification)." or, Vyakta, perishable and Avyakta, imperishable.

The Matsya Purana says, "Vyakta is said to be perishable and Avyakta, imperishable."

There are three kinds of Shivalingas. vyakta, avyakta and vyaktaavyakta; Devi is in all the forms. The three kinds of Lingas are described in the Brahma. Vaivarta Purana: "There are three Lingas, Svayambhuva (self-existing), Banalinga (got from a certain river) and S'ailalinga (made of stone), these are respectively called Vyakta, Avyakta, and Vyaktavyakta. Vyakta, they say, gives salvation, the Avyakta gives (worldly) happiness, and Vyaktavyakta gives both happiness and salvation.

व्यापिनी विविधाकारा विद्याविद्या-स्वरूपिणी।

महाकामेशनयनकुमुदाह्लादकौमुदी ॥८७॥

vyāpinī, vividhākārā, vidyā'vidyā svarūpiṇī॥

mahākāmēśa nayanā kumudāhlāda kaumudī॥87॥

400. vyāpinī:-All-pervading. Omnipresent.

With this nāma, we complete 400 Nāmas. Thus ends the fifth Kala, called *Jvalini* with the fourth hundred in the Saubhagyabhaskara composed by Bhāskararāya.

We continue to Nāma 401.

401. vividhākārā- having multiple forms.

402. vidyā'avidyā svarūpiṇī

Vidya and Avidya -In the form of knowledge and ignorance. Vidya and Avidya are explained in the Isa Upanishad (11): "One who knows both knowledge and ignorance having crossed over death by ignorance and attains immortality by knowledge."

The Devi Bhagavada Purana also says: "Devi is Brahman, very difficult to attain and in the form of Vidya and Avidya" In another place, it says "0 King, know, that Vidya and Avidya, are two forms of Devi; by which men are freed, by the other they are bound."

As per Vishnu Purana, सा विद्या या विमुक्तये, i.e. "Vidya is what liberates", which means any knowledge that leads to self-realization, is called as Vidya. In the same way, anything that does NOT help achieve self-realization is called 'Avidya'.

Both vidya and avidya are aspects of maya. Vidya refers to knowledge, learning. Avidya, the opposite of vidya refers to a state of confusion, delusion, and illusion: Sri Ramakrishna said that 'to know God is vidya and not to know Him, avidya'. Mahamaya contains both vidyamaya, the illusion of knowledge, and avidyamaya, the illusion of ignorance.'

403. mahākāmēśa nayanā kumudāhlāda kaumudī

Kumuda is a kind of waterlily that opens to the moonlight. Kaumuda means the month Kartika and Kaumudi the full moon of the month, Kartika.

Ambāl is like the full moon of Kaumuda that gladdens the Kumuda like eyes of Lord Maha Kamesha. Generally, the description of eyes goes to Ambāl as – as Meenakshi, Kamakshi, Visalakshi and so on. Here the eyes of Mahakamesha are described as Kumuda Like. Whereas Ambāl is seen as full moon -just as Abirama Battar saw- to please the eyes of Kamesha. In the next verse, Ambāl is compared to the Sun's rays.

Another interpretation by Bhāskararāya - Kaumuda also refers to those who long for worldly pleasures. They are called inferior because (their pleasures) are mixed with pain and for other reasons. Kaumuda means a miserable one. A man attains that stage by being led (nayana) to Mahakamesha.

Another meaning is that Devi becomes the guiding light, to them who are blind in worldly pursuits.

भक्तहार्दतमोभेदभानुमद्भानुसन्ततिः।

शिवदूती शिवाराध्या शिवमूर्तिः शिवङ्करी॥८८॥

bhaktahārda tamōbhēda bhānumad-bhānusantatiḥ||

śivadūtī, śivārādhyā, śivamūrti, śśivaṅkarī||88||

404. bhaktahārda tamōbhēda bhānumad-bhānusantatiḥ

bhaktahārda-in the heart of devotees. Tamobheda- removes the darkness, bhanumad bhanusantathi- like the sun's rays. Devi is like the sun's rays which remove the darkness from the heart of devotees.

405. śivadūtī: Shiva is her messenger.

The Markandeya Purana says, "As Shiva himself was made a messenger by that Devi, she was known in the world as Shivadhuti."

Devi Bhagavadam says Shakti sent Shiva as a messenger to the demons Shumba Nishumba to warn them of disastrous consequences if they chose to fight Devi. Thus, Devi became known as Shivaduthi.

406. śivārādhyā- Worshipped by Shiva.

407.śivamūrti- In the form of Shiva. Because there is no separation between Shiva and Shakti.

408. śśivaṅkarī

Giver of happiness. Shiva means auspiciousness and Kari giver. Devi makes her devotees happy by removing the noose of Avidya and leads them to Brahman which is to be attained by liberated souls.

शिवप्रिया शिवपरा शिष्टेष्टा शिष्टपूजिता।

अप्रमेया स्वप्रकाशा मनोवाचामगोचरा॥८९॥

śivapriyā, śivaparā, śiṣṭēṣṭā, śiṣṭapūjitā।

aprameyā, svaprakāśā, manōvāchāma gōcharā॥89॥

409. śivapriyā- Beloved of Shiva.

410. śivaparā- Beyond S'iva.Or, to whom S'iva is the supreme (Para)

411. śiṣṭēṣṭā

Desired by the Sistas -the wise. The word "shrestha" comes from the Sanskrit word sista, which means "noble" or "decent." According to the Vasistha-Sutras "The Shistas are those who always control their limbs, eyes, speech, and whole body, who receive the Vedas with their supplements by tradition, who are devotees to Brahman, and whose every motive directly depends on the scriptures."

412. śiṣṭapūjitā- This is an extension of the earlier naama. Worshipped by the shistas -great ones.

413. aprameyā- Immeasurable. Prameya, to be known, or measured

414. svaprakāśā- Self-luminous.

415.manōvāchāma gōcharā- Beyond mind and speech.

चिच्छक्तिश् चेतनारूपा जडशक्तिर्जडात्मिका।

गायत्री व्याहृतिः सन्ध्या द्विजबृन्दनिषेविता॥९०॥

chichChakti, śchētanārūpā, jaḍaśakti, rjaḍātmikā।

gāyatrī, vyāhṛti, ssandhyā, dvijabṛnda niṣēvitā ॥90॥

416. chichChakti

It is the power of removing Avidya or ignorance. It is also called Chaitanya. Bhāskararāya quotes the Devi Bhāgavada Puranam which says " O king, in all beings there is the Shakti with all its power, any being devoid of that Shakti becomes like a corpse. That Cit-Shakti is in all beings, that is but her form."

417. śchētanārūpā

In the form of Consciousness. The Devi Bhāgavada Purana says

या देवी सर्वभूतेषु चेतनेत्यभिधीयते।

नमस्तस्यै, नमस्तस्यै, नमस्तस्यै नमो नमः॥

"We meditate upon that primeval Vidya. which is in the form of Chaitanya of all."

418. jaḍaśakti

Jada has many meanings. It means inert, material, inanimate, immobile. The energy of inanimate creation. She is the strength of the immobile. She is worshipped in a stone that is inert material.

The Vishnu Purana. says, " The energies of all beings are not to be grasped by our intellects. The creative energies of Brahman are a hundred times more difficult to grasp they are in him as heat is in fire, 0 best of ascetics. He (Brahman) is only the instrumental cause of the creation of the world. Creative energies are the material cause.

Except for the instrumental cause, the creative energies depend on nothing. 0 best of ascetics, an object becomes itself by its own energy."

419. jaḍātmikā- The objective world. She is the world of immobile.

420. gāyatrī

It is the 24-syllabled Gāyatri Mantra. In Bhagavad Gita, Bhagavan Sri Krishna says, "I am Gāyatri among the metres"

बृहत्साम तथा साम्नां गायत्री छन्दसामहम्।

मासानां मार्गशीर्षोऽहमृतूनां कुसुमाकर:॥35॥

bṛihat-sāma tathā sāmnāṁ gāyatrī chhandasām aham

māsānāṁ mārga-śhīrṣho 'ham ṛitūnāṁ kusumākaraḥ

Gāyatri is the mother of the Vedas. According to. the Bharadvaja-Smriti "Because she protects (tra) the singer, (Gaa) she is called Gāyatri." As mother is inseparable from Gāyatri', she is thus named.

421. vyāhṛti- The utterance, or a certain Mantra.

422. sandhyā

It means, junction. When day meets night, the evening is called Sandhya Kalam. It also means meditation, the idea of the non-separation of ourselves and that of Caitanya.

Bhāskararāya comments: The explanation (of the word) is 'men meditate (Dhya) wholly Sam on her. She is called (Samdhya).'

Another interpretation given by Bhāskararāya- This (Samdhya) is the mind-born daughter of Brahma.

The Kalika Purana says "Born from his mind. Beautiful in form, having beautiful limbs, named Samdhya she. is the victorious deity of the twilights. Because she was born to Brahma, while he was engaged in meditation, she is known as Samdhya." "The word Samdhya also means the deity who is to be worshipped at the twilights."

423. dvijabṛnda niṣēvitā

Worshipped by all the twice born.

Brahmins and birds are called dwijas. Brahmin gets the title after Upanyanam which is considered another birth. Birds are first born in eggs and when the eggs hatch, it becomes their second birth.

Sandya, because it is between the other two states, indicates the dreaming state; The Sleeping State: As birds fatigued with flight,

        The Glory of Lalithā Sahasranāmam

fold their wings and enter their nests, so the tired Jivas quitting the waking and dreaming states, are absorbed in the supreme Brahman.

The Brihadaranyaka Upanishad (4-3-19) says,

तद्यथास्मिन्नाकाशे श्येनो वा सुपर्णो वा विपरिपत्य श्रान्तः संहत्य पक्षौ संलयायैव ध्रियते, एवमेवायं पुरुष एतस्मा अन्ताय धावति यत्र सुप्तो न कं चन कामं कामयते, न कं चन स्वप्नं पश्यति॥१९॥

Tadyathā asminnākāśe śhyeno vā suparṇo vā viparipatya śrāntaḥ saṃhatya pakśau saṃlayāyaiva dhriyate, evamevāyaṃ puruṣa etasmā antāya dhāvati yatra supto na kaṃ cana kāmaṃ kāmayate, na kaṃ cana svapnaṃ paśyati||

"Just as in this sky a hawk or an eagle after a long flight closing its Wings goes to its nest, so this person also rushes to that goal, where sleeping he neither desires anything, nor dreams any dream."

As the bird goes to its nest to remove the fatigue due to flight, so the Jīva (self), connected with the results of action done by the contact of the body and organs in the waking and dream states, is fatigued, as the bird with its flight, and in order to remove that fatigue enters his own nest or abode, that is, his own self, distinct from all relative attributes and devoid of all exertion caused by action with its factors and results.

तत्त्वासना तत्त्वमयी पञ्चकोशान्तरस्थिता।

निःसीममहिमा नित्ययौवना मदशालिनी॥९१॥ निस्सीम

tattvāsanā, tattvamayī, pañchakōśāntarasthitā|

nissīmamahimā, nityayauvanā, madaśālinī||91||

424. tattvāsanā- Tatvam means principles or categories. Devi is seated on principles.

425. tat- She who is that. What is that? The word 'Tat' signifies the revolution of mind as Devi revolves in all Buddhis she is signified by the- word Tat.

426. tvam

Thou. She is you. The word Tvam also signifies Devi.

Tattwamasi is also used as one word. Meaning "you are that." It is the famous expression of the relationship between the individual and the Absolute. It means that Brahman and Atman are one. The basic principle of Advaita philosophy is complex to understand. Tyagaraja Swami kRti *'tatvameruga taramA'* (set in rare Garudhwani Ragam) asking Rama, "Is it in one's capacity to realize the supreme reality as brought out in vEdas and SAstras?"

427. ayī- Devi is addressed by this word as she is the mother of all. In Marathi, mother is addressed as *Ayi*. Or ayi, fortunate one.

428. pañchakōśāntarasthitā

Residing in the five sheaths. These five (koshas) are the five employed in the worship of the five (deities). These five are:

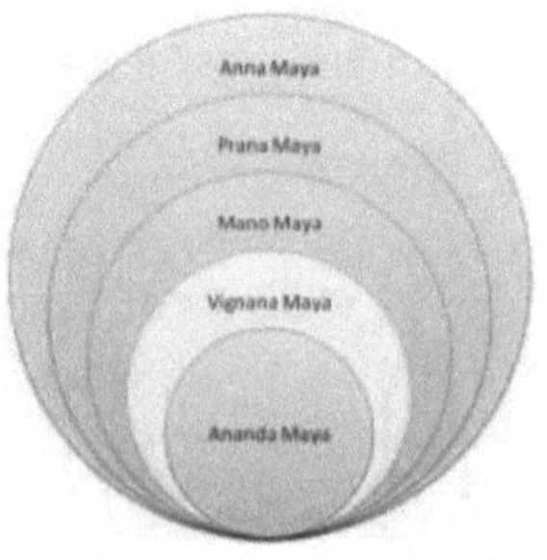

"Srividya, Paramjyotis, Para, Niskala Sambhavi, and the Ajapa mantra, and these are called the five sheaths." When we worship these five in the Sri Chakra, the last four Paranjyotis, etc., are to be worshipped individually and collectively and other Chakras which are surrounding (the Sri Chakra). But Srividya is the Bindu in the centre. Thus, she is amid the five sheaths.

There are in our bodies the five sheaths called *Annamaya, Pranamaya, Manomaya, Vijnamaya and Anandamaya,* each involved in the preceding one of these five, the innermost last is the Anandamaya, with that Devi is identified.

429. nissīmamahimā

Seema means boundary. Ni-no boundary. Mahima is fame. nissīmamahimā means Devi who has limitless fame

430. nityayauvanā: She who is ever young

431. madaśālinī: Shining with rapture. Mada, a kind of bliss, untainted by worldly things.

In Shyamala Dandakam, the word madaśālinī comes in the following verse:

माता मरकतश्यामा मातङ्गी मदशालिनी।

कुर्यात् कटाक्षं कल्याणी कदंबवनवासिनी॥३॥

432. madaghūrṇita raktākṣī- With reddened eyes rolling with rapture. Ghurnaana (rolling) turned away from worldly things.

433.madapāṭala gaṇḍabhūḥ- With cheeks blushing with rapture. Paatala, rose color.

434. chandana dravadigdhāṅgī- Her body smeared with sandal paste

435. chāmpēya kusuma priyā

Fond of the Champaka flower.

It is also known as Champanki flower. Champanki road in Malleswaram Bengaluru has many trees bearing this flower and hence named after this flower. This flower is not only beautiful but also very fragrant. Devi is very fond of this flower.

कुशला कोमलाकारा कुरुकुल्ला कुलेश्वरी।

कुलकुण्डालया कौलमार्गतत्परसेविता॥९३॥

kuśalā, kōmalākārā, kurukullā, kulēśvarī ||

kulakuṇḍālayā, kaula mārgatatpara sēvitā ||93||

436. kuśalā- Skilful. Intelligent.

437. kōmalākārā- Of graceful appearance.

438. kurukullā- This deity is in the tank, called Vimarsamaya, in the Srichakra, in the space between the walls of Cit and Ahankara

439.kulēśvarī- She who is the goddess for the kula or clan. Kula also means a triad the known, the knowing and the knowledge. Devi is the ruler of the triad.

440. kulakuṇḍālayā

Abiding in the Kulakunda. Kulakunda is the bindu, which is in centre of the pericarp of the Muladhara. It is like the small cavity in the centre of the pericarp of a lotus. Alaya, the place of rest (in the sleep) of Kundalini.

Acharya says in Saundarya Lahari "After reaching your own place assuming the form of a coiled serpent you sleep in the cavity of the Kulakunda."

441. kau_la mārgatatpara sēvitā

Worshipped by those devoted to the Kaula path. Marga, the path handed down by family tradition. Kula, it is so called because it relates to the Muladhara. There are three main modes in the worship of Devi- Samaya, Misra and Kaula. The first is shown in the Vedas and described in the five Agamas of Shuka, Vasistha, etc.

The second is that which is described in the eight Tantras, Gandrakala and others. It is called mixed because it partakes of both (modes).

The third called the Kaula mode differs from the above two. It is described in other Tantras. Kaula is so called because it is sought for by the Kaulas. The characteristics of these modes of worship and of their devotees are described in the corresponding Tantras

Chapter 9

Devi as Mother Goddess

We begin this chapter from Shlokam 94.

कुमारगणनाथाम्बा तुष्टिः पुष्टिर्मतिधृतिः।

शान्तिः स्वस्तिमती कान्तिर्नन्दिनी विघ्ननाशिनी॥९४॥

kumāra gaṇanāthāmbā, tuṣṭiḥ, puṣṭi, rmati, rdhṛtiḥ।

śāntiḥ, svastimatī, kānti, rnandinī, vighnanāśinī॥94॥

442. kumāra gaṇanāthāmbā: Mother of Kumara and Gananatha.

Kumara is Skanda; Gananatha is Ganesha. Ambāl is the mother of both Kumara and Ganesha.

In India, Sri Adi Sankara established six paths of worship - *Shaivism, Vaishnavism, Shaktism, Shouram, Gānapathyam and Kowmāram.*

So, he is called as *'Shanmatha Sthapakar."* Out of these six, Kowmāram, derived from Kumara refers to the worship of Kumara or Muruga as called by many. Gods generally do not have a previous birth. Not many people know that Kumara or Skanda had a previous birth or a past Janma.

There is an interesting story of Murugan's previous birth. This story is from a scripture called "Tripura Rahasyam." It is described in the 37th Chapter of the Mahatmya Kanda of the Tripura Rahasya. This scripture is considered by Bhagavan Sri Ramana Maharshi as one of the greatest works that expounded Advaita philosophy. It is said that Lord Vishnu incarnated on Earth as Sri Dattatreya, the Lord of the Avadhutas, and taught this Rahasya to Parasurama. The work was later written by Haritayana and is also called after his name Haritayana Samhita. It is said to consist of 12,000 slokas in three sections - The Mahatmya Khanda (Section on the Greatness of Sri Devi), Jnana Khanda (Section on Supreme Wisdom), and Charya Khanda (Section on Conduct).

I have heard this story about the origin of *'Shanmuka'* (the six-faced one or Subramanya) narrated by Kanchi Mahaperiyava.

Lord Brahma conceived four sons from his mind. They were called -*Sanaka, Sanandana, Sanat and Sanatana.* They are called Brahma's *manasika putras* (sons from the mind). They were all great jnanis, scholars who chose to remain celibate.

Sanatkumar is known as *Brahma jnani* - One who has attained the knowledge of Brahman. One day, he had a strange dream. He dreamt that there was a war between Devas and

Asuras. He fought in the war as Deva Senapathy, the Chief of Deva's army and killed the asuras. When he woke up, he felt surprised. He did not know the meaning of his dream and so asked his father Brahma what his dream meant.

Brahma said, "You are a Brahma Jnani, whatever you think, or dream will definitely come true someday, maybe it will happen in your next birth." The words of great jnanis come true. So, people seek their blessings.

Sanatkumar continued his deep meditation tapas on Parabrahmam. At that time, Parvathi Parameshwara visited his ashram and waited to get his attention, but Sanatkumar was totally immersed in his tapas, and so he did not even notice them. So, Parameshwara was annoyed. He called out and asked Sanatkumar, "How dare you ignore me and Parvathi? What if I curse you for your indifference?" Sanatkumar was least scared. He challenged Shiva boldly, "You can curse me as an angry Rudra. Your curse won't affect my Atma. Try it out."

Instead of getting angry, Parameswara felt happy at realizing that Sanatkumar was a true Jnani. So, he said, "I appreciate your Jnanam (knowledge). Ask me any boon you want." Sanatkumar replied, "I don't need any boon from you. On the other hand, if you need any boon from me, please ask and I shall give it to you." So, Parameshwara asked him a boon, "Please become my son in your next birth." So be it, said Sanatkumar on condition that he will not be born like humans through garbhavasa (pregnancy).

So, Sanatkumar was born as Parvati Parameshwara's son in a unique way. From Parmeshwara's third eye, six sparks of fire flew out and lodged in a pond called *'Saravana Poykai'* -

a pond in the forest of reeds, *Shara Vanam,* that was formed by Paravati melting herself when she could not bear the separation from Shiva.

The six sparks became six babies that were united together as one body and six heads- which became Arumugan (Six faces) or Skanda. He was also called Saravanan or Murugan who later preached *"Pranava Upadesam"* to his father Parameshwara.

We all know about Ganesha. He is the first one to be worshipped before starting any ritual activity. He is the leader of the Ganas – the army chieftain of Shiva. Hence called Ganaāntha. Ganesha is to be remembered as the remover of obstacles and be invoked before all undertakings.

Bhāskararāya gives other interpretations:

kumāra gaṇanāthāmbā: Split into Ku- inferior, Maaragana, the aggregate of passionate ideas (Vikara), Naathas, the lords, of the above. Amba, the binder (or destroyer). Ambāl is the binder or destroyer of all inferior ideas.

Kumāra, the Ahamkara (egoism) whose deity is Kumara.

The Varaha Purana says, "Vishnu is the Person, or Shiva by that name is called. Avyakta is Uma or Lakhsmi, the lotus eyed. Ahamkara arises from the interaction of these (two). This (egoism) is the Guha (Skanda), the leader of the army." She binds those who possess the qualities of egoism.

The next 7 naamas (443-449) तुष्टि:, पुष्टि, मंति, धृति:, शान्ति:, स्वस्तिमती, कान्ति *tuṣṭiḥ, puṣṭi, rmati, rdhṛtiḥ śāntiḥ, svastimatī, kānti* reflect 7 different qualities of Ambāl.

Let us see what they mean.

443. tuṣṭiḥ

Contentment.

Devi Mahatmiyam in the Markandeya Purana says,

या देवी सर्वभुतेषु तुष्टिरूपेण संस्थिता।

नमस्तस्यै नमस्तस्यै नमस्तस्यै नमो नमः ॥२४॥

"The goddess who resides as contentment in all beings, adoration to her."

Vedas describe *dosha trayam*- three kinds of defects which are natural to human beings

1. *dukha misri tatwam* - mixed with pain and pleasure. never pure joy -like for example you are happy with your daughter, but when she gets married and leaves for her husband's home, you feel sad.

2. *atrupti karatwam*- Never satisfied. Always wanting more. Money, car, furniture and so on. No tripti or satisfaction. No end to struggle. They perpetuate the struggle. like a rich man wants to become richer, not satisfied with one car, a woman wants more jewels. We see it every day. Companies use this trait of discontentment to sell more.

3. *'bandhakaratwam'*-dependence on a habit that binds a person -like smoking, drinking, gambling etc.

In these three doshas, discontentment and consequent unhappiness is a common thread. How can you overcome this dosha of atrupti? Only by praying to Ambāl who counters atrupti by being the goddess of contentment.

Real happiness comes only when one is contented. Those who worship Ambāl learn to be contented and overcome the dosha of atrupti.

 The Glory of Lalithā Sahasranāmam

444: puṣṭi

Nourishment. When you see a well-nourished plump child, you feel happy. Ambāl provides nourishment to her devotees. Baskrararya says Pushti is a deity in Devadāruvana (देवदारुवन). —A pine forest and sacred place.

445. mati

Mati means "intelligence," Knowledge" "understanding," "mindful," "intuition" and "perception."

Bhāskararāya explains: Mati is explained in the Vayu Purana as, "Purusa bears the measuring (rod), understands division and thinks himself composed of parts, hence he is known as Mati."

Ambāl makes a person sharpen his thinking and makes him a मतिमान or intelligent.

446. dhṛtiḥ

Fortitude. Courage. Ambāl provides courage as Dhairyalakshmi. My Guru used to tell me a story to explain the importance of constant courage in our lives.

There was a man who prayed Ambāl very sincerely for a long time. Eventually, Ambāl in the form of Ashtalakshmis blessed him with health, wealth, children- everything that he wanted.

After some time, Dhanyalakshmi (the goddess of grains) told him, "Now that you have all grains, I would like to go back. He said Ok. Next came Santana Lakshmi, She said now that you are blessed with good children, I would like to leave. He said Ok. Slowly, one by one, each Lakshmi took leave of him.

Lastly, Dhairyalakshmi (the goddess of courage), asked permission to leave him.

He said, no, you cannot leave me. She asked why. He said, because if I let you go, I will be devastated. I need you to remain with me always. So, Dhairyalakshmi stayed, and seeing her, the other Lakshmis automatically returned to him, and he was happy. So, one should never leave Dhairyalakshmi or courage. By worshipping Ambāl, we develop courage to face challenges in life.

Bhāskararāya adds: This is the deity 'dhriti' worshipped in the Pindaraka place. It is mentioned as one of the shakti peetas in Devi Bhagavadha Purana. It is a sacred place situated near Dvārakā in Saurāṣṭra.

447. śāntiḥ

Tranquility. Peace. Devi confers peace on Her devotees.

Bhāskararāya quotes the Saivagama that says, "That which gives place to a man (struggling with) the flood of impurity (of arm), illusion (of Maya), and change (of Karman), that Kala is called Santi. That is the abode which is the seat of dominion." Saint Thyagaraja Swami sings *"Shaanthamu Lekhaa, Soukyamu Lethu* "in Telugu. It means if there is no peace, there is no happiness. Where there is peace, there is happiness. But not the other way. One may be happy with material comforts but may not have peace of mind. So, in Sanatana Dharma Shanti has special significance and we say it three times before and after our rituals to remove obstacles caused by physical, divine and internal causes.

448. svastimatī

Ever True. Su, exceedingly, asti, being, mat, having. Because her being is supreme reality and not what ordinary people think to be reality. Svasti also means immortality.

449. kānti

Effulgent. Having a divine lustre. Ambāl in the Nellaippar Shiva temple in Tirunelveli is called "Kantimati." Many girls in Tirunelveli and around are named Kantimati. The name Kantimati comes again later in Nāma 465.

This concludes the seven nāmas that describe Ambāl's qualities.

Now we start with other names of special significance.

450. nandini

There are different interpretations.

The first one means Daughter of Nanda. Nanda here refers to Nandagopa.

There is a story behind this.

Lord Krishna was born in a prison. Krishna's father Vasudeva carried the baby Krishna across Yamuna River to the home of Nandagopa in Gokul where a baby girl was born to Yashoda. Vasudeva left Krishna in Nandagopa's home and carried back the baby girl. When Kamsa tried to kill this baby girl, she flew up as Mahamaya and warned kamsa that the child born to kill him is elsewhere. Ambāl born as Mahamaya to Nandagopal is called Nandini.

The word Nandini is derived from the Sanskrit verbal root nand, which means "to rejoice, delight". Nanda means "joy" in Sanskrit. The word Ananda is also an extension of nanda. a'nanda' -'a" means 'entire.' Nandagopal means one who brings joy.

Nandinī is a female gender, means a woman who brings joy. The name also specifically refers to a daughter, as a daughter brings joy to the family.

In Adi Sankara's Mahashisura Mardini Stotram, the very first line mentions Nandini as a daughter of Himavan.

अयि गिरिनन्दिनि नन्दितमेदिनि विश्वविनोदिनि नन्दिनुते गिरिवर विन्ध्यशिरोऽधि निवासिनि विष्णुविलासिनि जिष्णुनुते।

भगवति हे शितिकण्ठकुटुम्बिनि भूरिकुटुम्बिनि भूरिकृते जय जय हे महिषासुरमर्दिनि रम्यकपर्दिनि शैलसुते॥१॥

Here, Giri Nandini refers to the daughter of the mountain Himalayas.

Bhāskararāya says Nandini refers to the daughter of the celestial cow Kamadhenu. कामधेनू from kama desire, wish + dhenu milk cow could fulfil any desire. Nandini inherited her mother's qualities. Indra had gifted Nandini to Vashista Maharishi.

Once, the king Kaushika (later called Vishwamitra), visited Vashistha's ashram with his army and asked the Rishi for food.

Nandini, the divine cow provided food for the King and his entire army. The King was very impressed and tried to take the cow away from Vasishta by force but could not do so because of the divine powers of the Rishi. After being unable

The Glory of Lalithā Sahasranāmam

to get Nandini, the king renounced all his possessions and luxury and decided to acquire powers like Vasishta. So, he performed a tapas (penance) and became Vishwamitra to lead the life of a simple forest ascetic.

There is another story of the celestial powers of Nandini. The Raghuvamsa of Kalidasa mentions that king Dilipan had no children. On the advice of Vashista, he and his wife Sudakshina served Nandini cow and were blessed to have a son Raghu.

Raghu was the ruler of the Ikshvaku dynasty. His son was Aja, and Aja's son was King Dasaratha. Lord Rama is thus part of Raghuvamsa.

Like Nandini, Ambāl fulfills the desires of her devotees without any limit.

451. vighnanāśinī- Destroyer of obstacles.

तेजोवती त्रिनयना लोलाक्षीकामरूपिणी।

मालिनी हंसिनी माता मलयाचलवासिनी॥९५॥

tējōvatī, trinayanā, lōlākṣī kāmarūpiṇī।

mālinī, haṃsinī, mātā, malayāchala vāsinī॥95॥

452. tējōvatī- Devi is full of Because she is the support of the Sun and other luminaries. Bhāskararāya quotes The Sruti Brahadaranya Upanishad 3-3-11 "In this indestructible (Brahman) the Sun and Moon were established."

453. trinayanā

Three-eyed. The three eyes are the moon, the sun and the fire. Bhāskararāya gives different interpretations. We will mention a few of them. He says Trinayana, is another name for the word vaushat. When you do Nyasa, you say *"NetraTraye Vaushat" while* the index finger touches the right eye, ring finger touches the left eye, middle finger touches the third eye. It is for igniting the power of Divine vision, activating the third eye center

Bhāskararāya adds: Tri, three (paths), viz. south, north and the path of Brahman, Naya to lead. She leads those who are entitled to have one of the three paths. The Devi Purana says, "There are the Southern and Northern worlds, and the supreme abode of Brahman, as she leads those who follow the right way, she is called Trinayana."

454. lōlākṣī kāmarūpiṇī: In the form of the desire of women. Bhāskararāya comments:

To show her love is not limited to Shiva, Ambāl is so called as kāmarupini.

Or, she is in the form of Yogeshvari, who is the deity of desire.

The Varaha Purana says "(1) desire, (2) anger, (3) greed, (4) passion, (5) bewilderment, (6) envy, (7) calumny, (8) scorn, thus there are eight mothers. You should recognize desire as Yogeshvari, anger as Maheshvari, greed is said to be Vaishnavi, passion as Brahmani bewilderment is the self-existent Kalyani, envy as Indraja, the Devi, holding in her hand the death rod (Yamadanda) is herself calumny, and scorn is Varaha. Thus, they are mentioned."

455. mālinī

Wearing garlands.

Bhāskararāya says Mālini is the name of the deity of fifty-one letters.

Or Mālini is a companion of Devi, mentioned in the Vamana Purana in the section on the marriage ceremony of Parvati. Then Malini clasped the foot of Hara. Hara said "whatever you ask I will give but release my foot." Mālini, then replied to Shiva, "O Shiva, bestow your prosperity on my friend, then you will be released." Then Shiva said, "I have already given, release me."

Mālini has other meanings too. Mālini is a certain metre or the name of Ganga, a woman of the florist caste, the city of Campa, Gauri,and Ganga.

456. haṃsinī

Refers to Swan

Swan is a water bird which is revered in Sanatana Dharma. Hamsa is in the Sringeri Tradition. You will find the Swan logo here. If you open the website of svbfnorth, on the left side, you will find the circular logo with Hamsa pakshi.

Why is Hamsa so sacred? In the "tatvaloka' magazine of Sringeri Mutt (May 2016), Jagadguru Sri Sankaracharya of Sringeri explains: "Hamsa is a bird of elegance, beauty and purity. She is compared to a saintly person who is unattached to worldly desires, just as her feathers do not get wet although she is in water. It is believed that the swan separates water from milk.

This is its greatness. In a similar manner, a paramahamsa jnani separates the superimposed false jagat from real Brahman and immerses himself in the real. Jnanis alone can do this-like perceiving the real rope by negating the superimposed snake. It is because of this ability that Hamsa symbolizes a paramahamsa jnani."

The official seal of the Sringeri mutt shows a swan on a lotus.

Traditionally, the Hamsa symbol is attributed to the Peetam. The presiding deity of Sringeri Mutt is Devi Sharada. She is Brahmavidya Swarupini, the Goddess of Knowledge, Sarasvati. She is seated on the swan. She is referred to as Hamsa vahini, which means "she who has a Hamsa as her vehicle". The bird symbolizes Sattva Guna or purity par excellence.

Ramakrishna Mission too has Hamsa as its symbol with the words 'तन्नो हंस: प्रचोदयात् (Tanno hamsah prachodayat), meaning, "May the Paramatman, Supreme Self [symbolized by] the Swan (hamsa), awaken our [higher] understanding.".

So, hamsini is one of the most revered names for Ambāl.

457. mātā

Mother. See the similarity between Mata and Mother. Mom, Maa, Amma, all come from Mata. Because she is the mother of all. Or Mata in the form of letters (matrukas). She is the mother of all Mantras; hence the Supreme Eswari is called Matruka.

458. malayāchala vāsinī

Residing in the malaya mountain. In Kerala, there are Malaya mountains which are home to 'Bhagawati.' This deity is described in the Sabaracintamani as the MalayalayaBhagavadi

(Chi. Up., 4-14-2). Ambāl is hence known as Malayāchala Vāsini.

The other interpretation is Ambāl resides in the Himalaya mountains being the daughter of Himavan. In Lalithā Sahasranāmam we also see other names like 'Vindhya Vāsini', and 'Umā Śailēndra tanayā.'

सुमुखी नलिनी सुभ्रूः शोभना सुरनायिका।
कालकण्ठी कान्तिमती क्षोभिणी सूक्ष्मरूपिणी॥९६॥

sumukhī, naḻinī, subhrūḥ, śōbhanā, suranāyikā|

kālakaṇṭhī, kāntimatī, kṣōbhiṇī, sūkṣmarūpiṇī||96||

459. sumukhī

"Su" is a prefix that represents Good in Sanskrit. Sumithra = Good Friend, Subashshini = Good Speaker, Suhasini = Good Smiler and more. Here Sumuki means Beautiful-faced. You will find many more such words with *Su* as prefix coming up to describe Ambāl. Face is the index of mind. By wisdom, the beauty of the face increases. The Shrutis say, "One who knows this, his face shines." One can identify a Brahmavit - a sage whose face shines.

Sumukhi is also a deity to be worshipped as a part of Shodasi Mantra.

460. naḻinī

Means Lotus – a revered flower in our dharma. We explained it before. Devi is like the lotus. She is seated on Padmasana (naama 278). Her hands, feet, face, eyes and other limbs are gentle like the lotus.

461. subhrūḥ

Again, another word with Su as prefix. Here it means one with beautiful eyebrows. Note the similarity between the words bhruhu and the English word brow.

462. śōbhanā- Handsome, beautiful Devi

463. suranāyikā- Leader of the Devas. Sura refers to Devas. The opposite word is Asura -demon. The Shruti says, "(She is) the supreme power of the Devas."

464. kālakaṇṭī

Wife of Kālakanta. Kālakanta is Shiva: Kaala is black, kanta is neck. Shiva is called so because his throat is colored by poison. According to the Devi Purana, among the sixty-eight sacred places, Kalanjara is a place where Kālakantha is worshipped. This place is a fortress-city in Bundelkhand, in Banda District of Uttar Pradesh, in India. The Shiva temple here has a svāyambhuvaliṅga, one of the most sacred of liṅgas according to the Śaivāgamas. The presiding deity residing over the liṅga in this place (Kālañjara) is named Nīlakaṇṭha.

There is a story in the Linga Purana that to destroy the Daitya Daruka, "SiVa created Kali as well as Kapardini and Kālakanti."

465. kāntimatī

Radiant. Kāntimati is the radiant deity in Tirunelveli.

There are five places where Lord Shiva is said to have displayed his dance. All these places are called sabhas or Ambalams. Shiva is also called Ambalavanan.

These five places are Chithambaram- Golden Hall (Ponnambalam - kanaka sabha), Madurai - Silver Hall (Velli Ambalam - rajata sabha), ThiruvAlaNkAdu - Gem Hall (rathnasabai) ThirunelvEli - Copper Hall (thAmira sabai), KutrAlam - Picture Hall (chiththira sabai).

Tirunelveli (city in Tamil Nadu, India) is said to be the Thaamira Copper Ambalam Sabhai. Shiva is called Nellaiappar here and his consort is Kantimati.

Muthuswami Dikshitar has composed a rare kriti Sri Kantimatim in the Ragam: Hemavati praising Kantimati. *Sri Kanthimathim Shankara Yuvathim Shree Guruguha Jananeem Vandeham*

I pray before goddess Kantimati, the young ("Yuvathim") bride of Sankara, the mother ("Jananeem") of Guruguha.

He compares her face to the Bijakshara Hrim and speaks of her being enshrined in a golden mansion studded with gems.

He mentions a series of celestials – Indra, Himavan, Parasurama, Suka and Saunaka - associated with her. He concludes by mentioning the pure waters of the river and the deity being anointed with the waters from 108 Kalasas and conches.

What's in a name? A lot, particularly in India where there is wonderful system of naming children after local deities or local villages, or occupation. If you come across anyone with the name Kāntimati, you can be almost sure she has her origins in Tirunelveli area. Sankaran, Sankaranarayan or Gomathi are names from the Tirunelveli region.

Many Marathi surnames have the suffix 'kar' at the end of them. This 'kar' suffix usually denotes the village the person belongs to.

For example, Gavaskar refers to someone with their origins in the Gavaswadi village of Kolhapur district of Maharashtra. Mangeshkar refers to someone who belongs to the Mangeshi village in Goa. The singer Lata Mangeshkar is probably the most famous bearer of this surname. There are also occupational names related to the work one does like Divekar - one who makes lamps, Deshmukh means the 'head of the state' or 'head of the region.' Kamble - one who deals in blankets.

In Punjab, Sikh names are inspired by virtues or qualities. Like Harbhajan Singh-one who sings bhajans, Gurcharan Singh -one who is at the feet of the Guru, Paramjit Singh-one who is supremely victorious.

Each region had such an interesting system where a name meant something. The system is now changing to exotic short names like Lulu, Chiku, Dolly, and so on that have no meaning.

466. kṣōbhiṇī

One who causes emotion or excitement. Bhāskararāya adds:

By the agitation of (her) mind she created multitudes of deities. The Varaha Purana says, "Vaisnavi (the wife of Vishnu) once went to the Mandara mountain to perform penance; after she had performed penance for a long time, she became excited (by passion); from that excitement sprang young women of fair appearance, with blue curling hair, with lips red as the Bimba fruit, lotus-eyed, with body like the red lotus wearing a beautiful anklet. When the mind of Devi was agitated, hundreds and millions of such women arose with different faces.

467. sūkṣmarūpiṇī

Devi is of subtle form. Sukshma means difficult to perceive. The Shruti says "Subtler than the subtle, eternal."

Kathopanishad., 1-2-20. Says:

अणोरणीयान्महतो महीया-

aNor aNīyān mahato mahīyā-

नात्माऽस्य जन्तोर्निहितो गुहायाम्।

nā atmā'sya jantor nihito guhāyām

अणो: -than an atom; अणीयान्-more subtle; न्महतो महीया- greater than greatest

"More minute than an atom" Subtler than the subtle, greater than the great, in the heart of each living being, the *atman* reposes. We have said before that Devi has three forms, physical, subtle and supreme (and this refers to the second one).

वज्रेश्वरी वामदेवी वयोऽवस्थाविवर्जिता।

सिद्धेश्वरी सिद्धविद्या सिद्धमाता यशस्विनी॥९७॥

vajrēśvarī, vāmadēvī, vayō'vasthā vivarjitā।

siddhēśvarī, siddhavidyā, siddhamātā, yaśasvinī॥97॥

468. vajrēśvarī

The term vajra is a Sanskrit word that is usually defined as "diamond" or "thunderbolt which is a flash of lightning with a simultaneous crash of thunder." Both convey strength and indestructibility.

A thunderbolt carries high voltage electricity and is so powerful that it can break buildings and set them on fire. That is why we have special lightning protection in buildings.

Ambāl herself is described as lightning in verse 40.

तडिल्लतासमरुचिः षट्चक्रोपरिसंस्थिता।

महासक्तिः कुण्डलिनी बिसतन्तुतनीयसी॥४०॥

tadillatā samaruchiḥ, ṣaṭ-chakrōpari saṃsthitā।

mahāśaktiḥ, kuṇḍalinī, bisatantu tanīyasī॥40॥

107. tadillatA samaruchiH- She who is beautiful like a flash of lightning.

108. ShaT chakropari samsthitA - She who resides above the six chakrAs

109. mahAsaktiH - She who is greatly attached to the festive union of shiva and shakti

110. kuNDalinI- She who has the form a coiled serpentine power (within our spine)

111. bisa tantu tanIyasI

She who is fine and delicate as the fiber of the lotus

Bhāskararāya gives different interpretations. Devi herself gave Indra the weapon, Vajra. The Brahmānda Purana says when Indra performed penance in the water, "From that water Devi arose and gave Indra the bow called Vajra." So, she is called Vajreswari.

The Srichakra has twelve walls, all built of diamond; in the centre of the eleventh, there is a river called vajramayi and she is its deity.

Durvasas (Lalitastavaratna,44 and 45) says, "Let the overflowing river called Vajra, be everlasting, filled with the sound of the sweet notes of the swans gliding on the beautiful waves; on the pleasant bank of that river, Vajresi flourishes decked with diamond ornaments praised by the Devas headed by Indra, the hurler of the thunderbolt."

There is a town called Vajreshwari, 75 km away from Mumbai. It has a vajreswari temple. There are many hot water springs here which are named like Surya Kund (sun), Chandrakund(moon), Agnikund (fire), like trinayana.

469. vāmadēvī

The Wife of Vāmadeva

Bhāskararāya gives different meanings.

Vāmadeva is one of the (five) forms of Shiva as described in the Shiva Purana "Of beautiful appearance, red as the red paste (kumkuma), the north face of the Lord called Vama is firmly established."

Or Vāma, by left side, Deva, he shines. Ardhanarisvara svarupam has half body is S'iva and the other half is Devi on the left side or Vāmabaga). Hence called Vāmadeva.

Or Vāma, to be worshipped, deva, the deity. The Aitareya Shruti says, "The Devas addressed him; he indeed is to be worshipped by all of us, hence he is called Vamadeva."

Or Vāma, fair; Vama, the fruits of actions, Devi, the presiding deity.

Or Vāma, those devoted to the left-hand path (Vāmacara).

470. vayō'vasthā vivarjitā

Exempt from the different states of life.

Vayas, (in Tamil too we say Vayas to mean age) the states of childhood, boyhood, youth, old age. because she is eternal. Age does not apply to Ambāl.

471. siddhēśvarī

Queen of the Siddhas. Who are Siddhas? Siddha means "one who is accomplished." It refers to people who have achieved a high degree of physical and spiritual attainment.

There is also a deity of this name in Varanasi. There is a Sree Siddheswari Kali Temple in the city of Dhaka. There is also a Siddeshwar temple in Sholapur.

472. siddhavidyā- Eternal Science. meaning the Panchadasi

473. siddhamātā- The mother of Siddhas.

474. yaśasvinī

Famous. Yasho means fame. Not only is Devi famous but also grants fame to devotees.

In Argala Stotram we pray Devi as:

महिषासुरनिर्नाशि भक्तानां सुखदे नमः।

रूपं देहि जयं देहि यशो देहि द्विषो जहि॥४॥

Mahissaasura-Nirnaashi Bhaktaanaam Sukhade Namah|

Ruupam Dehi Jayam Dehi Yasho Dehi Dvisso Jahi||4|

O Devi, Please Grant me Beauty, Please Grant me Victory, Please Grant me Glory and Destroy my (Inner) Enemies.

विशुद्धिचक्रनिलयाऽऽरक्तवर्णा त्रिलोचना।

खट्वाङ्गादिप्रहरणा वदनैकसमन्विता॥९८॥

viśuddhi chakranilayā, raktavarṇā, trilōchanā।

khaṭvāṅgādi praharaṇā, vadanaika samanvitā॥98॥

475. viśuddhi chakranilayā

Abiding in the Vishuddhi Chakra.

One of the distinctive and unique features of Sanatana Dharma is it sees the Divine present in all existence. It believes in the divinity of each living being. Mundaka Upanishad declares Aham Brahmasmi. It means "I am Brahman" or less literally as "I am divine." देहो देवालयः प्रोक्तः जीवो देवस्सनातनः। Deho Devalayaha Proktaha Jivo Deva Sanatanah. It means our body is a Temple and the life enshrined in it is the Almighty. Lalithā Sahasranāmam describes divine aspects of our body.

In Lalithā Sahasranāmam, you will find descriptions of Ambāl with different names associated with chakras in the human body. Chakras are points of energy running along our spine. Each of the chakras is associated with a particular body part and its proper functioning.

These are energy-centres frequently described in Sanskrit literature, in some of the minor Upanishads, in the Puranas and in Tantric works.

From this nāma 475 to 534 (60 nāma-s), you will find the description about the chakra-s or psychic centres of kuṇḍalinī and sahasrārā. Each chakra or psychic centre is presided over by a deity called yogini. There are seven such yoginis.

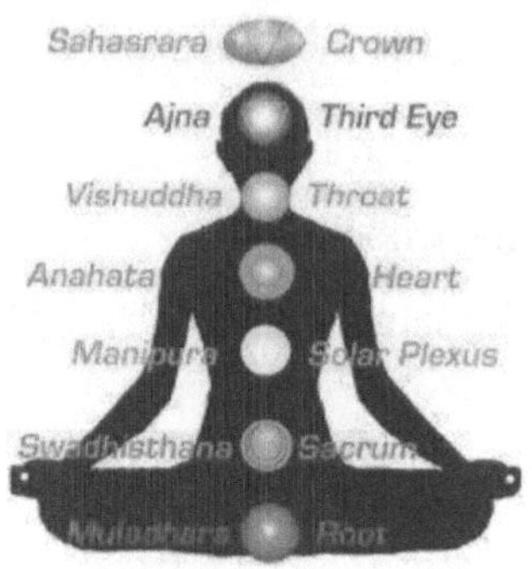

There are 7 chakras in the body of a human being are called Mulādhāra, Swadhisthana, Manipoorabja, Anahata, Vishuddhi, Ajna, and Sahasrara.

The order in which these names follow is not from the base chakra to the crown chakra or from the crown chakra to the base chakra. Each chakra is especially connected with one of the elements earth, water, fire, air, ether and mind. It begins with viśuddhi chakra, goes down to the lower chakra-s then to ājñā and ends with sahasrāra at the top.

Also, Sanskrit has fifty alphabets that include sixteen vowels. Each chakra has a certain number of lotus petals and each of these petals represent a particular alphabet of Sanskrit. For example, the throat chakra or viśuddhi cakra has sixteen lotus petals, which represent sixteen vowels. There are totally 50 petals of the Chakras as one goes from the base (muladhara) to the ajna Chakra. The specific number of lotuses is 4, 6, 10, 12, 16, and 2. The Sahasrara Chakra, which is at the top has 1,000 petals and it is associated with the innermost triangle of the Sri Chakra. That is also called Bramandha or Bindumandala. Ambāl is called *bindumaṇḍala vāsinī.*

Divine mother is called by different names and forms linked to those chakras. We saw earlier a shlokam that describes Ambāl as षट्चक्रोपरिसंस्थिता – *(shatchakoparisamsthita)* She who resides above the six chakrAs. (This excludes Sahasrara).

 The Glory of Lalithā Sahasranāmam

In one form she has one face in another two faces etc. In one form she is red and in another she is in golden color.

In another form she likes pāyasam (kheer in Hindi) and in one more form she likes Ghee mixed rice etc. Lalithā Sahasranāmam describes her forms in detail. It starts here with Vishuddhi chakra.

What is Visuddhichakra? The phrase vishuddha translates to visha – impurity or poison; and suddhi – purify. the word Chakra translates as "the wheel." A wheel represents the flow of prana, or life force through the body, from the Root Chakra to the Crown Chakra.

It is a symbol of wholeness, eternity, and an infinite, cyclical exchange of energy. The Vishuddhi Chakra is a center of physical and spiritual purification. It is in the vicinity of the Larynx – and is therefore also known as the Throat Chakra.

The breath that flows through the throat, and therefore through this Chakra, plays a big role in humans. The throat chakra, *vishuddha,* is associated with the element of ether that represents communication, authenticity and purification. The Yoga technique of Prānāyāma (regulation of the breath) exerts a strong influence on the Vishuddhi Chakra and improves a person's health and mind.

Every chakra is said to have a different number of lotus petals. The combination of these petals is the thousand petalled lotus (sahasrāra-padma). Ambāl, known by different names, is said to be residing in those lotus petals. You will find more references to this later -like anāhatābja nilayā, maṇipūrābja nilayā and so on.

Why Lotus? The lotus, commonly called Padma, is a sacred flower in Sanatana Dharma. You will see Lakshmi Devi standing on it. The Lotus appears from the navel of Mahavishnu. So, Mahavishnu is called Padmanabha. The Lotus is a symbol of purity and perfect beauty. It is the national flower of both India and Vietnam. A lotus is a perfect analogy for the human condition: even when its roots are in the dirtiest waters, the Lotus produces the most beautiful flower.

In the Bhagavad Gita Chapter 5, verse 10, a human is advised to be like the lotus leaf; they should work without attachment, dedicating their actions to God, untouched by sin like water on a lotus leaf.

ब्रह्मण्याधाय कर्माणि सङ्गं त्यक्त्वा करोति य:।

लिप्यते न स पापेन पद्मपत्रमिवाम्भसा॥10॥

brahmaṇyādhāya karmāṇi saṅgaṁ tyaktvā karoti yaḥ

lipyate na sa pāpena padma-patram ivāmbhasā

brahmaṇi-to God; *ādhāya*-dedicating; *karmāṇi*-all actions; *saṅgam*-attachment; *tyaktvā*—abandoning; *karoti*—performs; *yaḥ*—who; *lipyate*—is affected; *na*—never; *saḥ*—that person; *pāpena*—by sin; *padma-patram*—a lotus leaf; *iva*—like; *ambhasā*—by water

The Lotus represents spiritual blossoming, the elevation of the mind, body, and spirit. We consider the lotus flower a symbol of divinity, fertility, life, beauty and prosperity. That is why lotus is used very often in our scriptures. Ambāl is described as बिसतन्तु - तनीयसी – *Bisatantutaniyasi*- She who is fine and delicate as the fiber of the lotus.

Vishuddha chakra resembles a mandala lotus with 16 petals - *shodasha dala padma.* Ambāl has her abode in the pericarp of the sixteen-petalled lotus. The sixteen petals of the throat chakra are associated with the sixteen vowels of Sanskrit. The vowel letters are called 'Aksharas.' Akshara means indestructible. The vowels are most important in communication, and hence the Vishudda Chakra is key to speech. It is the abode of the Devī of speech. A blocked throat chakra influences the ability to communicate.

In each of the six chakras there is one of these divinities like Dākini, Rākini, and others. According to the Yogini Nyasa, under the forms of the seven Yogini deities who preside over the seven cakras, the names begin with the syllables Da, ra, la, ka, sa, ha, ya (respectively).

They are *Dākini, Rākini, Lākini, Kākini, Sākini, Hākini, and Yākini.*

These yoginis are the adhishtana Devatha of each chakra in our body and the seven yoginies also represent the dathus in the body – like Dākini for the skin, Rākini for the blood, Lakini for the muscles, Kākini for the fat, Sākini for the bones, Hākini for the Majja or bone marrow and Yākini for the Shuklam (semen) of the human body.

Each of the yogini is surrounded by parivara Devathas also. The yoginis represent any of the many forms and/or qualities of Devi. They have individual and collective powers.

The meditation on the Dākini is, "In the Vishuddhi centre which is in the cavity of the throat, in the sixteen-petalled lotus, I adore Dākini, the rosy, three-eyed, armed with club, the sword, the trident and a large skin, having one face, striking the ignorant with terror, ever fond of Payasanna milk-food, the deity presiding over the organ of touch, whose form is surrounded by Amrita and other deities, and worshipped by warriors."

Mantras represent deities in the form of 'aksharas' or sound. Hidden in each of them is the energy of a particular deity, which remains latent until the Mantra is pronounced accurately with the right intention, intonation and aspiration as prescribed in the scriptures. The deity of the Mantra awakens only if the sounds create the right frequencies.

476. raktavarṇā- Ambāl is of light red complexion.

477. trilōchanā- Three-eyed. As she is the spouse of Shiva.

478. khaṭvāṅgādi praharaṇā

Armed with khatvanga - the club.

Khatvanga also means the foot of a cot. The word cot and khat are similar. The term Khat and the English word Cut are also similar. So, khatva anga means a part of the body cut- here it means a club with a human skull at its end.

479. vadanaika samanvitā- Having one face. Dākini devi is one-faced.

पायसान्नप्रिया त्वक्स्था पशुलोकभयङ्करी।

अमृतादिमहाशक्तिसंवृता डाकिनीश्वरी॥९९॥

pāyasānnapriyā, tvaksthā, paśulōka bhayaṅkarī|

amṛtādi mahāśakti saṃvṛtā, ḍākinīśvarī||99||

480. pāyasānnapriyā

She likes sweet rice (Pāyasam). Nutrition is important for us and Pāyasanna is a nutritious saatvic food. In Kerala, Paal Pāyasam made with milk is a well-known dish. This dessert is a famous Naivedyam/Prasadham at Sree Krishna Temple in Ambālapuzha (Kerala). The taste of this pāyasam is unbeatable. In North India, it is called kheer, which came from क्षीर (ksheer), the Sanskrit word for milk.

481. tvaksthā

Tvak refers to skin. Ambāl is the deity of organ of touch. She lives in the sensibility of the skin.

The Vedas envisage the human body as a replica of the Cosmic Person, Purusha. The body is an abode of gods. They are an inseparable part of our existence.

The Atma Bodha by Sri Adi Sankaracharya describes the different aspects of our personality. First comes the physical body. It is called sthula shariram or the gross body. The human body, just like the entire universe, is formed by a combination of the five great elements—earth, water, fire, air and space.

The Earth element is Bones and Muscles, Water element is Blood, Air element is Breath, Fire element is the Heat, and Space element is the Emptiness within.

482. paśulōka bhayaṅkarī

What is meant by Pasu? Pasu is an animal. Animals are ignorant. Here it refers to humans who are ignorant like animals. Pasuloka bhayankari means Ambāl fills such ignorant people with fear. Bhāskararāya adds- Pasus are those devoid of the knowledge of Advaitam or non—duality. The

Shrutis (Brahataranya Upanishad, 1-4-10) say, "now one who worships another deity (saying) 'the deity is different, and I am different,' he knows not, he is like a beast (Pasu)." "Fear comes when there is duality" (Br. Up. 1-4-2).

483. amṛtādi mahāśakti saṃvṛtā

Surrounded by Amrita and other Shaktis.

Amrta and others are the sixteen great Shaktis from Amrtakarsani to Aksara, each seated in each of the sixteen petals of the Visuddha Chakra. The Svacchanda Tantra, describing Shaiva rituals says, "One finger above that (Anahata) is the Vishuddhi with sixteen petals. Dākini, the supreme ruler is in the center. Amrita to Aksara is in the sixteen petals. Above that is Chandrabimba."

484. ḍākinīśvarī

The goddess of the south. Also refers to the famous temple Dakshineswar Kali temple where Ramakrishna Paramahamsa and his wife Sharada Devi were attached to it.

This concludes the nine (475 to 483) attributes of Devi.

अनाहताब्जनिलया श्यामाभा वदनद्वया।

दंष्ट्रोज्ज्वलाऽक्षमालादिधरा रुधिरसंस्थिता॥१००॥

anāhatābja nilayā, śyāmābhā, vadanadvayā |

daṃṣṭrōjjvalā, 'kṣamālādhidharā, rudhira saṃsthitā || 100 ||

485. anāhatābja nilayā

Abiding in the Anāhata lotus.

In the heart, in the twelve-petalled lotus, called Anahata chakra, the Yogini named Rākini, resides.

Her meditation is as follows: "We meditate upon Rākini who is in the twelve-petalled lotus of the heart, having two faces, with protruding tusks, black colored, bearing the disc, the trident, the skull, and the drum in her hands, three-eyed, presiding over the blood, attended by Kalaratri and other deities, fond of greasy food, worshipped by warriors, and the giver of desired objects."

486. śyāmābhā- Black in hue. Ambāl is called Kāli meaning black

487. vadanadvayā

Two-faced. Ambāl's name is also Rākini. Rākini has two heads to represent the duality between one's internal landscape and the external environment who has two faces.

488. damṣṭrōjjvalā

Damstro refers to tusks or long teeth. The elephant has beautiful tusks. The wild boar too has long teeth. Ujva means shining. Devi is with shining tusks.

489. Akṣamālādhidharā

Devi is Wearing a garland of Aksa beads.

The akshamala denotes a string made up of beads where each bead represents the 50 letters of the alphabet, a (अ) to ksha (क्ष), hence it is known, Akshamala. There is an Upanishad called Akshamalika Upanishad. It is a part of Rig Veda.

490. rudhira saṃsthitā

Residing in the blood. Blood is important for the body and just as we saw Devi resides in skin, here it is said Devi is also in the blood.

कालरात्र्यादिशक्त्यौघवृता स्निग्धौदनप्रिया।

महावीरेन्द्रवरदा राकिण्यम्बास्वरूपिणी॥१०१॥

kālarātryādi śaktyōghavṛtā, snigdhaudanapriyā|

mahāvīrēndra varadā, rākiṇyambā svarūpiṇī||101||

491. kālarātryādi śaktyōghavṛtā

Ambāl is attended by hosts of Shaktis, Kalaratri and others.

There is a certain Shakti called *Kalaratri*. Concerning the three forms (of Devi) says the Varaha Purana, The Shakti of Rudra (Raudri) born from darkness, who went to the blue mountain determined to perform penance, O earth, hear her vow... That Raudri, the supreme Shakti ever devoted to penance, causing destruction, is called Kālaratri." Adi refers to all: twelve Shaktis from Kālaratri to Tamkaari one in each petal (of Anāhata).

492. snigdhaudanapriyā- Fond of greasy food. Ambāl is fond of cooked rice mixed with ghee. For growing children, food with some fat content like ghee is nutritious.

493. mahāvīrēndra varadā

Ambāl grants boons (varada) to Mahaveer -great warriors.

Vi is many, Eera or ira means excited or intoxicated; the meaning is the Veeras are the (trained orators) gifted with eloquence. In Tamil, they call them as *'Sol Veerarkal.'*

Indras mean those who know Brahman. Idam, those who directly realise (dra) Brahman, which is the Self, the witness of all, saying 'I am He.'

The Shruti says, "He perceived; hence he is called Indra."

Or Mahavira is Prahlada, and Indra, the lord of the Devas. The Devi Bhagavada Purana (Book IV) says that Indra and Prahlada praised Devi after their fight which lasted a hundred divine years, and she granted them boons. So, She is called Mahavirendra Varada.

494. rākiṇyambā svarūpiṇī

Assuming the form of the Mother Rākini.

Rākinyamba is said to be residing in a lotus of 12 petals.

मणिपूराब्जनिलया वदनत्रयसंयुता।

वज्रादिकायुधोपेता डामर्यादिभिरावृता॥१०२॥

maṇipūrābja nilayā, vadanatraya saṃyuta |

vajrādhikāyudhōpēta, ḍāmaryādibhi rāvṛtā || 102 ||

495. maṇipūrābja nilayā

Abiding in the Manipura lotus. Manipura is the ten-petalled lotus in the navel. Here the Yogini named Lākini resides. Here meditation is: "Let us meditate on Lākini in the eight-petalled lotus of the navel, three-faced, tusked, red-colored, bearing in her hands, the dart (Shakti), the thunderbolt, club, and abhaya (a weapon), most terrible, attended by Damari and other Shaktis, inspiring the ignorant with terror, presiding over the flesh, fond of sweetmeat, doing good to all."

496. vadanatraya saṃyutā- Three-faced.

497. vajrādhikāyudhōpēta- Armed with a thunderbolt and other weapons.

498. ḍāmaryādibhi rāvṛtā- Attended by Damari and others.
Adi includes the ten Shaktis from Damari to Phatkarini.

रक्तवर्णा मांसनिष्ठा गुडान्नप्रीतमानसा।

समस्तभक्तसुखदा लाकिन्यम्बास्वरूपिणी॥१०३॥

raktavarṇā, māṃsaniṣṭhā, guḍānna prītamānasā|

samasta bhaktasukhadā, lākinyambā svarūpiṇī||103||

499. raktavarṇā- Blood-colored.

500. māṃsaniṣṭhā- Presiding over flesh.

This is the 500th naama that ends the sixth Kāla called *Ruci* in the Saubhagyabhaskara composed by Bhāskararāya.

501. guḍānna prītamānasā- Fond of sweetmeats, jaggery sweets

502. samasta bhaktasukhadā- Conferring happiness on all her devotees.

503. lākinyambā svarūpiṇī- Assuming the form of the mother Lākini

स्वाधिष्ठानाम्बुजगता चतुर्वक्त्रमनोहरा।

शूलाद्यायुधसम्पन्ना पीतवर्णाऽतिगर्विता॥१०४॥

svādhiṣṭhānāmbu jagatā, chaturvaktra manōharā|

śūlādyāyudha sampannā, pītavarṇā,'tigarvitā||104||

504. svādhiṣṭhānāmbu jagatā

Residing in the Svadhisthana lotus. The Yogini called Kākini' resides in the six-petalled Svadhisthana lotus; her meditation is: " We meditate upon Kākini who resides in the six-petalled Svidhisthana lotus, four-faced, three-eyed, bearing in her hands the trident, the noose, skull and ahhaya (weapon), ever proud, presiding over the fat (or lymph), fond of mead,

    The Glory of Lalithā Sahasranāmam

attended by Bandhani and others, yellow, fond of food mixed with curd, giver of desired objects."

505. chaturvaktra manōharā- Four-faced and fascinating

506. śūlādyāyudha sampannā- Armed with the trident and other weapons.

507. pītavarṇā- yellow colored

508. Atigarvitā- Very proud

मेदोनिष्ठा मधुप्रीता बन्धिन्यादिसमन्विता।

दध्यन्नासक्तहृदया काकिनीरूपधारिणी॥१०५॥

mēdōniṣṭhā, madhuprītā, bandinyādi samanvitā|

dadhyannāsakta hṛdayā, kākinī rūpadhāriṇī||105||

509. mēdōniṣṭhā- Presiding over fat.

510. madhuprītā- Fond of mead.

Madhu, honey or spirituous liquor. The Shruti says, "One who presents an oblation with honey (Madhu) pleases the great Devi."

511. bandinyādi samanvitā- Attended by Bandhani and others. These are the six deities from Bandhani to Lambosthi.

512. dadhyannāsakta hṛdayā- Fond of food mixed with curd. Curd rice is a common food item in many South Indian homes.

513. kākinī rūpadhāriṇī- Assuming the form of Kākini

Chapter 10

The Secret of Chakras

Lalithā Sahasranāmam continues to describe the various Chakras, the energy centers in the human body, from nāma 475 (viśuddhi chakranilayā) to 534 (60 nāma-s).

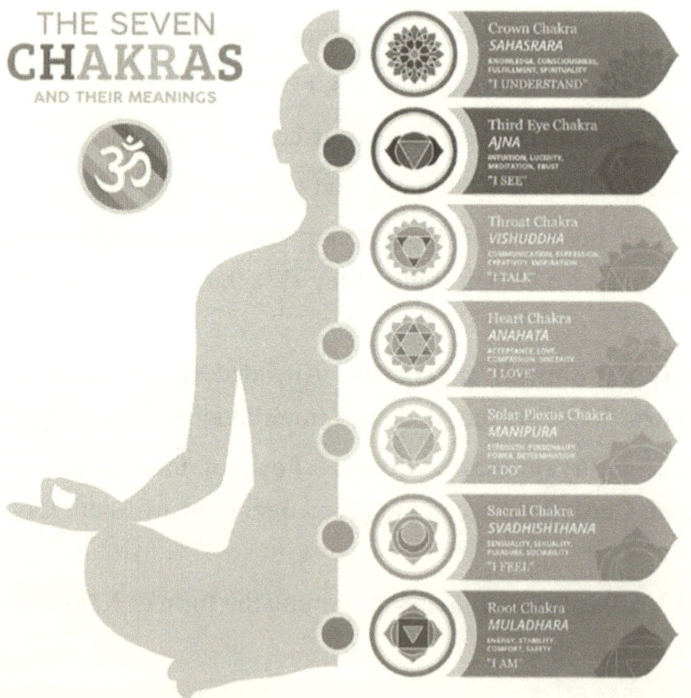

Chakras symbolize the flow of energy in our body and refer to the energy centers in our body. There are numerous such chakras in our body (some say 114) but seven of them are most important (see illustration). In Chapter 9, we explained these seven Chakras.

Each chakra or psychic center is presided over by a deity called yogini and there are seven such yogini-s which are certain aspects of the Devi.

We will continue with the nāmas that describe the chakras or psychic centers and the associated yoginis.

There is a strong connection between Lalithā Sahasranāmam and Yoga. To appreciate this and enjoy reciting the naamas, we must clearly understand the terms like Yoga, Prana, Nadis, and Chakras. These are fundamental elements that relate to our body.

LalithAmbāl is described as Yoginī योगिनी (653). She is in the form of yoga.

Yogadā योगदा (654): She bestows yoga on Her devotees. Yogyā योग्या (655): She can be attained by yoga. The Divine dwells in the human body. Just as Yoga describes Chakras, so does Lalithā Sahasranāmam describe the Chakras. Now let us see.

What is Yoga? The word Yoga is derived from the root yuj- to connect. It is a means to connect the Jeevatma with the Paramatma.

Yoga is a process of union with the divine. It is concerned with integrating the physical, spiritual, as well as mental well-being of a person. According to Sanatana Dharma, the goal is Moksha or liberation. (Dharma, Artha, Kama, Moksham). It is to attain the ultimate bliss. Yoga helps to achieve it. Bhagavad

Gita shows the way through Karma Yoga, Bhakti Yoga and Jnana Yoga.

About Yoga, Kanchi Mahaperiyava says: "The direct meaning of Yoga is 'to combine or merge'. In our lives we need to merge (combine) with many things. But none of these combinations are permanent. The mind is also constantly wavering. On the contrary, if we can join with the thing that is the ultimate and if we remain inseparable from it, that is true yoga. Paramatma, the origin of our mind is that 'ultimate thing'."

What Is Prana? The word prana is a Sanskrit word that means life energy. Yama is control. Pranayama that we perform means control of life-giving energy by breathing exercises.

Prana forms part of our bodies and moves through channels or nadis.

What is Nādi? Nādi is a Sanskrit word which translates as 'tube,' 'channel,' or 'flow. 'In our body, Nadis are subtle energy channels through which prana or life-force energy flows.

There are thousands of Nādis in our body but there are three important "Nādis" called "Ida", "Pingala" and "Sushumna", within the spine. "Ida" is lunar channel and associated with "feminine" properties. "Pingala" is solar channel and associated with "masculine" properties.

Both these Nādis represent the "duality" in existence which we may call as "Shakthi" and "Shiva". The "Sushumna" nādi is in the center, between Ida and Pingala. At the lower end of this "Sushumna" Nadi, lies the "Root" chakra. This is where

   The Glory of Lalithā Sahasranāmam

the dormant "Kundalini" energy rests. The term "Kundalini" comes from the Sanskrit word "kundal," which means "circular." Here it refers to a coiled serpent. Through proper and systematic yogic practices, this energy is awakened. Once awakened, this energy must be carefully taken step by step to the upper chakras. A yogi can attain ultimate bliss, when he takes "kundalini" to the top "Crown" chakra, the seat of Shiva and Shakti.

Someone can ask, Is this true?

Let me narrate an incident. Sir John George Woodroffe, a judge of the Calcutta High court, once tested a Yogi to see if he indeed had supernatural powers. He locked him up in a room and asked him to tell him what was happening at that moment in the judge's family home in England. The yogi emerged from the room and told the judge exactly what he wanted. Much later, the judge had a letter from his daughter, which said a yogi had visited the judge's home in England, and she had told the yogi about what was happening in England. The judge came to believe in Hindu tantric traditions and wrote a book on Kundalini yoga titled 'The Serpent Power – The Secrets of Tantric and Shaktic Yoga.' He lived barely 100 years ago and died in 1936.

What is a chakra? Chakra means "wheel" and it refers to the key energy points in our body. They are like spinning disks of energy. They should stay aligned, as they correspond to bundles of nerves, major body organs, and areas that impact our emotional and physical well-being.

Lalithā Sahasranāmam describes Ambāl in Nāmas connected with the seven key chakras, each of which has a presiding Yogini. Today, we will cover many verses that talk about the Chakras.

Let us proceed to verse 106.

मूलाधाराम्बुजारूढा पञ्चवक्त्राऽस्थिसंस्थिता।
अङ्कुशादिप्रहरणा वरदादिनिषेविता॥१०६॥

mūlā dhārāmbujārūḍhā, pañchavaktrā,'sthisaṃsthitā।

aṅkuśādi praharaṇā, varadādi niṣēvitā ॥ 106 ॥

514. mūlā dhārāmbujārūḍhā

Ascending the Mulādhāra lotus. Ambuja is lotus.

The Mulādhāra means "root support." It is the bottom most chakra of the Chakra system. It has a presiding deity called Sākini. Chakras are allegorically represented as lotuses, having a different number of petals.

Bhāskararāya explains: The Yogini called Sākini resides in the four-petalled Mulādhāra lotus. Her meditation is: "We meditate upon Sākini who resides in the four-petalled Mulādhāra lotus, five-faced, three-eyed, smoke-colored, presiding over the bones, bearing in her hands the elephant-hook, lotus, book, and Jnanamudra (a gesture), attended by gentle Varada and other deities, fond of eating mudgabeans, intoxicated with mead." Let us see the meaning of each word in this shlokam.

515. pañchavaktrā- This devata has five faces -representing the four directions and the sky.

516. Asthisaṃsthitā

Presiding over bones. Ambāl exists in every part of the body as is believed in our dharma. Someone can ask, how can

   The Glory of Lalithā Sahasranāmam

she be present in bones. Look at it scientifically. What is the immune system? Everybody has their own immune system to resist diseases. What are antibodies and who created them? Science tells us that we are born with it. Obviously, this is a part of Mother's creation.

517. aṅkuśādi praharaṇā

Armed with angusam-the hook that controls an elephant, and other implements. Elephant is a huge animal. Yet it is controlled by a small bull-hook called Angusam. The elephant must have respect for its handler; and to be blunt, this quality begins with fear: fear of punishment! Like the elephant handler, *'Yanai Pāhan'* as he is called in Tamil, Ambāl is armed with an angusam to control our elephant like powerful mind that tends to run wild. The elephant represents the power of human drive and the libido.

518. varadādi niṣēvitā

Attended by Varada and others.

After the letters य(ya) र(ra) ल(la) comes व(va) followed by the letters श(sha) ष(sha) स(sa). Ambāl is surrounded by four shaktis; Varada who fulfills our desires, Sridevi, who is the shakti who provides wealth, Shanda is the third deity, and Sarasvati, the fourth one who provides knowledge. Thus, there are four Shaktis from व(va) Varada to स(sa) Sarasvati. Ambāl is attended by these four Shaktis.

मुद्गौदनासक्तचित्ता साकिन्यम्बास्वरूपिणी।

आज्ञाचक्राब्जनिलया शुक्लवर्णा षडाननI ॥ १०७ ॥

mudgaudanāsakta chittā, sākinyambāsvarūpiṇī।

ājñā chakrābjanilayā, śuklavarṇā, ṣaḍānanā ॥ 107 ॥

519. mudgaudanāsakta chittā

Fond of food mixed with mudga-beans or 'Mung' as it is commonly called in Hindi. Food and mood are closely related. Research linking the two is growing at a rapid rate. Food can contribute not only to physical well-being but also to management of mental health conditions, including depression and anxiety disorders. If Ambāl likes a type of food, there is certainly some great value in it. Let us see how mung can help as a food. Mung is a legume plant and mung beans are recognized for their high nutritive value. It is composed of about 20%-50% protein of total dry weight. They have lower calories compared to other cereals, which makes it more attractive to obese and diabetic individuals. Mung or moong dal is the split version of the whole mung bean.

520. sākinyambāsvarūpiṇī- Assuming the form of Sākini. She is another Yogini.

521. ājñā chakrābjanilayā

Residing over the Ajna chakra lotus. The presiding yogini for this chakra is called Hākini.

This Gate is the sixth chakra on the path of Kundalini between and above the eyebrows (ajnya), referred to as the "third eye." The literal meaning of "Ajna" is to command. The location of this chakra is behind the forehead, which is the seat of consciousness. We can say that this chakra is of extreme importance just as Shiva's third eye. It is the point where two Nadis, Ida and Pingala (which were separate all along) merge with the central Sushumna. The duality represented by two petals ends and pure consciousness with the supreme being is established.

Bhāskararāya comments: There is a two-petalled lotus in the Ajna centre between the eyebrows; there resides the Yogini, called Hākini.

The meditation on her is: "We meditate upon Hākini, residing between the eyebrows, in the two-petalled Bindu lotus, white, holding the Jnanamudra, Damaru (drum), lotus, Rudrakhsa bead, and skull, residing in the marrow, six-faced, three-eyed, attended by Hamsavati and other Shaktis, fond of saffron-flavoured food, doing good to all."

In Yoga, there is a mudra called Hākini Mudra. It is one of the hasta mudra or hand gestures performed for stimulating various parts of the mind and enhance our emotional and mental quotient inside our brain.

This mudra is believed to significantly remove depression and enhance power over the mind.

522. śuklavarṇā- White faced. White signifies purity. Both Shiva and Saraswathi are white in color.

523. ṣhaḍānanā- Shad is six. Anana is face (like you have in Gajanana). Hākini is a deity having six faces.

मज्जासंस्था हंसवतीमुख्यशक्तिसमन्विता।

हरिद्रान्नैकरसिका हाकिनीरूपधारिणी॥१०८॥

majjāsamsthā, hamsavatī mukhyaśakti samanvitā।

haridrānnaika rasikā, hākinī rūpadhāriṇī॥108॥

524. majjāsaṃstha- Presiding over the marrow. What is marrow? It is a soft fatty substance in the cavities of bones.

Blood cells are produced here. It is a source of strength and vitality.

525. haṃsavatī mukhyaśakti samanvitā- Attended by Hamsavati and other mukya (important) Shaktis. Hākini is on a two-petaled lotus for which the akshara devathas are Hamsavati and Khsamavati representing the letters ह*(ha) and* Khṣa (क्ष).

526. haridrānnaika rasikā

Fond of Haridrānna (हरिद्रान्न) refers to rice cooked with turmeric. Haridra or turmeric is a natural and powerful antibiotic from nature with a strong antibacterial, anti-inflammatory, antioxidant and anti-allergic effect. We use it in our food preparations. Bhāskararāya interprets it as saffron flavored food.

527. hākinī rūpadhāriṇī

Assuming the form of Hākini.

We learnt earlier about Dākini, Rākini, Lākini, Kākani, Sākini, the devathas of the various chakras. Now we are learning about Hākini.

Hākini is the goddess of the third eye depicted as a two-petal lotus symbolizing two hemispheres of the brain. She is the deity who personifies the energy of the ajna (third eye) chakra and the name of the energy itself.

In Sanskrit, Hākini means "power" or "rule." Hākini is the goddess of the third eye, the chakra of intuition and mind.

Hākini Shakti is one form of Shakti, the divine feminine and consort of Lord Shiva who represents the creative energy and power of the universe. She is depicted with pale pink skin, four arms and six heads and sitting on a lotus flower. Three of her hands hold Shiva's drum, a skull and a mala (prayer beads). Her fourth hand is raised in a gesture of dispelling fear.

सहस्रदलपद्मस्था सर्ववर्णोपशोभिता।

सर्वायुधधरा शुक्लसंस्थिता सर्वतोमुखी॥ १०९॥

sahasradaḻa padmasthā, sarvavarṇōpa śōbhitā|

sarvāyudhadharā, śukla saṃsthitā, sarvatōmukhī||109||

528. sahasradaḻa padmasthā

Residing in the thousand-petalled lotus. The presiding deity here is a Yogini named Yākini.

After Ajna Chakra comes the Sahasrara Chakra which is the seventh and highest centre of the subtle body and is located at the crown of the head. When a person's sahasrara opens, he experiences Self-realization. One experiences heightened intuition, and profound tranquility. It is sheer bliss. The merging of Kundalini in the seventh chakra at the top of the brain (Sahasrara) is the abode of the awakened Shakti (divine energy.) This chakra has been described in the great mandala of the Sri Chakra in Shri Shankaracharya's Saundarya-Lahari.

Bhāskararāya comments: In the Brahmarandhra, within the thousand-petalled lotus, resides the Yogini named Yākini. The meditation for her is: "We meditate upon the beneficent Devi, Yākini, residing in the moon of the pericarp of the thousand-petalled lotus in the Brahmarandhra, armed with all kinds of weapons, facing on every side, attended by the host of the Shaktis of the letters from A to Khsa (fifty-one), all colored, fond of all kinds of food, and devoted to the supreme Shiva."

529. sarvavarṇōpa śōbhitā

Ambāl is Brilliant, shining with 'sarva varnam' -all colors.

When pure white light passes through a prism, it separates into different visible colors. We call it VIBGYOR. Colors are powerful forces in our lives. It has an impact on our Moods, Feelings, and Behaviors.

We feel good when we wear colorful clothes. We present flower bouquets to honor someone. In our tradition, we perform Puja with colorful flowers. We make garlands with flowers and are happy to see Ambāl decorated with flowers of different colors. That's why floral decorations are part of our culture.

Bhāskararāya adds: Sarva, all, Varna (the fifty-one) letters from A to Ksha, that is the fifty Shaktis from Amrita to Kshmavati;upa, in the petals. Counting these (fifty) backwards and forwards we obtain a hundred Shaktis; these each reside in ten petals. Upa means ten (according to the Vararuchi's rule pa one and u ciphor), i.e. each residing in ten petals. Hence some repeat in the Yogininyasa ten times each of those Shaktis to make up a thousand.

530. sarvāyudhadharā- Armed with all kinds of weapons.

531. śukla saṃsthitā- Residing in the Semen, the reproductive force.

532. sarvatōmukhī- Facing on every side.

सर्वौदनप्रीतचित्ता याकिन्यम्बास्वरूपिणी।

स्वाहा स्वधाऽमतिर्मेधा श्रुतिः स्मृतिरनुत्तमा॥११०॥

sarvaudana prītachittā, yākinyambā svarūpiṇī।

svāhā, svadhā, amati, rmēdhā, śrutiḥ, smṛti,

ranuttamā ॥ 110 ॥

                    The Glory of Lalithā Sahasranāmam

533. sarvaudana prītachittā- Fond of all kinds of cooked food.

534. yākinyambā svarūpiṇī- Assuming the form of the mother Yakini.

Thus, having described Devi under the forms of Yoginis, Lalithā Sahasranāmam proceeds to describe Her with other qualities.

535. svāhā

536. svadhā

Bhāskararāya explains: The words Svaha and Svadha are used in Homam when "Ahudis" oblations are offered to gods. The Kosha says, "The words Svāhā, Shrausat, Vausat, Vasat and Svadhā are used when the oblations are offered to Devas." Hence these two words indicate Devi herself.

The Markandeya Purana says, "There are seven words which are used in the Some. (sacrifice), in the oblation and in the cooking. By repeating (or uttering) your name (only), O Devi, the merit of repeating these names is obtained by Brahmavadins."

In another place (Devi Māhatmiyam): "By uttering your name all the host of gods, 0 Devi, is satisfied in all sacrifices, for you are Svaha and you are named Svadha, the word which gives satisfaction to the hosts of Pitrus." The Prapanchasara explains the meaning of these words thus: "Sva means heaven and also the Self, aka, the attainment... and Svaha is the Wife of fire."

According to the Taittreya S'ruti, "Your own (Sva) speech (aha) " means one's own speech. The Samaveda Bra. and the

Yiska Nirukta also explain 'Svaha' thus, "Su means well, Aha is speech, or Sva, Self, aha, to speak." Some others explain this, Su, good, aha, to be given as an oblation.

Or Sva one's own people, Aha to go. She recognizes the people as her own Self.

The Linga Purana says, "The wife of Shiva in the form of fire is said to be Svaha. The divine six-faced one (Skanda) is called by the wise the son." The same confirms the Vayu Purana also. According to the Padma Purana this is the presiding deity of the city of Maheshvara.

537. amati

Amati, is Avidya, or A little, mati is knowledge. she is in the form of the knowledge of modifications. Durgacharya in his commentary (on Shukla Yajus) explains the word amati, as the knowledge of the Self. Amati, as said before (No. 397 Moolaprakriti) refers to the first creation which was devoid of intelligence.

538. mēdhā- Intelligence. The next creation was accompanied by intelligence.

Or, Medha, individual intelligence. There is a term *"medhavi"* in Tamil that refers to someone who is considered very intelligent.

The Devi Māhatmiyam says:

या देवी सर्वभुतेषु बुद्धिरूपेण संस्थिता।

नमस्तस्यै नमस्तस्यै नमस्तस्यै नमो नमः॥८॥

Yaa Devii Sarva-Bhutessu Buddhi-Ruupenna Samsthitaa|

Namas-Tasyai Namas-Tasyai Namas-Tasyai Namo Namah||8||

To that Devi Who in All Beings is Abiding in the Form of Intelligence, we offer repeated namskarams. Devi resides in all beings in the form of intelligence.

According to the Padma Purana the deity is called Medha in Kashmir.

539.śrutiḥ

540.smṛti

Shruti refers to the Vedas. They were heard by the Rishis and hence called Shruti which means what was heard. The Vedas are referred to as Veda Mātha. Smrtis refers to what was remembered and told (like Manusmriti). Both Shruti and Smriti are ancient scriptures of Ambāl's forms.

Bhāskararāya adds:

Shruti and Smrti, the knowledge in the form of hearing and recollection.

The Vayu Purana says, "As Devi recollects all actions, present, past, and future, she is called Smrti."

The Kurma Purana says, "Rik, Yajus, Sama, and Atharvana are the inherent forms of Brahman, thus is the eternal Shakti."

541. anuttamā- The best. Because there is none superior to Ambāl.

Bhāskararāya quotes: The Shruti and Smrti (Svetaranya Upanishad, 6:8, Bhagavad Gita 11:43), "Nothing is to be found equal or superior to him."

पितासि लोकस्य चराचरस्य

त्वमस्य पूज्यश्च गुरुर्गरीयान्।

न त्वत्समो ऽस्त्यभ्यधिक: कुतोऽन्यो

लोकत्रयेऽप्यप्रतिमप्रभाव॥43॥

pitāsi lokasya charācharasya

tvam asya pūjyaśh cha gurur garīyān

na tvat-samo 'sty abhyadhikaḥ kuto 'nyo

loka-traye 'py apratima-prabhāva

You are the father of the entire universe, of all moving and non-moving beings. You are the most deserving of worship and the Supreme Spiritual Master. When there is no equal to You in all the three worlds, then who can possibly be greater than You, O Possessor of incomparable power?

The Devi Bhagavadam Purana (Book III): "People never say of a man devoid of strength 'he is deprived of Rudra or of Vishnu,' but say 'deprived of Shakti' (energy)."

पुण्यकीर्तिः पुण्यलभ्या पुण्यश्रवणकीर्तना।

पुलोमजार्चिता बन्धमोचनी बर्बरालका॥१११॥

puṇyakīrtiḥ, puṇyalabhyā, puṇyaśravaṇa kīrtanā।

pulōmajārchitā, bandhamōchanī, barbarālakā॥111॥

542. puṇyakīrtih- Famed for righteousness. Whose fame sanctifies.

543. puṇyalabhyā

Attained through righteousness. Punya, good actions performed. The Devi Bhagavada Puranam says, "Only those ever-righteous ascetics, who are devoted to wisdom, see; but the men of desire see not the holy and beneficent Devi."

544. puṇyaśravaṇa kīrtanā- Hearing of and praising Devi are holy.

545. pulōmajārchitā

Worshipped by Indra's wife.

Bhāskararāya adds a story. This story occurs in the Deva Bhagavada Purana (Book VI): When Nahusa was ruling heaven, the wife of Indra worshipped Devi that Indra might be restored. "Thus addressed, the wife of Indra with cheerful mind received the powerful mantra of Devi, from the teacher (Brhaspati) and worshipped earnestly Tripurasundari, by oblations of food, flowers, etc.."

546. bandhamōchani

Remover of bonds.

Bandha, bonds of ignorance or prison. Bhāskararāya says:

In the Harivamsa, Aniruddha says, "O Samkari, you are praised by these and other names by me; by thy grace, let me be soon freed from prison. 0 large-eyed one, behold, I take refuge in thy feet. You are to liberate me from every bond... Durga, the powerful one, thus praised, set free the brave Aniruddha, who was confined in the town of Bana."

The Devi Bhagavada Purana (Book VI) says, "Once a princess named Ekavali was imprisoned by a Daitya called Kalaketu and was freed by Devi who Was worshipped by Yashovati, the friend of the princess."

547. barbarālakā: Devi with wavy hair. Curly hair.

विमर्शरूपिणी विद्या वियदादिजगत्प्रसू: ।

सर्वव्याधिप्रशमनी सर्वमृत्युनिवारिणी ॥ ११२ ॥

vimarśarūpiṇī, vidyā, viyadādi jagatprasūḥ ।

sarvavyādhi praśamanī, sarvamṛtyu nivāriṇī ॥ 112 ॥

548. vimarśarūpiṇī

In the Vimarsa form. Bhāskararāya comments:

Vimarsa is the (first) inherent vibration of Parabrahman who is in the Prakasa aspect. The Saubhagya Sudhodaya says, "In that (Brahman) there is an inherent Shakti in the form of vibration called Vimarsa. That Shakti produces the animate and inanimate universe, the same also destroys it."

Or Vimarsa means significant words like a speech. (*Vimarsanam* in Tamil)

The Matrkaviveka says, "Without Vimarsa (speech) how is thought manifested? Without thought to be spoken of, how can there be speech? Therefore, thought is required for the existence of speech, and thought, even when there is self-consciousness (for its own existence) required speech."

549. vidya

Because she is the Vidya (knowledge) which confers salvation.

The Devi Māhatmiyam says, "The holy supreme Devi is Vidya."

The Gaudapada Sutra says, "She herself is Vidya." She refers to Devi as described in the previous Sutra as "in the form of absolute consciousness."

Or Vidya, a certain kind of Kalā, which is in the light-(Tejas) and its nature is described in the Shaiva Tantras. "By the discrimination of the products of Maya, one recognizes the state of Wisdom, that supreme Kalā is known as Vidya consisting of knowledge and action."

550. viyadādi jagatprasūḥ: The mother of the universe (consisting) of ether, etc.

The Shruti (Taitriya Upanishad., II, 2) says, " Ether arose from Atman."

    The Glory of Lalithā Sahasranāmam

551. sarvavyādhi praśamanī: Alleviating all diseases.

552. sarvamṛtyu nivāriṇī: Dispelling all death.

Mrtyu, untimely death, fatal disease, etc. The Shrutis (Svetarnya Upanishad, 4-15, Kathopanishad, 3-15) say: "Knowing Him thus, he tears up the nooses of death"; "He is freed from the power of death."

अग्रगण्याऽचिन्त्यरूपा कलिकल्मषनाशिनी।

कात्यायनी कालहन्त्री कमलाक्षनिषेविता॥११३॥

agragaṇyā,'chintyarūpā, kalikalmaṣa nāśinī।

kātyāyinī, kālahantrī, kamalākṣa niṣēvitā॥113॥

553. agragaṇyā

She is considered the first and foremost.

As she is the root cause of the whole universe, she is the first to be enumerated.

Or agra means foremost point, tip, or top. Ganyā means belonging to a multitude or class or troop. She is the first commander of these.

554. Achintyarūpā- Of unthinkable form. Her nature is unthinkable.

555. kalikalmaṣa nāśinī

Destroyer of sin in Kaliyuga.

She destroys the sin which necessarily predominates in the Kali Yuga and which cannot be destroyed by others.

Bhāskararāya adds:

The Kurma Purana says, "Water is able to quench the fire, the presence of the sun to dispel darkness, and the repetition of the names of Devi to destroy the multitude of sins in the Kali age."

The Brahmānda Purana: "The remembrance of the feet of Supreme Shakti is said to be the highest expiation for sins consciously or unconsciously committed.

556. kātyāyinī

The daughter of a Rishi named Kata. This is the name of the deity in the collective form of the brightness (Tejas) of all the Devas.

The Vamana Purana says,

"That brightness, which is the best, and the greatest, is known in the world by the name of Katyayani. Under that name she shines and is celebrated in the world." In Tamil Nadu, the village folks call Her as *Kātayi-the one who protects*. Saraswathi is called *Petchayi-the one who speaks*.

557. kālahantrī: The destroyer of time.

Kaala refers to death. The Shruti (Svetaranya Upanishad 6-2) says, "Omniscient, time of time, possessed of all qualities, all-knowing."

558. kamalākṣa niṣēvitā: Worshipped by Kamalāksa.

Chapter 11

Vibhuti Vistaram

Starting from Nāma 542 Punyakirti (Shlokam 111), we enter a long part called *Vibhuti Vistaram and Margabhedam*. It bears a lot of similarity with what is said from the 10th chapter of Vibhuti Yoga and leading up to Chapter 18 of Moksha Sanyas Yoga in Bhagavad Geetha.

Ambāl is called **Sri Chakraraja Simhasaneswari**. Chakrararja includes all the nine Chakras beginning from the Bindu. The path of yoga Sadhana constituting various chakras namely **Mulādhāra, Svādhishthana, Manipura, Anāhata, Vishuddhi, Ajna, Sahasrara** is extensively described in Lalithā Sahasranāmam. Because the thousand names of Ambāl contain the secret of Chakra, and of Mantra, Lalithā Sahasranāmam is well-known as the thousand secret names (Rahasya-Nama-Sahasra). As I said before, each name is a mantra.

Bhāskararāya quotes the Devi-Bhagavada Purana that says, "Devi has countless names, which have been composed by Brahma and other Devatas according to her different qualities and activities."

What more do we want? Brahman itself is Shabda (sound). Hence some names are here used, to correspond with the different states of human beings (Jivas), such as, 'She is the Jiva in the waking "state' (Visvarupa No. 256); and Taijasa (No. 259), (11.6., Devi is the Jiva of the dreaming state). Some names signify the attributes of Jiva, such as 'Mālini ' (Wearing garlands, No. 455). Some signify immovable things, such as Māhi (earth, No. 718); some are attributes of the qualified Brahman, such as Mukunda (one of. the aspects of Vishnu, (N0. 338). Some indicate different aspects of Devi, such as Rama. etc., (No. 313). Some denote the actions performed by her in various incarnations, (Avataras such as fighting with Bhandasura), Some denote the unconditioned Brahman, such as Paramjyotis (supreme light, No. 806). In this way many other meanings of the names are to be made out.

Bhāskararāya asks questions and answers: Here an objector might say: This collection consisting of a thousand names is useless, for all words (Shabdas) in one way or another denote Brahman.

The answer is, amongst all other names by which, the great virtuous old men who were the devotees of Devi—praised Her and fulfilled their desired objects, these names, Devi declared to be endowed with power, and capable of conferring boons; and the devotees themselves blessed the names; Such names alone are collected and arranged into a thousand. Though the same is common to all collections of thousands, yet this one is superior to the rest and has been accepted by many great men, because by it quickly gets the reward which cannot be gained using other collections of thousand names, and for many other reasons. According to the objects in view, the powers are different.

The Glory of Lalithā Sahasranāmam

By repeating such names, the corresponding results are to be obtained. Whatever power belongs to a name, it is effective in that sphere.

Bhāskararāya says:

"Anna Kamo Annadaaya Naama ithi

Baddo Bandhamochinyai Naama ithi Japet"

From this it follows: One who desires food should repeat the name "Annada" (giver of food, No. 669); he who desires wealth, the name "Vasudha "giver of wealth, No. 670); he who is afraid, "Bhayapaha "(the remover of fears, No. 121) and he who is imprisoned, "Bandhamochani" (the liberator from bondage, No. 546).

The Vayu Purana thus gives the common effect of all names: "One should repeat Devi's names in the forest, in water, on dry land, in places where fear arises from tigers, wild animals, or thieves, and in all diseases. That the name Devi should be continually repeated When walking, sleeping, standing and eating; thus doing, he liberates himself from bondage."

The Vaamakesvara tantra says, "If one aspirant thinks in his mind one single name of hers, in that moment he knows the chakra of the mother, 0 beloved one." This indicates that mere mental repetition of her names confers on one the boons even up to the knowledge of her Chakra.

Bhāskararāya questions again. An objector might say: In the Phalashruti chapter of a work it is invariably said that one will obtain whatever he desires by reading the book in question.

Then, what is the use of saying that one will be relieved if he repeats a certain name like 'O remover of all diseases. "The answer is that though each name produces a result corresponding to its specific power, yet it may also produce a general result.' For, Devi says, "One should always repeat these thousand names to please me, and by my grace one will undoubtedly obtain all his desires."

Thus, according to the Scriptures any of the names of Devi may be repeated, yet if anyone desires a particular object to be fulfilled, he must invoke the goddess by the corresponding name. For example:

For Marriage: *"Kamesa bhadda mangalya soothra shobitha khandhara"*

For Good Health/Health Related problems: *"Sarva vyaadhi prasamani sarva mruthyunivarini"* In conclusion, if any worshipper invokes Devi by any name such as "Annada," etc., he will soon obtain the corresponding result. In mantra form, each name is said individually, preceded by "Aum" and followed by "Namah".

When chanted in mantra form, the ending of each nāma is generally changed to "A" or "Yai". Example: Om Sri Mhatre Namaha, Om Sri Lalithāmbikyai Namaha. Mantra form is commonly used to recite Lalithā Sahasranāmam during archana.

We will now start from Shlokam 114 and Nāma 559.

ताम्बूलपूरितमुखी दाडिमीकुसुमप्रभा।

मृगाक्षी मोहिनी मुख्या मृडानी मित्ररूपिणी॥११४॥

tāmbūla pūrita mukhī, dāḍimī kusumaprabhā।

mṛgākṣī, mōhinī, mukhyā, mṛdānī, mitrarūpiṇī॥114॥

          The Glory of Lalithā Sahasranāmam

559. tāmbūla pūrita mukhī

Ambāl is having Her mouth full of Tāmbulam, called betel in English or "paan" as it is known in Hindi. Let me explain the importance of Tāmbulam in the context of our most ancient tradition.

Tāmbulam or Betel leaves with betel nut or supari (called *Vettilai Paaku* in Tamil, and *Paan Supari* in Hindi) are offered as a mark of respect and at auspicious events in traditional Indian culture.

According to Hindu scriptures, this leaf was obtained by the gods during the churning of ocean for Amrutam -the elixir for immortality. Thus, the leaf is used in every puja ritual and given to guests after a meal at events like weddings. In India, many restaurants offer 'Paan.' In Pujas, after Naivedyam, we offer Tāmbulam to the deity and say,

"Pugiphala Samaa yuktam Nagavalli Dalair UtamKarpoora Choorna Samyuktam Tamboolam Parigruhyataam"

'Pugiphala' is a Sanskrit word for 'betel nut' or Supari. 'Nagavalli dalam' is the Sanskrit word for tender betel leaves. In addition to its importance in rituals, betel leaves has very good medicinal properties too. It's called Tāmbula or Nagavalli (in Sanskrit), Paan (Hindi), vetrilai (Tamil), vettila (Malayalam) or Tamalapaku (Telugu). In Tamil, it is called

'Vetrilai' meaning 'just leaf' as the plant does not have any flowers. The leaf is also used as a remedy against various diseases.

Verse 10, Naama 26 also says कर्पूरवीटिकामोध-समाकर्षि-दिगन्तरा *'Karpura veetikamoda-smakarshi-digantara.* (26). Karpūravītikā is a combination of fragrant ingredients, used to chew along with the betel leaves. Ambāl attracts devotees with the fragrance of Tāmbulam. Legends indicate that Devi has blessed her devotees with betel juice.

Many of you may have heard about the famous poet Kalidas. It is believed that he got his wisdom by kali writing on his tongue with the juice of Her betel leaves. He is then said to have become the most brilliant poet at the court of the king Vikramaditya of Ujjain. Shyamala Dandakam is supposed to be the first prayer. Dandakam is poetry where some of the lines have more than 26 syllables. It very much resembles prose. This entire Dandakam is like a single sentence from start to the end. *"Manika Veenam Upalalayanthim."* In this, Kalidasa describes Ambāl as Tāmbula Purita Mukhi.

सर्वविश्वात्मिके सर्वसिद्ध्यात्मिके कालिके.

मुग्ध मन्दस्मितोदारवक्त्र स्फुरत् पूग ताम्बूल कर्पूर खण्डोत्करे

ज्ञानमुद्राकरे सर्वसम्पत्करे पद्मभास्वत्करे श्रीकरे!

Sarva Vishwathmikey Sarva Siddhyathmikey Kalikey

Mugdha Mandhasmithodhara Vakthra-Spurath Puga Tāmbula Karpoora Khandothkarey

Gnana Mudrakarey Sarva Sampathkarey

Padmabhasvathkarey Shrikarey

Goddess Sri Kali who is the soul of the Universe and all psychic powers. (Victory to the Divine Mother) whose face is lighted up by a beautiful smile, whose mouth is fragrant with betel leaf areca nut and camphor pieces, who sports the gnana mudra on her hand, who showers riches (on her devotees) and whose hands are beautiful and soft like the lotus.

So also, it is believed that the Tamil Poet Kalamegam too got his poetic skills through Ambāl's betel leaves juice.

Soundarya Lahiri verse 65 mentions Devas receiving Devi's partially chewed Tamboolam as prasadam.

रणे जित्वा दैत्यान पहृत शिरस्त्रैः कवचिभिः
निवृत्तै श्चण्डांश त्रिपुरहर निर्माल्यविमुखैः।
विशाखेन्द्रोपेन्द्रैः शशिविशद कर्पूरशकलाः
विलीयन्ते मातस्तव वदनताम्बूलकबलाः॥

rane jitvā daityāna pahṛta śirastraiḥ kavacibhiḥ
nivṛttai ścaṇḍāṁśa tripurahara nirmālyavimukhaiḥ|
viśākhendropendraiḥ śaśiviśada karpūraśakalāḥ
vilīyante mātastava vadanatāmbūlakabalāḥ||

rane jitvā daityā - victorious in war with demons; apahṛta śirastraiḥ - having taken their head gears; kavacibhiḥ - remaining only with armours on their chests; nivṛttaiḥ - returning (from wars); caṇḍa aṁśa – that portion meant for Caṇḍikeśvara; tripura hara nirmālya vimukhaiḥ - ignoring the remains of Śiva's food (which is meant for Caṇḍikeśvara); viśākha indra upendraiḥ - Skanda (son of Śiva), Indra, Viṣṇu; śaśi viśada karpūra śakalāḥ - camphor, (edible camphor) as pure white as moon; vilīyante – melting away (due to proper chewing); mātaḥ - O! Divine Mother! tava – Yours; vadana tāmbūla kabalāḥ - mouth full of betel leaves.

In this sixty fifth sloka of Soundarya Lahari, Adi Sankara speaks of the grace of Ambāl to Devas who defeated the asuras. Says Sankara, "O Mother! After victory over the asuras, the Devas removed the helmets and kavachas, prostrated before You! They ignored "Siva nirmalya" -- the remnants of puja and worship (that was before Chandikeswara!)

On the other hand, Skanda, Vishnu and Devendra have taken the remnants of your half chewed tāmbula with white camphor bits! That is the reward that Devi grants to those that have won Her grace!" The half chewed Tāmbula is the prasadam for the Devas!

So, that's the greatness of Ambāl's *Tāmbula Purita Mukhi!*

560. dāḍimī kusumaprabhā

dāḍimī refers to pomegranate; *Anar* in Hindi, *Mathulai* in Tamil. Kusumaprabha (कुसुमपुरभ) refers to "that which shines like a flower." Flower colors range from brilliant red to orange. Ambāl has the hue of pomegranate flower. The Vedas consider the pomegranate, with its inner treasure of edible seeds, a symbol for fertility and prosperity. It is revered for its healthful qualities.

561. mṛgākṣi- Mrga refers to a fawn. Akshi means eyes. A fawn is a young deer with beautiful eyes. Ambāl is described here as Fawn-eyed.

562. mōhinī

Enchanting Devi. Bhāskararāya quotes the Laghu Naradiya Purana that describes, "Because O beautiful one, this whole universe is enchanted with you, your name shall be the enchanting one, which is derived from its own qualities."

The story of Mohini avatara is well-known. At the time of 'Samudra Manthan,' the churning of the ocean, Vishnu assumed the form of Mohini. Bhāskararāya quotes the Brahmānda Purana that says: "As the result of Brahma's meditation, there first appeared to him, the Shakti who is called Prakrti, who fulfils the desires of the gods.

Her second appearance causing enchantment of all, transcending mind and speech, was during the churning (of the ocean) for nectar, seeing which even Lord Shiva was enchanted... The form obtained as the result of meditation, unequalled, marvelous, meditating with one mind on that Mohini form you will be emancipated."

563.mukhyā- The first. Or the most important. Bhāskararāya cites Taittreya Upanishad 3-10-6 which declares *Aham asmi prathamaja ritasya* - I am more ancient than the effulgent Gods. For I am the first – born of truth."

564. mṛḍānī

The Wife of Mrda. Mṛḍa (मृड) is another name for Shiva. The root mṛḍ means to be pleased or delighted, Mrda, means the giver of happiness, i.e., Paramashiva. Shiva is pleased instantly and hence called *Asuthoshi.* Bengalis use the word Asutosh as first name.

565. mitrarūpiṇī

The friend. Or Mitra – The sun. Mitra is an Indian family name and surname found mostly amongst Bengali Hindus. Mitra refers to the Sun. It is repeated many times in our daily

Sandhyavandhanam ritual. It comes in the Surya Upasthanam (Pratahkala) paying a tribute to Sun God:

ॐ मित्रस्य' चर्षणी धृत:, श्रवो' देवस्य' सान सिं| सत्यं चित्रश्र' वस्तमं| मित्रो जनान्' यातयति प्रजानन्, मित्रो दा'धार पृथिवी मुतद्यां,| मित्रः कृष्टी रनि'मिषाऽभि च'ष्टे, सत्याय' हव्यं घृतव'द्विधेम| प्रसमित्र मर्तो 'अस्तु प्रय'स्वा न्यस्त' आदित्य शिक्ष'ति व्रतेन'| न ह'न्यते न जी'यते त्वोतोनैनम अगंहो' अश्नोत्यन्तितो न दूरात्|

Mitrasya charshani dhritah sravo devasya saanasim /

Satyam Chitrasravastamam // Mitro janam yaatayati prajaanan Mitro daadhaara Prithivee mutadyaam /

Mitrah krishteeranimishaabhichashte Satyaaya havyam ghritavadvidhema//

Pra Sa Mitra Marto Astu Payaswaan Yasta Aditya Sikshati Vratena /

Na Hanyate Na Jeeyate Toto Nainam agumho Asnotyantito Na Dooraat//

In this prayer, we worship Surya to get blessings from that Supreme God for our longevity and happiness. In the same way, we worship Ambāl as *Mitraupini* or Universal friend to receive her blessings.

नित्यतृप्ता भक्तनिधिर्नियन्त्री निखिलेश्वरी।

मैत्र्यादिवासनालभ्या महाप्रलयसाक्षिणी॥११५॥

nityatṛptā, bhaktanidhi, rniyantrī, nikhilēśvarī|

maitryādi vāsanālabhyā, mahāpralaya sākṣiṇī||115||

566. nityatṛptā

Eternally pleased. Always contented.

It is an inner state of peace and contentment. It is a state of joy and satisfaction, regardless of pleasure, pain, gain, loss, prosperity or poorness. In Yoga, it is practiced as a niyama and with a positive mind.

567. bhaktanidhi- Ambāl is a treasure of the devotees.

568. niyantrī- Guide. Ambāl is the guide of the universe.

569. nikhilēśvarī- Ruler of all. Some women have name as Nikila. Akilam means universe. She is the supreme Goddess of the universe.

570. maitryādi vāsanālabhyā

Ambāl has a name 'Maitri.' She is attained by those with an intense desire for friendship or by the idea of cheerfulness. Bhāskararāya says: There are four ideas or qualities: friendship, compassion, complacency and indifference; these apply respectively to the happy, the miserable, the virtuous, and the sinful. Devi helps them all in different ways.

571. mahāpralaya sākṣiṇī

Witness to mahapralaya - the great dissolution.

In the Lalithā Sahasranāma sthotra, Goddess Sakthi is mentioned as *Maha Thandava sākshini and Maha Pralaya sākshini.* She is the witness to Lord shiva's Maha Thandavam (the great dance) and also, She is the witness to Maha Pralayam (the great dissolution).

In the end of everything, only the consciousness (Lord Shiva), and energy (Goddess Sakthi) remain. Lord Shiva performs the great dance, at the end of all the worlds, Maha Thandavam, as it is described. Ambāl is a witness to it. The end of everything, that is the end of all worlds is at the occurrence of the great deluge. Ambāl is also a witness to this great deluge. After the great deluge, the Universe is again created.

Goddess Sakthi is also a witness to this Creation. She is also Viswa Sākshini. Even in Christianity, the story of Noah's Ark and the Great Flood is most famous from the Bible.

Bhāskararāya adds: As Brahma, Vishnu, and others perish at that time of the dance of Shiva at the great dissolution, Ambāl alone was the witness (of that dance). It is said, "Bearing the *Paasa Angusha*, the noose and the elephant hook, the bow of sugar-cane, and the arrow of flowers, Ambāl's form alone remains victorious, witnessing the dance of the divine Para bhairava, bearing the axe at the time of dissolution of the universe."

परा शक्तिः परा निष्ठा प्रज्ञानघनरूपिणी।

माध्वीपानालसा मत्ता मातृकावर्णरूपिणी॥११६॥

parāśaktiḥ, parāniṣṭhā, prajñāna ghanarūpiṇī।

mādhvīpānālasā, mattā, mātṛkā varṇa rūpiṇī॥116॥

572. parāśaktiḥ

The Supreme energy. Para is superlative. like in Parameswaran. Bhāskararāya offers different interpretations to this term.

In the body the tenth elementary substance (Dhātu)is called Para Shakti. The Kaamika Agama says, "Skin, blood, flesh, fat and bone, these (five) substances are derived from

                    The Glory of Lalithā Sahasranāmam

Devi; marrow, semen, breath, vitality (Jiva), these (four) substances are derived from Shiva. Thus, this body consists of nine substances derived from nine origins. The tenth substance alone is called Parā-Shakti."

Or the Shruti (Svetaranya Upanishad 6-8) says, "His supreme Shakti is known in different forms."

The Linga Purana: "Whatever energy is attributed to any substance that is Devi, the ruler of all energized substance is the great Shiva. Those substances which possess energy are the manifestations of Shiva. The wise recognize the energies in substance to be Devi."

Or Parāmantra also is called Parāshakti.

573. parāniṣṭhā

Ambāl is the Supreme end. or Parā nistha: a certain kind of knowledge. This alone is the goal of all desires and all worlds.

There are different stages to reach this end. There is some philosophy behind this.

The senses dissolve in the mind. Mind dissolves in Intellect (Buddhi). Buddhi dissolves in Atman. Reaching this state and realizing the Atman is called Parānishta.

Bhāskararāya quotes a verse from the Bhagavad Gita (4-33) that says:

श्रेयान्द्रव्यमयाद्यज्ञा ज्ञानयज्ञः परन्तप|

shreyān dravya-mayād yajñāj jñāna-yajñaḥ parantapa

सर्वं कर्माखिलं पार्थ ज्ञाने परिसमाप्यते||

sarvaṁ karmākhilaṁ pārtha jñāne parisamāpyate

"O Partha, all kinds of actions end in knowledge." What kind of knowledge? That kind of knowledge is described in Suta Gita, 5-50 to 54: "Convinced by instruction derived from the scriptures and from teachers, and by reasoning in conformity with the scriptures, that he is himself the witness of all, his mind becomes fixed, knowing the whole which appears different from Self as his own Self, again fully convinced by his own experience that he himself is the pure, non-dual Brahman; merging that conviction in his own pure consciousness which is unchangeable and non-dual: knowing that even that merging is of the nature of thought (chitrupa), he should remain as the absolute. This ascetic is indeed the best of those who know Brahman; this is the highest end the result of scriptural teachings and of experience."

574. prajñāna ghanarūpiṇī

Ambāl is the personification of knowledge and consciousness. In other words, Concentrated knowledge. Pra, means superior, jnana, the eternal wisdom, ghana. concentrated meaning not contaminated by Avidya.

Some learned pandits are called "Ghanapaatis". This means that they are learned in the Vedas to the extent of chanting of the Vedas in the pattern called "Ghanam".

When we listen to a Ghanapaati reciting Vedas in Ghana form, we note that he repeats the syllables in various ways back and forth and in different patterns. This would be not only pleasant to the ears, creating a sense of happiness but, in a deeper zone, it generates a great feeling transporting the listener to new heights. The natural grandeur of the Veda mantras is augmented manifold, as it were. This chanting requires superior knowledge.

The Shruti (Brahadaranya Upanishad, 4-5-18): "Just as taste of a quantity of salt is neither inside nor outside but everywhere, this Self is neither within nor without but is full and concentrated knowledge."

575. mādhvīpānālasā- Madhvi is grape juice or wine. Weary of drinking wine

576. mattā- Cool, Intoxicated. *Matham* in Tamil.

577. mātṛkā varṇa rūpiṇī

Lalithā is also known as Matrika Devi, the Goddess of the Letters of the Alphabet called Aksharam. Ambāl holds Akshamala in her hand. She is in the form of Matruka letters. It is said that the matruka letters have colors.

In Sanskrit there are 36 consonants and 15 vowels. The combination of the 15 Vowels (the 15 Nityās) and the consonants (the 36 Tattvās) produces all sound, all mantra, all vibration, all word, and all music. Akshara (अक्षर) means a letter in Sanskrit. It has three syllables, a+ksha+ra. 'A' (अ) and 'Ksha' (क्ष) are the first and last letter of the Sanskrit alphabet. Ra (र) is the lord or Isvara or Shiva who supports them. Together they are known as Matrka Chakra (the wheel of matras) in Shaivism. Matrka Chakra is the wheel of creation or the force matrix of the cosmic ocean (the universe) which is filled with vibrations or waves of energy.

Akshara also means imperishable. It represents the sound (nada) form of Shiva as Isvara or Brahman (akshara brahma) who has Prakriti or Parāshakti as his dynamic force.

If you reverse the syllables in Akshara it becomes Raksha (ra+ksha). 'Ra' means Shiva. 'Ksha' means Shakti. Raksha means protecting or guarding.

As the upholder of the whole creation, Shiva along with Parashakti (ra+ksha) acts as the protecting and upholding (Raksha or ra+ksha) force of the universe. The same protective force is also hidden in the letters (aksharas) and sacred chants (mantras) which protects us from evil (rākshasas).

Each letter in the Sanskrit alphabet contains a shakti as its presiding deity. When it is uttered, the shakti manifests and travels through space (chidakasam) of Shiva to produce vibrations.

Bhāskararāya adds:

Matruka letters from A to Khsa, have varna colors, White, etc., Rupini, Devi is in the form of these. The Sanatkumara Samhita says, "Vowels beginning with A (16) are smoke-colored; Ka and others (to da, 13) are red.

Dha to pha (9) are yellowish; the five letters: Ba etc., are crimson; Sa etc., (5) are of the color of gold; Ha and the last (Khsa) are of the color of lightning."

Some Tantras differ in this: "The vowels (16), are the color of crystal Ka to Ma (25) are the color of coral, Ya and others (to ha, 9) are yellowish, and Ken. is crimson." Some say all the letters are white.

The Matrkaviveka says, "A is all divinity, red, controlling all things..."

Thus, to each letter a different color is given.

Or, the fifty-one letters (A to Ksa) are her form, 'Varna', the letters, Rupa, indicates her. Just as the Supreme Shiva is twofold as Shakti and Shiva, so this Matruka Devi herself shines in two. The vowels indicate one form of Shakti, the others (consonants) indicate Shiva. Thus the (Devi) of Vidya under the form of letters indicates Shiva.

महाकैलासनिलया मृणालमृदुदोर्लता।

महनीया दयामूर्तिर्महासाम्राज्यशालिनी॥ ११७॥

mahākailāsa nilayā, mṛṇāla mṛdudōrlatā।

mahanīyā, dayāmūrtī, rmahāsāmrājyaśālinī॥ 117॥

578. mahākailāsa nilayā- Ambāl is said to be residing in the great Kailāsa. Mahakailāsa is a place far beyond the present known Kailāsa mountain.

Or Kailāsa is the Sahasraara which is in the Brahmarandhra.

579. mṛṇāla mṛdudōrlatā

Mrnala refers to the slender stem of lotus. Some women have Mrinalini as their name. Mrudu is soft. Even in Tamil we say *'miridu'* for softness. Lata refers to creeper.

Ambāl has creeper-like arms that are soft as the lotus stem.

580. mahanīyā- Illustrious. Worthy of worship.

581. dayāmūrtī- Personification of mercy.

582. mahāsāmrājyaśālinī

Resplendent with wide dominion-Mahasamrajyam.

Lalithā Sahasranāmam begins with maharajhni.

आत्मविद्या महाविद्या श्रीविद्या कामसेविता।

श्रीषोडशाक्षरीविद्या त्रिकूटा कामकोटिका॥ ११८॥

ātmavidyā, mahāvidyā, śrīvidyā, kāmasēvitā l

śrīṣōḍaśākṣarī vidyā, trikūṭā, kāmakōṭikā ll 118 ll

We have many names ending with Vidya. These indicate different sciences or knowledge. -Yagnavidya -yagams, Guhyavidya-secret mantras, Upasana vidya-Rituals, finally Atmavidya-realizing the self as brahman.

583. ātmavidyā- Spiritual knowledge. Atmavidya may mean eight-syllabled Mantra. (Atma—staksaramantra.)

584. mahāvidyā- Exalted science. Because it removes all sorrows.

585. śrīvidyā

Sacred science.

Bhāskararāya says it could mean the Panchadasi mantra.

The Vishnu Purana says, "0 fair one, the sacrificial science, exalted science, secret science, and spiritual science, 0, Devi thou art all these, the bestower of salvation; also thou art Logic, Trayi, Vārtā, trade and justice."

The commentators on the above say: "The meaning of the 1st four namely Sacrificial science, exalted science, secret science and spiritual science are—Science of action, Devotion to deities, the Science of Mantras, and the Science of Brahman, Varta, architecture, medicine etc."

586. kāmasēvitā

Worshipped by Kāma

Kāma is also known as Kāmadeva and Madana, is the Hindu god of love. He is Manmata (Churner of Mind). He is also considered as the son of Lakshmi and Vishnu. Since he was burnt by Shiva, he is called Ananga-without body. We have covered his worship of Kamakshi earlier.

Bhāskararāya quotes from Aruneyi Upanishad:

Kāma, the bodiless one (God of love). "The bodiless son of Lakshmi, though without mind, has animation. He knew that jewel (Srividya). He, though without fingers, worshipped (folding his hands). Though without a neck, he adorned himself.

Though Without tongue, he tasted it. Without knowing that Rishi(seer) one should enter the city. When one enters, he should enter after performing secret rites. This is the vow of Manmatha." Without mind (Achetas), without eyes he saw the jewel.'

Since he saw it without eyes, he touched it without fingers, wore the necklace without a neck, tasted without tongue, he is the seer or Rishi. The external cakra (worship) can be entered (performed) by knowledge of him alone; since no ceremonial worship is necessary to enter the internal cakra, the Rishi need not be known. Secret rites, i.e., the knowledge of the essential equality of Shiva with Devi. The meaning is that worship performed without the knowledge of the essential equality of Shiva with Devi cannot be fully effective.

587. śrīṣōḍaśākṣarī vidya

The science of sixteen syllabled Mantra.

Bhāskararāya adds:

The Gaudapada-Sutra says, "This Mantra consists of twenty-eight syllables," yet there will be no contradiction, if we divide the Mantra into three divisions (add some syllables more between the divisions).

It is in fact a 28-letter mantra and Om is added in the beginning and Namah is added at the end. Without Om and Namah, it is called Shodasi and with Om and Namah it is called Mahashodasi. Though it has 28 letters it is called Shodasi or Shodasakshari meaning 16 letters. This is because though the lines 4, 5 & 6 have 5, 6 & 4 bijas, they are called 3 Kootas or combined bijas. The word Mantranam is used in the plural to show that these are composed of three groups (Kootas). Panchadasi has 15 letters of three kutas (Parts) first with 5, second with six and third, with 4 bijaaksharas.

The Normal form of shodasi is to add Srim bija at the end of Panchadasi.There are variations like mahasodasi, Guhya Sodasi, Sowbhagya Panchadasi and so on. You will find many variations with different Bijas as practiced by different guru paramparas.

Shodasi Mantra is known as Mantra-raj, the King of Mantras. Many believe that Shodasi worship grants the sadhaka both iham and param, i.e., Material and spiritual benefits.

Maha Shodashi Mantra महाषोडशी मन्त्र

1. Om – ॐ

2. śrīṁ – hrīṁ – klīṁ – aiṁ – sauḥ: श्रीं ह्रीं क्लीं ऐं सौः

3. om – hrīṁ – śrīṁ ॐ ह्रीं श्रीं (3 bījas)

4. ka – e – ī – la- hrīṁ क ए ई ल ह्रीं (5 bījas)

5. ha – sa – ka – ha – la – hrīṁ ह स क ह ल ह्रीं (6 bījas)

6. sa – ka – la – hrīṁ स क ल ह्रीं (4 bījas)

7. sauḥ – aiṁ – klīṁ – hrīṁ – śrīṁ सौः ऐं क्लीं ह्रीं श्रीं (5 bījas)

           The Glory of Lalithā Sahasranāmam

8.   Namah नमः

The second line of this mantra has five bijas or seeds. They are called śrī bīja, then māyā bīja, then kāma bīja, then vāgbhava bīja and finally parā bīja.

śrīṁ (श्रीं), which is known as śrī bīja or Lakṣmī bīja. Bīja śrīṁ can provide auspiciousness. It promotes a positive attitude and growth in the mind of the aspirant. This bīja is the root cause for faith, devotion, love and ultimate surrender unto Her.

Next to श्रीं is hrīṁ ह्रीं, which is known as māyā bīja. Hrīṁ ह्रीं is also known as Bhuvaneśvarī bīja. Bhuvana means the earth and Īśvarī means the ruler.

She is known as Bhuvaneśvarī because, She rules the earth.

Next to hrīṁ ह्रीं is klīṁ क्लीं, which is known as kāma bīja. This bīja draws divine energy towards the aspirant. It acts like a magnet. This bīja is known as a power of attraction.

Next to क्लीं is aiṁ ऐं, known as vāgbhava bīja. It is the bīja of Sarasvati, Goddess of Knowledge. This bīja is the cause for spiritual intellect (buddhi).

Next to ऐं is sauḥ सौः, known as parā bīja. This is also known as hṛdayabīja or amṛtabīja.This is known as nirvāṇa dīkṣā as it is meant to be initiation for final liberation, where nirvāṇa means emancipation.

588. trikūṭa

Three peaked. Bhāskararāya says: Tri, may mean Brahma, Vishnu Shiva, or the three states (Rajas, Tamas and Satva), the three seats (Jalandhara, etc.), the three worlds, three qualities, etc"; or Trikuta means Vagbhava and other Kutas.

589. kāmakōṭikā- The spirit of Kāma.

कटाक्षकिङ्करीभूतकमलाकोटिसेविता।

शिरःस्थिता चन्द्रनिभा भालस्थेन्द्रधनुःप्रभा॥११९॥

kaṭākṣakiṅkarī bhūta kamalā kōṭisēvitā|

śiraḥsthitā, chandranibhā, phālasthēndra dhanuḥprabhā||119||

590. kaṭākṣakiṅkarī bhūta kamalā kōṭisēvitā- This is one long nāma. meaning Ambāl is attended by millions of Lakshmis subdued by Her glances.

591. śiraḥsthitā- Siras means head, Sthitha means resides. Ambāl resides in the head which is the Brahmarandhra.

592. chandranibhā- Ambāl is like the Moon. There is a moon in the lower part of the Brahmarandhra, that is the third division of the Vidya. (Panchadasi).

593. phālasthēndra- Phala is the forehead.

She resides in the forehead in the form of the Bindu of the syllable Hrim.

594. Indradhanusprabhā- Indradhanus is the Rainbow. Ambāl is rain-bow hued.

हृदयस्था रविप्रख्या त्रिकोणान्तरदीपिका।

दाक्षायणी दैत्यहन्त्री दक्षयज्ञविनाशिनी॥१२०॥

hṛdayasthā, raviprakhyā, trikōṇāntara dīpikā|

dākṣāyaṇī, daityahantrī, dakṣayajña vināśinī||120||

595. hṛdayasthā

Ambāl resides in the heart. Because she is to be contemplated as in the heart.

Bhāskararāya adds:

Or Hrudaya, the seed of the universe, because it is the seed of all.

The Anuttar trimsika Sastra: "Just as a great Banyan tree is contained potentially in a tiny seed, so the animate and inanimate universe resides as a seed in the heart."

596. raviprakhyā- Resembling the Sun.

597. trikōṇāntara dīpikā

The light within the triangle.

Bhāskararāya explains:

There is a triangle in the pericarp of the Muladhara, in that there is a disc of fire, that is the first division (of the Panchadasi). The Tantraraja says, "In the centre of the eternally manifested Muladhara of all beings, there is a fire; similarly in the heart, there is the sun. In the head below the Brahmarandhra, there is the moon. Thus, the first, the ancient (Mantra) is threefold."

Or, when the sun circumambulates the eight-angled Meru Mountain, he illuminates only three angles (at a time); for when the sun is at zenith in the city of Indra, it is sunset and sunrise in the cities of Soma and of Yama respectively. The Vishnu Purana says, "When the sun (at midday) passes over either of the cities of the gods, his light extends to three cities and two intermediate points: when situated in an intermediate point, he illuminates two of the cities and three intermediate points."'

The meaning is that she illuminates at a time the three cities which are in the triangular form.

598. dākṣāyaṇī

Daughter of Daksha.

The name Daksha means "skilled one". Daksha was a Prajapati, a manasika putra of Brahma and a divine King. He had numerous daughters including the youngest one named Sati. The word Sati is derived from 'Sat' which means truth. So, Sati means truthful or virtuous. Legends describe Sati as the favorite child of Daksha. Since she was the daughter of Daksha, she was also called Dakshayani.

In Sanskrit, a son or daughter may have a name aligned to the father – like Rama was called Dasarathi, son of Dasaratha.

Sita was called Janaki, daughter of Janaka. Dakshayani loved Shiva and eventually married him much against her father's wishes. As Shiva's spouse, Dakshayani finds a place in Lalithā Sahasranāmam. She was also responsible for the destruction of a great Yajna that was performed by her father Daksha.

599. daityahantrī

Slayer of Daityas.

The word Daitya is derived from Diti who was also a daughter of Daksha. She was married to the sage Kashyapa and the children born to them were called Daityas. They were Asuras like Hiranyakashipu and Hiranyaksha who were born to them. Daityas is a common name applied to Asuras.

As Ambāl killed many asuras like Bhandasura, Mahishasura, Chanda and Munda, She is described as Daityahantri.

600. dakṣayajña vināśinī

Destroyer of the sacrifice of Daksha.

Bhāskararāya says: There are two Dakshas, one is known as Prajapati and the other is a human king, an incarnation of the former. Though Shiva destroyed both of their sacrifices, Devi was the instrument (of the destruction).

The Brahmānda and Vayu Puranas say, "After consulting the seven Rishis, Shiva cursed Daksha (saying), you will become a human king in the Chaakshusa cycle. You will be born of a Marisa caste woman, as the son of Prachetas, and as the grandson of Praachina barhis, and you will be known by the name of Daksha. Desiring to please Devi, I shall destroy your sacrifice."

Daksha-Yajna is narrated in various Hindu scriptures. It refers to a great yajna (sacrifice) organized by Daksha who did not intentionally invite his daughter Sati and son in law Shiva. Daksha never liked his son-in-law Shiva and consequently Daksha did not invite shiva for one of the great 'Yajyams' fire sacrifices that he conducted. However, Sati still believed in her father (postal delay!) and went to attend that event despite shiva's warning not to do so. Daksha did not even welcome his daughter and in fact insulted her and Shiva. Sati felt shattered! Unable to bear the humiliation, She warned Daksha that the wrath of Shiva would destroy him and his empire.

Even the Bhagavada Purana that reveres Vishnu, talks about Dākshayani and the destruction of Daksha Yajnam. In Bhagavadam, there is a beautiful verse in which the humiliated Sati addresses her father Daksha at the Yajnam. We mentioned this verse before and repeat it because it is relevant to this nāma here.

यद्व्यक्षरं नाम गिरेरितं नृणां सकृत्प्रसङ्गादघमाशु हन्ति तत्

पवित्रकीर्तिं तमलङ्घ्यशासनं भवानहो द्वेष्टि शिवं शिवेतरः

yad dvy-akṣaraṁ nāma gireritaṁ nṛṇām, sakṛt prasaṅgād agham āśu hanti tat, pavitra-kīrtiṁ tam alaṅghya-śāsanaṁ, bhavān aho dveṣṭi śivaṁ śivetaraḥ

भवान् Respected father, yad dvy-akṣaraṁ nāma The two-lettered name of 'Shi-va' even if uttered accidentally just once instantly frees one from sin. His order is never neglected. Lord Shiva is always pure, no one else but you alone hate him.

The last word is, 'sivetara: = siva +itara:', means Anti-Siva. Unable to bear the humiliation, in sheer disgust and disappointment, Sati jumped into the holy fire and ended her life. On hearing this Shiva got furious and he ordered his Bhutaganas to kill Daksha and destroy the yajna.

There are several versions of this story but what is important is that Shiva went to isolation and solitude for ages

 The Glory of Lalithā Sahasranāmam

and wandered all around until Sati reincarnated as Parvati, the daughter of the King Himavan. Pārvatī sought and married Shiva.

This story forms the basis of the establishment of the Shakti Peethas, temples of the Hindu Divine Mother.

Legends say that Lord Vishnu had cut Sati's body into 51 body parts, using his Sudarshana Chakra, which fell on Earth to become sacred sites where people can pay homage to the Goddess. These sites came to be known as Shakti Peetas. There are 51 Shakti Peetas as per the puranas denoting the 51 Sanskrit alphabets.

These Shakti Peetas are in different parts of SE Asia including India, Nepal, Bangladesh, Tibet, Pakistan and Sri Lanka. Some of the most popular Shakti Peetas include Kamakshi Temple, Kanchipuram, Chamundeswari Temple, Mysuru, Srisailam Temple, Kamakhya Temple in Assam.

There are paintings and inscriptions that illustrate the relationship between Ambāl and Aksharas. The devis corresponding to each Sanskrit Alphabet are painted in the inner ceiling of Harsiddhi temple of Ujjain, Madhya Pradesh. Ujjain Mahakali is an important Shakti Peetam.

In the Shiva temple at Tiruvarur in TamilNadu, Parvathy is worshipped as Kamalamba. Behind the sannidhi, there is an akshara peetam, which has the 51 letters of sanskrit engraved on it. It is believed that Sage Durvasha engraved the mathruka beejam on this peetam.

Thus ends the seventh Kaala called 'Susumna' with the sixth hundred naama in the Saubhagyabhaskara composed by Bhāskararāya.

Chapter 12

The Panchadasi Mantra

The arrangement of letters in Sanskrit alphabet is called Varnamaala (वर्णमाला) which means Garland of Letters. In the Tantra Shastra worship of Devi, Sanskrit letters are hidden in the Sri Chakra and Lalithā Sahasranāmam. Hence, Devi is described as 'Mathruka Varna Roopini.'

Akshara (अक्षर) means a letter in Sanskrit. It has three syllables, a+ksha+ra. 'A' (अ) is the starting letter, and 'Ksha' (क्ष) as the last letter. Akshamala Upanishad gives the meanings of every letter. The akshamala that Ambāl holds is a string made up of beads where each bead represents the 50 letters of the alphabet, a (अ) to ksha (क्ष). Each letter in the Sanskrit alphabet contains a shakti as its presiding deity.

(Note: you will see in various texts a count of 51— reached by the inclusion of the the obscure letter ळ, which rarely appears except in Vedika texts as a specific sandhi for ḍa ड.)

Shodasi Mantra is known as Mantra-raj, the King of Mantras. It is an essential part of Lalithā Sahasranāmam and should be taught (*Upadesam*) only by a competent Guru.

मन्त्र मातृका पुष्पमाला स्तवः *Mantra matṛka pushpamala stavaḥ* is a composition by Sri Adi Śaṁkarācārya that is most relevant to Shodasi Mantra.

The special feature of this composition is that it is a unique combination of Shodasa Upacharam (16 services) and shodasi mantra. It consists of a total of seventeen verses. Mantra pushpamala means a mantra in praise of Ambāl -the Divine Mother in the form of a pushpamala -a garland- woven with alphabets.

What are these alphabets?

These are the bījākṣara-s of pañcadaśākṣarī mantra. The first alphabet of the first fifteen verses this pushpamala form the fifteen bījkṣara-s of Pancha Dasakshri mantra. Each of the first 15 verses begins with one letter of *Panchadasi* mantra contained in the three Kutas; the first verse with क Ka, the second verse with ए Ai, the third with ई EE, and so on.

The 16th verse begins with bīja śrīm श्रीं, which, if appended to the Pañcadaśī mantra, Pañcadaśī mantra becomes ṣoḍaśākṣarī mahā mantra.

It is a Phalashruti, फलश्रुति that means the "fruits of listening." The Phalashruti indicates the merit that accrues to the devotee who chants this mantra every day regularly. In the 16 verses Adi Sankara offers the Shodasa Upacharas (16 types of services) to Devi. The 16 upacharams include Aavaahanam (invocation), Aasanam (offering a seat), Paadyam (offering water to cleanse the feet), Arghyam (offering water to rinse hands and mouth), Aachamanam (offering water to drink),

Snaanam (bathing the deity), Vasthram (garments for the deity), Yagnopaveetham (offering the sacred thread), Gandham (offering sandal paste), Pushpam (offering flowers), Dhoopam (offering fragrant smoke), Deepam (waving oil lamp to illuminate), Naivedyam (announcing the food for the deity), Taambulam (offering betel nut and leaves), Pradakshinam & Namaskaram (circumambulation and homage).

The seventeenth and last verse is a eulogy of the prayer. It is in the form of a submission of this maala at Devi's feet. It says इति गिरिवरपुत्री पाद राजीवभूषा- *iti girivara putri paada raajivabhusha* - Devi is described as Girivaraputri- the daughter of King of Mountains. Śaṁkarācārya places this mantramātṛkāpuṣpamālā at Her feet. It is a brilliant composition by Adi Shankara in praise of Ambāl. To understand this pushpamala, we need to know what the three Kutas are and what is Panchadasi Mantra.

Panchadasi means 15. Since this mantra has fifteen letters it is called Panchadasi. The understanding of this mantra may be a little complex. The Panchadasi Mantra has three lines of bijas and each line is called 'kuta' or group. The three kutas are vakbhava kuta, madhya kuta and shakthi kuta. The whole form of Lalithambigai is made up of these three kutas as described in the following verses:

Srimadvagbhava-kootaika-swarupa-mukha-pankaja

Her lotus face corresponds to the great vagbhava kuta

Kantadha-katiparyantha-madhyakuta-swarupini

From the throat to the waist, she represents the madhyakuta.

shakti-kutaikatapanna katyadhobhaga dharinee

Devi's portion lower from the waist is identical to Saktikuta

Vakbhava kuta consists of five bijas viz. क ए ई ल हरीं -ka-Ai-Ee-la-hreem.

Madhya kuta consists of six bijas ह स क ह ल हरीं ha-sa-ka-ha-la-hreem.

Shakthi kuta consists of four bijas स क ल हरीं sa-ka-la-hreem.

Each Syllable stands for a devata like Shiva, Shakti, Vishnu, Brahma etc.

The 15 bijas of Panchadasi are the most secretive mantra of Lalithambigai. All the three kutas end with 'hreem' and this hreem is called 'hreelekha.' Many other details of the kutas are beyond the scope of this book. There are many interpretations of the bijas from different scholars. We will describe the significance of each Kuta and the hidden meanings.

The first kuta, namely 'vakbhava kuta' has five bijas. This kuta indicates jnana shakthi of Lalithambigai. क -Ka refers to Brahma, the creator. 'ए' -Ai means Sarawathi the goddess of jnana. ई- 'Ee' means Lakshmi, ल 'la' means Indra and हरीं 'hrim' means the merger of Shiva and Shakthi. As Brahma is mentioned, the first kuta refers to creation.

The second kuta is kamaraja kuta or Madhya kuta is to be meditated upon Lalithambigai's neck to hip. This kuta has the highest number of bijas viz 6. We have two new bijas ह and स in this kuta. Out of the new bijas 'ha' has been repeated twice. The first 'ha' means Shiva; the second 'ha' means akash element. 'sa' in this refers to Vishnu. In this kuta of sustenance, Vishnu is mentioned as he is the lord of sustenance.

     The Glory of Lalithā Sahasranāmam

The third and the last kuta, which is called shakthi kuta, has only four bijas. This kuta is to be meditated upon the portion between hip and the feet of Lalithambigai. In this kuta, the 'ha' bija is not there. This kuta forms the third act of Brahman, pralayam or the dissolution. The dissolution is represented by the bija 'la' which refers to destructive weapons. There are three 'hrim's in Panchadasi. Each of the three 'hrim's represent creation, sustenance and dissolution.

Sri Lalitha Maha Tripurasundari *is "Maha Tantra, Maha Mantra, Maha Yantra* Mahasana." She is the greatest Tantra, mantra and Yantra!

Sarva yantratmika sarva tantra rupa manonmani. There is a lot of emphasis on the Panchadasi mantra.

We will now see just two sample shlokas from the mantramātṛkāpuṣpamālā – the first and the fifteenth. Let us look at the first shlokam of this pushpamala. (slide) It starts with क, the first bija letter of the panchadasi mantra.

कल्लोलोल्लसितामृताब्धिलहरीमध्ये विराजन्मणि-
द्वीपे कल्पक वाटिका परिवृते कादम्ब वाट्युज्ज्वले।
रत्न स्तम्भ सहस्र निर्मित सभामध्ये विमानोत्तमे
चिन्तारत्न विनिर्मितं जननि ते सिंहमासनं भावये॥१॥

kallola ullasita amṛtābdhi laharī madhye virājat-maṇi-dvīpe

kalpakavāṭikā-parivṛte kādamba-vāṭi-ujjvale

ratna-staṁbha-sahasra-nirmita-sabhā-madhye vimānotame

cintāratna-vinirmitaṁ Janani te simhāsanaṁ bhāvaye

In this shlokam, Adi Shankara visualizes the mother in a Simhāsanam. Why is it called a Simhāsanam? Because its legs are carved in the shape of four lions. Here the Simhāsanam, a throne is made up of cintāratna. Cintāratna is a type of precious stone which can fulfill all the desires. This throne is placed under a vimāna. Vimāna means a seven-tier construction under which the throne is placed. It is said to be excellent vimāna, which means that it is built with gold and precious gems. It is in the middle of an island, called Maṇidvīpa or the island of precious stones. This island is in the middle of an illuminating cosmic ocean full of nectar and the waves of the ocean are too high. The same narration is there in Soundaryalaharī verse 8. Nectar here means Bliss. The devotee's mind is totally pervaded by Her thoughts. He totally gets isolated from the material world at this stage.

The second shlokam goes on to describe Devi's gross form to enable the devotee to invoke Her in his mind. It says the central point of Śrī chakra is called bindu which is the Abode of Parāśakti.

Earlier, I had explained the meaning of Tāmbula Purita Mukhi and gave several references of how Ambāl gets happy with Tāmbulam. In this pushpamala too, in the 12th verse, Adi Sankara refers to Ambāl's desire for Tāmbulam and says:

सच्छायैर्वरकेतकीदलरुचा ताम्बूलवल्लीदलैः

पूगैर्भूरिगुणैः सुगन्धिमधुरैः कर्पूरखण्डोज्ज्वलैः।

sacchāyaiḥr varaketakīdalarucā tāmbūlavallīdalaiḥ

pūgaiḥr bhūriguṇaiḥ sugandhimadhuraiḥ
karpūrakhaṇḍojjvalaiḥ|

Adi Sankara places the Tāmbulam box before Ambāl containing betel leaves, karpura vitika (condiments like saffron, cardamom, clove, camphor, kastūri, nutmeg) - all for Devi's happiness.

Now, let us see the shloka number 15:

ह्रीङ्कार त्रय सम्पुटेन मनु नोपास्ये त्रयी मौलिभि-
र्वाक्यैर्लक्ष्यतनो तव स्तुति विधौ को वा क्षमेताम्बिके।
सल्लापाः स्तुतयः प्रदक्षिणशतं सञ्चार एवास्तु ते
संवेशो नमसः सहस्रमखिलं त्वत्प्रीतये कल्पताम्॥१५॥

hrīṁkārā trayasaṁpuṭena manunopāsye trayīmaulibhiḥ

vākyairlakṣyatano tava stutividhau ko vā kṣametāmbike|

sallāpāḥ stutayaḥ pradakṣiṇaśataṁ saṁcāra evāstu te

saṁveśo namasaḥ sahasramakhilaṁ tvatprītaye
kalpatām||15||

This verse begins with the fourth and the last bīja हरीं Hreem of the third and last kūṭa viz. śakti kūṭa of Pañcadaśī mantra. This is the 15th and the last bīja of the Pañcadaśī mantra. At the end of this verse Pañcadaśī mantra, if the first bīja-s of these verses are taken, entire Pañcadaśī mantra consisting of 15 bīja-s is formed.

ह्रीङ्कार त्रय सम्पुटेन मनु नोपास्ये means "Oh Goddess Ambika, the one who should be meditated upon by the three mantras with Hreem"

The verse goes on to say, "O Mother, You can be realized through the subtle teaching of Upanishads, which are considered as the head of Vedas. Who is an expert at composing hymns in Your praise? Let my spoken words be prayers to you; let all my movements be pradakshina for You; let my lying down be like thousands of namaskarams for You. Let all these be for Your Grace." At the end of this shloka, a devotee has attained such a maturity that he offers all his talks as prayers in Devi's praise. Speech normally reflects one's thinking and mental status. Since his entire mind is filled with Ambāl, he speaks only auspicious words. He offers all his body movements as pradakshina namaskāra.

In short, he realizes Ambāl within himself and thus radiates positive energy all around. That is why mere presence near Mahaans gives us a good feeling. Similarly, the chanting of Lalithā Sahasranāmam fills our mind with Ambāl and we get a positive feeling.

Let us move on to shloka 121.

दरान्दोलितदीर्घाक्षी दरहासोज्ज्वलन्मुखी।

गुरुमूर्तिर्गुणनिधिर्गोमाता गुहजन्मभूः॥१२१॥

darāndōḷita dīrghākṣī, darahāsōjjvalanmukhī।

gurumūrti, rguṇanidhi, rgōmātā, guhajanmabhūḥ॥121॥

601. darāndōḷita dīrghākṣī

This may be split into Darā, Andolita, and Deergakshi. Darā means slowly moving or feeling of fear, Andolita, driving out, Deergakshi, large eyes i.e., Ambāl's glances dispel the fear of her devotees. Her eyes express Her compassion and concern for Her devotees.

Mūka was a dumb person but with the blessing of Goddess Kamakshi he became a great poet. He composed Mūka Pañcaśatī (मूक पञ्चशती) consisting of 500 verses glorifying the divine beauty of Goddess Kamakshi. Mūka Panchashati consists of five Satakams, each Satakam containing 100 verses (The Sanskrit word śatakam means one hundred). One of them is Kataksha Satakam having 101 verses that are dedicated to Ambāl's eyes. Later, Mūka became one of the Sankaracharyas of the Kanchi Mutt. In Saundarya Laharī also there are verses praising Ambāl's beautiful eyes.

602. darahāsōjjvalanmukhī

Dara, Haso, Jvalanmukhi – Dara is gentle, little, (like *jhara* in Hindi), Haso – laugh (Haso means laugh in Hindi too), Jvalanmukhi -Shining face. It means Ambāl's face shines with a gentle smile. When you see a smiling face, you feel very happy.

Nowadays, people use smiling face emojis to spread happiness. Smiles beget smiles. This nāma teaches us a lesson – keep a smiling face! A smile costs nothing.

603. gurumūrti

Devi is a window for knowledge. She assumes the form of the teacher.

Bhāskararāya quotes The Sundari Tapaniya Upanishad which says, "Just as the words, pot, vessel, etc., mean the same thing, so (the words) Mantra, Devata and Guru mean the same thing."

The meaning of the word 'Guru' is given in the Shaktirahasya. "Gu means darkness, and 'ru removes that." In another place, "Gu, existence (13.6., Brahman,) and no knowledge, because he is one with the knowledge of Brahman, he is called Guru."

The Nitya hrdaya also says: "One should meditate upon that Devi who assumes all forms at will, as the Guru."

604. guṇanidhi

Treasure house of qualities. Bhāskararāya explains the treasure of nine qualities:

The Saamkhya doctrine is that though the Sattva, Rajas and Tamas are specifically three, they have endless modifications. Samkhya is a school of Indian philosophy that is known for its theory of Gunas viz Satva, Rajas and Tamas. All matters have these three Gunas but in different proportions.

Guṇa-s also mean conglomeration of nine qualities. Shiva is said to possess nine qualities. These nine qualities are: 1. time (kalā), 2. lineage (kula), 3. names (nāma), 4. Knowledge (jñāna), 5. consciousness or mind (cit), 6. nāda (subtle sounds arising within the body while practicing prāṇāyāma), 7. bindu (consisting of sixteen kalā-s that include prāṇa, sincerity, five elements, indriyas - karmendriya-s and jñānendriya-s, mind, food, vitality, penance, mantra-s, karma-s, worlds and names. 8. kalpa and 9. jīva.

There is a story associated with this nāma. Guna also means rope. During great pralya, Vishnu took Matsyavataram (the form of a fish), placed the entire seeds of jīvas in a boat and pulled them with a rope that was tied to the nose of the fish. Devi took the form of the rope making the rope strong. So, the Guna here also refers to Devi as a rope.

Navadurga represents nine forms of Durga Devi with nine different qualities.

     The Glory of Lalithā Sahasranāmam

605. gōmātā

Mother of cow or a collection of cows.

Surabhi is the divine cow. Another meaning of the word Ghau or Go is speech. This may also be taken here as Mother of Speech. Go has several other meanings such as heaven, bull, rays, thunderbolt, moon, collyrium, eye, the quarters, bow, earth, speech, and water. The Aneka arthadhvani manjari also says, "mother, fire, face, truth, and path."

In Sanatana Dharma, Cows are considered sacred. This nāma could also mean the holy cow kāmadhenu capable of yielding any quantity of food at anytime

606.guhajanmabhūḥ

Guha means a cave – a place to hide, conceal or secret. Janma-bhūḥ means the birthplace. It means the mother of Guha or Subramanya. She personifies the birthplace of Lord Subrahmanya.

Bhāskararāya adds:

Guha that which is covered, the Jivas veiled by Avidya (ignorance); Janmabhu, the birthplace. The Shruti (Bṛhadāraṇayaka Upaniṣad 2, 1, 20) says, "Just as from fire small sparks arise, etc., Souls are the tiny sparks and the Self is the Brahman, or Lalithambika."

The Yajnavalkya Smriti. also, says "Just as sparks come from the hot iron so the souls have come out from the Self."

It supports our belief that every living being is a tiny spark of the Brahman just as the dew on grass reflects the Sun in the early morning.

देवेशी दण्डनीतिस्था दहराकाशरूपिणी।

प्रतिपन्मुख्यराकान्ततिथिमण्डलपूजिता॥१२२॥

dēvēśī, daṇḍanītisthā, daharākāśa rūpiṇī|

pratipanmukhya rākānta tithimaṇḍala pūjitā||122||

607. dēvēśī- She is the Īśvarī for Deva-s (gods), which means that She is the Supreme among all gods and goddesses. She is the source for all divinities.

608. daṇḍanītisthā

Daṇḍa-nīti – Danda or *Dandanai* in Tamil means punishment. *Niti-* is justice.

Dandam also means a stick. In the good old days, teachers used a stick to punish errant students.

Dandaniti means making evil people pursue the path of goodness. Devi punishes those ignorant men who are unwilling to pursue the virtuous path.

Krishna says in Bhagavad Gīta (10.38):

दण्डो दमयतामस्मि नीतिरस्मि जिगीषताम्।

मौनं चैवास्मि गुह्यानां ज्ञानं ज्ञानवतामहम्॥38॥

daṇḍo damayatām asmi nītir asmi jigīṣhatām

maunaṁ chaivāsmi guhyānāṁ jñānaṁ jñānavatām aham

I am punishment amongst means of preventing lawlessness, and proper conduct amongst those who seek victory. Amongst secrets I am silence, and in the wise I am their wisdom.

Bhāskararāya quotes the Devi Puranam which says, "Because Devi leads to certainty men who wander into good and bad ways by restraining and by soothing them, she (Devi) is called Dandaniti (justice)."

Punishment is necessary to instill fear amongst evil people. This is the reason why we have police, laws and justice.

609. daharākāśa rūpiṇī

The subtle ether in the heart. She is in a subtle form in the hearts of all beings.

Bhāskararāya cites Chāndogya Upaniṣhad that says,

"There is in this city of Brahman the small lotus house and in it that small ether, that should be sought for." Here the ether of the heart is said to be Brahman. This nāma confirms that Ambāl is in that form of the Brahman, that can only be realized by devotion.

610. pratipanmukhya rākānta tithimaṇḍala pūjitā

Pratipad means the first lunar day and rākā means the full moon.

Each lunar day is represented by one tithi nitya devi. In Śrī Chakra, She is surrounded by fifteen Avarana Devatas called Nitya Devis.

Their names are Kameshwari, Bhagamalini, Nityaklinna, Bherunda, Vahnivasini, Mahavajreshwari, Shivaaduti, Tvarita, Kulasundari, Nitya, Neelapataka, Vijaya, Sarvamangala, Jvalaamalini, and Chitra.

Tithi maṇḍala is also referred to in Vedas, which mentions fifteen names representing fifteen lunar days or tithi-s of waxing moon. In Śrī vidyā Upasana, all these deities are worshipped during the ritual worship of Śrī Chakra. She is worshipped by the aggregate of the Nitya deities of the first to fifteenth.

So, *pratipanmukhya rākānta tithimaṇḍala pūjitā* means Devi is to be worshipped by the modes laid down for the different days from the Pratipad to the full moon as described by the Tantras. Purnima tithi (Full Moon Day) is auspicious to Ambāl.

कलात्मिका कलानाथा काव्यालापविनोदिनी।

सचामररमावाणीसव्यदक्षिणसेविता॥१२३॥

kalātmikā, kalānāthā, kāvyālāpa vinōdinī|

sachāmara ramāvāṇī savyadakṣiṇa sēvitā||123||

611. kalātmikā

Devi is in the form of Kala.

Kalā means minute parts of an entity. Kalā also means Arts. Bhāskararāya says that Kalā here refers to the ten Kalās of fire, the twelve of the sun, and the sixteen of the moon; and the other well-known sixty-four Kalais (arts) are also to be taken here.

He adds many more kalās:

"In the waking state there are four Kalās, namely, rising, waking, thinking, (Bodha) and the continuous mental action, thus there are four Kalās belonging to the waking state. The waking state is said to be Devi accompanied with all qualities." These four kalās belong to Shakti.

Likewise, these are four Kalās of the sleeping state, "death, oblivion (unconscious of what is happening), indifference and sleep abounding with darkness. All these belong to Shiva.

 The Glory of Lalithā Sahasranāmam

Then there are four other Kalās, that belong to Shiva as well as to Shakti. These are: Desire, confusion, anxiety and recollection of sense objects, also dispassion, desire of salvation, the mind purified by concentrated meditation (Samadhi) and determination of reality and unreality; these are the Kalās of the Turiya state." Some describe Turiya as pure consciousness, a state of liberation

In the Dutiiyaga chapter sixteen Kamakalas are described. In the Antara duti chapter sixteen Kalās are attributed to the Srividya. Also some more, such as the Kalās of Bindu, Ardhacandra are described in Svacchanda-Bhairava and other works; and all these are to be taken here.

612. kalānāthā- Ruler of kalā that we described in the earlier Naama 611.

613. kāvyālāpa vinōdinī

Kāvyā-s mean the great epics. In Tamil also we say Kavyam. In Marathi too we say Kavya for Poetry. Vinodini means Happy.

Kāvyās have eighteen characteristics. These include serenity, regularity, absence of vanity, sincerity, simplicity, veracity, equanimity, fixity, non-irritability, adaptability, humility, tenacity, integrity, nobility, magnanimity, charity, generosity and purity. Valmiki Rāmāyaṇa has all the eighteen qualities and is said to be the first among the epics. Devi is happy to listen to such great epics that fulfil all the eighteen qualities.

When Devi is worshipped sincerely, one attains poetic abilities. A well-known example is the poet Kālidāsa. I told you about him earlier. He composed the Shaymala Dandakam in praise of Devi and wrote many plays like Śakuntalām, Megha-dūta, and Raghu-vaṁśa.

Another example is Mūka kavi who was dumb but with Ambāl's grace, he turned into a poet and author of Muka Panchasati.

Saundarya Laharī (verse 17) says:

सवित्रीभिर्वाचां शशिमणिशिला भङ्गरुचिभिः

वशिन्याद्या भिस्त्वां सह जननि सञ्चिन्तयति यः।

स कर्ता काव्यानां भवति महतां भङ्गिरुचिभिः

वचोभिर्वाग्देवी वदन कमलामोद मधुरैः॥

savitrībhirvācāṁ śaśimaṇiśilābhaṅgarucibhiḥ

vaśinyādyābhistvāṁ saha janani sañcintayati yaḥ|

sa kartā kāvyānāṁ bhavati mahatāṁ bhaṅgirucibhiḥ

vacobhir vāgdevī vadana kamalāmoda madhuraiḥ||

"The one who meditates on You, surrounded by eight vāk devi-s appearing like a cutout moonstone, attain the capacity to compose splendorous poetic works like epics, stotrams etc adding luster to Sarasvati's lotus like face."

Meaning:

savitrībhir vācāṁ - source of speech or formation of words; śaśi maṇi śilābhaṅga rucibhiḥ - the splendorous beauty of the moonstone after cutting it; vaśinya adyābhis – Vaśini and other vāc devi-s (eight in number) worshiped in the seventh āvaraṇa of śrīvidhyā navāvaraṇa pūjā tvāṁ - You; saha – in company; janani – Parāśakti, the Supreme Mother; sañcintayati yaḥ - who contemplates You; sa kartā kāvyānāṁ bhavati mahatām - he becomes a composer of excellent poetic works; bhaṅgirucibhiḥ - dressed with splendor; vacobhir – words; vāgdevī vadana kamala āmoda madhuraiḥ - adding luster to the lotus like face of Sarasvatī.

In short, Ambāl is very happy to listen to Kavyams and poetry.

614. sachāmara ramāvāṇī savyadakṣiṇa sēvitā

Attended on either side by Lakshmi and Sarasvati bearing Chamaras (ceremonial fans).

आदिशक्तिरमेयाऽऽत्मा परमा पावनाकृतिः।

अनेककोटिब्रह्माण्डजननी दिव्यविग्रहा॥१२४॥

ādiśakti, ramēyā,"tmā, paramā, pāvanākṛtiḥ।

anēkakōṭi brahmāṇḍa jananī, divyavigrahā॥124॥

615. ādiśakti- The Primordial energy. Adi, because she is the cause of the origin of the universe.

616. Amēyā

Devi is immeasurable. Except Herself there is none to measure her. Bhāskararāya cites the Linga Purana which says, "Heaven, Pātala, the end of the world, in these eight coverings of the Brahmānda, all that can be measured, is in the form of Uma, and the measurer is the great Lord (Shiva)."

617. Atman

Atman means here the Jiva and the next name Parama means the supreme Self.

The Linga Purana says, "Just as the different sparks are said to be in the fire, so the Jivas are all in Shiva and He is the Supreme Self."

Atman has several meanings such as body, mind, Brahman, nature, firmness, and intelligence. Durga Saptasati says,

या देवी सर्वभुतेषु बुद्धिरूपेण संस्थिता।

नमस्तस्यै नमस्तस्यै नमस्तस्यै नमो नमः॥८॥

ya devi sarvabhuteshu vidya-rupen sansthita

Namasthasyai, Namasthasyai, Namasthasyai,

Namaonamaha ॥8॥

"Devi who is in all beings in the form of intelligence."

The 207th name of the goddess in Sri Lalithā Sahasranāmam is Manonmani, where she is the mind beyond the mind.

Srinivasa Ramanujan was a mathematical genius. It is said that Ambāl would appear in his dream and give him the intuitive push. From Thiru Gnana Sambandar to Kalidasa, Kalamegam to Srinivasa Ramanujan-Ambāl is believed to be the divine phenomenon to make the inherent intelligence shine.

618. paramā

The Supreme. Bhāskararāya says: There are four forms of Para-Brahman. The Vishnu Purana says, "The first form of supreme Brahman is Purusha, the Second is the unmanifested; the third is manifested and the fourth is time. Thus, that which is higher than unmanifested, Purusha, manifested, and time is seen by the Wise to be the pure supreme abode of Vishnu. The forms called Pradhana and others are the cause of the manifestation of the universe."

Ambāl has transcended all these four forms to remain as parama - the Supreme.

619. pāvanākṛtiḥ

Of pure form. Ambāl is the embodiment of purity.

Bhāskararāya adds: Akriti, may also mean her actions, or her knowledge.

The Yajnavalkya Smriti says, "Penance and knowledge are the means of purifying the soul (Bhutatman), the knowledge purifies intellect, the Kshetrajna is said to be completely purified by the knowledge of the Lord." Thus, Her actions lead to purification of the soul.

620. anēkakōṭi brahmāṇḍa jananī

The creator of many crores of worlds (Brahmāndam – the giant egg, refers to the Cosmos). She is the mother of Virat, who are the deities of many crores of Brahmāndas.

What is Virat? Described as 'Virata Purusha', Virat is the Primeval Force of Creation that has countless heads, eyes and feet pervading the entire Universe, far beyond the miniscule level of human comprehension. Purusha Suktam says *"Sahasraseersha Purusha Saharaksha Sahasrapat."* It describes the emergence of Virata from the conscious being (Purusha) having thousands of heads, thousands of eyes and thousands of feet (and hands).

Everything in the world, including sentient creatures and insentient matter (sasanasane), is the manifestation of one foot (paada) or a quarter. It is further stated in Purusha Suktam that hardly one quarter of the Purusha is comprehended as the totality of His Creation and the rest of Him is unmanifested. The following verses from the Purusha Suktam are relevant here:

पुरुष एवेदं सर्वं यद्भूतं यच्च भव्यम्।

उतामृतत्वस्येशानो यदन्नेनातिरोहति॥२॥

एतावानस्य महिमातो ज्यायाँश्च पूरुषः।

पादोऽस्य विश्वा भूतानि त्रिपादस्यामृतं दिवि॥३॥

puruṣa evedaṁ sarvaṁ yad bhūtaṁ yacca bhavyam,

utāmṛtattvasyeśāno yadannenātirohati.

etāvānasya mahimāto jyāyāṁśca pūruṣaḥ,

pādo'sya viśvā bhūtāni tripādasyā'mṛtaṁ divi

From the manifested part sprang the 'Brahmānda' or the Cosmos, the countless forms of living or non-living species and the Five Elements (Earth, Water, Fire, Air, and Sky) as also the Divine Architect,'Visva Karma', The Master-Builder.

621. divyavigrahā

Divinely shaped.

Another interpretation by Bhāskararāya: Divya, in the ether, Vigraha, quarrel or war.

The Markandeya Purana says, "Even there (in the ether) without support Chandika fought with him." meaning she fought the battle against the demon Śuṁbha, climbing to the sky without any support.

क्लीङ्कारी केवला गुह्या कैवल्यपददायिनी।

त्रिपुरा त्रिजगद्वन्द्या त्रिमूर्तिस्त्रिदशेश्वरी॥१२५॥

klīṅkārī, kēvalā, guhyā, kaivalya padadāyinī।

tripurā, trijagadvandyā, trimūrti, stridaśēśvarī॥125॥

622. klīṅkārī

Creator of the syllable Kleem.

Kleem is the Kamabija; or she is the Kleem itself; or Kleemkara is Shivakama and she is his wife. She is in the form of kāma bīja klīṁ (क्लीं). It is also known as Manmatha (Kāmadeva) bīja.

623. kēvalā

The absolute. Because she is single as she is devoid of attributes. It is the unique feature of the nirguṇa Brahman.

Śhiva sūtra (III.34) explains thus "Completely free from the influence of pleasure and pain, he is rather alone – fully established in his real Self as sheer consciousness. Sutra (III, 35): "That which is freed from that is the absolute (Kevala)."

The bīja klīṁ discussed in the previous nāma is made up of ka + la + īṁ. When the two bīja-s ka and la are removed from klīṁ, the bīja that remains is im which is Kevala meaning the Kamakala capable of giving liberation. Kāmakalā, which forms part of klīṁ can liberate a soul.

The meaning is, the three objects (Dharma, Artha and Kaama) are attained by Kamabija, and Moksa through Kamakala alone.

624. guhyā

The secret. Ambāl is secretive both in form and in nature. It is repeatedly said that Her worship should be secretive in nature.

We surrender to the Devi with this mantra

गुह्याति-गुह्य-गोप्त्री-त्वं

गृहाणास्मित्कृतम् जपं।

सिद्धिर्भवतु मे देवी

त्वत्प्रसादान्मयि स्थिरा॥

oM guhyAti guhya goptrI tvaM gRhAN Asmat kRtaM japam|

siddhir bhavatu me devi tvat prasAdAtan mayistira||

You are the Protector of the secret of the secrets; O Devi! please accept the Japa that is done by me. By your grace may I receive Sthira Siddhi (the accomplishment that is permanent).

625. kaivalya padadāyinī

Kaivalya, the state of singleness Without attributes. That is the fifth state (of consciousness). Dāyini, the bestower.

Kaivalya is the final stage of life of a living being. The soul is about to leave its present body and getting ready to merge with the Brahman. Kaivalya is liberation or salvation and hence it is called the final stage.

Bhāskararāya comments:

The Yoga-Sutra (IV, 38) says, "Kaivalya is the establishment in its own nature of the energy of consciousness."

Pada means the four kinds of salvation, namely Saalokya, Saarupya, Saamipiya and Sayujya, because they are of the nature of fixed abodes. This is to be known here.

1. Saalokya (lit. remaining with the god in the same world) state is to be attained by the worship of idol, etc.

 The Glory of Lalithā Sahasranāmam

2. Saarupya (receiving the same form with the god) is the worship, without using images, of deities regarded as different from oneself and as endowed with dominion and of the nature of equality between the deity and the worshipper. Some call this (state) Saarastita, equality of dominion.

3. Saamipiya (lit. remaining near the deity) is attained by those celibates who perform the duties as ordained to their states in life.

The authority for the first three kinds of salvation is the Chandogya Upanishad (2-20-2)

4. Saayuja (lit. becoming one with the deity) worshipping as himself the, deity with attributes and he becomes one with the deity.

The authority for the fourth is the Mundaka Upanishad. (1-2-11): "Those who are peaceful, learned, who live on alms, in the forest performing penance and having faith, without passion, proceed through the sun to the place where is the immortal person, the eternal Self."

These four kinds of salvation are the result of action, transitory, and conditioned. Hence these are described by the words Pada (abode).

The Kaivalya salvation which is the result of knowledge and is unconditioned, permanent.

Singing the praise of Ambika, Adi Sankara says in Soundarya Lahari:

भवानि त्वं दासे मयि वितर दृष्टिं सकरुणां

इति स्तोतुं वाञ्छन् कथयति भवानि त्वमिति यः।

तदैव त्वं तस्मै दिशसि निजसायुज्य-पदवीं

मुकुन्द-ब्रम्हेन्द्र स्फुट मकुट नीराजितपदाम्

Bhavaani tvam daase mayi vitara drishtim sakarunaam

Iti stotum vaanchan kathayati bhavani tvamitiyah;

Tadaiva tvam tasmai disasi nija-saayujya-padaveem

Mukunda-brahmendra   sphuta-makuta   neeraajita padaam.

So great is the mercy of the mother that the moment the Bhakta (devotee) begins his prayer with the words, Bhavaani tvam, Ambika does not even wait till he completes his prayer, but confers on him saayujya, viz., the merger of the soul with the Mother.

So great is Kaivalya Pada Dāyini.

626. tripurā

Bhāskararāya gives different interpretations.

Devi is called Tripura because she is older to the three key deities (Brahma, Vishnu and Rudra)

The Tripurarnava says. "Tripura, means the three Nadis, Susumna, Pingali and Ida; and Manas, Buddhi and Chitta! as Devi dwells in them she is called Tripura."

The Gaudapada-Sutra says, "The difference is by- the three Tattvas." The meaning is that the one Brahman is divided into three by the three Tattvas.

"Tattvas' are explained variously as qualities, forms, states of consciousness, - worlds, Pitha, Bija divisions (of the Pancadas'i)

The Laghustava (8'10. 16). "There are three Devas, three Vedas, three fires, three energies, three notes (Svaras), three worlds, three abodes, (or according to another reading, three cities), three sacred lakes, three castes, whatever in the World is threefold, such as the three objects of human desire, all "these, O divine one, really belong to your name." Because everything is three-fold you are called Tripura.

She is in the form of all triads. Brahma, Vishnu and Rudra; Icchā, jñāna and kriyā Shakti-s; the three kūṭa-s of Pañcadaśī; creation, sustenance and destruction; the three nādi-s, iḍā, piṅgala and suṣumna; three worlds, bhūr, bhuva, suvaḥ; three guṇa-s sattvic, rajasic and tamsic.

Tri in Sanskrit is Three in English. The number three is important having different meanings.

627. trijagadvandyā

Ambāl is adored by the three worlds. bhūr, bhuvar, suvar. The three worlds are represented by three vyāhṛti-s of Gāyatrī mantra. bhur, bhuvar and suvar are known as the Vyaahruthis uttered after OM (PraNavam) in Sandhya Vandanam.

Bhur-Loka – Inhabited by us-Humans, Bhuvar-Loka – Sphere of Sky right above us, Swar-Loka – Planetary sphere where Devas and Indira live

These three worlds are nothing but the three stages of consciousness. The lowest level of consciousness is materialistic in nature and the highest-level consciousness is pure in nature.

The purest form of consciousness is the Brahman.

628. trimūrti

Triple-formed. Trimurti-s are Brahma, Vishnu and Rudra. She is the combined form of these three Gods. Bhāskararāya tells a story from the Varaha Purana.

"Brahma looked at Shiva and called to mind Narayana. Then the divine Narayana stood between the two. They became Brahma, Vishnu and Shiva. Then a threefold vision appeared to them; from that sight, sprang a young girl of divine form seeing that girl, Brahma, Vishnu and Shiva asked her – 'who are you? What are you doing, 0 smiling one?' Thus questioned, that girl of three colors, namely black, white, and red, replied, '0 best ones, do you not know me, I am your own Shakti, supreme dominion, of beautiful shape, born from your gaze.'

Then the triad, Brahma, and others were pleased, and they granted her boons. They said, 'Your name is the triple Devi, ever protecting the world, O sinless one, you will have many other names derived from your qualities. Hear from us, O Devi, another thing. Make your body threefold according to the three colors you possess, white, red and black.' Devi thus addressed by the gods made her body threefold. Thus, she assumed three forms, white, red and black." White color is Brahma. He is sattvic in nature and hence described as white. Next is black representing Vishnu's rajo guṇa. The third color

　　　　The Glory of Lalithā Sahasranāmam

is red, representing the red color of Rudra, a form of Śiva, tamo guṇa.

The Devi Bhagavadam also says "Sambhavi is white hued, SriVidya red, and Shyama black. Thus, the Shaktis are of three qualities."

629. tridaśēśvarī

Tridasa is three times ten. Ruler of the thrice-ten.

Tridasas are the devas; Ambāl is the chief of all tri-daśas. Tri three, dasa, or ten, i.e., thirteen. or triple ten, she is the ruler of the thirty-three ganas of gods (of course three is understood). Each gana is ten million or one crore.

त्र्यक्षरी दिव्यगन्धाढ्या सिन्दूरतिलकाञ्चिता।
उमा शैलेन्द्रतनया गौरी गन्धर्वसेविता॥१२६॥

tryakṣarī, divyagandhāḍhyā, sindhūra tilakāñchitā |

umā, śailēndratanayā, gaurī, gandharva sēvitā || 126 ||

630. tryakṣarī

Three syllabled.

The syllables are the Bijas of the three kuta or divisions (of the Pancadasi), namely, Vagbhava, Kamaraja and Shakti.

Bhāskararāya quotes the The Vamakesvara Tantra that says, "Vagisvari is the Jnana-Shakti which is in the Vaghbava division and confers Salvation. Kamaraja is the Kriya-Shakti, the ruler of desires and fulfils desire.

The Shakti division is the Iccha Shakti, the supreme energy and is in the form of Shiva. Thus Devi, the great Tripurasundari, is three-syllabled."

Tryaksari also refers to Hrdaya and Sattva -heart or truth.

The Bṛhadāraṇayaka Upaniṣad (5-8-1 and 5-5~1) says, "The words heart and truth are each three-syllabled."

Hṛdaya (हृदय) has three syllables (hṛ + da+ ya). Satya (सत्य) has three syllables (sa + t + ya). Both heart and truth mean the Brahman. All those that have three syllables lead to Her.

631. divyagandhāḍhyā

Endowed with the divine perfume

Divya, the divine beings such as gods and other animated beings. She is surrounded by celestial things and not like the (ordinary) kings who surround themselves with terrestrial objects. Gandham refers to perfume or fragrance.

Divyagandha, the perfumes, Harichandana. Devi possesses perfumes that are not easily perceived.

632. sindhūra tilakāñchitā

Decorated with a red forehead mark

Another interpretation is Sindura means elephant, tilaka she elephant, anchita- worshipped; or worshipped by females whose gait resembles that of an elephant.

633. umā

Bhāskararāya gives many interpretations to this word.

U, Shiva, Ma, Lakshmi or U. Shiva Ma, limits. Or,

Uma rose color, also saffron color, fame, brightness.

For it is said (Mark. Pr.), "Devi who resides as brightness in all creatures. "

Umā is the combination of three letters of OM – U + M + A, the praṇava. U refers to creation, M refers to destruction and A refers to sustenance.

In Linga Purana. Shiva says to Devi, "In my Pranava there are A-U-Ma and U-M-and A are in the order in your Pranava, meaning respectively, Brahma, Rudra andVishnu

According to the Shiva-Sutra, (I, 13) Uma means the Iccha-Shakti of Yogins. "The young Uma is called the Iccha-Shakti."

634. śailēndratanayā

Daughter of the king of mountains.

Shailendra refers to Himavan; Tanaya is offspring.

The Devi Puranam says, "Being born in the abode of the king of mountains, she is called the daughter of the king of the mountains"

635. gaurī

Because her color is yellowish. The Maha-Vasista,

"She is called Gauri because her body is yellow."

The Devi Puranam says, "She who was burned by the fire of Yoga (Sati), was again born of Himalaya, as she has the color of the conch, jasmine and the moon, she is called Gauri."

636. gandharva sēvitā

Attended by the Gandharvas. They have exceptional musical skills.

Liṅga Purāṇa refers to twelve excellent gandharvas. They are set to reside in sky, or the region of the air and the heavenly waters. Gandharvas are celestial singers. Devi is worshipped by Gandharvas.

Chapter 13

Devi is Parashakti

This chapter begins with shlokam 127.

विश्वगर्भा स्वर्णगर्भाऽवरदा वागधीश्वरी।

ध्यानगम्याऽपरिच्छेद्या ज्ञानदा ज्ञानविग्रहा॥१२७॥

viśvagarbhā, svarṇagarbhā,'varadā vāgadhīśvarī |

dhyānagamyā,' parichChēdyā, jñānadā, jñānavigrahā ॥127॥

637. viśvagarbhā

Viswa refers to the Universe.

Garbha is the womb. Viswagarbha means one whose womb contains the Universe. Ambāl is the mother of everyone. We start Lalithā Sahasranāmam with the words Om Sri Maatha. Another thing we should all know. In our temples, there is a Garbagriha. It is the sanctum sanctorum or the innermost part of a Hindu temple where the idol of the main deity is installed. It is the nucleus of the temple. It has only one opening in the front. It is unique in our temple architecture. It is the place from where the 'divine energy' radiates towards the devotees who seek darshan of the deity.

638. svarṇagarbhā

Literally means Golden Womb.

The Vayu Purana says, "Ambāl's womb is golden and born from gold, hence she is called Hiranyagarbha." Ambāl arose from the Chitagni kunda on a golden plate. Our Solar system is called Brahmāndam. Brahm means great. Anda means an egg. Creation emerged from Hiranyagarbha, a golden egg, the shape of which is oval. Vedanta Paribhasha says,"Hiranyagarbha is the first soul to be born and is different from Brahma, Vishnu and Shiva." All beings evolved from Hiranyagarbha. Ambāl is the origin of the Universe and hence called Svarna or Hiranyagarbha. Swarnagarbha also refers to the Mother of Vedas and Bijaaksharaas.

There is a Sri Kanakadurga Devi temple in Vijayawada on the banks of river Krishnaveni. Kanaka means gold. Vijayawada is known as Kanakapuri. His holiness Sri Sri Vidyashankara, the 10th Acharya of Sringeri Sharada Peetham, visited this temple, and praised Amba with a beautiful stotram known as श्रीकनकदुर्गाऽऽनन्दलहरी.- Sri KanakadurgA Ananda Lahari.

639. Avaradā

Varada is one who gives boons. '*Varada abhaya hasta Dhāreem*' means Ambal has hands that give boons and protection. Avarada is just the opposite. It means Punisher. Ambāl is a punisher of Asuras. Ambāl came up from *Chitagnikunda* to punish or destroy the Asuras.

640. vāgadhīśvarī

Eshwari of Vaak (speech). Ruler of speech.

The 100th verse of Soundarya Lahari concludes as

त्वदीयाभि र्वाग्भि स्तव जननि वाचां स्तुतिरियम्॥100॥

tvadīyābhir vāgbhiḥ stava janani vācāṁ stutiriyam||

All these words (of Soundaryalaharī) are only Your own words."

This is the last verse of Soundaryalaharī, one of the greatest hymns on Parāśakti ever composed.

Those who worship Devi have fluency of speech. Just listen to some of the Devi Upasakas and you will find how true it is.

641. dhyānagamyā

Ambāl is to be attained by meditation. There is a belief that you attain what you keep thinking constantly. Meditation is a complex process that enables one to explore the entire human potential within. On the importance of meditation, Kanchi Mahaperiyava said:

"It is not enough if the house is free from dirt. It is not enough if the clothes are clean. It is not enough if the body is clean. Our mind should become free from impurities. For this, the only way is meditation on the lotus feet of Ambāl, the consort of Parameswara and the Supreme Shakthi (Parasakthi). If we keep on meditating on Ambāl's feet, the impurities will go, all wants will be fulfilled and we will become complete and full. What we must start is meditation on the lotus feet of Ambāl. Even if meditation is done a little, its taste will be known. It will become clear that there is nothing that can give greater Shanthi than the lotus feet of Ambāl. All of you should meditate on Her for your athma kshemam (welfare of self) and the welfare of the world."

If Ambāl can be attained by meditation, the next question that arises is: How to do this meditation? There are different ways of meditation. There are three approaches, each progressively increasing in complexity.

1. First is to visualize Ambāl in a physical form what is called Sthula Roopam. When you think of your close friend, you can easily imagine his face. Think of Ganesha, immediately you see an elephant's face with a bent trunk. Likewise, you may start to see Ambāl in full colorful form seated on a throne with Paasangusam Cha Varada Bhaya Hastadareem.

   If you find it difficult, start with visualizing just the lotus feet of Ambāl. "Charana Yugala Ambayaha." Surrender to the twin feet of Ambāl.

2. The second approach, slightly more difficult, is to meditate Ambāl through Her Shookshma Roopam – what is hidden. Ambāl is hidden in mantras and yantras like a seed hides a plant. A seed and a plant may look different, but it is the tiny seed that produces a plant or a huge tree. Chanting Lalithā Sahasranāmam worshipping Ambāl on Sri Chakra with dedication forms the second approach.

3. The third approach is the most difficult and it is like reaching the Sahasrara Ecstasy. It is called "Para Dhyanam." Para is Superlative-like in Parameswaran. The first two approaches ultimately lead to gradual enlightenment and a firm belief that there is nothing above Ambāl. As the famous Sanskrit saying goes, *'Ekam Sath Viparha Bahuda Vadanti.'* There is only one truth (Brahman), the wise call it by different names. It takes a long time to reach this ultimate dyanam.

642. aparichChēdyā

Unlimited. Ched is to cut. Chedam means broken or damaged. Parichedam is fragmented. Aparichedyam is just the opposite. It means completely whole beyond measurement. Ambāl is beyond any measurements. She is incomprehensible, hence, infinite.

643. jñānadā

Bestower of knowledge. Gnana means knowledge of that which is utmost superior. It is the form of Paramatma or Brahman. That is why Paramatma is explained as a brilliant self-luminous light.

Bhāskararāya quotes a shlokam 25 from Kena Upanishad:

स तस्मिन्नेवाकाशे स्त्रियमा जगाम बहुशोभमाना मुमाँहैमवतीं ताँहोवाच किमेतद्यक्षमिति॥२५॥

sa tasmin nevākāśe striyamā jagāma bahuśobhamānā

mumām̐ haimavatīṃ tām̐hovāca kimeta dyakṣamiti||25||

The meaning is-

Indra saw in that very spot a woman, Uma, very beautiful and of golden hue, daughter of Himavat. He said to her "What is this Great Yaksha?

Story: In a battle between the Devas and the Asuras, the Brahman defeated the Asuras. But Indra and the other Devas thought the victory was theirs and they cherished this false notion. So, the Brahman appeared before them as a Yaksha, a Great Spirit. The Devas asked Agni the Fire to find out who this Great Spirit was. So, Agni ran to that Yaksha. The Yaksha asked him "Who are you?" He replied, "I am Agni

    The Glory of Lalithā Sahasranāmam

or Jataveda." The Yaksha asked him, "what can you do?" He replied, "I can burn everything even all this, on the earth." The Yaksha placed a straw before him and said: 'Burn this.' Agni tried his level best but was not able to burn it. He immediately returned to the Devas and said I was not able to learn what this Great Spirit is." The Devas then said to Vayu: "O Vayu! find out who this Great Spirit is" He said: "yes." The Yaksha asked him, "Who are you?" He said, "I am Vayu or Matarisva" The Yaksha asked him, "what is your power?" He replied: "I can blow away all the universe and all that is on the earth." The Yaksha placed a straw before him and said, "Blow it away." He approached it with all speed but was not able to blow it. He returned immediately from there and told the Devas "I was not able to learn who this Great Spirit is."

Finally, Indra himself went there but the Yaksha vanished. Instead, Indra saw in that very spot a woman, Uma, very beautiful and of golden hue, daughter of Himavat. He said to her "What is this Great Spirit? She said "It is Brahman indeed. Attain glory in the victory of Brahman." From her words only, he learned that it was Brahman. So, Ambāl is Brahman!

The Suta Samhitai (4-47-58), "Such is the supreme Vidya Sankari, destroyer of Samsara, arises in men by the grace of Shakti alone."

In Suta Gita 8-80, "She who is in the form of Vidya, to be known by the Vedas, is existence, bliss, infinity, and knowledge, by the grace of that speech, Ambika, the one mother of the Universe (one obtains salvation) through devotion."

Another interpretation is jnana, the knowledge which leads to the bondage, da, the slayer (the remover).

The Shiva-Sutra (I, 2) says,

"Jnana is bondage "some commentators say jnana in this Sutra should be taken as Ajnana. Ambāl is the giver of knowledge and hence remover of ignorance. Those who have attained Jnana are called Jnani. They see the supreme Mother in everything.

644. jñānavigrahā

Ambāl whose body is knowledge. Vigraha means "a sacred image." In temples, we have vigrahas (idols). Ambāl is the personification of knowledge.

The Vishnu Purana (Book II): "Jnana alone is the supreme Brahman. This universe consists of knowledge. There is nothing beyond knowledge."

There is a shiva temple in Kalahasti, famous for its Vayu Lingam (Wind Lingam). It is one of the Panchabhoota Sthalams, representing wind. Ambāl at this temple is known as Sri Jnana Prasoonambika. She is the consort of Sri Kalahastishwara Swamy (Lord Shiva of Srikalahasti Temple). She is jñānavigrahā.

सर्ववेदान्तसंवेद्या सत्यानन्दस्वरूपिणी।

लोपामुद्रार्चिता लीलाक्कॢप्तब्रह्माण्डमण्डला॥१२८॥

sarvavēdānta saṃvēdyā, satyānanda svarūpiṇī |

lōpāmudrārchitā, līlāklupta brahmāṇḍamaṇḍalā || 128 ||

645. sarvavēdānta saṃvēdyā

Ambāl is to be known through all the Vedantas.

Vedas have 4 main parts. Vedantam comes at the end.

1. **Samhita:** Samhitas are the main text of the Vedas. Samhita means "systematised and collected together". This has all the mantras and stotras or Poetic hymns of praise. "Veda-adhyayana" (the study or chanting of the Vedas) is normally the Samhita part.

2. **Braahmanaas:** The Brahmana lays down the various rites - karma - to be performed and explains the procedure for the same. It interprets the words of the mantras occurring in the Samhita, how they are to be understood in the conduct of sacrifices. The Brahmanas constitute a guide for the conduct of yajnas.

3. **Aranyakas:** The word "Aranyaka" is derived from "aranya". You must have heard of places like "Dandakaranya" and "Vedaranya". "Aranya" means a "forest". Neither in the Samhita nor in the Brahmana is one urged to go and live in a forest. Vedic rites like sacrifices are to be performed by the householder (grhastha) living in a village. But after his mind is rendered pure through such rites, he goes to a forest as a recluse to engage himself in meditation. It is to qualify for this stage of vanaprastha, to become inwardly pure and mellow. For the Aranyakas, more important than the performance of sacrifices is awareness of their inner meaning and significance. It explains various karmas like Braahmanaas. But it focuses more on the internal meaning of these karmas than the physical interpretation.

4. **Upanishad:** If the Samhita is the tree, the Brahmana the flower and the Aranyaka the raw fruit, the Upanishads

are the mellow fruit - the final fruit or "phala." This is a profuse philosophy called Brahma vidya. It explains about jeevatma, paramatma, gnana and moksha. The Upanishads try to explain various aspects of Divine Mother.

The essence of all the upanishads is Divine Mother. Upanishads come at the end of vedas. So, they are called Vedantham.

Ambāl is the core knowledge in Vedantas. Hence, she is called Sarwa Vedanta Sam Vedya.

Bhāskararāya quotes the Varaha Purana that says,

"This (Devi) is explained as the threefold energy and set forth as the end of logic. She is the energy of wisdom, set forth in all the Vedantas."

646. satyānanda svarūpiṇī

Satya is Truth; Anandam is bliss. She is in the form of truth (satya) and eternal happiness (ānanda). Ambāl is true existence and bliss. Bhāskararāya explains: Some divide this name into two. as 'Satya' and 'Anandasvarupini.' Satya, she is good to the wise, or sat means brightness.

Anandasvarupini: Ambāl is Form of Happiness, Bliss. i.e.Brahman.

In the Vedanta Sutra (III, 3-11) it is explained that the qualities, bliss, etc. are the qualities of Brahman itself.

आनन्दादयः प्रधानस्य॥११॥

ānandādayaḥ pradhānasya||11||

ānandādayaḥ—Bliss and other attributes; pradhānasya—of the subject (i.e. Brahman). Bliss and other (qualities) must be attributed to Brahman everywhere.

Pleasure/Joy is of two types:

1. Loukika

2. Para

1. Loukika represents all the pleasures that come from material attachments. Though they look like pleasures, they always carry the shadow of sorrow with them.

2. Para represents the bliss of Atma. When a Yati becomes yogi by taking kundalini to sahasrara, he experiences Satya Ananda. It cannot be explained. It has to be experienced. That is Divine Mother.

647. lōpāmudrārchitā

Worshipped by Lopamudra. Who is Lopamudra?

Lopamudra was the wife of Agastya, the great sage who is considered to have traveled from north to south of India. Lopamudra was a worshipper of Devi.

When Hayagrīva was reluctant to share Lalithā Sahasranāmam with sage Agastya, Lalithāmbikā, appeared along with Śhiva before Hayagrīva and asked him to initiate sage Agastya into Lalitha Triśatī. Lalitha Trisati (I, 15) says, "Agastya's wife named Lopamudra worships me with so much devotion."

The Tripura-Siddhanta also says, "As the supreme ruler was pleased with the wife of Agastya, named Lopamudra, this Devi is involved under the name of Lopamudra."

648. līlāklupta brahmāṇḍamaṇḍalā

Devi who formed the world systems as if they were some kind of sport. She created the universe effortlessly. She is described as "Aneka Koti Brahmānda Janani." Lalitha name itself means playful.

Devīstava (देवीस्तव) is the name of a work on the topic of Stotra ascribed to Bhāskararāya. He said in Devistava "Even Shiva is powerless to create, preserve or destroy. Brahma, Vishnu and other gods, but O mother, the regulation of the universe is just a sport to you."

अदृश्या दृश्यरहिता विज्ञात्री वेद्यवर्जिता।

योगिनी योगदा योग्या योगानन्दा युगन्धरा॥१२९॥

adṛśyā, dṛśyarahitā, vijñātrī, vēdyavarjitā|

yōginī, yōgadā, yōgyā, yōgānandā, yugandharā||129||

649. adṛśyā

Invisible. Not perceived by our eyes and other senses. (We say Adhirstam in Tamil for a fortune that comes unseen). The Devi Bhagavada Puranam (Book III): "Your unqualified form is not an object of visual perception... Shakti is without quality (Nirguna); difficult of approach. The supreme Person also is without qualities."

650. dṛśyarahitā

Transcending the visible. Ambāl is beyond our visual perception. This is an extension of the previous nāma. Her presence must be experienced. Or, she is freed from Drshya, the wordly things because they are not eternal.

651. vijñātrī-Perceiver. Vijnanam means Science. Here, it denotes special knowledge perceived by Her. She knows all sciences.

652. vēdyavarjitā- Transcending the Vedas. Veda comes from the root Vid-to know. Ambāl is beyond knowledge contained in the Vedas.

The next few names relate Ambāl to Yoga.

653. yōginī- The term is the feminine Sanskrit word of the masculine yogi. Ambāl is personification of Yoga. She stands united with Śiva. (She also bestows it on others, as the next Naama reveals). So, she is called Yogini.

654. yōgadā- Bestower of Yoga. Divine Mother helps us to pursue the path of Yoga

655. yōgyā

Powerful, able. Fit or proper for Yoga, or for religious meditation. She who can be reached by yoga

The meaning of the Yoga is given in the Vishnu Purana:

"Having controlled all the senses with the mind, the idea of unity of the soul with the supreme Self is Yoga"

The Bhagavad Gita (6-23): "One should know that Yoga which, frees from the attachment of the pain."

The Yoga Sutra (1-2), "Yoga means the restraint of mental modifications."

or Yoga means (lit.) enjoyment of objects, hence of three names (653-655), the first is enjoyer, the second, the bestower of enjoyment, and the third, the object of the enjoyment.

For the Bhagavad Gita. (14-10) says,

रजस्तमश्चाभिभूय सत्त्वं भवति भारत|

रज: सत्त्वं तमश्चैव तम: सत्त्वं रजस्तथा||10||

rajas tamaśh chābhibhūya sattvaṁ bhavati bhārata

rajaḥ sattvaṁ tamaśh chaiva tamaḥ sattvaṁ rajas tathā

There are three gunas Sattva (goodness), Rajas (Passion) and Tamas (Ignorance). Krishna says: Sometimes sattva prevails over rajas and tamas. Sometimes rajas dominate sattva and tamas, and at other times tamas overcomes sattva and rajas.

All three guṇas are present in our mind as well. They are like three wrestlers competing. Each keeps throwing the others down, and so, sometimes the first is on top, sometimes the second, and sometimes the third. Of these the first called Sattva, is meant by the name Yogada, the bestower of enjoyment (654).

The energy possessed with the second (Rajas) called jiva, is the enjoyer and expressed by the Word Yogini (653).

The same possessed with the third (Tamas) called the material universe (Jadavastu) is expressed by the word Yogya. Thus, they should be distinguished.

656. yōgānandā

Bliss of Yoga. She is in the form of bliss that is attained through yoga.

Yoga + Ananda is called Yoga sleep, because bliss chiefly pervades in sleep. Don't we all love to sleep? We rest and forget everything while we sleep.

That state belongs to Devi.

Devi Māhatmyam says:

या देवी सर्वभूतेषु निद्रा रूपेण संस्थिता,

नमस्तस्यै नमस्तस्यै नमस्तस्यै नमो नमः।

To that goddess who abides in all beings as sleep: Salutations to Thee,

The Glory of Lalithā Sahasranāmam

The Hari vamsa says, "She who is a mass of bliss and is known in the world as sleep."

657. yugandharā

Yugam means double. What to do in a crisis?

स्मरणीयं चरणयुगलम्बायाः Remember the twin Lotus Feet of Devi. Yugalam here refers to the twin feet of Ambāl.

The yoke that binds the two bulls in a bullock cart is called 'Yugam.'

Ambāl is described as the Bearer of the yoke. Yuga has many other meanings.

According to the Visvaprakasa "Yuga means a measure consisting of four cubits, chariot yoke, a plough, also the four yugams or cycles like Krita, Treta, Dvapara, and Kali, a pair, and a species of medicinal plant."

The meaning here is as the bearer of the yoke, yugam-the pair refers to Shiva and Shakti. She is also the controller of the cycle of yugas.

इच्छाशक्ति ज्ञानशक्ति क्रियाशक्ति स्वरूपिणी।

सर्वाधारा सुप्रतिष्ठा सदसद्रूपधारिणी॥१३०॥

ichChāśakti jñānaśakti kriyāśakti svarūpiṇī।

sarvādhārā, supratiṣṭhā, sadasad-rūpadhāriṇī॥130॥

658. ichChāśakti jñānaśakti kriyāśakti svarūpiṇī

Shakti means energy. Ambāl represents a unique combination of three types of energies- The energies of Icha-desire, Jnana-wisdom, and Kriya-action

These correspond to the three qualities. Bhāskararāya quotes several scriptures.

The Samketa paddhati says. "Desire is her head, wisdom her trunk, action her feet, thus her body consists of three energies."

Vamakeshvara Tantra is said to be the most important tantra for Sri Vidya worship. This tantra discusses on internal worship of Shakthi.

The Vamakeshvara Tantra also says, "Tripura is threefold, viz" Brahma, Vishnu, and Eesa and she, O beloved one, is the energy of desire, wisdom and action." Of these energies, the preceding one is the cause of success. Like desire leads to wisdom, and wisdom in turn leads to action.

The Kriyasakti is fivefold according to the Suta samhita (4-14-28) namely, "Spanda, Parispanda, Prakrama, Parisilana, and Pracara, thus there are five actions." Spanda is the pulsation of the ecstasy of the divine consciousness. It is the energy behind the breath, the heartbeat, and the movement of our thoughts and feelings. It is also the source of all our inner experiences. Likewise, the other four describe different kinds of actions.

The Malini Vijaya Tantra says, "That supreme divine energy becomes the energy of desire when Brahman, the supporter of the universe, wishes to create. This should be known thus and in no other way. She becomes the energy of knowledge when she reminds him saying 'let this be thus.' When thus knowing he acts, she becomes the energy of actions."

The One who is the possessor of all three shakthis or energies is known as 'para-shakthi' or the Supreme energy.

659. sarvādhārā

Sarva, the whole world, Adhara, support, Supporter of all. she is in all. The Markendaya Tantra says, "In reality it is

     The Glory of Lalithā Sahasranāmam

Devi herself who is perceived in all things, permanent or impermanent, gross or subtle or more subtle, embodied or dis-embodied, one or many, in earth, in the heaven or elsewhere." She supports the universe with the aid of three energies.

660. supratiṣṭha- Pratishta means to establish. Ambāl is firmly established. She is the foundation of all existence.

661. sadasad-rūpadhāriṇī

The foundation of being (sat) and non-being (asat)

Sat, Brahman, asat, universe which is different from sat. Though the universe, which is very difficult to define (one Way or other) as sat or asat (Anirvacaniya) is different both from the Sat and Asat; yet here the word asat represents the universe.

For the Shruti (Taitreya Upanishad. 2-7-1): "In the beginning this was indeed asat-." Another Shruti (Chi. Up., 6-2-2). "How did sat come to exist from asat." In these places asat means the universe.Sat and Asat may mean existence and non-existence. Existence is what is permanent and unchangeable.

The Suta Samhita (4-12-16). "Whatever appears either as existent or non-existent all is caused by the Maya of Mahadeva."

अष्टमूर्ति रजाजैत्री लोकयात्राविधायिनी।

एकाकिनी भूमरूपा निर्द्वैता द्वैतवर्जिता॥१३१॥

aṣṭamūrti, rajājaitrī, lōkayātrā vidhāyinī।

ēkākinī, bhūmarūpā, nirdvaitā, dvaitavarjitā॥131॥

662. aṣṭamūrti: Ashta means eight. Devi is of eight forms; She is also a combination of eight virtues.

Bhāskararāya provides different interpretations.

The Matsya Purana says, "Wealth, intelligence, earth, nourishment, gauri, contentment, radiance, stability, protect me, O Sarasvati, by these eight forms."

Or her eight forms are to be known by mantras. The Yoga-Sastra says, "The self is of eight kinds according to the difference of qualities, namely, embodied soul (Jivatman), inner Self (Antaratman), supreme Self (Paramatman), unstained Self (Nirmalatman), pure Self (Suddhatman), wisdom Self (Jnanatman), great Self (Mahatman), and elemental Self (Bhutatman). Thus, there are eight Selves."

Or the five elements plus the sun, moon, and Jiva, or heaven or sacrificer; these are eight bodies. The Shaktirahasya says, "The five elements sun, moon and heaven (are the eight bodies)." The Vishnu Purana also: "The Sun, water, earth, fire, air, ether, the Brahmana the sacrificer and the moon, these are the eight bodies.

The Wives of these eight are respectively—Umia, Sukesi, Apara, Siva, Svaha, Diti, Diksha and Rohini. Their sons are respectively —

Saturn, Venus, Lohitinga, Manojava, Skanda, Svarga, Santana, and Budha." But the Linga Purana says, "The eight Prakrtis are said to form the body of Devi, also the (eight kinds) of products (vikrtis) are manifestations of her body in order to mould the bodies."

According to the Bhagavad Gita (7-4), Earth, water, fire, air, ether, mind, intellect, and egoism thus eightfold is her Prakrti.

The eight Kulas (The eight kinds of women). The Samayachara Smriti says,

"Ganika, Shaundika, Kaivarti, Rajaki, Takrakiri, Karmari, Matangi, and Pumscali."

In the Rudrayamala the characteristics of the following eight women are given, namely, "Ananga kusuma, who has symmetrical limbs and long hair." The name of each woman is given in the third chapter of the same book. The eight forms may mean the eight Vasinis. Brahmi, etc.

663. ajājaitrī

Ajā means ignorance and jetri means victory. (Aja means a goat typically known to be dull, ajam also means unborn) The conqueror of the unborn or ignorance (avidya).

Bhāskararāya quotes the Svetasvatara Upanishad Chapter 4 verse 5 that says:

"ajām ekām lohita śukla kṛṣhṇām bahvīḥ prajāḥ sṛjamānām sarūpāḥ"/

There is one unborn prakriti - red, white and black - which gives birth to many creatures like itself. Unborn here refers to ignorance. The meaning is as she is wisdom she destroys ignorance.

664. lōkayātrā vidhāyinī- loka-yātrā means the journey of the worlds. Vidhayini -one who has achieved. Ambāl is one who directs the course of the worlds. Lokas, the fourteen worlds, Yatra, direction or protection.

665. ēkākinī: Ambāl is One.

Because she is without a second. The Devi Purana says, "Alone she consumes the worlds, alone she establishes them, alone she creates the universe, hence she is called the one." Chāndogya Upaniṣad (VI.ii.1) says "ekam eva advitiyam" which means 'the one without a second'.

666. bhūmarūpā

Bhuma means the Brahman. Bhāskararāya says it means Ambāl is the aggregate of all existing things.

The previous name means 'She is one,' but this says, 'she is aggregate of many things.' The Devi Purana says, "Though she is one by limitations she is everywhere seen as many (Bhuma). As the crystal is colored by the transmission of different colors, so by the qualities Devi is described as Bhuma.

Just as one cloud becomes many retaining the same nature and colors, so Uma becomes many through the qualities. Just as the rain from the sky assumes various tastes according to the soil, so is Uma is through the qualities. Just as the wind, which is one takes on different odors, fragrant and otherwise, so is Uma through the qualities. Just as the one Gaarhapatya fire takes different names such as Daksina and Ahavaniya fires, so Devi is said by the wise to be one and many. Hence, supreme devotion to her should be practiced for the attainment of all objects."

667. nirdvaitā

Without duality. Dvaita means two, which means dualism.

In nir-dvaita or advaita as propagated by Adi Sankaracharya, the belief is that soul Jeevatma is no different from God Paramatma.

Devi is the Brahman without duality.

668. dvaitavarjitā- Transcending duality. This nāma is an extension of the previous nāma and confirms Ambāl is devoid of duality.

अन्नदा वसुदा वृद्धा ब्रह्मात्मैक्यस्वरूपिणी।

बृहती ब्राह्मणी ब्राह्मी ब्रह्मानन्दा बलिप्रिया॥१३२॥

annadā, vasudā, vṛddhā, brahmātmaikya svarūpiṇī।

bṛhatī, brāhmaṇī, brāhmī, brahmānandā, balipriyā॥132॥

669. annadā

Giver of food.

In this world, every living being needs food. This name extols the motherly nature of Ambāl in as much as it supplies food to all the living beings by way of crops, fruits, nuts, vegetables and others.

I had mentioned earlier that each Nāma in Lalithā Sahasranāmam is a Mantra. According to the Nāma in view the powers are different.

By repeating the names, the corresponding results are obtained. Whatever power belongs to a name, in that sphere alone it is effective. From this it follows: Those who desire food should repeat the name "Annada"

670. vasudā

Giver of wealth.

The Brahadaranya Upanishad (4-4-24) says: "This indeed is the great birthless Self, the giver of food and giver of wealth (the fruits of one's work). He who knows this, obtains food and wealth."

671. vṛddhā

The word Vraddha has two meanings, Old and Ancient. No doubt, Ambāl is the oldest, and the most ancient Goddess. In another sense, it could mean 'one who nourishes and gives an occupation.' So, Vrddha may also mean that she nourishes the world.

The next few Naamas that begin with the alphabet B are related to Brahman, the supreme consciousness (paramatma) or absolute reality.

672. brahmātmaikya svarūpiṇī: Brahman + ātman + aikya + sva + rūpiṇī.

Ambāl represents the union of Brahman and Atman.

Brahma, meaning Shiva here, Atman is Jiva, Sva, the Hamsa-Mantra, which unites the souls with Siva; rupa, is her form. Paramesvara is known to be in every object. From the greatest to the smallest, in the whole universe animates and inanimates are born, live and die in the supreme Lord.

The Jiva who manifests through earthly existence is also the supreme Lord. Aham Brahmasmi is a term that is well-known. It is typically translated as "I am Brahman" or less literally as "I am divine." It is advaita!

673. bṛhatī

Simply means Vastness or Great.

Brhati has several other meanings. Bṛhatī (बृहती) is one of the twenty-six varieties of Sanskrit metres (chandas) mentioned in the Chandaśśāstra. Brahati is also a certain metre of thirty-six syllables.

Chandas (छन्दस्) refers to Sanskrit prosody and represents one of the six Vedangas (auxiliary disciplines belonging to the study of the Vedas).

"Gāyatrim Chandasam mata". "Chandas" means the Vedas. So Gāyatri is the mother of all Vedic mantras. Kurma Purana says: "You are the Gāyatri among the metres," because Devi is both the metres.

Bhagavad Gita (10-35) says:

बृहत्साम तथा साम्नां गायत्री छन्दसामहम्।

मासानां मार्गशीर्षोऽहमृतूनां कुसुमाकर:॥35॥

brihat-sāma tathā sāmnaṁ gāyatrī chhandasām aham

māsānāṁ mārga-śhīrṣho aham ṛitūnāṁ

kusumākaraḥ॥35॥

I am Brhatsama among the Samans (Samaveda); amongst poetic meters Chandas I am the Gāyatri. Among the months, I am Margsheersh, and of seasons I am spring, which brings forth flowers.

So, Ambāl is bigger than the Universe and greatest amongst all!

674. brāhmaṇī

The word Braahmani has at least ten different meanings.

Brahmani means a Brahmin's wife, or a certain medicinal plant Or wisdom.

The Samayacara-Paddhati says, "Brahmani means divine wisdom crowned with the white flower (Sattva)." Brahmani also means the wife of Shiva. The Chandogya Upanishad (8-14-1) says: स आत्मा प्रजापतेः, sहं भवामि ब्राह्मणानां यशो

That Self is of Prajapati; May I attain the fame of a Brahmin

"You are Brahmana among the Devas, I wish to be the Brahmana among men"

Parasara, Aditya, Kurma, Vasistha and Linga Puranas also confirm this:

"The divine Sambhu the consort of Devi, is Brahmana and is the deity of Brahmanas. A Brahmana especially should take refuge in Rudra, the Lord."

So, brahmani may be taken as the energy of Brahman.

675. brāhmī: Again, this word has many meanings.

The Brāhmī alphabet is the ancestor of most of the 40 or so modern Indian alphabets.

➤ Brāhmī refers to a medicinal plant.

➤ Brāhmī also means "The Śhakti of Brāhma"

➤ Brahmi - "the power of the immense being" —One of the names of Sarasvatī, the goddess of speech, eloquence and all forms of knowledge. So, Brahmi

     The Glory of Lalithā Sahasranāmam

here refers to the female counterpart of Brahman, or speech.

> Ambāl is the Goddess of Speech. (Vaageeswari)

676. brahmānandā

Bliss of Brahman. It is that state of perfect and infinite bliss that is sought to be achieved as the goal of spirituality. It comes with the realization of oneself. Devi is the possessor and dispenser of the bliss of Brahman.

677. balipriyā

Bali has two meanings.

1. It means mighty warriors who can overcome and conquer both internal (senses) and external enemies. बलिष्ठ [baliṣṭha]: Balavan, Most powerful, strongest. Ambāl delights in such people of great strength.

2. Bali accessories of ceremonial worship such as offering daily food to all creatures as bhuta yagna. In our temples, we can find the "Bali Peetam" near the Dwajasthambham (flagstaff). The word Bali means "Sacrifice." It doesn't mean physical sacrifices as the name implies but it refers to the sacrifice of our six bad qualities Kama (Lust), Krodha (Anger), Lobha (Selfishness), Moha (Delusion), Madha (Pride), and Matsarya (Envy) in front of the Bali Peetam. It is also considered as a "Seat of offerings." The priests at the temple normally offer the Prasadam (Naivedhyam) at the Bali Peetam to the Aavarana devatas. This is normally done after offering the Naivedhyam to the main deities of the temple. Ambāl is fond of such offerings.

भाषारूपा बृहत्सेना भावाभावविवर्जिता।

सुखाराध्या शुभकरी शोभना सुलभा गतिः॥१३३॥

bhāṣārūpā, bṛhatsēnā, bhāvābhāva vivarjitā।

sukhārādhyā, śubhakarī, śōbhanā sulabhāgatiḥ ॥133॥

678. bhāṣārūpā- In the form of languages. She is the cause for learning and understanding. She is the Śabda Brahman.

679. bṛhatsēnā- With mighty army. She administers the universe with the help of this army.

680. bhāvābhāvavivarjitā

The Sanskrit word Bhāva worldly existence. Abhava is the opposite word meaning non-existence. These are Vedantic terms.

Ambāl is devoid of existence and non-existence. Bhaava also refers to our emotional frame or state of mind.

Abhava is non-existent. As Abhava is non-existence, Devi cannot be said to be devoid of it. But the holy Vyasa answers this objection in the Suta Samhita. (4-2-8 and 9), "Destruction of artificial things means their substratum alone remains. For destruction is the non-existence of the existent. It is also the existence of the non-existent. The substratum is different from these two, viz" existence and non-existence. The substratum is not destroyed because it is ever real."

681. sukhārādhyā

Sukha + Aradhya: Easily worshipped.

Sukha, without bodily pain by fasting, elaborate rituals etc., and without restrictions on the mode of meditation. In other words, She can be worshipped without any difficulties.

 The Glory of Lalithā Sahasranāmam

682. śubhakarī- Devi does good. That is even to someone who but imperfectly worships her. She does only auspicious things for devotees.

683. śōbhanā sulabhāgatiḥ

The right path and easily attained. Sobhana, Salvation; Sulabha, easy modes of worship; Gati, result or means. Ambāl offers an easy mode of worship to attain Her. It is an extension of earlier naama.

Nāma-s 684 to 689 begin with the word 'Rāja'

राजराजेश्वरी राज्यदायिनी राज्यवल्लभा।

राजत्कृपा राजपीठनिवेशितनिजाश्रिता॥१३४॥

rājarājēśvarī, rājyadāyinī, rājyavallabhā।

rājat-kṛpā, rājapīṭha nivēśita nijāśritāḥ ॥134॥

684. rājarājēśvarī- Ruler of the king of kings

Brahma, Vishnu, Rudra, Indra and others are the Rajas or kings of the Devas. Devi is the Ruler of all such kings

685. rājyadāyinī- Bestower of dominion. Dominion includes territories like Vaikuṇṭha (the abode of Viṣṇu) or Kailāsa (the abode of Shiva).

686. rājyavallabhā- Delighting in dominion. She is the ruler of Śrī Chakra, the abode of all gods and goddesses.

687. rājat-kṛpā- Radiating compassion.

688. rājapīṭha nivēśita nijāśritāḥ- Her dependents are established in thrones. That is Indra's and other thrones.

राज्यलक्ष्मीः कोशनाथा चतुरङ्गबलेश्वरी।

साम्राज्यदायिनी सत्यसन्धा सागरमेखला॥१३५॥

rājyalakṣmīḥ, kōśanāthā, chaturaṅga balēśvarī|

sāmrājyadāyinī, satyasandhā, sāgaramēkhalā||135||

689. rājyalakṣmīḥ- Royal wealth; the glory of sovereignty. She holds the entire wealth of this universe.

690. kōśanāthā

Master of the five koshas (sheaths). As per Vedānta, there are five superimposed layers covering the human soul. They are prāṇa-maya mano-maya, vijñāna-maya, ānanda-maya and anna-maya kośa. The Self-illuminating Ātman inside our self is covered by these layers or coverings. She is in the form of That Ātman.

Kośa also means the wealth of a government. Since She is in total control of various Rājya-s or kingdoms, She is known as Kośanāthā.

691. chaturaṅga balēśvarī

Ruler of the four armies.

Chaturanga, four divisions of armies consisting of chariots, elephants, cavalry, and soldiers. Ratha, Gaja, Thuraka, Padathi. Chess is called Chaturangam – a game that is believed to have originated in India. She rules army (external) as well as antaḥkaraṇa (internal tools) of mind, intellect, conscience and ego.

692. sāmrājyadāyinī

Bestower of Samrajya. Samrajya is the kingdom of a king who performs the Rajasuya sacrifice, or a king of the earth, or the king of kings. It is said in the Agni Purana that "He who has performed the Rajasuya sacrifice, one who is the lord of the earth and who rules over kings is called Samrat.

693. satyasandhā- Devoted to truth. This nāma stresses the importance of Truth.

694. sāgaramēkhalā- Girdled by ocean. She is in the form of earth, and the entire water bodies of the planet earth forming Her girdle.

दीक्षिता दैत्यशमनी सर्वलोकवशङ्करी।

सर्वार्थदात्री सावित्री सच्चिदानन्दरूपिणी॥१३६॥

dīkṣitā, daityaśamanī, sarvalōka vaśaṅkarī|

sarvārthadātrī, sāvitrī, sachchidānanda rūpiṇī||136||

695. dīkṣitā

Initiated. Dīkṣā is initiation of a disciple by a Guru to knowledge. Ambāl gives dīkṣā to Her disciples. Di, wisdom, ksi, to give. The Atharva-Brahmana says, "Next, therefore Diksa, from which root Diksit-a is derived... They call the man who is initiated as Diksita."

Or Diksita: she destroys the sin of her disciples by imparting the mantra. "Out of compassion she imparts (diyate) to her disciples(consequently) she destroys (kshiyate) their sins; hence she is called Diksita."

696. daityaśamanī

Destroyer of Daityas. Who are Daityas? They are demons. Kashyapa was an ancient rishi, who is one of the Saptarishis in the present Manvantara; He was the father of the Devas, Asuras, Nagas and all of humanity. He married Aditi, who gave birth to Agni, the Adityas (Devas), and most importantly Lord Vishnu's Avatar as Vamana. With his second wife, Diti, he begot the Daityas who were asuras.

697. sarvalōka vaśankarī

Subjugating all the worlds. In the Puranas and in the Atharvaveda, there are 14 lokas or worlds.viz. bhur, bhuvas, suvar, mahas, janas, tapas, and satya above and atala, vitala, sutala, rasātala, talātala, mahātala, pātāla at the bottom. She subjugates all the worlds.

698. sarvārthadātrī

Sarva + artha + datri.

Bestowing all objects of desire. Sarva, the four objects of human desires. Dharma, Artha, Kama, Moksha are the four classifications of objects of desire in Sanatana Dharma. Artha refers to wealth and materialistic desires.

The Devi Purana says, "In all the works she gives Dharma or righteousness and the other desired objects, hence she is called by all by the word Sarvartha-sadhini, (fulfiller of all objects including Moksha)."

699. sāvitrī

The creator of the universe, i.e. the supreme Shiva whose wife she is. The Vishnudharmottara Purana says, "He is called Savita because he creates beings." The Bharadvaja Smriti also says, "As she gives light to the sun, or because she creates the Universe, she is called Savitri." The Vasistha-Ramayana also repeats the same.

The Devi Purana says, "Devi is worshipped by Devas, and worshipped by Yoga and in the Scriptures and she is naturally pure, hence she is called Savitri." The Devi Bhagavada Purana says: "The root Sra means flowing, from the flow, arises brightness (Tejas), hence she is called Savitri."

 The Glory of Lalithā Sahasranāmam

700. sachchidānanda rūpiṇī- Sat + Chit+ Ananda: Existence, consciousness and bliss

Thus ends the eighth Kala, called Bhogada with the seventh hundred shloka in the Saubhagyabhaskara composed by Bhāskararāya.

Chapter 14

The Omnipresent Ambāl

We begin this chapter with Shlokam 137.

देशकालापरिच्छिन्ना सर्वगा सर्वमोहिनी।

सरस्वती शास्त्रमयी गुहाम्बा गुह्यरूपिणी॥१३७॥

dēśakālā'parichChinnā, sarvagā, sarvamōhinī।

sarasvatī, śāstramayī, guhāmbā, guhyarūpiṇī॥137॥

701. dēśakālā'parichChinnā

To know the meaning, this naama should be split into Desa + Kālā+ Parichinna.

Desa relates to Space. Desa also means country. Kaala is time. Chinna means divided or split. In Tamil, we say Chinna Pinnam. Pari enforces it Parichinna means totally split, indeterminate or unlimited. Ambāl is unlimited by space and time.

When you say this book was not here in this place-it relates to space. It is called Desa Bhavam. When you say this book was not here yesterday-it relates to time. It is called Kaala Bhavam. Ambāl is beyond such limitations.

Among the six religious divisions that Adi Sankara established, the one called Shauram relates to the worship of the Sun.

In the Shaura sect, the god Surya is the lord of the Trimurti, the eternal Brahman and the supreme spirit, the soul of all creatures, self-existent, unborn, the cause of all things and the foundation of the world. Shaura followers worship Surya as the Saguna Brahman. The most important text of the Shaura sect is the Shaura Samhita. It has 16 chapters and is mainly a Shiva Purana.

In the first 7 chapters it deals with Shiva and related rituals and in the remaining 9 chapters it deals with philosophical issues such as Brahma-jnana, the nature of Shiva and Ishwara etc.

Bhāskararāya quotes Shaura Samhita. He says, "The Person is omnipresent like ether. Everything, except himself, is illusory, as he is said to be unlimited as to space, time and things."

Limited by space, means the absolute non-existence of a thing in a certain place (saying) 'This is not here.' Limited by time, 'this was not before and it will not exist in future,' a thing having no antecedence nor precedence.

The gist of this nāma is that Ambāl is not limited by space and time.

702. sarvagā

Omnipresent. Ambāl is everywhere, in every substance.

This Nāma confirms the core belief of Sanatana Dharma that everything is divine. Sankara said *'Sarvam Vishnumayam Jagat,'* the entire world is filled with Vishnu.

When Hiranyakashipu asked his son Prahlada, 'Where is your Narayana?' Prahlada said that He is in everything right from a small particle to a pillar. Pointing to the pillar, Hiranyakashipu asked, 'Is he in this pillar?' Prahlada said, "Yes.' When Hiranyakashipu stuck the pillar with his sword, out came the Lord as Narasimha, proving what was said by Prahlada.

Likewise, Ambāl exhibits to us the innumerable substances of the Universe. Divinity is inherent in everything that we see, smell, hear, touch or feel. We do not spit or step on paper or money, enter a house or temple with our footwear on and so on. It's because we feel that each of these have divinity in them. It is the core belief of our Sanatana Dharma. We worship the bell, a pot of water, trees, cows, elephant, books and various implements on Ayuda Puja day. What is the background story behind Ambāl in every substance?

Let's hear from Bhāskararāya. He quotes the Varaha Purana:

When Devi in the form of the creative Shakti, was performing tapas (penance) in the Shveta Mountain, Brahma was pleased and he said, "Devi, ask a boon." Devi replied, "O holy one, I cannot bear to remain in one place, hence please grant me the boon of omnipresence." Brahma then replied to the creative Devi, "You of all forms, shall become omnipresent. Your qualified forms will be in all bodies, or you will become the soul of all."

The Devi Purana also says, "This is the true established doctrine about Devi, she is certainly the Vedas, sacrifices, heaven; all this Universe, animate and inanimate, is pervaded by Devi. She is sacrificed to, and she is worshipped, she is food and drink. Everywhere Devi is present under different

 The Glory of Lalithā Sahasranāmam

forms and names as in the trees, in the earth, wind, ether, water, fire. Bhumi Puja is done before construction starts. Thus, this Devi is to be worshipped according to the rules; one who thus knows her, will be absorbed into her."

In Devi Māhatmiyam, we chant Devi Stuti as being in many forms.

या देवी सर्वभूतेषु विष्णुमायेति शब्दिता।

नमस्तस्यै नमस्तस्यै नमस्तस्यै नमो नमः॥६॥

या देवी सर्वभूतेषु चेतनेत्यभिधीयते।

नमस्तस्यै नमस्तस्यै नमस्तस्यै नमो नमः॥७॥

She is in the form of Vishnumaaya and in our consciousness.

703. sarvamōhinī

All-bewildering. Moham (desire) attracts like a magnet. It also means to bewilder. Bewilders means cause someone to become perplexed and confused. Sometimes the naamas may be confusing.

Bhāskararāya questions- how can this Devi be said to possess contradictory attributes such as, permanence, and impermanence, animation and non-animation, and so on. This naama answers this question. She bewilders (Mohini) all the ordinary people (Sarva), who believe in the reality of the apparent duality, that is she makes them devoid of the knowledge of Unity. The meaning is that the apparent difference between Brahman and the Universe is illusory or Maya.

In the Kurma Purana, Shiva says, "This supreme Shakti is in me and is Brahman itself. This Maya is dear to me, infinite, by which this world is bewildered. I bewilder the whole Universe with the Devas, Daityas, and men; and I create them, and I cause them to exist."

In another place Devi says to Himavat, "whatever different scriptures are found in the world, opposed to Sruti and Smrti, devoted to the position of duality, via, Kapala, Bhairava, Saakala, Gautama, and many similar ones, they are for the purpose of bewilderment; those who are confused by the false scriptures, also confuse the world, in another cycle; these were all created by me for the sake of bewilderment."

Sarvamohini means Ambāl bewilders (Moha) the three worlds (Sarva).

704. sarasvatī

Sarasvati is a Sanskrit fusion word of saras meaning "lake, pond, pool", but also means as "speech"; and vati meaning "she who possesses". Sarasvati is the deity who presides over knowledge, i.e., she is in the form of the ocean of knowledge.

Bhagavad Gita (5-15) says,

नादत्ते कस्यचित्पापं न चैव सुकृतं विभु:।

अज्ञानेनावृतं ज्ञानं तेन मुह्यन्ति जन्तव:॥15॥

nādatte kasyachit pāpaṁ na chaiva sukṛitaṁ vibhuḥ

ajñānenāvṛitaṁ jñānam tena muhyanti jantavaḥ॥15॥

Meaning: The omnipresent God does not involve Himself in the sinful or virtuous deeds of anyone. The living entities are deluded because their inner knowledge is covered by ignorance.

"Knowledge is covered by ignorance hence people are bewildered." It is necessary to confuse sinful men because

      The Glory of Lalithā Sahasranāmam

they are devoid of divine grace; to conceal from them the knowledge of non-duality which is the highest of human desires and which removes all sorrow.

Bhāskararāya adds: The Bharadvaja Smriti says, "Sarasvati is she who ever resides in the tongue of all beings and who causes speech, hence she is called Sarasvati by great Rishis." The Vasistha-Ramayana, says "She is called Sarasvati because she is the stream of sense-impressions."

Ambāl is Sarasvati who is the pool of knowledge and causes speech. The Sankaracharyas of Kanchi Kamakoti Peetam have 'Sarasvati' in their names. Goddess Sharada in Sringeri is the goddess of learning. Sharada devi is also known as Sarasvati.

705. śāstramayī

Sastra means Learned Discipline or Sciences. And sciences mean knowledge by modern standards also.

Sastramayi means She who is in the form of the scriptures; She whose limbs are the scriptures. The Brahmānda Purana says, "She created from her breath, the Vedas, via, Rik, Saman, Yajus, and Atharvan; from her sweet words she created poetry, drama, Rhetoric, etc.; from her tongue, created Sarasvati. From her chin, whose eyes resemble the Chakora bird, the six supplementary of the Vedas; from the top of her throat, Mimansa, Nyayasastra, Puranas, Dharma-Sastra; from the middle of her throat Medicine and Archery; from the bottom of her throat the Sixty-four Sciences; from the rest of her limbs all other Tantras; and from her shoulders the Science of love."

One of the names of Ambāl in Lalithā Sahasranāmam is Veda Janani.

706. guhāmbā

The Mother of Guhaa or Subramanya.

Guha refers to a "cave." guh (darkness) is the dhātu (root) of guhā. The cave is dark and a secret place. Guhai in Tamil means a cave. Guhaa also means Subrahmanya. In one of my earlier sessions, I had told the story of Sanat Kumar who was later born as Subramanya. The Mahabharata gives the reason in the Anusasana Parva.

To destroy the Daitya Taraka Asuras at the request of the Devas, Subramanya was born in a forest at Saravana Poigai (Saravana Lake).

Because of his birth in the solitude of a forest of reeds he came to be called by the name of Guha (the secret-born). As he was reared by Krittikas, he came to be also known throughout the three worlds as Kartikeya.

Guhamba also means Ambāl is one who resides in the Guha (heart or cavity) of all living beings

707. guhyarūpiṇī

An extension of Guha is guhyam - a confidential subject. Guhyarupini means Ambāl is in the secret form. Shlokam in Japa Vidanam praying to Ambāl

गुह्याति-गुह्य-गोप्ता-त्वं गृहाणास्मितकृतम् जपं।

सिद्धिर्भवतु मे देवी त्वत्प्रसादान्मयि स्थिरा॥

GuhyAti guhya goptrI tvaM gRhAN Asmat kRtaM japam|

siddhir bhavatu me devi tvat prasAdAtan mayastira||

You are the secret of all secrets. Please accept this Japa performed by me and bestow Your perpetual Grace on me.

All the ordinary ideas, i.e. of duality, are only true for a time, but non-duality or Advaitam is ever true. This (non-duality) is the most secret (Guhya) not perceivable by ordinary vision; rupa, the form (her nature).

Bhāskararāya quotes a verse from the Sutasamhita that forms part of the huge Skanda Purana, which consists of 100,000 slokas.

The Suta Samhita. (4-47-69) says, "We adore Devi who assumes the form of the Guru, secret, in the form of secret knowledge, beloved by her secret devotees, residing in the secret place." Thus, by attributing two forms to the one Brahman the two kinds of scriptures are reconciled. Guhya means the Guhya Upanishad which is her form.

"Gu means ignorance, and Ru means dispeller," with guru meaning the one who "dispels ignorance.

The Kurma Purana in describing the glory of Devi says, "Among the Upanishads. O Devi you are the Guhyopanishad."

सर्वोपाधिविनिर्मुक्ता सदाशिवपतिव्रता।

सम्प्रदायेश्वरी साध्वी गुरुमण्डलरूपिणी॥१३८॥

sarvōpādhi vinirmuktā, sadāśiva pativratā।

sampradāyēśvarī, sādhvī, gurumaṇḍala rūpiṇī॥138॥

708. sarvōpādhi vinirmuktā

Sarva-Upadi, Vinirmukta. Ambāl is free from all limitations. Naama 701 Desakalaparichinna is stressed again.

Bhāskararāya comments: Sarvopadhi, all limitations or attributes such as, the Mother of Skanda, shadow, and light, etc., whether conditioned or unconditioned. The relation between the qualities and the thing which is qualified is illusory (or false) like the relation of the silver in the mother-of-pearl. To establish the authority of the scriptures as truth-indicating, it must be explained that all the Vedantas mean directly or indirectly one and the same supreme Brahman, which is non-duality.

The other scriptures which advocate duality are to be taken as explaining the ordinary vision as we find the same in the science of eclipse where it is indicated (by the words) 5 or 6 fingers about the consumption (of the sun and moon). In ancient days, Time intervals, were measured with the aid of a water clock, an ancient device for measuring time by the gradual flow of water. Time intervals were expressed in time-degrees, equal to four minutes, while eclipse magnitudes were expressed in "fingers," each equal to 1/12 of the lunar diameter. So, both the scriptures one advocating the duality and the other-nonduality, are not to be dealt with equally.

709. sadāśiva pativrata

Totally devoted to Shiva. It means ever remaining with him in all the times.

Shristi Kartri BrahmaRupa, goptri govinda rupini samhaarini rudra rupa tirodhanakarishvari sadashivanugrahada pancha kritya paraayana.

Among her five functions, 'Sadashiva Anugrahata' is the last one.

The Glory of Lalithā Sahasranāmam

Śiva is Nirguna Brahman or the Brahman without attributes and Ambāl belongs to Brahman, endowed with all the energies for creation, sustenance and dissolution.

710. sampradāyēśvarī

What is Sampradayam? It means a tradition followed by a group of people for a long time. Sampradāya is a sacred tradition in families since generations. It usually starts with the advice of a Guru and continues through generations as a tradition. Ambāl is the Eswari of traditional wisdom.

Bhāskararāya comments: Sampradaya, the wisdom regularly (Sam) imparted (Pradaya) to the disciples (by the teachers); Eswari, ruling. This knowledge is arrived at by reason and by tradition.

Ambāl is the ruler of traditional knowledge.

Sādhvī The word Sadhvi was in shlokam 43 earlier.

शाङ्करी श्रीकरी साध्वी शरच्चन्द्र-निभानना।

शातोदरी शान्तिमती निराधारा निरञ्जना॥ ४३॥

Here it is to be split into two Namas: 711.Sadhu and 712.I (pronounced Ee).

711. Sadhu

It has several meanings. It comes from the root sādh, which means "reach one's goal", "make straight", or "gain power over". sādhu as an adjective means good; virtuous; pious. One who is pious is called 'Sadhu.' The same root sadh is used in the word sādhanā, which means "spiritual practice".

It literally means one who practises a "sadhana" or a path of spiritual discipline.

Bhāskararāya interprets it as 'well done.' He calls Ambāl's inherent quality as parāhaṃta just as burning is the inherent quality of fire.

What is parāhaṃta? Both intellect and ego evolve from three guṇa-s (sattvic, rajas and tamas). The Brahman stands covered by the sheath of ego. Ego is a functional quality and hence Śhaktī is called parāhaṃta. Shiva is static in nature and Śhaktī is functional in nature. Functionality is the inherent quality of Śhaktī. She is the cause of accomplishments and dispelling ignorance. Hence, She is called Sādhu.

712. I: ई (i but pronounced as e) Bhāskararāya says it refers to Kamakala. We have seen earlier that Kāmakalā is mentioned in nāma 322. kāmakalā rūpā. 'kamakala' is the root of Panchadasi and it represents Ambāl's subtle form and Her subtlest form kuṇḍalinī.

Bhāskararāya comments on the philosophy behind this Nāma:

This name proceeds to say that quality (parāhaṃta) has two forms. This name is one-syllabled belonging to the Turiya known as Kamakala meaning "the fourth" derived from chaturiya, chaturtha, which is pure consciousness. अ represents Vishnu and ई represents Ambāl as Vishnu's sister. The derivation of the ई is from अ that represents Vishnu. The meaning of ई is she partakes the nature of Vishnu (A), as his sister playing the role of Preservation or Sthiti.

Interestingly, most female names end in ई or ā. Examples: Meenakshi, Kamakshi, Kantimathi, Vaishnavi, Gāyatri, Savithri, Aarti, Parvati, Dharini, -even western names like

Mary, Nancy, Natalie, Sophie, Molly, Ellie and so on. Names that end in ā include Vidya, Aparna, Ramya, Saroja, Sindhuja, Durga and so on. Let me say more about the importance of the aksharams or letters in Sanskrit.

We have seen before that Ambāl is in every one of the aksharams. Aksharam, meaning non-diminishing entity. Shyamala Dandakam by Kalidasa says *Sarva Mantrathmike, Sarva Yantrathmike, Sarva shakthyathmike, Sarva peedathmike, Sarva thathwathmike.* Lalitha is also known as Matrika Devi, the Goddess of the Letters of the Alphabet. Matrika or Matruka (मातृका) is the collective term for all letters and sounds. They are Mother-like, because they form the basis or the source for all forms of knowledge as also of the planes of existence (Lokas). Matrika-s are the subtle form of force that is behind every thought, speech and Mantra.

The arrangement of letters in Sanskrit alphabet is called as वर्णमाला -Varnamala which means Garland of Letters. The aksharas are not just mumbo-jumbo. When you utter them, they release the power of Parashakti (Matrka) who is hidden in them and energize speech, mind, breath and other organs in the body. The combination of the 15 Vowels (the Nityas) and the consonants (the 36 Tattvas) produces all sound, all mantra, all vibration, all word, and all music to the entire universe. The Soundaryalahari contains the 51 Aksharas hidden in 51 slokas. That's why Ambāl's Peetam is called Akshara Peetam. In Tiruvarur Kamalamba Temple, there is an Akshara Peetam. There is no vigraham of Ambāl in this Peetam. Ambāl is Guhyarupini and devotees can imagine Ambāl here in any form. Muthuswami Deekshitar worshipped Ambāl here and one of his songs on Ambāl's peetams is *"Panchasath Peeta Rupini"* set in Devgandhari ragam.

The Panchadashi-mantra of very potent fifteen letters or syllables (Bijakshara), composed of three segments (Kūṭa), is indeed the very heart of the Sri Vidya Upasana.

Also, Devi Māhatmiyam Chapter 4 Shlokam 4 explains the greatness of Devi who is in different forms in different people. It speaks

या श्रीः स्वयं सुकृतिनां भवनेष्वलक्ष्मीः

पापात्मनां कृतधियां हृदयेषु बुद्धिः।

श्रद्धा सतां कुलजनप्रभवस्य लज्जा

तां त्वां नताः स्म परिपालय देवि विश्वम्॥4.4॥

yā śrīḥ svayaṃ sukṛtinām bhavanēṣvalakṣmīḥ

pāpātmanāṃ kṛtadhiyāṃ hṛdayēṣu buddhiḥ।

śradthā satāṃ kulajanaprabhavasya lajjā

tāṃ tvāṃ natāḥ sma paripālaya dēvi viśvam॥5॥

Devi is herself a good-fortune in the virtuous, and misfortune in the evil-minded; she is the intelligence in the learned, and shraddha in the saintly; and she is the modesty of the distinguished noble-hearted ones, to her we ever bow down in reverence; O devi, please protect and sustain this world by your power.

O Devī, तां त्वां नताः we bow before you श्रीः Good fortune, स्वयं सुकृतिनां (She Who) Herself (is Good-Fortune in the Dwellings of the Virtuous) भवनेष्वलक्ष्मीः bhavanēṣva Alakṣmīḥ- पापात्मनां misfortune in the wicked, and कृतधियां good fortune in the dwellings of the stable-minded, virtuous, and हृदयेषु बुद्धि: hṛdayēṣu buddhiḥ-intelligence in the hearts of the learned, श्रद्धा सतां -faith in the hearts of the good, and कुलजनप्रभवस्य लज्जा -modesty in the hearts of the high-born. परिपालय देवि विश्वम्- May you protect and sustain the universe!

Bhāskararāya adds:

The Brahman becomes twofold by becoming both the quality and the thing qualified. Again, the quality is divided into two, masculine and feminine. The feminine became the Wife of Paramashiva, the masculine became Vishnu as the material cause of the Universe.

These three together, according to Shaiva doctrine form the partless Brahman. This doctrine is supported by the Kurma and other Puranas. Appayadiksitar elaborately deals with it in his work Ratnatrayapariksa.

Sri Adi Sankaracharya in his work Saundarya Lahari (Sl. 19), gives the mode of the worship of Kamakala.

713. gurumaṇḍala rūpiṇī

Ambāl is in the company of Gurus.

Talking about Gurus, we say in our dhyana shlokam, *Sadashiva Samarambam*-beginning with Sadashiva who was the first teacher, and ending up with *Asmad Acharya Paryantaam,* our present teacher.

Gurus, from Paramashiva to one's own teacher, form the mandala or group, the regular succession of them. The meaning is that this secret (of Vedas or scriptures) was handed down uninterruptedly from teacher to pupil and was not written in books.

Yogini hradaya (1, 3) says. "Into this world (this secret) was handed down from ear to ear." Ambāl is worshipped in such Guru Mandalam.

कुलोत्तीर्णा भगाराध्या माया मधुमती मही।

गणाम्बा गुह्यकाराध्या कोमलाङ्गी गुरुप्रिया॥१३९॥

kulōttīrṇā, bhagārādhyā, māyā, madhumatī, mahī।

gaṇāmbā, guhyakārādhyā, kōmalāṅgī, gurupriyā॥139॥

714. kulōttīrṇā

Transcending the senses. In this nāma kula means the group of senses, both internal (antahkarana) and external. She has transcended all the senses (saguna Brahman or as nirguna Brahman and merely remains as a witness).

715. bhagārādhyā

Bhaga + Aradhya. Bhaga has several meanings. "Wealth," "power" or "fortune." Bhaga is one of the 12 Adityas, a group of deities known as the sun gods, as described in the ancient text, the "Bhagavada Purana."

The Adityas are different avatars of Lord Vishnu in the form of the sun god, Surya, also known in Vedic traditions as Bhagavan. As Bhaga, he resides in the body of all living things. In this nāma, Bhaga means the Sun's disc (suryamandala). There are many forms of the Sun God in Vedic thought, which reflect various aspects of Dharma or cosmic law.

These include Surya (he who revolves and expands), Savitri (the transforming will), Aditya (primal intelligence), Mitra (the Divine Friend), Aryaman (the servant of Dharma), and Bhaga (the giver of bliss). Bhaga, the sun's disc is the object of secret adoration. Aradhya means worshipped. Ambāl is worshipped as a part of the Solar disc.

Or, Bhaga, the letter E., i.e.She is to be worshipped through the letter ए (Ai). The first alphabet of Sanskrit अ (a) in conjunction with ई gives rise to alphabet ए (Ai), the eleventh alpabhet. It is said, "The eleventh letter of her (Mantra ए) is the support and the seed and is in the triangle form."

716. māyā

Māyā means "that which is not." It means Illusion.

The energy that obscures what is plain, *Māyā* is a mystery of omnipresent power. It appears in the form of deceptive masks producing only illusionary effects.

Bhāskararāya comments:

In the Devi Purana it is said, "It is called Māyā because it is the instrument of marvellous actions, producing unheard of results, like dreams or jugglery."

Kanchi Periva says: Ambāl, the Brahma Shakti, is the power of Maya, who confers us Brahma Jnyana. Though She wraps us in delusions of Maya, She also possesses absolute compassion to liberate us from the clutches of Maya. We divert our minds through the pleasures of our sensory organs. In the process, we forget our inherent inner happiness. All our five senses thus begin ruling us. To cleanse our mind and liberate us from the control of our senses, and to also free us from our wavering and wandering mind, Ambāl appears as Kamakshi.

Ambāl is Maya. Ambāl is the powerful force that creates the cosmic illusion that the phenomenal world is real. In

Hardwar, there is a temple for Maya Devi. Haridwar was previously known as *Mayapuri* in reverence to this deity.

717. madhumatī

Madhu means honey and mati means intellect.

The Shruti says, "The nature of the great deity is honey-like." Bees produce honey by collecting the sugary secretions of plants (floral nectar). You can store honey for a long time. Honey is naturally antimicrobial; it has been used throughout history for almost every illness of mind and body.

Honey is so sweet that Americans use the term 'honey' to call someone they love intensely.

Another interpretation given by Bhāskararāya is:

"There are four kinds of Yogins as mentioned in the Yoga-Sastras. Of these the fourth is he who is called Atikrantabhavana (who) transcends even the state of meditation. He is the highest of them all. He also should overcome the seven steps or foundations (Bhumikas), of these the seventh step is called Madhumati, hence her name. That wisdom alone which arises from this foundation causes one to cross over the ocean of the Samsara."

In Saundarya Lahari - Verse 3, Adi Sankara says this shlokam is for attainment of all knowledge:

अविद्यानां-मन्त-स्तिमिर-मिहिर द्वीपनगरी

जडानां चैतन्य-स्तबक मकरन्द श्रुतिझरी।

दरिद्राणां चिन्तामणि गुणनिका जन्मजलधौ

निमग्नानां दंष्ट्रा मुररिपु वराहस्य भवति

avidyanam antas timira mihira dvipa nagari

jadanam chaitanya stabaka makaranda sruti chari

daridranam cintamani gunanika janma jaladhau

nimagnanam damstra muraripu varahasya bhavati

avidyanam: for the ignorant, antas timira mihira, you banish the inner darkness; dvipa nagari. Like an island city of lights. Ambāl is like brilliant sun that removes the darkness of ignorance; For Jhadanam- the dull-witted, chaitanya stabaka, to establish Chaitanyam, the 'makaranda shruti jari'- the gush of nectar of intelligence from the cluster of flowers gushes the nectar of intelligence. She grants Chaitanyam to the dull-witted like honey from the flowers.

Such is the greatness of Ambāl as Madhumati.

Madhumati is the name of a river too.

718. mahī- Mahī means earth. She manifests as planet earth (Bhumadevi). The Devi Purana says, "It is great because it pervades all, hence Prakrti is called Mahi." Mahi is also the name of a river.

719. gaṇāmbā- Troops of Shiva are known as Ganas. Ambāl is the mother of Ganas. Gana also refers to Ganesha. She is mother of Gaṇeśa who the chief of Śhiva's gaṇas and is known as Gaṇapati.

720. guhyakārādhyā

Worshipped by Guyahakas. Guhyakā-s are the warriors of Kubera, the lord of wealth, who is one of greatest devotees of Lalitāmbikā. Guhya means secret and ārādhya means worship.

In this context, this nāma means that She is worshipped in a secret place known as mūlādhāra, in Her subtlest form kuṇḍalinī.

721. kōmalāṅgī- Komala means tender and Angi refers to limbs. Ambāl is described as Tender limbed. She is also called Nalini.

722. gurupriyā

The guru here refers to Shiva. She is the wife of Shiva and is fond of him.

स्वतन्त्रा सर्वतन्त्रेशी दक्षिणामूर्तिरूपिणी।

सनकादिसमाराध्या शिवज्ञानप्रदायिनी॥१४०॥

svatantrā, sarvatantrēśī, dakṣiṇāmūrti rūpiṇī।

sanakādi samārādhyā, śivajñāna pradāyinī॥140॥

723. svatantrā

Independent. As Ambāl creates without depending on any instruments, she is called Svatantra.

Svatantra: Sva + Tantra- all the Tantras belong to her; even in the Shaiva, Vaisnava, Ganapatya, her glory only is described, hence all Tantras are Hers. She is the embodiment of sixty-four tantra-s, that have been described in nāma 236 catuḥ-saṣti-kalā-mayī.

Sva, Self, i.e.Paramashiva, Tantra depending. The meaning is that each depends on the other.

The Kalika Purana says, "Shiva ever lives in that place sporting with Devi. In the centre is the abode of Devi, Sankara remains there. In the north-east of that mountain is

 The Glory of Lalithā Sahasranāmam

the hermitage of Sankara Where he lives forever. Parvati also remains there."

724. sarvatantrēśī- Sarva + tantra + īśvarī = The ruler of all Tantras.

She is the presiding deity of all tantra-s that are sixty-four in number.

725. dakṣiṇāmūrti rūpiṇī

Ambāl is in the form of Dakshinamurthi.

Dakshinamurti is Guru form of Shiva sitting and facing southwards. well-known as the instructor of Brahma, Narayana, whose mantras are found described in the Tantras. Adi Sankara wrote the Dakshinamurthi Ashtakam.

726. sanakādi samārādhyā

Worshipped by Sanaka and others.

Who are Sanaka and others? Sanaka, Sana, Sanatkumāra, and Sanāndana are the four great sages who are manasika Putras of Brahma. They are described as the first mind-born creations of the creator-god Brahma.

Born from Brahma's mind, they are included in the succession of gurus. There is a story that Sanatkumar was born as Murugan in his next birth.

The Brahmānda Purana says, "You are the beginningless, the whole in the form of cause and effect, the Yogins, Sanaka are searching after you alone."

727. śivajñāna pradāyinī

She imparts the knowledge of Shva

The Vasistha-Ramayanam says, "Wind is recognized by motion, fire by heat, Shiva who is consciousness, purity and tranquillity, is known by his vibratory energy. There is no other way (to know him)." Shiva can be realized only through Shaktī.

Or, it can be said that Shiva is the bestower of the knowledge of Devi.

The Varaha Purana says, "These three (Trimurtis) are attained by one who really knows Rudra (Shiva)."

चित्कलाऽऽनन्दकलिका प्रेमरूपा प्रियङ्करी।

नामपारायणप्रीता नन्दिविद्या नटेश्वरी॥१४१॥

chitkalā,'nandakalikā, prēmarūpā, priyankarī।

nāmapārāyaṇa prītā, nandividyā, naṭēśvarī॥141॥

728. chitkalā

Chit, Brahman which is existence, knowledge, and bliss, and Kala is part. It is the power of consciousness that causes limitation in respect of activities (existence). Sri Krishna says in Bhagavad Gita, "My part alone in the world are the eternal Jivas."

ममैवांशो जीवलोके जीवभूत: सनातन:।

मन:षष्ठानीन्द्रियाणि प्रकृतिस्थानि कर्षति॥7॥

mamaivānsho jīva-loke jīva-bhūtaḥ sanātanaḥ

manaḥ-ṣhaṣhṭhānī indriyāṇi prakriti-sthāni karṣhati

mama—My; eva—only; anśhah—fragmental part; jīva-loke—in the material world; jīva-bhūtaḥ—the embodied souls; sanātanaḥ—eternal; manaḥ—with the mind; shashthāni—the six; indriyāṇi—senses; prakṛiti-sthāni—bound by material nature; karṣhati—struggling

The souls in this material world are My eternal fragmental parts. But bound by material nature, they are struggling with the six senses including the mind.

The Padma Purana too while enumerating the (different) forms of Devi, says, "In the mind of all embodied souls, resides the energy called Citkala."

729. Anandakalikā

Germ of bliss. She is one portion of the bliss enjoyed by Jivas. The Shruti (Tai. Up., 2-7-1) says, "Other beings live by a part of this bliss." She is in the form of bliss basked by humans.

Or it means the bud of the Anandamaya Kosa (sheath).

730. prēmarūpā- In the form of affection. She is the embodiment of love, the quality of being the Supreme Mother (Śrī Mātā).

731. priyaṅkarī- Because of being an embodiment of love, she causes love in humans.

732. nāmapārāyaṇa prītā

Ambāl is very happy in the repetition of (Her) names.

As we said before, Ambāl resides in each Aksharam. Bhāskararāya explains:

From अ A to Ksha are her names, A is one and Ka and the rest are thirty-five, in all thirty-six, these thirty-six represent thirty-six years. When we multiply this 36 with 16 vowels, we get 576. These are 576 and are the first letters. Again this 576 is multiplied by 36 letters in second place of each letter in order, we get 20,736. Add with this the first letter अ, 20737 is arrived at. There are 20,737 combinations of letters that should be recited. The Devi Bhagavadam. (Book III): "When from A to Ksa the vowels are joined to the consonants, countless names are obtained."

The repetition of these Akshara names in five ways is described in the Srividya tantra of Kaadimata. "By day, week, fortnight, month and year. etc." It is the ceremony of the repetition of the names in either in a day, a week, a month, in six months (ayana) or in a year. *"Keertayan Nama Sahasram, idam mathpreetaye Sadha."* Ambāl is pleased with the repetition of Akshara Naama Parayanam just as She is with Lalithā Sahasranāmam.

733. nandividyā

The Science of Nandi. The Vidya is worshipped by Nandi. Nandividya is a science of mantras revealed by Nandi, the bull of Lord Shiva.

Srisaila Kshetra is called an abode' of Hadi Vidya-Kadi Vidya' but also to Nandi Vidya. By saying 'Nandividya Nateshwari ', it emphasizes the fact that Nandi is dear to Lord Shiva but also is the first one to worship Sri Vidya, which is the vidya that belongs to Goddess Parvati.

734. naṭēśvarī

She is the wife of the Dancer, the Nataraja of Chidambaram.

Saundarya Laharī (verse 41) describes this dance as nava rasa mahā tāṇḍava naṭam which means the great dance with nine types of rasa-s (nine types of expressions).

तवाधारे मूले सह समयया लास्यपरया

नवात्मानं मन्ये नवरसमहाताण्डवनटम्।

tavādhāre mūle saha samayayā lāsyaparayā

navātmānaṃ manye navarasamahātāṇḍavanaṭam।

In your Mulādhāra I meditate on the Navatman (Maha Bhairava) who express nine sentiments (Navarasas) and engaged in Maha Tandava along with Samaya (Maha Bhairavi) whose dance form is Lasya.

मिथ्याजगदधिष्ठाना मुक्तिदा मुक्तिरूपिणी।

लास्यप्रिया लयकरी लज्जा रम्भादिवन्दिता॥१४२॥

mithyā jagadadhiṣṭhānā muktidā, muktirūpiṇī।

lāsyapriyā, layakarī, lajjā, rambhādi vanditā॥142॥

735. mithyā jagadadhiṣṭhānā

She is the basis of the illusory universe, the effect of māyā. Just as the mother-of-pearl based on its shine is illusorily perceived as the basis of silver.

Mithyā means false, jagad means universe and adhiṣṭānā means support or basis. This nāma means that She is the basis for false appearance of the universe, or She supports this delusive (illusionary) universe with the power of Her māyā.

The cause for the illusionary universe is explained in Bṛhadāraṇayaka Upaniṣad (IV.iv.19) which says "Through the mind alone the Brahman is to be realized. Here there is no manifoldness whatever. There is no diversity."

Universe is the manifestation of the Brahman. When Brahman is real, the universe also is bound to be real. A pot is made of clay; hence clay and pot are not different. In the same way, the Brahman and universe are not different. They are one. Though they are the same, because of illusion they appear different. The illusion becomes a reality here. This is the argument of Vedānta. However, Pot and clay are considered as different and the cause for the pot, the clay is ignored. The cause for the universe, the Brahman is ignored as illusion binds a person with visible objects.

736. muktidā

Giver of salvation

Bhāskararāya comments:

The Kurma Purana says, "Hence one desirous of salvation should take refuge in Parvati, Paramesvari, the Soul of all beings and also of Shiva."

The Shiva Purana "If one recites the names of the supreme Lord even unconsciously, Shiva gives him salvation. Why say more?"

The Brahmānda Purana also says, "Those who worship the supreme Shakti whether regularly or irregularly, are not entangled in Samsara. There is no doubt, they are the liberated souls."

737. muktirūpiṇī

In the form of salvation

Acquiring knowledge alone does not give salvation. It should be said only when one remains in his own bliss, (the real) salvation comes to him. She is the embodiment of liberation. Salvation is the culmination of the process of realizing Self.

738. lāsyapriyā- Fond of dancing. Lasyam refers to the dancing by women while Thandavam is the dancing of men.

739. layakarī

Causing absorption

Laya, a peculiar state of mind, is a stage beyond meditation. "Laya (mental absorption) is equal to ten meditations." In music, if svara (musical note) is the father, then laya is the mother. Laya is the balancing act between the primary music and the supporting music.

740. lajjā- Lajjā means bashfulness.

It is considered as one of the basic qualities of women. It is said (Markendeya Purana) 'Devi who resides in all beings in the form of bashfulness."

741. rambhādi vanditā

Adored by Rambha and others like Urvasi, all beautiful celestial damsels

भवदावसुधावृष्टिः पापारण्यदवानला।

दौर्भाग्यतूलवातूला जराध्वान्तरविप्रभा॥ १४३॥

bhavadāva sudhāvṛṣṭiḥ, pāpāraṇya davānalā|

daurbhāgyatūla vātūlā, jarādhvānta raviprabhā||143||

742. bhavadāva sudhāvṛṣṭiḥ

It can be divided into भव-दाव-सुधा-वृष्टिः Bhava means samsāra, dhāva means forest fire. Sudha is nectar. Vrishti means shower.

Material life is compared to forest fire, and She extinguishes it by rain of nectar. She is the rain of nectar (falling) in the forest-fire of worldly existence.

It can also be divided into three names (as Bhavada, Vasudha, Vrstih). Bhava also means Shiva, therefore bhavadā means She is the giver of Śiva. AttainingShivameans liberation. Vasudhā means wealth. She is the giver of wealth. Vṛṣṭiḥ means giver. That is, she is the bestower of worldly enjoyment and Salvation. The Rudrayamala and the Mangala rajastava say, "Where there is worldly enjoyment there is no salvation, where there is salvation there is no worldly enjoyment. To the best devotees of Ambāl, salvation and enjoyment are both in their hands"

743. pāpāraṇya davānalā

Pāpa means sins. Aranya means forest. Dava is forest fire. When a forest catches fire, it destroys the trees and homes very rapidly-like you see the raging fires in California. Ambāl is the forest fire who blows away sins that cause miseries. She is papanasini -the destroyer of sins.

The Naradiya Purana says, "The supreme name of Ganga is the fire that consumes the forest of Sin because Ganga is the remover of the disease of Samsara. Therefore, it should be sought with much effort."

Or, Dava (forest fire) means devotion, etc., which are the means of destroying sin. Ana, life—energy, la, receive, that is she reveals the actions which remove sin.

Rudra Yāmala says "Indra! This supreme secret which destroys all sins immediately is to repeat Pañcadaśī mantra

1008 times by standing in water after taking bath with total devotion and faith."

744. daurbhāgyatūla vātūlā

Daurbhgya means durbhagyam -misfortune. Vatu refers to Vayu or Air. In India, you will see Airconditioned coaches in railways marked as 'Vatanukula.' It means Vatam (Air) is Anukulam (comfortable). Here, Ambāl is described as a gale or storm blowing away misfortune. Vatula refers to certain good actions like blowing the light fluffy attached to thistle seeds in the wind. You can see them floating in the air during springtime. She removes the miseries like whirlwind blowing away thistledown.

745. jarādhvānta raviprabhā

Jarā means old age, ravi means sun, dhvānta means darkness, and prabha means to illuminate. The body is subjected to decay. People start worrying when they become old.

They develop fear of death. Ambāl is like the sun beam dispelling the darkness of decay.

भाग्याब्धिचन्द्रिका भक्तचित्तकेकिघनाघना।

रोगपर्वतदम्भोलिर्मृत्युदारुकुठारिका॥ १४४ ॥

bhāgyābdhichandrikā, bhaktachittakēki ghanāghanā।

rōgaparvata dambhōḻi, rmṛtyudāru kuṭhārikā ॥ 144 ॥

746. bhāgyābdhichandrikā- Previous nāma referred to sun and this nāma refers to moon. Sun and Moon are Ambāl's eyes. The moon is cool and delightful. Ambāl is like the moonbeams illuminating the ocean of good fortune.

747. bhaktachittakēki ghanāghanā

बक्त-चित्त- minds of her devotees. केकि means peacock, घना घना - means rain bearing clouds (dark clouds). On seeing the clouds, the peacocks cry with the sound of keki and dance on seeing dark rain bearing clouds. Ambāl is compared to the clouds. The minds of Her devotees are compared to peacocks.

So, Ambāl is like the cloud that nourishes the peacocks which are the minds of her devotees. Make the mind happy and dance.

748. rōgaparvata dambhōḻi

Roga means disease, parvata means mountain and dhambholi means thunderbolt. She is like a thunderbolt to diseases. Thunderbolts are very powerful and capable of even breaking the mountains. Thunderbolt also refers to the vajrāyudha of Lord Indra, a potent weapon that can annihilate the opponents. This nāma says that Ambāl is like the thunderbolt that destroys the mountain of disease.

749. rmṛtyudāru kuṭhārikā: मृत्यु-means death दारु refers to wood-कुठारिका is the axe. (kodali in Tamil). Ambāl is like an axe to the tree of death.

We have already seen earlier that Ambāl is सर्वव्याधि - प्रशमनी सर्वमृत्यु - निवारिणी in naamas 551 and 552.She cures all diseases. By sarva-vyādhi it means disease of both body and mind. Sarva mrtyu means premature or untimely deaths – like what happens in riots and violence. The nāmas 748 and 749 emphasize that Ambāl saves us from the mountain of diseases and untimely deaths. Let us pray to her to protect us from such calamities.

 The Glory of Lalithā Sahasranāmam

Chapter 15

The Great Maheswari

We begin this chapter with shlokam 145.

महेश्वरी महाकाली महाग्रासा महाशना।

अपर्णा चण्डिका चण्डमुण्डासुरनिषूदिनी॥१४५॥

maheśvarī, mahākāḻī, mahāgrāsā, mahā'śanā।

aparṇā, chaṇḍikā, chaṇḍamuṇḍā'sura niṣūdinī॥145॥

750. Maheśvarī

The great Goddess Devi, spouse of Maheswara. Maha means great -like in Mahavishnu, Mahalakshmi. Maheshwari is one among the seven mother goddesses or Sapta Matrikas: Brahmani, Vaishnavi, Maheshvari, Indrani, Kaumari, Varahi, and Chamunda or Narasimhi. She takes Her name from Lord Shiva (Maheshwara). She is believed to have been born from the body of Lord Shiva. She is armed with similar weapons to Shiva and has numerous other symbols and characteristics of Shiva. She is usually depicted as "*Varada Abhaya Hasta* Dhaarim"-having four arms with one arm in Varada Mudra (granting wishes)

and one in Abhaya Mudra (protection). The other two arms are depicted as holding the Shula (Trident) and Damaru (drum) just like Shiva. The Vahana (vehicle) of Goddess Maheswari is 'Rishabam' - a bull like Shiva's.

751. mahākāḷī

Maha is great, and Kāli means "She Who Is Black." काळा Kāḷā in Hindi and Marathi also means black. Kāli also means goddess of time or fate. She is called great because she rules over even death. Devi is also referred to as Mahakāli, Bhadrakāli and Kālika (Sanskrit: कालिका).

She is considered a ferocious form of Devi. The very name of Kāli induces fear in the minds of people as She is most often portrayed as a fearful fighting figure with popping eyes, a necklace of skulls, protruding red tongue, and armed with weapons.

However, Maa Kaali is Mother Goddess, who destroyed evil asuras as we understand from our ancient scriptures. Besides being a dark colored goddess, Devi is seen as a great power of time (Kaala). We will see how she is described in various scriptures and how her greatness was realized by various devotees even in the recent centuries.

How did Kāli appear first? There is a legend. It is said that Kāli 's earliest appearance was when she emerged from Shiva.

At one time, Devas were harassed and hurt deeply by an asura called Daruka. None could fight and destroy him because of a boon he got from Brahma that would allow only a female

　　The Glory of Lalithā Sahasranāmam

to kill him. Parvati merges with Shiva's body, reappearing as Kāli to defeat Daruka and his armies.

Bhāskararāya quotes Liṅga Purāṇa (Chap.106) "Having entered the body of the lord of Deva-s, Pārvatī made Her own body out of poison in the neck of Shiva.

Shiva created Kālī, the dark necked Goddess with matted hair from His third eye.... On seeing Kālī who resembled fire and whose black neck was embellished with poison, Devas including Vishnu, Brahma, and Indra fled due to fear."

In Devī Māhātmyam chapter 7, Verses 5-6 describe the emergence of Kālī and how the asuras Chanda and Munda were killed. On seeing the armies led by them approach her, Devi becomes very angry.

ततः कोपं चकारोच्चैर अम्बिका तान अरीन्प्रति।

कोपेन चास्या वदनं मषीवर्णम अभूत्तदा॥

भ्रुकुटीकुटिलात्तस्या ललाटफलकाद्द्रुतम।

काली करालवदना विनिष्क्रान्तासिपाशिनी॥

tataḥ kopaṃ cakāroccair ambikā tān arīn prati,

kopena cāsyā vadanaṃ maṣīvarṇam abhūt tadā.

bhrukuṭīkuṭilāt tasyā lalāṭaphalakād drutam,

kālī karālavadanā viniṣkrāntāsipāśinī.

Meaning: Ambikā then became very angry (ततः कोपं, Kopam in Tamizh too) with those enemies, and in her anger her face became dark as (मषीवर्णम) ink (mashi, is ink in Tamil).

From the surface of her forehead, bent with frown, suddenly Kālī Karālavadanā leapt out, with a sword and a noose.

The word kālī is used repeatedly in chapters 7, 8, and 9 of Devi Māhatmiyam.

In Chapter 12, the Phalashruti part of Devi Māhatmiyam, there is more description of the form mahākālī – "great Kālī" or "great dark goddess" or "great power of time" – in verse 38. The verse declares that mahākālī pervades the universe.

व्याप्तं तयैतत्सकलं ब्रह्माण्डं मनुजेश्वर।

महाकाल्या महाकाले महामारीस्वरूपया॥38॥

vyāptaṃ tayaitat sakalam brahmāṇḍam manujeśvara,

mahākālyā mahākāle mahāmārīsvarūpayā. ॥38॥

The Rishi Sumedhas tells the King Suratha: "Your majesty, the whole universe is pervaded by Mahākālī (the great dark goddess) who appears in the form of the great catastrophe महामारीस्वरूपया or Samharini at the time of the Mahākāla or Pralayam."

The next verse uses the word kāla twice (in the locative form kāle) and can be read as an explanation of the term mahākālī. She who destroys at the appropriate time and creates and sustains at the appropriate time is called "the great power of time."

सैव काले महामारी सैव सृष्टिर्भवत्यजा।

स्थितिं करोति भूतानां सैव काले सनातनी॥39॥

saiva kāle mahāmārī saiva sṛṣṭir bhavatyajā,

sthitiṃ karoti bhūtānāṃ saiva kāle sanātanī.

 The Glory of Lalithā Sahasranāmam

It is she who is the great catastrophe महामारी (Pralyakale Shakti:). It is she, the birthless one, creates. It is she, the eternal one, who maintains the life of all beings in their time. (Covid 19, the epidemic is called Mahamari in Hindi)

Parvati is addressed as the fair one, Gauri, as well as Kali, the dark one. Isn't it a contradiction? The twin opposite colors, white and black, represent the two-opposing nature of the Goddess. Parvati is also the goddess of love, or Kamakshi. In times of danger, She can become a fierce and angry Kali. Śrī Kāñcī Mahaperiva (Deivathin Kural – Volume I) says "Shiva gets to the task of saṃhāra (destruction) after taking black colored Pārvatī as Śhaktī. When we refer to Ambāl Herself as saṃhāramūrtī, we call Her as Kālī."

In India, there is a famous Mahakaleshwar temple, one of the twelve Jyotirlingas in Ujjain. MahaKāli is the Devi at this temple. She is called Hara Sidhi Mata.

This Maha Kāli was worshipped by the great King Vikramadithya. This is the kshetra where Kāli dasa who was an illiterate gained wisdom by the Grace of MahaKāli.

Let me say a few words about the great poet Kālidasa. There is an interesting story about how he became a Mahakavi. Kālidasa was once a foolish shepherd who eventually became a great poet by the grace of MahaKāli. The story goes that he was brought by some jealous ministers before a proud princess Vidyottama for marrying her. Vidyottama tested him with signs. She raised her index finger to mean God is one without a second. Kālidasa, quickly replied by showing two fingers. He had thought that she was meaning to poke him in one eye. Vidyottama interpreted Kālidasa's answer as God has two parts -one as Paramatma the supreme God and the other as Jeevatma, the individual soul. Venturing further, she showed her five fingers to indicate five senses. Kālidasa thought she was about to slap him, so he showed his fist. This time Vidyottama thought it to mean that controlling the five senses can lead to ultimate happiness. She was surprised by his wisdom and agreed to marry Kālidasa but found out later that he was a fool and drove him out. Kalidas went inside a temple and prayed to Kāli to grant him wisdom. Kali wrote on his tongue, and he instantly became a Mahakavi, a scholar poet. Kalidasa means Kali's servant. His very first prayer to Kāli was Shyamala Dandakam beginning with *"Manikhya veenaam upalalayanthim."*

He wrote many great dramas like Shakunthalam and great epics like Raghu Vamsam, Kumara Sambhavam, Megha Sandesham etc. With Kali's grace, he became one of the "nine jewels" of the court of King Vikramaditya.

Ramakrishna Paramahamsa (1836-1886), Swami Vivekananda (1863-1902), and Ramprasad Sen (1718-1785), all from Bengal, are some of the legendary devotees of Kāli.

They lived barely 150-250 years ago and demonstrated spiritual realizations of Kali.

Their stories show how greatness was achieved with the grace of Devi. They are an inspiration to worship Devi.

To ward off fear, Durga Saptasati says:

                    The Glory of Lalithā Sahasranāmam

ॐ सर्व स्वरूपे सर्वेशे,

सर्व शक्ति समन्विते,

भये भ्यस्त्राहि नो देवी,

दुर्गे देवी नमोस्तुते.

Meaning: O Goddess of all Goddesses, you take many forms, you are all powerful and worshipped by all. O Goddess Durga, I Salute you and pray to save and protect us from all fears.

752. mahāgrāsā

The great devourer. Brahmasutram (1-2-9) says

ॐ अत्ता चराचरग्रहणात् ॐ॥ १.२.९॥.

oṃ attā carācaragrahaṇāt oṃ.. 1.2.9.

attā—The eater; charā achara grahaṇāt—because the movable and immovable (i.e. the whole universe) is taken (as his food). Who is he? The eater of such a stupendous thing can be Brahman alone and no one else.

The eater (is the Supreme Lord), on account of the appropriation of all that moves and does not move.

This nāma refers to the act of annihilation or the great dissolution (mahā pralaya) when everything is devoured by Ambāl who is maha samharini.

753. mahā'śanā

This is an add-on to the previous nāma. Mahat, because consuming both the animate and the inanimate Universe. Ashana is 'to eat'. Mahā-ashanā means a great eater. Possibly the earlier nāma refers to the great dissolution (the deluge) and this nāma refers to the capability of Devi.

Both the naamas 752 and 753 mean Devi is a great devourer or great eater.

You will find that Devi's glory is described in detail in the Devi and other Shakta Upanishads. Devi is not only the principle of creation, she is also the principle of auspiciousness, the principle of cosmic energy, and the principle of austerity, (Thapasi Jwalathi), of destruction too. She is also the principle of Divine knowledge. She is Jada Sakti and Chit Sakti.

754. aparṇā

There are different interpretations. Bhāskararāya says:

Apa means removing; Rna is debt. Aparna means without debts. Devi does not owe anything to anybody.

Parna means leaf. A-parna is just the opposite. Means without leaf! The Kāli ka Purana says, "Devi renounced eating even leaves as food when doing Tapas, hence the daughter of Himavan is called Aparna."

The same is repeated in Brahmānda Purana.

There is another story. Lord Shiva at the temple in Suchindram in South India is called 'Sthanumurthy, also Sthanumalayan." Sthanu means still- something that appears to be like dead wood but has life in it. Ambāl was entwining Shiva as a tender creeper. She looked at the still form of Sthanumurthy and thought why she alone should be glamorous with nice leaves. So, shed all her leaves and became without leaf. Hence, she is called Aparna.

755. chaṇḍikā

The name "Chandi" is derived from the Sanskrit word "chand" which means "tear apart." (I think the Tamil word Chandai has come from this word). The Goddess Chandi is described as "She Who Tears Apart" Chandi also refers to anger. Ambāl becomes angry at her enemies.

Devi Māhatmyam is a part of the Markandeya Purana (one of the oldest 18 mahapuranas). It is also called Durga Saptasati and Chandi Path. It is popularly known as Chandi because it describes the glory of the Goddess as Chandika, the terrible. Like the god Rudra, the Goddess too has two forms- a malevolent form and another benevolent form. In Her terrible form She destroys the evil demons. Yet in Her destruction, one can see the light of a resplendent regeneration too. The benevolent form is Her compassionate form as the Mother of the Universe. The recitation of the Chandi Path is designed to guide the reader's awareness into the presence of Chandi – the Divine Mother Herself – so that all conflict of mind may settle down and return to Peace.

As per Devi Bhagawada Purana, Goddess Parvati is the progenitor of all other goddesses. She is one who is the source of all forms of goddesses. She is worshiped as one with many forms and names. Her different mood brings different forms or incarnation.

According to Devi Bhagavadam, a girl of seven years is called Chandika.

756. chaṇḍamuṇḍā'sura niṣūdinī

Devi is the destroyer of Daityas (Asuras) Chanda and Munda. Hence, she was called Chamundeswari.

The Markendeya Puranam says,

यस्माच्चण्डं च मुण्डं च गृहीत्वा त्वमुपागता।

चामुण्डेति ततो लोके ख्याता देवी भविष्यसि।।

"Because you captured Chanda and Munda, you shall be called Chamunda."

Chāmuṇḍa is one of the sapta mātā-s (seven mothers). In the previous nāma, we saw that she was Chandika- the angry one. It is said that She is angered on seeing evil doers. To prove this point, she destroyed the two demons, Chanda and Munda who were the great evil doers.

Devi Māhatmyam identifies Chamunda with Kāli. As per Devi Māhatmyam, Chamunda emerged as Chandika from the eyebrow of goddess Kaushiki, a goddess created from "sheath" of Durga and was assigned the task of eliminating the demons Chanda and Munda, the army generals of demon kings Shumbha-Nishumbha. She fought a fierce battle with the demons, ultimately killing them.

The second portion of Devi Māhatmyam is the most popular one and it describes Durga's destruction of Mahisha. Durga in this form is the recipient of the valor and strength of all gods and she kills demon Mahishasura.

The name Mysore—or Mysuru is derived from Mahishooru, Place of Mahisha, who was destroyed by the goddess Chamunda. The famous Chamundeshwari Temple is on Chamundi Hill, Mysore.

There is also another interpretation from the Varaha Purana. There is a sloka on how Devi got the name Chamunda.

When Devi fought with Ruru, a daitya (asura) king, she pierced him with her Shoolayudham (Trident) whereby the head (Mundam) and the body (Charmam) got parted. She took away the two body parts charma-munda and so, Devi got the name Chamunda. Also called Chamundeswari.

Harikesanallur Muthiah Bhagavadhar has composed a nice song on Chamudeshwari. It is *sarasamukhi* set in rAgA: gauDa malhAr.

क्षराक्षरात्मिका सर्वलोकेशी विश्वधारिणी।

त्रिवर्गदात्री सुभगा त्र्यम्बका त्रिगुणात्मिका॥१४६॥

kṣarākṣarātmikā, sarvalōkēśī, viśvadhāriṇī|

trivargadātrī, subhagā, tryambakā, triguṇātmikā ॥ 146 ॥

757. kṣarākṣarātmikā

Ksharam means perishable. Aksharam is just the opposite which means imperishable. It also means syllables.

The Varaha Purana says, "Though Devi is all-syllabled, yet she is called one-syllabled as she is the ruler of the Universe."

We have seen before that She is in the form of all alphabets and words. She is śabda Brahman! Every word in Lalitha Saharanamam is a mantra.

Devi Upanishad (9.6) says *mantrāṇāṁ mātṛkādevī śabdānāṁ jñāna rūpiṇī* (मन्त्राणां मातृकादेवी शब्दानां ज्ञान रूपिणी) (She is in the form *matṛkā*-s in *mantra*-s and in the form of *jñāna* in sound.) Nāma 577 says mātṛkā varṇa rūpiṇī. *Matṛkā* means source or origin.

In this context it means the alphabet. The realization of *matṛkā* by the soul means liberation to the soul. Soul realizes *matṛkā* by means of *mantra*, the origin of which is *matṛkā* or Sanskrit letters from *a* to *kṣa* (अ to क्ष).

In Bhagavad Gita, Shri Krishna says (15.16):

द्वाविमौ पुरुषौ लोके क्षरश्चाक्षर एव च।

क्षर: सर्वाणि भूतानि कूटस्थोऽक्षर उच्यते॥16॥

dvāv imau purushau loke kṣharaśh chākṣhara eva cha

kṣharaḥ sarvāṇi bhūtāni kūṭa-stho 'kṣhara uchyate

Shri Krishna says that there are two kinds of beings: the kṣhar (perishable) and the akṣhar (imperishable). All beings in the material realm are perishable, and those liberated are imperishable. Although all souls are eternal; in the material realm, Maya binds the individual soul to a material body. From the tiniest insect to the celestial gods, all embodied living entities in the material world are kṣhar (perishable). They must go through the repetitive cycle of birth and death of their material body. Whereas the akṣhar (imperishable) souls possess an immortal body, which is free from the cycle of birth and death. They reside forever in the divine realm, the Abode of God.

Thus, Ksharaa refers to body and a-ksharaa refers to soul.

Being and non-being (Sat and Asat) are also called Kshara and Akshara.

Vishnu Sahasranamam shlokam 51 reads:

धर्मगुब्धर्मकृद्धर्मी सदसत्क्षरमक्षरम्।

अविज्ञाता सहस्रांशु विधाता कृतलक्षण: ॥५१॥

Dharmagub dharmakṛddharmī sadasat akṣaramakṣaram.

avijñātā sahasrāṃśur vidhātā kṛtalakṣaṇaḥ. ॥51॥

Sat: sat, means "that which is true." The Parabrahman who is truth. The word 'Satyam' comes from Sat. India's national

                    The Glory of Lalithā Sahasranāmam

motto is 'Satyameva Jayate.' Truth alone Triumphs from Mundaka Upanishad.

The Central element of the Upanishads is the reality termed as Brahman. Brahman is of the nature of Sat, Chit which is consciousness and Ananda which is bliss. Asat is hidden or not having reality.

Kṣaram: All beings subjected to change.

Akṣaram: The changeless one.

758. sarvalōkēśī

Ambāl is the ruler of all worlds. There are seven worlds each world is represented by one vyāhṛti. (bhūr, bhuvar, svar, mahar, janar, tapar, satya as described in our Gāyatri Mantra).

She is the Sarveshwari.

759. viśvadhāriṇī- Supporter or Holder of the Universe.

760. trivargadātrī

Tri-varga means puruṣārtha-s. She is the giver of three puruṣārtha-s. Puruṣārtha-s are dharma (righteousness), artha (wealth or purpose), kāma (desire) and mokṣa (liberation). The last one, mokṣa is not included here, hence instead of puruṣārtha-s, the nāma only says tri-varga.

Kanchi Mahaperiyava says, "Religion is the instrument for Dharma-Artha-Kama-Moksa commonly called Purushartham (Goal of Man). Man thinks of living a life full of joy and plenty.

Happiness is of two kinds: A temporary one and another, the irreducible one. Kāmam is one that gives a temporary joy; it is a common denominator for all worldly pleasures.

Perinpam (Great Joy = Eternal Bliss) stays put, never leaves once received and is Moksa or Vīdu (Liberation).

Adi Sankaracharya asserts in Bhajagovindam that this Arththam is Anarththam (Wealth is meaningless).

अर्थमनर्थं भावय नित्य, नास्ततत:सु खलेशः सत्यम्।

सत्यम् पुत्रादपि धनभाजां भीति:, सर्वत्रैषा विहिता रीति:॥

Wealth is meaningless, truly there is no joy in it. Always reflect this. A rich man fears even his own son. This is the way of wealth everywhere.

Artham = Meaning; wealth. These temporary and trivial pleasures of life, conferred by wealth and objects, rob us of eternal and fulfilling Moksa or liberation.

If we were to make Nishkāma Dharma, it would become the means to Moksha or Vīdu (heaven) and eternal Bliss. Moksha is irrevocable liberation from bonds and attainment of Eternal Bliss.

The purpose of our Religion is to take us back to our Home of Eternal Bliss. Moksha is the Eternal Abode of Joy."

Ambāl is the giver of the three objects of desire. Dharma, Artha, Kama are the three objects. It does not mean she does not offer Moksha. The Nama Muktidā मुक्तिदा (736) says she offers liberation to those who are worthy of it.

761. subhagā

The Sanskrit word Shubam has several meanings like 1. Propitious 2. promising 3. Beneficial 4. Good luck, all denoting positivity. Likewise, Subaga has several meanings as Bhāskararāya comments:

    The Glory of Lalithā Sahasranāmam

It can mean good fortune.

A girl of five years of age is called Subhaga.

Bhaga, means wealth, desire, magnanimity, strength, effort, fame, etc... su, excellent (remain in Her).

The Viswa Purana says, "Bhaga means dominion, Wisdom, dispassion, fame, strength, effort, desire, wealth, virtue, sun, and salvation."

We have seen earlier that Bhaga means the sun, by her the sun is illuminated. Because she resides in the sun and causes all its works. Devi is known as Kushmanda. Kushmanda is the fourth aspect in Navadurga forms of Mahadevi. Ku means "a little", Ushma means "warmth" or "energy" and Anda means "cosmic egg".

She is the Goddess who has the power and capability to live inside the Sun. The glow and radiance of her body is as luminous as that of the Sun.

The Whole and supreme energy of Vishnu, which is called the three Vedas, Rig, Yajus and Saman lightens the Whole universe and destroys its iniquity. Wherever every month the sun exists there is this energy of Vishnu, composed of the three Vedas. The Rigs shine in the morning, the Yajus at noon, Brhad ratha and other portions of the Saman at the end of the day.

Thus, the manifestation (of the energy) of Vishnu is threefold known as Rig, Yajus and Saman. The energy of Vishnu ever does not abide in the sun.

The threefold energy Vishnu only exists in the sun, but is also manifest in Brahma, Vishnu and Rudra. Thus these (three gods) are also the three Vedas. The sun possessed with the energy neither rises nor sets.

In this way the energy of Vishnu exists in the sun encircled by seven troops. As a man, nearing a mirror kept on a stand, observes in it his own image so the energy of Vishnu is never disjoined but remains month by month in the sun which is there placed." "The seven troops are, Devas, Rishis, Gandharvas, Apsaras, Yaksas, Saadyas and Raksasas (Saptakiranas)." You can see Surya in a cart being driven by seven horses. So also, the seven rays or Saptakiranas are called VIBGYOR. The collective meaning of the above passage is the seven troops are the causes of the sun's monthly changes, but the energy, as she is the foundation of all, does not change.

Subhaga may also mean 'acharavastus' (motionless) of the eight things used in auspicious occasions, as the Padma Purana says,

ikshuvas tarurajam cha nishbhava jeeratanyake,

vikaravacha go ksheeram kusumbham kusumam thata

lavanam che iti sowbhagya ashtakam sthavara muchyate

"Sugarcane,Taruraaja (The palmyra tree or panai maram), sprouted Jeera and Coriander seeds, the cow's milk (with all its transformation curd and butter), Yellow garment, Kusumbha flowers and salt ";

or Devi herself; for the same Padma Purana says,

trivishtaba sowbhagyamayeem bhukti mukti pradaam Umaam

aaradhya subhagaam bhaktya naari vaa kim na vindhati?

"What else should not one——whether a man or woman—obtain by worshipping Uma with devotion, who is the conferrer of blessings to Devas. and bestower of enjoyment and salvation on all humankind"?

762. tryambakā

Three-eyed. Shiva has three eyes. It is quoted in Vedas.

The very first word in the Maha Mruntajaya Mantram is 'Trayambakam.'

ॐ त्र्यम्बकं यजामहे सुगन्धिं पुष्टिवर्धनम्

उर्वारुकमिव बन्धनान् मृत्योर्मुक्षीय मामृतात्

Om Tryambakam yajamahe sugandhim pushtivardanam

Urvarukamiva bandanaan mrtyormukshiya maamrutat.

Tryambakeshwar Jyotirling temple is in Tryambak near Nashik.Ambāl is a part of Shiva, and hence She is called Traymbaka. There is also a Tryambakeshwari Temple in Karnataka, the only one I know of. it is near Chamarajanagar about 60 miles from Mysore. Bhāskararāya quotes Devi Purana that says, "The moon, the sun and the fire are the three eyes of Devi, and called by sages three-eyed. "त्रयाणां ब्रह्म विष्णु रुद्राणां अम्बिका माता वा"- Tri, Brahma,Vishnu and Rudra, amba', mother, (i.e., mother of Brahma, etc.)

763. triguṇātmikā

Possessed of the three qualities- Sattva, Rajas and Tamas. Satva as in Parvathi, Rajas as Durga, and Tamas as in Kāli. She is the equilibrium of the three qualities Sattva, Rajas and Tamas.

स्वर्गापवर्गदा शुद्धा जपापुष्पनिभाकृतिः।

ओजोवती द्युतिधरा यज्ञरूपा प्रियव्रता॥ १४७॥

svargāpavargadā, śuddhā, japāpuṣpa nibhākṛtiḥ।

ōjōvatī, dyutidharā, yajñarūpā, priyavratā॥147॥

764. svargāpavargadā

Ambāl is the bestower of Swargam and Moksham -heaven and salvation respectively.

Svarga is heaven and apavarga means liberation, the emancipation of the soul from bodily existence, exempted from further transmigration also known as mokṣa.

Swargam gives Anitya sukam; Moksham provides Nitya Sukam that is Brahmanandam or Bliss called Apavarga in Sanskrit.

The Shruti says, "That happiness which is not interrupted by pain (now) or in future, attained through desire, is called Svarga."

This happiness is temporary as Krishna says in Bhagavad Gita (9-21):

ते तं भुक्त्वा स्वर्गलोकं विशालं

क्षीणे पुण्ये मर्त्यलोकं विशन्ति।

एवं त्रयीधर्ममनुप्रपन्ना

गतागतं कामकामा लभन्ते॥ 21॥

te taṁ bhuktvā swarga-lokaṁ viśhālaṁ

kṣhīṇe puṇye martya-lokaṁ viśhanti

evaṁ trayī-dharmam anuprapannā

gatāgataṁ kāma-śāmā labhante

          The Glory of Lalithā Sahasranāmam

After enjoying the vast pleasures of heaven, when their stock of Punya or merits get exhausted, they return to the earthly plane. Thus, those who follow the Vedic rituals (the duty enjoined by the three Vedas), desiring objects of enjoyment, repeatedly come and go in this world.

All the Vedic scriptures support this belief.

The happiness in Moksham or salvation is an eternal one. Ambāl gives both svarga or heaven and liberation.

765. śuddhā- Pure. Free from the stains of Avidya.

766. japāpuṣpa nibhākṛtiḥ

Whose body is like the Hibiscus flower or China-rose. China-rose is the Hibiscus flower called Gurhal गुढल (Hindi), Chemparati (Malayalam), Sembaruthi (Tamil), Jaswand जासवंद(Marathi). It is generally in a bright red color.

The other interpretation given by Bhāskararāya is:

This name may be taken as two, adding the syllable 'a' before, as 'Ajapa ' and 'Puspani bhaakritih.'

Ajapa, is a mantra and the description of its 'nature is given in the Daksinamurthy Samhita. Japa starts in Vaikhari or vocal form. Ajapa is just the opposite. It means without chanting. The efficacy of the Japa depends upon the dedication and the attentiveness of the person performing the Japa.

After long years of constant practice, done with devotion and commitment, an extraordinary thing happens. Now, the Japa no longer depends on the will or the state of activity of the practitioner.

It seeps into his consciousness; and it goes on automatically, ceaselessly and inwardly without any effort of the person, whether he is awake or asleep. Such instinctive and continuous recitation is called Ajapa.

"Without repetition (Japa), that which brings to the practitioners of Mantra the attainment (the result) of the repetition, is called Ajapa, which breaks as under the noose of the Samsara."

It is also called Hamsa mantra. There is another definition of A person exhales with the sound 'Sa'; and he inhales with the sound 'Ha'. This virtually becomes Aham-sa: mantra (I am He; I am Shiva). A person is said to inhale and exhale 21,600 times during a day and night. Thus, the Hamsa mantra is repeated (Japa) by everyone, each day, continuously, spontaneously without any effort, with every round of breathing in and out. And, this also is called *Ajapa-japa.*

In Tiruvarur, Lord Nataraja is said to be performing the dance called *ajapa natanam* in Vishnu's hrudayam to match the rhythm of his breathing.

The idol of Sri Thyagaraja is covered with flowers and a piece of cloth in such a manner that only his face can be seen. It is just to ensure that devotees should not mistake that Shiva is dancing over Vishnu.

Pushpa, according to the Hema-Kosa, means the flowering season, chariot of Kubera, flower and the beauty of the eyes.

767. ōjōvatī

It means Vitality.

Ojas is explained as the eighth substance (Dhatu) in the Vedic Commentaries. She is the one to nurture Ojass (Vital, Strength, Attracting Power, Powerful Aura) in the human

　　　　The Glory of Lalithā Sahasranāmam

body. Ojass is being created through a systematic process viz: Medhass, Thejass, Varchass, Ayus and Ojass. This powerful Ojass will uphold the life energy (Prana) in a damaged body. It is the vitality and sharpness of the senses. The Visva says: "Ojas means light, the vitality of the substances, splendour, strength and radiance;" as Ambāl possesses all these qualities she is called Ojovati. Devi is full of vitality and strength. Devotees who worship her constantly may also expect to be active and strong.

768. dyutidharā- Dyuti means light. Dhara means holding. Dyutidhara means the light bearer. In Hindi, electricity board is called Vidyut Mandal.

769. yajñarūpā

Ambāl is the form of Yajna. What does yajna mean?

Yagna is a Sanskrit word meaning "worship," "sacrifice" or "offering." It is derived from "yaj," meaning divine worship.

It refers to any activity performed to please the Almighty Bhagvan.

Taitreya Samhita says Yajna means Vishnu. Scholars have interpreted this Nāma to say that Devi is the form of Vishnu. In my ancestral village of Maharajapuram, Devi is in the form of Vishnu and called *'VishnuDurga'*.

Yajnas are of different kinds. There are five great yajnas (pañcamahāyajña) to be performed by a householder, according to Manu.

1. **Brahma Yajna:** Part of a daily ritual. It is an offering to Devas, Rishis and Pithrus supposed to be done daily. It includes chanting Vedic manthras, Each from One

Veda, Rig, Yajur, Sama and Atharva after completing the Madhyahnika

2. **Deva Yajna:** For the pleasure of the Devas- Ganapathy Homam, etc.

3. **Pitru Yajna:** For ancestors -Tarpanam, Shraddam etc.

4. **Bhauitika Yajna:** Feeding animals, birds,

5. **Manushya Yajna:** Athithi Bhojan, Anna Dhanam, and others.

According to the Mukhyam naya rahasya, Yajnarupa, "The great sacrifice is worshipping one's own Self with much devotion, by perfumes, etc., which he recognises by his own senses."

770. priyavratā

Fond of vows. Ambāl is fond of all vows, even those which are made to other deities.

The Bhavisyottara Purana says, "He who makes a vow to any god or to goddess, all is for the delight of Shiva and Devi who are the creators of the world. There is no difference here because the whole world is Shiva and Shakti."

दुराराध्या दुराधर्षा पाटलीकुसुमप्रिया।

महती मेरुनिलया मन्दारकुसुमप्रिया॥ १४८॥

durārādhyā, durādarṣā, pāṭalī kusumapriyā |

mahatī, mērunilayā, mandāra kusumapriyā || 148 ||

771. durārādhyā

Dura means difficult. Durdasai. Duradistam are some examples where Dura is connected. Aradhya is worship. Ambāl is difficult to worship. For whom? For the fickle-minded.

Saundarya Laharī (verse 95) says "It is difficult for those who cannot control their senses, to come near your sacred feet and worship you."

पुरारन्ते-रन्तः पुरमसि तत-स्त्वचरणयोः

सपर्या-मर्यादा तरलकरणाना-मसुलभा।

तथा ह्येते नीताः शतमखमुखाः सिद्धिमतुलां

तव द्वारोपान्तः स्थितिभि-रणिमाद्याभि-रमराः

purārāterantaḥ puramasi tat astvaccharaṇayoḥ

saparyāmaryādā taralakaraṇānā masulabhā.

tathā hyete nītāḥ śatamakhamukhāḥ siddhimatulāṃ

tava dvāropānta: sthitibhir aṇimādyābhi ramarāḥ. 95

You are the consort of Shiva, मसुलभा it is very difficult indeed for unsettled minds to attain the equivalent of the way of Your worship. Whatever limitless gains they, the divinities such as Indra and others might have had, all those psychic powers such as Anima, they got them from just outside Your door.

Most people, who are referred to as being of unsettled mind and incapable of the proper way of worshipping the Absolute Goddess. Adi Sankara intends to sound a warning here. He says that there could be a majority of people for whom this way of looking at beauty, from a feminine and negative standpoint, might be prejudicial to their spiritual progress.

Bottomline: Worshipping Her is very difficult without controlling mind and senses. It does not yield any result.

772. durādarṣa- Difficult of control. Dur, difficult, Adarsha. controlling. It is very difficult to perceive her.

773. pāṭalī kusumapriyā

Fond of Paatali flowers. It is pale yellow with a red tinge. Yellow Trumpet Flower (English), PaadhiriPu (Tamil) The padma purana says, "Shiva is fond of Bilva leaves and Devi of Patala flowers."

774. mahatī

Means the great! As she manifests in the form of the things she is called Mahat. She is addressed as mahat by Vāc Devi-s because She manifests in all living beings as She is also known as prakṛti. Mahat is also known as buddhi or intellect, the great and exclusive principle of humanity. Intellect is an essential component for attaining knowledge.

The Saakapurni explains it is the Mahat by which all things are measured. Mahati means (also) the Veena of Narada.

775. mērunilayā

Residing on Meru.

Meru has already been discussed in nāma 55 sumeru madhya śṛṅgasthā. Three-dimensional form of Śrī Chakra is known as Meru or Mahā Meru. She lives atop Meru.

It is described in the Tantraraja in the 28th chapter thus, "Now I shall describe to you the sixteen Nitya deities which are the Lokas," After describing their world with all its oceans and islands it continues. "In the midst of Meru, the great shining Lalita, ever remains," around it (the Meru) there are fourteen continents up to the ocean where the other deities (remain). Beyond them in the last supreme ether, is the Chitra's and other deities' abode.

Another interpretation by Bhāskararāya says:

Srichakra has three aspects (Prastaras) Bhumi, Kailasa and Meru.

The Bhuprastara is when it is identified with the eight deities, viz" Vasini, etc., when it is with the Matruka letters, it is the Kailasa, and the Meru is when it is with the sixteen Nitya deities. Merunilaya means she abides in the (mental) identification with sixteen Nitya deities. The mode of the meditation is given threefold in the three Samhitas of Sanatkumara, Sanandana and Vasistha.

Or, Meru, the nine-syllabled mantra as described in the Jnanarnava indicated by the following words, "Bhumi, Chandra, Shiva, Maya, Shakti, Krsnadhvan, Madana, Ardhacandra and Bindu." Nilaya, the place wherefrom all other mantras arise.

776. mandāra kusumapriyā- Fond of Mandara flowers. Mandara. Devadaru. Mandāra tree is in Devaloka.

वीराराध्या विराड्रूपा विरजा विश्वतोमुखी।

प्रत्यग्रूपा पराकाशा प्राणदा प्राणरूपिणी॥१४९॥

vīrārādhyā, virāḍrūpā, virajā, viśvatōmukhī।

pratyagrūpā, parākāśā, prāṇadā, prāṇarūpiṇī॥149॥

777. vīrārādhyā

Vira means warriors, those who fight in a battle. The Tamil word Veeran also means a warrior or a brave person.

Aradhya is worshipped. Ambāl is worshipped by warriors. What type of warriors – not those who carry weapons but courageous devotees.

The characteristic of the Viras is given thus: "One who enjoys (realizes) the Self, the remover of pain, brings about the dissolution of egoism and of what is opposed (to the Self, i.e., duality), devoted to bravery."

778. virāḍrūpā- She who is in the form of the cosmic whole. Viraad encompasses the entire visible and tangible world. Devi is in the form of the entire universe.

779. virajā

Vi means without and rajas means impurity. She is without impurity. Virajaa has two meanings. One is without any impurity or blemish. Another meaning is "Without passion".

Viraja, is the presiding deity at the Utkalaksetra.

Brahmānda Purana says, "At Viraja, the goddess Viraja is established by Brahma. By seeing her a mortal purifies as far as seven generations." 'Raja-s' also means light, water and worlds.

780. viśvatōmukhī

Facing every direction.

She has faces in all directions. The Shruti (Svetaranya Upanishad 3-3) says, "Having eyes and mouths on all sides." When a form is created by devotees through meditation, then alone she becomes manifest as having hands, feet on all sides, and eyes, mouth and head everywhere.

781. pratyagrūpā

Interior.

Pratyak, tending inwards; the direction of the senses towards objects is called Bahirmukhatva and Paraanmukhatva (external); their inward direction towards the Self is called Antarmukhatva and Pratyanmukhatva.

The Shruti (Kathopanishad 4-1) says, "The Self-existent made senses. Hence one sees externally but not internally." The meaning is that Her nature is to be seen internally.

Devi is visible to those who see inwardly. She can be realized within, and this is known as self-realization. Experienced seniors say "to attain God, look within yourselves. God resides in everyone's minds, only we must find the Almighty" This is the core belief in Sanatana Brahma. Every being is divine.

782. parākāśā

Para is supreme. Akasa is ether. The supreme ether.

Because she is Without quality, i.e. she is Parabrahman.

The Chandogya Upanishad (1-9-1) in the following passages means ether as Para-Brahman, "He said that is ether, ether is the greatest of all these things. This ether is the supreme rest." It is also declared in the Veda Sutra (1-1-22), "The ether is Brahman on account of characteristic marks." That is, it does not mean the elemental ether. The Kurma Purana says, "Whose (of Brahman) supreme divine energy is called ether." Thus, she is the origin of the Universe, namely one, all, all controlling, Mahesvari, energy, without beginning, called ether, as if shining in the heavens.

783. prāṇadā

The giver of life.

Primal, the five kinds of vital breath or the eleven senses da to destroy or control. In the Ved. Sutra (I, 1, 23), "For the same reason breath is Brahman,"

784. prāṇarūpiṇī

The life

Hence Prana- means Brahman. Shruti also (Chandogya Up., 4-10-5) says, "Prana is Brahman, Ka is Brahman, ether is Brahman."

Manu Smriti (12-123): "The same (Brahman) some call fire, others Manu, others Prajapati, others Indra, others breath and others Paramatman."

मार्ताण्डभैरवाराध्या मन्त्रिणीन्यस्तराज्यधूः।

त्रिपुरेशी जयत्सेना निस्त्रैगुण्या परापरा॥१५०॥

mārtāṇḍa bhairavārādhyā, mantriṇī nyastarājyadhūḥ |

tripurēśī, jayatsēnā, nistraiguṇyā, parāparā || 150 ||

785. mārtāṇḍa bhairavārādhyā

Worshipped by Martandabhairava.

Bhāskararāya comments:

In the Sri Chakra between the 22nd and 23rd walls there is a devotee of Devi named Martandabhairava. The Lord of the teachers, Sage Durvasa says in his Lalitha Stava Ratna, "In my heart I adore Martandabhairava, decked with the jewelled crown, sporting with (his wife) Chaya who is the energy which supplies light to the eye."

Or, Shiva, to kill the Daitya called Manimalla, mounted a horse and descended to Earth, is called in Maharashtra by name Mallari and by name Martandabhairava. The Tantrachintamani also repeats the same. The worship of Devi performed by Shiva is described in the Mallari Mahatmya.

Marthanda, the Sun. The Skanda Purana says: "Because he was born from the inert egg (Mrta and Anda) he is called Martanda." Bhairava means Vatuka and other different kinds. Concerning the worship of Devi by the sun, the Padma Purana says: "The sun after worshipping daily a jeweled image of Devi obtained his pure divine lofty position." As regards the worship by Bhairava, the Kāli ka Purana describes it at length.

Bhairava: according to the Shiva Sutra (I-5) "effort is called Bhairava," it is the sun (Martanda) because it destroys the darkness of confusion; for Shiva Sutra (III-7) says: "By conquering confusion, by the expansion of the endless, victory over innate knowledge." The Vaarttikakaara explains thus:"confusion means darkness,i.e. inborn egoism, by overcoming this, the Sun of effort is produced; ' endless ' Samskaras (good mental tendencies); Expansion means the expansion of the Samskaras. To the Yogin who thus understands victory means attainment of the innate knowledge." The meaning is, Devi is to be attained by that rising sun-like effort which is called Bhairava.

786. mantriṇī nyastarājyadhūḥ

Who has entrusted her kingdom to Mantrini.

Bhāskararāya comments:

Mantrini, Shyamalamba. The Brahmānda Purana says speaking about Rajashyamala, "The care of the dominion and of the Shaktis of Lalita, the supreme ruler, all are in the power of Mantrini."

Or Mantrini, those who worship (Devi) by Mantras, or Mantra is a pure thought, because it has the quality of protecting the man during meditation. (manana trayete iti mantra:) Those who possess this are called Mantrins. Mantrini, a certain effort which leads them to union with Bhagavadi; in that effort depends on the power of attaining universal dominion. The meaning is the attainment of unity by devotees and Yogins depends upon Devi alone.

The Shiva-Sutras (II-L2 and 3) say: "Thought is Mantra; effort is the means; knowledge is the body: and manifestation is the secret of the Mantra."

The holy Krishnadasa explains the Sutras as follows: "Thought, by this the supreme truth of the Self is experienced. Thus, the thought is the experience of the grace of the manifested Self. Thought is Mantra. The same experience is thought secretly, i.e. Eswara and one's own nature without distinction, hence it is called Mantra. It is called Mantra because through their teachers by the manifested qualities of the Self meditated upon, the complete egoism (Purnahamta), and by the power of protecting through destruction of Samsara. The man attains equal mindedness by divine experience through the Mantra. The thought of the aspirant also is called Mantra for it has union with that quality. The effort of fixing the mind continuously on the Mantra just said above which has the quality of protecting the man during (meditation) is called Prayatna (effort). Prayatna means internal agitation; this alone it means. Thus, the man who practises the Mantra attains the unity with deity (the Self). The Yogin Who practises thus obtains the power of the Mantra, which makes him forever continue meditation on the Purnahamta as said above. Vidya, the experience of the highest unity. Body the divine hosts of

          The Glory of Lalithā Sahasranāmam

words. Manifestation of the Purnahamta in all directions. That is the meditation by the Mantras which have the power of protecting one. Secret, that it is a secret to ordinary people."

787. tripurēśī

The deity of the SarvAsapAripuraka chakra is called Tripuresi. The second avarana is the 16 petals circle known as Sarvasaparipuraka Chakra. Sarva Aasa Paripuraka means fulfills all desires. The presiding form of Lalita in this Avarana is Tripureshi. She is ornamented with gems, carries a book and a rosary.

788. jayatsēnā- With victorious army. Jayat, refers to the conquest of Bhandasura and others. Sena, her attendant Shaktis.

789. nistraiguṇyā- Devoid of three qualities

790. parāparā

Para and Apara. Superior and Inferior.

Bhāskararāya gives many interpretations.

Para, apara and paratpara: Para, others, apara, the Self; or Para, foe, apara friend. The Bhagavad Gita (9-29) says I have neither foe nor friend.

समोऽहं सर्वभूतेषु न मे द्वेष्योऽस्ति न प्रिय:।

ये भजन्ति तु मां भक्त्या मयि ते तेषु चाप्यहम्॥29॥

samo 'haṁ sarva-bhūteshu na me dveṣhyo 'sti na priyaḥ

ye bhajanti tu māṁ bhaktyā mayi te teshu chāpyaham.

Also, Para means, he who is far off, Apara he Who is near." Bhagavad Gita (13-15) says "I am far and near." Para and apara, the two forms of Brahman. the unconditioned and the conditioned.

The Prasna Upanishad (5-2): "This is indeed, O Satyakama, Para and Apara." As the name suggests, it is an Upanishad of six main questions, asked by six seekers of truth and answered by sage Pippalapada, son of sage Dadhichi, a great teacher of the Atahrvaveda.

एतद्वै सत्यकाम परं चापरं च ब्रह्म यदोङ्कारः।

तस्माद्विद्वानेतेनैवायतनेनैकतरमन्वेति॥५.२॥

etadvai satyakāma paraṃ cāparaṃ ca brahma yadoṅkāraḥ.

tasmād vidvānetenaivāyatane naikataramanveti ॥5.2॥

Para (literally means posterior) quality, energy; apara the thing qualified, i.e. Shiva who is anterior.

Shiva conjoined with Shakti only is called Para-Brahman. Or Para and Apara, the twofold ether, or the twofold knowledge, as described in the Mundoka Upanishad (1-1-4).

Mundaka means shaven head referring to Sanyasis. The Mundaka Upanishad is embedded in Atharva Veda. It contains three Mundakams (parts), each with two sections. The first Mundakam defines the science of "Higher Knowledge" and "Lower Knowledge"- para and apara.

Angirasa Rishi – a sanyasi is telling Saunaka - a grahastan

तस्मै स होवाच।

द्वे विद्ये वेदितव्ये इति ह स्म

यद्ब्रह्मविदो वदन्ति परा चैवापरा च॥४॥

    The Glory of Lalithā Sahasranāmam

tasmai sa hovāca.

dve vidye veditavye iti ha sma

yadbrahma vido vadanti parā caivāparā ca ||4||

To him he said: Two kinds of knowledge must be known-that is what the knowers of Brahman tell us. They are the Higher Knowledge and the lower knowledge.

It is further described that the lower knowledge is the Rig-Veda, the Yajur-Veda, the Sama-Veda, the Atharva-Veda, siksha (phonetics), kalpa (rituals), vyakaranam (grammar), nirukta (etymology), chhandas (metre) and jyotis (astronomy); and the Higher Knowledge is that by which the Imperishable Brahman is attained. Linga Puranam also confirms this.

Or the twofold meaning of the scriptures. Sushruta Samhita 4.2.2 says, "The meaning of the scripture is divided into Para and Apara. The Para means the supreme which is beyond (all the things). Apara is dharma, (religion) the means of obtaining the supreme."

Or in the Yoga-sastras also knowledge is divided into three—Para, Apara and Parapara.

It is said, "Knowledge is said to be threefold by the division of Para, Apara, and Parapara. Of these, the first is the Supreme Knowledge and is the cause of cognising the Lord. the bondage, and the Self. The second, Apara knowledge is simply the cause of cognising bondage. The Paratpara knowledge is, just as the change of the sight between a man and cat in the night, it does not distinguish the marks (Vilaksana).

Or the worship is also of three kinds, Para, Apara and Parapara. The Nityahrdaya says, "Your worship described in the Nitya '(Tantra) is declared to be of three kinds, 0 Gauri, Para, Apara, and Parapara.

The first is the remaining in non—duality whatever method is practised; the second is the worship by means of the (Sri)Chakra which I ever perform; 0 Devi, full of wisdom, the third is worship of all the manifestations of Her."

Devi is also threefold, Para, Apara. and Parapara.

The Varaha Purana says when speaking about the Trimurtis: "The creative (energy) is said to be Para which has the White color. Vaisnavi who is red and long eyed is Apara. The Raudri (energy) is called Parapara. These three are attained by one who really knows Rudra."

　　　　The Glory of Lalithā Sahasranāmam

Chapter 16

Ambāl is Brahman

There are many nāmas of Ambāl that affirms Her status as Brahman. In Devi Atharva Shirsha - a Shakta Upanishad, the very first verse says, साब्रवीत्- अहं ब्रह्मस्वरूपिणी। "I am the very same Svarupini (form) of the Brahman.'

Bhāskararāya, also mentions that the Goddess Devi is indeed the Brahman, the Supreme non-dual reality.

What is Brahman? Brahman is defined as *"satyam jnanam anantam brahma,"* which can be translated as "that which is truth, knowledge, never changes and infinity"

Kanchi Maha Periava explained that anything that does not change is sathyam. Brahman is sathyam. It doesn't end in all three kalas (avasthai).

The movie appears on the support of the white screen. Still that very movie hides the screen itself which is its support. The screen is in no way affected; it is still the screen, and it remains as the screen. Brahman is like the screen.

The Vedas say *"brahmam satyaM jagan-mithyety-evaM rUpo vinishcayaH"* Brahman is the only Reality. The Universe is mithyA, that is, it may appear real but will become unreal. *"Jeevo Brahmaiva Na aparahaa."* The jeevan that is inside us is nothing but brahman. The jeevan learns the attributes of the jagad from the indryaas and enjoys the world (jagad). It retains the name "jeevan" if he has the knowledge of the jagad. Once that is gone, that jeevan is brahman! Our Sanatana Dharma believes that the Absolute Truth that is called Brahman – is the only thing to be aimed. Ambāl is Brahman!

Let us always keep this in mind while we chant the Lalithā Sahasranāmam.

सत्यज्ञानानन्दरूपा सामरस्यपरायणा।

कपर्दिनी कलामाला कामधुक् कामरूपिणी॥१५१॥

satyajñānā'nandarūpā, sāmarasya parāyaṇā|

kapardinī, kalāmālā, kāmadhuk,kāmarūpiṇī||151||

791. satyajñānā'nandarūpā

Satya is Truth; Jnana is Wisdom, and Ananda is bliss. Ambāl is the embodiment of all three combined. Bhāskararāya cites several Upanishads to explain this Naama.

Taitreya Upanishad II-0,

ॐ ब्रह्मविदाप्नोति परम्। तदेषाऽभ्युक्ता।

सत्यं ज्ञानमनन्तं ब्रह्म।

om brahma vidāpnoti param, tadeṣā' abhyuktā, satyaṃ jñānam anantaṃ brahma.

The knower of Brahman reaches the Supreme. On that, this is spoken: 'Real, Consciousness, Infinite is Brahman; "The Brahman is Truth, Wisdom, infinity."

Brahadaranya Upanishad (3-9-28-7) says विज्ञानमानन्दं ब्रह्म "vijnAnam Anandam brahma: "knowledge/omniscience; bliss is Brahman. "Brahman is eternal, wisdom, bliss."

satyajñānā' may be split as Saty and ajnana: Sati refers to Devi, Ajnana, ignorance—those who are ignorant of Devi, to those she assigns Ananda Rupa, the world called Ananda is devoid of Bliss.

Brahadaranya Upanishad 4-4-11 says,

अनन्दा नाम ते लोका अन्धेन तमसावृताः।

तांस्ते प्रेत्याभिगच्छन्त्यविद्वांसोऽबुधो जनाः ॥११॥

anandā nāma te lokā andhena tamasāvṛtāḥ|

tāṃste pretyā abhigachanty avidvāṃso abudho janāḥ||11||

"Those worlds are called Ananda. which are covered with deep darkness; the ignorant and unwise men go to those worlds after death."

Lalithāmba is formed of pure and concentrated Sattva Without any admixture of Rajas and Tamas, whereas the other Saktis merely have a preponderance of the Sattva, quality over the other two (Rajas and Tamas) and not of pure Sattva. Hence, she is the highest, the prototype of Para-Brahman.

792. sāmarasya parāyaṇā

The word 'Samarasam' literally means equal taste. This nāma means "The supreme abode of the equal nature (of Shiva and Shakti)."

The Shruti says, "Equally pre-eminent, equally fundamental, both are equal."

Or Samarasya, the worlds of Devas, with them, Parayana, abode or refuge.

Or Rasya, songs, Sama, Sama~Veda songs, Parayana, fond of. "Parayana means, fond of, devoted to, dependent."

793. kapardinī

This nāma is derived from the word Kaparda. Hair of Shiva is known as Kaparda. Kaparda means braided and knotted hair. If you see Nataraja statue, you will find hair braids flying on both sides of the head.

Bhāskararāya comments:

Ka, water, i.e. of Ganga, Para, the flow, da, sanctifies. Shiva's matted hair sanctifies even the water of the Ganga that falls on his head.

According to Devi Purana, Kapardini is the wife of Kaparda (Shiva), a deity worshipped at one of the sixty-eight sacred places. There is a reference to 68 sacred shrines of pilgrimage in India even in Siri Guru Granth Sahib Jee. There are 4 Dhams Char Dhams four abodes: Badrinath, Dwarka, Puri and Rameswaram and 12 Jyotirlingams along with 52 Shakti Peeths in India. [68 in all]

Bhāskararāya gives another interesting interpretation. Kapardini means decked with the garland of cow-dung cakes. When Shiva incarnated as Mailara, his wife called Mahalasa, was decked with a garland of cow-dung cakes. Mailara Linga is also known as Mallappa, Mallanna, Mallara or Mallayya. These names are popular in Karnataka. Mailara Shiva is known as Khandoba in Marathi. There is a shrine constructed for Khandoba at Jejuri, near Pune.

Kapardini also means greatly praised.

794. kalāmālā

Kalā refers to arts. Mala is Garland. Ambāl wears a garland made from sixty-four Kalā-s (arts). Kalā also means beauty, ma means limitless, and la means to bring. Based on this, it can also be interpreted that Ambāl is of limitless beauty.

795. kāmadhuk

The cow that gives plenty. Or Ambāl is the celestial cow (Kamadhenu).

In Bhagavad Gita 10.28, Krishna says: धेनूनामस्मि कामधुक् among cows I am Kamadhuk, the cow that gives plenty.

Saundarya Laharī (verse 4) says:

शरण्ये लोकानां, तव हि चरणावेव निपुणौ॥४॥

Sharanye Lokaanaam Thava Hi Charanaav-eva Nipunau!"

"She grants refuge and wishes more than what is asked for and that too through Her holy feet." In short, Ambāl fulfils all desires.

796. kāmarūpiṇī

Kāma means desire and rūpiṇī means form. Ambāl is in the form of desire.

Kāma refers to the supreme Shiva. Ambāl is in the form of Shiva. They are not different. Kamesvara is Shiva He who desires to create the Universe as described in Taittreya Upanishad, II, 5.

सोऽकामयत। बहुस्यां प्रजायेयेति। स तपोऽतप्यत।
स तपस्तप्त्वा। इदसर्वमसृजत। यदिदं किञ्च।

so'kāmayata. bahusyāṃ prajāyeyeti. sa tapo'tapyata.

sa tapastaptvā. idagͫum sarvam sṛjata. yadidaṃ kiñca

He desired, 'I shall become many and be born. He performed Tapas. having performed Tapas, He created all this. Having created it, He entered it.

Brahadaranyaka Upanishad, (3-9-11) describes a dialogue between Yajnavalkya and Sakalya, two great saints in which Yagnavalkya describes Shiva: "I know that loving person. But tell me, Sakalya, who is his devata?"

य एवायं काममयः पुरुषः स एषः, वदैव शाकल्य;

तस्य का देवतेति; स्त्रिय इति होवाच॥११॥

"He is the Person consisting of desire, it is He, 0 Sakalya, who is His deity? He replied, woman is His deity." The woman he refers is Ambāl.

Thus, Ambāl becomes the source of desire for creation.

कलानिधिः काव्यकला रसज्ञा रसशेवधिः।

पुष्टा पुरातना पूज्या पुष्करा पुष्करेक्षणा॥१५२॥

kalānidhih, kāvyakalā, rasajñā, rasaśēvadhih |

puṣṭā, purātanā, pūjyā, puṣkarā, puṣkarēkṣaṇā ॥152॥

797. kalānidhih

Ambāl is the Reservoir of sciences. Kalās are already described as *"Chasushasti kalamayi."* Kalās are Jivas.

Bhāskararāya explains Kalā means action (Karman); hence all actions end in her (Nidhi); He quotes Bhagavad Gita 4-33 that says all actions end in wisdom.

श्रेयान्द्रव्य मयाद्यज्ञा ज्ञानयज्ञः परन्तप।

सर्वं कर्माखिलं पार्थ ज्ञाने परिसमाप्यते॥33॥

shreyān dravya-mayād yajñāj jñāna-yajñah parantapa

sarvaṁ karmākhilaṁ pārtha jñāne parisamāpyate

After all, O Partha, all sacrifices of work culminate in wisdom.

798. kāvyaka<u>l</u>ā

The poetic art. Kala, the inspiration which produces poetry; because as described in the Tantras variously, a certain kind of meditation confers the power of poetical composition. This nāma means Ambāl is the inspiration or the source for kāvyas-poetry or plays.

Kālidasa's Kavyas or creations were inspired by Kali. The very first Kavya he composed soon after he was blessed by Kāli was the Shyamala Dandakam starting with *Manikya Veenam Upalalyantim.* He was the author of Mahakavyas Epic poems Kumārasambhava, Raghuvaṃśa. and Meghadūta.

Many kāvyas are composed by providing an eminent place for Devi - like Sita in Ramayana.

799. rasajñā

Rasa means essence or taste or flavor. (Example: Rasam, the spicy and delicious South Indian lentil soup). In performing arts, Rasa also means sentiment or emotion.

There are different modes of rasa, typically called as Navarasas viz Sringara, Haasyam, Raudram, etc. Saundra Lahari Verse 51 describes the various rasas displayed by Ambāl.

> शिवे शृङ्गा रार्द्रा तदित रजने कुत्सनपरा - *śive śṛṅgārārdrā taditarajane kutsanaparā*

> सरोषा गङ्गायां गिरिश चरिते विस्मयवती। *saroṣā gaṅgāyāṃ giriśacarite vismayavatī*

> हरा हिभ्यो भीता सरसिरुह सौभाग्यजयिनी *harāhibhyo bhītā sarasiruha saubhāgyajayinī*

➤ सखीषु स्मेरा ते मयि जननी दृष्टिः सकरुणा *sakhīṣu smerā te mayi janani dṛṣṭiḥ sakaruṇā*

O, Mother of Universe, when looking at Shiva, your eyes are filled with love, with dislike at other men, envy when looking at Ganga, with wonder when hearing stories of Shiva, with fear when looking at the snakes worn by Shiva, with friendliness at your sakhis, and with mercy when seeing me.

Rasajna means Ambāl is possessed of the various rasas or sense of taste. (Muthuswamy Dikshitar kritis 'compositions' in praise of Ambāl are sweet and melodious).

800. rasaśēvadhiḥ

Ambāl is the treasure of Rasa.

Here Rasa means, the nectar of Brahman. Bhāskararāya comments:

The Shruti (Taitreya Upanishad 2-6-1): "He is the Rasa, when this essence is obtained one becomes blessed."

तदात्मान स्वयमकुरुत। तस्मात्तत्सुकृत मुच्यत इति।

यद्वै तत् सुकृतम्। रसो वै सः।

रस-ह्येवायं लब्ध्वाssनन्दी भवति।

tadātmāna svayamkuruta. tasmāt tatsukṛta mucyatha iti.

yadvai tat sukṛtam. raso vai saḥ.

rasa͞um hyevāyaṃ labdhvā Anandī bhavati.

This which was Self-made. It is called the Self-made… that is taste (joy). Having obtained this taste man becomes blessed.

The Brahmānda Purana also says, "Rasa is the supreme Brahman. Rasa is the supreme way, Rasa is the giver of light to man, Rasa is said to be the seed.

He is the Rasa, one having obtained the Rasa becomes blessed. This, on the authority of the scriptures. Rasa represents the vital breath. Who can live or who can breathe (without Him).

With this Nāma 800, the ninth Kala called Visva ends in the Saubhagya Bhaskaram composed by Bhāskararāya.

801. puṣṭā

Nourished. Puṣhṭi (पुष्टि, means "prosperous, well-nourished") Because she is the possessor of the body consisting of thirty-six Tattvas, or possessed of many qualities, or by Brahmarasa, or by Brahmanas. The Smriti says, "Brahman is nourished by Brahmanas."

What is meant by Tatvam and what is Brahmana?

Tatvam means the core belief. "Tattvamsi (तत् त्वम् असि} is a popular expression found in the Upanishads. It comes in the sixth chapter of the Chandogya Upanishad. It means "I am that" generally understood as a reflection of one's connection with a Higher Self. It is to recognize that Brahman and Atman are one. There is also another saying Aham Brahmasmi - I am Brahman, or I am Divine. It is the core belief of Advaitam.

Shaivism identifies 36 tattvas. 1- 5 are Iswara-tattvas. They belong to the pure worlds, 6-10 are Shakti-tattvas, 11-16 are recognized as atma-tattvas and finally 17 - 36 are prakriti-tattvas.

Ambāl is said to be well-nourished with these 36 tatvas.

Each veda has three parts - Samhita, the Brahmana and the Aranyaka. When we speak of "Veda-adhyayana," we normally have in mind the Samhita part only. Apart from them, each Sakha has a Brahmana and an Aranyaka.

The Brahmana lays down the various rites - karma - to be performed and explains the procedure for the same. It interprets the words of the mantras occurring in the Samhita, how they are to be understood in the conduct of sacrifices. The Brahmanas constitute a guide for the conduct of yajnas. So, in this context, Brahmanas are considered as nourishments to the Brahman or Ambāl.

"Aranya" means a "forest". In India, there are places like "Dandakaranya" and "Vedaranya". Neither in the Samhita nor in the Brahmana is one urged to go and live in a forest. Vedic rites like sacrifices are to be performed by the householder (grahastha) living in a village. But after his mind is rendered pure through such rites, he goes to a forest as a recluse to engage himself in meditation. It is to qualify for this stage of vanaprastha, to become inwardly pure and mellow, that Vedic practices like sacrifices are to be followed.

802. purātanā- Ancient. Ambāl is the first. In Tamil too, the word Puratanam means ancient.

803. Pūjyā

Worth to be worshipped or worshipful. Ambāl is to be worshipped by all. She is also called Maha Pujya (Nama 213)

Generally, the form and inherent qualities make a person worshipful. For example, if you visit Sringeri, you will find the Acharyas are full of positive energies that radiate through their bodily form and talks.

                    The Glory of Lalithā Sahasranāmam

804. puṣkarā

Lotus. Pushkarini-a pond where lotuses bloom.

Puska, nourishment, ra, recover. Puskara is the deity of Puskara Tirtha. As there is no difference between ra and la, Puskala, means complete.

Pushkarini or the temple tank literally means "Koil Kulam" in Tamil

These temple theerthams or ponds or pushkarinis are said to cure various diseases, also get us free from various curses and gives us boons. In Tirupathi, many devotees take a dip in the Pushkarini near the Balaji temple.

805. puṣkarēkṣaṇā: Lotus-eyed. She has eyes like lotus petals.

Bhāskararāya quotes from Puranas:

In Sanskrit, the word पुष्कर has numerous meanings.

"Puskara means lotus, ether, water, elephant's trunk, end, herb, island, bird, place of pilgrimage, a certain musical note, a kind of serpent, the drum, head, sword and a fruit called Khadgaphala."

According to the Padma Purana, Puskara, is a certain planetary conjunction. When the sun is in the asterism called Visakhi, and the moon is in the Krttika, the conjunction is called Puskara, and it is very rare at the place of Puskara." Puskara also means the earth.

The Padma Purana says, "The Devas call the pericarp of the lotus earth, the saaragurus in the lotus, they call divine mountains. The (upper) petals of the lotus became the Mileccha country.

The lower petals are the worlds of the serpents and the Daityas. Thus, by the wish of Narayana the earth came out from the lotus. Hence the earth is called Puskara."

Pushkara also means the Banyan tree; Matsya Purana says, "Because there is a banyan tree in the Pushkara Island, it is called Pushkara."

The Vishnu Purana says, "The banyan tree is in the Pushkara country, that is the supreme abode of Brahman."

Because Vishnu slept on the Banyan leaf, Vishnu himself is called Pushkara.

In बालमुकुन्दाष्टकम्, Bālamukundashtakam, a verse says:

करारविन्देन पदारविन्दं मुखारविन्दे विनिवेशयन्तं

वटस्य पत्रस्य पुटे शयानं बालं मुकुन्दं मनसा स्मरामि॥

Kara-Aravindena Pada-Aravindam

Mukha-Aravinde Vi-Niveshay-Antam|

Vatasya Patrasya Putte Shayaanam

Baalam Mukundam Manasaa Smaraami||

My mind remembers that beautiful bala mukundam who rests on the Banyan leaf (Vatasya Patram).

Ikashana means compassionate look. So, Pushakarekshana is explained in Devi Bhagavada Purana as, "Devi's Adoration of Vishnu in the form of a child asleep on banyan-leaf.

परञ्ज्योतिः परन्धाम परमाणुः परात्परा।

पाशहस्ता पाशहन्त्री परमन्त्रविभेदिनी॥१५३॥

parañjyōtiḥ, parandhāma, paramāṇuḥ, parātparā।

pāśahastā, pāśahantrī, paramantra vibhēdinī॥153॥

806. parañjyōtiḥ

Para means supreme, Jyoti means light and paramjyotiḥ means 'Supreme Light'.

Bhāskararāya cites various Upanishads explaining this light. The Bṛhadāraṇayaka Upanishad (4-4-16) says, "That is light of light."

यस्मादर्वाक्संवत्सरोऽहोभिः परिवर्तते।

तद्देवा ज्योतिषां ज्योतिरायुर्होपासतेऽमृतम्॥१६॥

Yasmād arvāksaṃ vatsaro'hobhiḥ parivartate।

taddevā jyotiṣāṃ jyotirāyur hopāsate'mṛtam॥16॥

taddevā jyotiṣāṃ jyotirāyur hopāsate amṛtam means upon that immortal Light of all lights the gods meditate as longevity. This means that gods meditate on this Supreme Light for their immortality.

Kathopanishad (2-2-15) says:

तत्र सूर्यः न भाति। चन्द्र तारकं नेमा विद्युतो भान्ति कुतोऽयमग्निः।

तमेव भान्त मनुभाति सर्वं तस्य भासा सर्वमिदं विभाति॥

tatra sūryo na bhāti. Chandra tārakaṃ nemā vidyuto bhānti kuto 'yamagniḥ।

tameva bhāntamanubhāti sarvaṃ tasya bhāsā sarvamidaṃ vibhāti॥

"There no sun shines, nor moon, nor stars, nor these lightnings, nor the fire. All that is bright is but the shadow of His brightness and only when he is illuminated by Him." When Brahman shines, everything shines.

Chandogya Upanishad 8-3-4 says परं ज्योति रुप सम्पद्य *param jyothirupa sampadyate* meaning "The supreme light one attains." The Upanishad says here "Then, this person, who is the embodiment of happiness, emerging from the body and attaining the highest light, assumes his real nature. This is the Self."

Knowledge is very often associated with light. We sometimes repeat the prayer, '*Tamasaḥ mā jyotiḥ gamaya*— lead us from darkness to light.' Lead us from the darkness of ignorance to the light of knowledge. Jyoti here means illuminator, for we see the same meaning given in many places.

Brahadaranya Upanishad 3-9-10 says

पृथिव्येव यस्यायतनम्, अग्निर्लोकः, मनोज्योतिः

pṛthivyeva yasyāyatanam, agnirlokaḥ, manojyotiḥ

'He who knows that being whose abode is the earth, whose instrument of vision is fire, whose light is the Manas.

When we are attached to the body, we are always trying to enjoy more and more sense objects. For that reason, we are always disturbed and unhappy.

When the self leaves the body during deep sleep, it assumes its real nature. What is that nature? Does it have any form? Not exactly. It attains its real nature as light.

    The Glory of Lalithā Sahasranāmam

Once Sharada Devi was in a state of ecstasy and saw herself outside her body. She thought to herself: 'How can I go back to such a body?' For people like her and great mahans, leaving the body is a matter of choice.

807. parandhāma

Ambāl is the Supreme abode. Param+ dhāma = paramdhāma. Param means Supreme and dhāma means brilliance or abode.

Bhāskararāya explains: Dhaman means light.

The Bhagavad Gita (15-6) says:

न तद्भासयते सूर्यो न शशाङ्को न पावक:|

यद्गत्वा न निवर्तन्ते तद्धाम परमं मम॥6॥

na tad bhāsayate sūryo na śaśhāṅko na pāvakaḥ

yad gatvā na nivartante tad dhāma paramaṁ mama

"The sun nor moon, nor fire never illumines That (supreme abode). After reaching it one does not return, that is my supreme abode."

Dhaman, the states of consciousness, Para, beyond—Devi is beyond the states of consciousness. Gaudapadacarya (1-5), "The man who knows both the object of enjoyment as well as the enjoyer is never stained though he enjoys in the three states."

The Suta Samhita (4-11-32 and 33) says, "He who knows the three states, namely, Jagrat-Swapna-Sushupti Avastha; Waking, Dreaming, and Sleeping he is the Self, that is not the object, the object is super-imposed upon that. I take three abodes, characterised by reality, wisdom, bliss, etc. and is the meaning of the word 'I'."

Dhaman abode. Katha Upanishad (3-9) says, *"tad Viṣṇoḥ paramaṃ padam "'*. "That is the supreme abode of Vishnu." Viṣṇu is known as Paraṃdhāman. In India, the old time 'snakes and ladders' game was played on an illustrated picture called "paramapada shobaana patam"- the top most place being 'parama padam' - the supreme abode.

The Kurma Purana also says, "My energy is, Mahesvari, Gauri, spotless, tranquil, reality, knowledge, bliss, the supreme abode.

808. paramāṇuḥ

Supreme atom.

Kathopanishad (2-20) "More subtle than the atom," that is, difficult to know.

In the song *'Sreeman nArAyaNa,'* Annamacharya sings:

parama yOgijana bhAga dhEya Sree

parama purusha parAtparA

paramAtmA paramANu roopa Sree

tiru venkaTagiri dEvA SaraNu||

You are the destination for supreme sages. You are the supreme personality. You are transcendental. You are the supreme soul. You manifest yourself even in the tiniest atom. Oh Lord of holy Venkata hill, I surrender to you.

Anu also means mantra. Para means Supreme. Paramanu, the Supreme mantra is always Her Pañcadaśī mantra.

809. parātparā

The supreme most of the supreme. She is supreme over Brahma, Vishnu and Rudra. Or, Para, the age of Brahma—she is beyond that.

The Kaali Purana says, "The day and night to the Brahma is called Para, the half of that is called Parardha. Such is the day to the Lord, so also the night. He who is grosser than the gross and subtler than the subtle has neither day nor night, nor years.

There is nothing superior to parātpara. Papanasam Sivan sings *"Paratpara Parameswara"* in Vachaspati Ragam.

810. pāśahastā

Bearing a noose of Pāsam in her hand. The noose is in her left lower hand; or she removes the bonds (Paasa) with her hand.

811. pāśahantrī

She is the Destroyer of Pāsam. Pāśa here means bondage, attachment,

The Harivamsa says, "When she Devi had burst the bonds of Anirudha who was bound by Nagastra the serpent-noose (released by Banasura), which was like a thunderbolt, who was distressed in mind, she addressed him, offering to confer boons on him."

812. paramantra vibhēdinī

Bhāskararāya defines this naama as Destroyer of hostile charms.

There are two meanings to the word 'para.' One meaning is alien or hostile. The other is supreme. Let's see the application of the first one.

Para mantra means mantra-s that cause enmity. What are these mantras? These mantras are used in witchcraft and black magic. Vibhedini means breaks apart. By destroying such evil mantra-s, Ambāl protects Her devotees.

Those who hate Ambāl's devotees, i.e., Kings; and mantra, certain forces which are included in the three energies, viz. the energy of lordship (Prabhushakti), council (Mantrasakti) and armed force (Utsahashakti); In other words, abusing their powers-Ambāl destroys such hostile charms.

Now let us apply the meaning superior. Then mantra refers to the fifteen-syllabled mantra* (Panchadasi) Vibhedini, (she) divides into twelve kinds.

For it is said in the Tantras "Mann, Chandra, Kubera, Lopamudra, Manmatha, Agastya, Agni, Surya, Nandi, Skanda, Shiva and Krodhabhattāraka (Durvasa), these twelve are the devotees of Devi.

*The famous Panchadashi-has three sections (kutas), each ending with Hrim, which mantra by itself can be used to worship Tripura Lalita.

KA E(Aye) I(EEE) LA HRIM

HA SA KA HA LA HRIM

SA KA LA HRIM

These fifteen lettered Pancha-dasakshari mantras is revered as the verbal form of the Mother Goddess. By adding to it the secret syllable śrīm (श्रीं) it is transformed into the sixteen lettered Shodasi mantra.

"Para, superior, Mantra', those who meditate (on Devi), avi their sins, Bhedini, destroys.

The Linga Purana says, "The word avi in the scriptures means sins, say the Braahmanas. It is called Avimukta (freed from sins) because it is freed from that (sin) and freed also from illusion."

 The Glory of Lalithā Sahasranāmam

मूर्ताऽमूर्ताऽनित्यतृप्ता मुनिमानसहंसिका।

सत्यव्रता सत्यरूपा सर्वान्तर्यामिनी सती॥१५४॥

mūrtā,'mūrtā,'nityatṛptā, muni mānasa haṃsikā।

satyavratā, satyarūpā, sarvāntaryāminī, satī॥154॥

813. mūrtā- Having a shape or form.

814. Amūrtā

Shapeless or formless. That which has form is called Murta. (Earth, water and fire); Amurta means formless air and ether.

Or, Murta, the five gross elements mingled with each other; Amurta, the subtle elements which are not mingled with each other. For we see the above two explanations given in Brahadaranya Upanishad (2-8-1), "Brahman has two forms, Murta and Amurta."

Or, Murta, Universe, Amurta, Brahman. The Vishnu Purana says, "That Brahman has two forms, Murta and Amurta, these two respectively perishable and imperishable and both are in all beings. The imperishable is the ever-remaining Brahman, the perishable is the whole Universe."

Verse 77 of Vishnu Sahasranamam says "Vishvamurthy Mahamurthy, Deeptamurthiramurtimaan." The nāma to note is a-mūrtimān.

"Vishnu has no defined form and is formless as He assumes any Form He please, hence He is also off multiform who is Inscrutable and appears in hundreds of forms with hundreds of faces."

815. Anityatṛptā

Satisfied with the perishables (offerings).

A-nitya means things that are perishable. She is happy with the offerings of perishables. She is pleased only by devotion. Bhagavad Gita (9-26) says:

पत्रं पुष्पं फलं तोयं यो मे भक्त्या प्रयच्छति।

तदहं भक्त्युपहृतमश्नामि प्रयतात्मन:॥26॥

patraṁ pushpaṁ phalaṁ toyaṁ yo me bhaktyā prayachchhati

tadahaṁ bhaktyupahṛitam aśhnāmi prayatātmanaḥ॥26॥

"He who offers with devotion a leaf a flower, a fruit, or water, I accept from the striving Self."

Whatever is given with devotion to Devi gives Her satisfaction.

816. muni mānasa haṃsikā

The swan of the Manasa Lake of the Muni's mind. Muni means sages, mānasa means expressed in mind and haṃsikā means swans. Devi appears as swans in the minds of sages. Nāma 372 says *Bhakta manasa hamsika*, As the mythical swans live in the celestial lake called Manasa, so she lives in the minds of her devotees. The Swan is a symbol of purity, beauty, grace, love and elegance, and divinity.

817. satyavratā

One who has a fixed vow. Bhāskararāya gives different interpretations.

Satya truth alone is her vow. The meaning is she is attained by the vow of observing the utterances of truth alone. Satyavrata means what Sri Rama said (in the Ramayana VI),

     The Glory of Lalithā Sahasranāmam

"One who once approaches me, with a request 'I am yours,' on him I confer fearlessness from all beings. This is my vow."

According to the Shiva-Sutra (III, 27) "The cure of the body is a vow." (Satyavrata.) The commentator says, "To take care of the body which is filled with the nectar of devotion to Shiva is a vow, that should be performed, hence the care of the body should not be neglected." Such a vow is necessary. Hence Bhattotpala asks for bodily health in these words: "May this body, nourished by the nectar derived from the pure Shakti (another reading, from pure devotion) manifested in me, remain long to enjoy thy worship."

Satyavrata is a Brahmana who is frightened by a boar exclaimed, ai, ai, and through his penance became a devotee of Devi and a great poet.

This story is related in the Devi Bhagavada Puranam (Book III): "There was a Brahmana named Satyavrata, illiterate, very foolish, hearing the syllable from the mouth of the boar, and repeating from that time this syllable without the final m, in course of time became the best of the wise. By merely uttering the word ai, Devi became pleased and made him the king of poets.

There was a saint called Satyavrata. He served as the head of Shri Uttaradi Math from 1635–1638. He was the 18th in succession from Madhvacharya. He wrote a commentary on Nyaya Sudha of Jayatirtha called Sudha Vivruthi.

818. satyarūpā- Reality. Satya is truth, Rupa, form. She is the embodiment of truth. Ambāl is fully Satva.

819. sarvāntaryāminī

Pervading all hearts. Sarva, all beings, anta, the senses, yamini, directs.

The Brahadranya Upanishad (3-7-3): "This is thy Self which is within all and is immortal."

Māṇḍūkya Upaniṣad (Āgama prakaran-6) also says, *antaryāmi*. "This is within all and is the origin of all."

Or Sarva, all and antaryamini, entered in all. Devi is in all and entered in all.

The Taitreya Upanishad (2-6-1): Having created that, he entered into it, after entering it, he became animate and inanimate."

Smrti also gives explanation to the word Sarva thus: "Because She always knows the beginning and the end of everything and as she creates being and nonbeing, She is called sarva."

820. satī

Faithful spouse. Pathivrata. Sati, reality.

Sati is the name of the daughter of Daksha, also called Dakshayani. She was disregarded by her own father Daksha who did not invite her nor her husband Shiva for a yagna he was performing. Unable to bear the insult of her father, Sati destroyed the yajñā of Dakṣa (Dakshayajnavinasini - nāma 600) and then immolated herself. She was reborn as Umā to Himavān (nāma 633).

The Brahmānda Purana says 'concerning the daughter of the Himavan, "She, who was before, Devi the faithful spouse

(Sati), became Uma, she ever dwells with Shiva and he is never deserted by her."

In Saundarya Lahari (verse 96), Ādi Śaṁkara addresses Her as Satī.

महादेवं हित्वा तव सति सतीना-मचरमे

mahādevaṁ hitvā – except Śiva; tava – Your (Parāśakti); sati (satī) – faithful wife; satīnāma carame – foremost amongst chaste women

In this context, Satī means virtuous wife.

There is a temple called Daksha Mahadev temple, about 4 kms from Haridwar where King Daksha Prajapati, is said to have performed yajna where Sati immolated herself.

ब्रह्माणी ब्रह्मजननी बहुरूपा बुधार्चिता।

प्रसवित्री प्रचण्डाऽऽज्ञा प्रतिष्ठा प्रकटाकृतिः॥१५५॥

brahmāṇī, brahmajananī, bahurūpā, budhārchitā।

prasavitrī, prachaṇḍā'jñā, pratiṣṭhā, prakaṭākṛtiḥ ॥ 155 ॥

821. brahmāṇī

She is the energy of the Brahman (*Śiva*).

Aṇī means the pin of the axle of a cart. Without this aṇī the cart cannot run. In this context, the nāma means that Brahman (Śiva) cannot function without Shakti (aṇī).

Brahma; ani: tail (of a bird). She is the Brahman which forms the tail of the Anandamaya sheath (compared to a bird)

Brahma, ani gives life——she gives life to Brahma. The Devi Puranam says, "She is called Brahmani because she creates or gives life to Brahma."

822. brahman

That which is to be attained by liberated souls; or

Brahman is the knowledge of the undifferentiated Self.

The Vishnu Puranam says, "That knowledge is called Brahman which annihilates duality, mere being, transcending speech, recognized by the Self alone."

Brahman is the highest level of consciousness that is – nirviśeṣā (non-characterization), nirguṇa (devoid of qualities),

nirvikārā (without any modifications), śuddha (purity absolute) and sat-cit-ānanda (existence, consciousness and bliss). At this level, Shaktī merges into Shiva and they are one known as Brahman.

Since there is no difference between Shiva and Shaktī, She is addressed here as Brahman. There are many nāma-s in this Sahasranāma which affirm Her Brahman status.

823. jananī- The mother. She is the creator of the whole Universe. This name may relate to the previous name 'Brahmajanani'. One of Papanasam Sivan's compositions in Tamil starts with *paraashakti jananee*.

Nāma 264 says srṣṭi-kartrī- the creator.

824. bahurūpā

Devi is of manifold form. Bhāskararāya cites many scriptures.

The Devi Bhagavada Puranam says, "She is formless because she is supreme, she has many forms because of her activity."

Though she is of the nature of Para-Brahman, she is the agent of action, such as the slaying of Bhandasura, and other asuras. As she assumes many such forms, she is said to be 'bahurupa' many—formed.

The Gaudapada-Sutra (8) says, "Though one, she becomes many in order to destroy Bhandasura."

The Devi Puranam also says, "Her forms are many, immovable and movable, devas, men, animals, hence Devi is called many formed."

The Vamana Puaranam also says, "This Universe is known as manifold, she is everywhere, hence Shiva is said to be many formed."

Sri Rudram 11-1 says

सहस्राणि सहस्रशो ये रुद्रा अधि भूम्याम्।

तेषाहूं सहस्रयोजनेवधन्वानि तन्मसि॥११.१॥

Sahasrani sahasrashoye Rudra Adhi bhumyaam,

teshahum Sahasra yojane vadhanvani tanmasi‖

Sahasrani sahasrasho you Rudra - means thousands of Rudra-s in thousands of forms. Their wives are known as Rudrāṇī-s. Thus, "she is many formed."

The Varaha Puranam says "The dark (Tamas) energy called Raudri is said to be Chamunda. There are nine crores of different Chamundas. The Rajasi, passionate energy, the protector of the Universe, called Vaishnavi, has differentiated into eighteen crores of energies. The energy of Brahma belonging to Satva is said to be infinite in number, of all these energies, O earth, the divine Rudra is the husband as he is in all. All these great energies are forms created by Shiva, and he attends to all as their husband. One who worships these (energies), Rudra becomes pleased with him; these energies are also delighted with him; of this there is no doubt.'

Concerning these things, the Narasimha Purana. says, "Uma alone in many forms is the wife (of all the forms of Shiva)."

Viṣṇu Sahasranāma nāma 721 is aneka-mūrtī. Ambāl is worshipped in different forms and each form has certain specific qualities. For example, Sarasvatī is worshipped for knowledge, Lakṣmī worshipped for wealth, etc.

825. budhārchitā

Adored by the Wise.

She is (Archita) worshipped by the (Budha) knowledgeable people.

The Bhagavad Gita (7-16) says,

चतुर्विधा भजन्ते मां जना: सुकृतिनोऽर्जुन।
आर्तो जिज्ञासुरर्थार्थी ज्ञानी च भरतर्षभ॥16॥

chatur-vidhā bhajante mām janāḥ sukṛitino 'rjuna

ārto jijñāsur arthārthī jñānī cha bharatarṣhabha

"O Arjuna, good men of four kinds worship me, he who is distressed, he who desires knowledge, he who desires wealth, and the Wise man."

The Glory of Lalithā Sahasranāmam

826. prasavitrī

Creator.

Ambāl is the Mother of the world consisting of the five elements and of the people. The Tamil word *'prasavam'* referring to delivery comes from this. In Hindi and Marathi, they call it *prasuti*. Because she generates the beings, she is called Savita.

The Bhagavadi Purana also says, "From her proceeded all things from Brahma to the inanimate creation and the Universe also proceeded from her, from Mahat to substance, I adore that supreme mother."

827. prachaṇḍā

Wrathful. Ambāl inspires fear just as Shiva does too.

The word 'Chanda' refers to the fiery power of anger. The name "Chandi" is derived from the Sanskrit word "chand" which means "tear apart."

The very first line of Sri Rudram says:

॥ ओं नमो भगवते रुद्राय॥

नमस्ते रुद्रमन्यव उतोत इषवेनमः।

Om Namo Bhagavade Rudraya.

Namaste Rudramanyava Utota Ishavenamah

O Rudra, prostrations to your wrath and your arrow

Kathopanishad (2.3.3) says,

भयादस्याग्निस्तपति भयात्तपति सूर्यः।

भयादिन्द्रश्च वायुश्च मृत्युर्धावति पञ्चमः॥३॥

Bhayād asyāgnistapati bhayāt tapati sūryaḥ.

Bhayād indraśca vāyuśca mṛtyur dhāvati pañcamaḥ.2.3.3.

From the terror of Brahman, fire burns; from terror of It, the sun shines; from terror of It, Indra and Vayu and Death, the five, run.

In the Veda Sutra (1-3-39) Prana is explained as the Brahman because of vibration in which everything trembles.

Why is Ambāl angry? Anger is a quality necessary to induce fear and to enforce discipline. Don't we give 'Time-out' for our children?

Ramakrishna Paramahamsa told a parable to illustrate how one has to show anger. A holy man arrived in a village. The people there said that a snake was terrorizing them. The snake was biting them, and they were afraid to go out. The swamiji asked the snake with love and compassion to stop biting the villagers and the snake agreed. Soon the villagers discovered that the snake would no longer hurt them, so they beat and trampled him. One day the Swamiji found the snake bleeding. He asked the snake what happened. The snake said I followed your advice, and this is what happened to me. The Swamiji said "I told you not to bite, but I never told you not to hiss."

So, anger has a place in our lives. At least, pretend you are angry without hurting.

Or Pra, fond of, chanda, a kind of flower called Sankha flower; Prachanda, shining one.

828. Ajna

Ordinance or commandment. She commands.

The desire of the Lord in the form of command and prohibition as expressed in the Vedas. So, in the Linga Purana

I.87.9-11, Shiva says, "She is the power of knowledge, kriya (rite) and icchā (will). She is Ājñā. For she is not to be taken as Prakrti (matter) not Jiva (life), nor Vikriti (a secondary product). At Her ājñā (here it means command), I think about the welfare of the worlds. I am Śiva. My eternal five-faced (Gāyatri), holy ordinance which delivers the world from fear, proceeded of old from my mouth."

The Shiva Puarana also says, "Through this established divine ordinance of Rudra alone comes salvation."

Or this name may be taken as ' Jna,' the knower— She is the person who is the enjoyer of the Gunas: The Linga Purana says: "They say that by the word jna is meant the Person, the enjoyer of Gunas." "Jna also means Brahma, Mercury and a wise man."

829. pratiṣṭhā

Foundation.

Because she is the foundation of the whole Universe. This foundation is made up of dharma and righteousness. The universe is created and sustained only on the principle of interdependence.

The Supreme authorities, Shiva and Shaktī are also interdependent.

830. prakaṭākṛtiḥ

Of form experienced. Prakaṭa means evident, manifest, clear, experienced by all, made public (Prakatanam in Tamil) and ākṛti (Akruti in Tamil) means form, figure shape or nature.

In Śrī Chakra worship, deities of first āvaraṇa are known as prakaṭa yogini-s. Possibly, these prakaṭa yogini-s reveal Her form or her true nature.

प्राणेश्वरी प्राणदात्री पञ्चाशत्पीठरूपिणी।

विशृङ्खला विविक्तस्था वीरमाता वियत्प्रसूः॥१५६॥

prāṇeśvarī, prāṇadātrī, pañchāśat-pīṭharūpiṇī।

viśṛṁkhalā, viviktasthā, vīramātā, viyatprasūḥ ॥156॥

831. prāṇeśvarī

Goddess of senses. Brahma-Sutra 2.4.14 says

ज्योतिराद्यधिष्ठानं तु तदामननात्॥१४॥

Jyotirādya adhiṣṭhānaṁ tu tadāmananāt ॥14॥

Prana, senses, in the Veda Sutra (2-4-14) "There is guidance of pranas by fire, etc.," it is established by discussion, the existence of the ruling deity.

Prana, the five vital breaths.

The Shruti says, "He is the breath of breath." Or Pra exalted, ana; Vedas. The Shruti (Kathopanishad., 2-15) says, "All Vedas point out the same abode."

832. prāṇadātrī

Nourisher of senses. She is the giver of prāṇa. Previous naama said She is Praneswari. Brahma Sutra 2-4-5 says ॐ सप्त गतेर्वि शेषितत्वाच्च -oṃ sapta gater viśheṣitat vāccha. The pranas are seven in number, on accounzt of this being understood from scriptures and of the specification of those seven."

 The Glory of Lalithā Sahasranāmam

Muṇḍaka Upaniṣad (II.i.8) says, *tasmāt sapta prāṇaḥ prabhavanti* which means 'from That (Brahman) seven prāṇa-s (prāṇa here means seven organs - two eyes, two nostrils, two ears, and mouth) have come. This Upanishad confirms the statement of KathoUpanishad in the previous nāma.

She gives that 'vital force' called prāṇa, without which life is not sustainable.

833. pañchāśat-pīṭharūpiṇī

Ambāl is in Fifty seats. Pancāśa means fifty, pīṭha means seat and rupiṇī means form. Though Panchasat is fifty, the expression here generally stands for fifty-one. Sanskrit alphabets are fifty or fifty-one depending upon the number of vowels or consonants (inclusion of ॡ (lū).

Hence, Harsha dikshita comments on the first verse of the Sharada tilakam 'His body is eternal bliss' explains fifty as fifty-one. Her manifestation in alphabets is known as Śabda Brahman. The energy in matter is called 'Shakti'. The foundation of energy in matter are the 51 letters of Universe, which drive the evolution of Universe in various ways and creates matter locked with lot of energy. Hence these 51 letters are called shakti pIta or foundation/pedestal of shakti. Puranas say after Sakti immolates herself in dakSa Yajna, her body is cut into 51 pieces by Vishnu and the places where these 51 pieces fell became 51 shakti pItas. These 51 pithas are said to be linked to the 51 letters of the Sanskrit alphabet.

834. viśṛṅkhalā

Unfettered. Without bondage. Shrinkala means fetters, or bondage vi means without.

So great men say, "O Lord, destroy my good actions as well as my bad actions; when the fetters are on the feet it makes no difference whether they are of gold or iron." The meaning is that ordinances and prohibitions only apply to the ignorant.

835. viviktasthā

Abiding in lonely places. Vivikta, according to the Kosa, means lonely and holy places. The Harita Smriti says, "The ground is everywhere, holy where no people are seen." Even an inhabited region becomes sanctified. Though the word Vivikta means both the region of righteous people as well as an uninhabited place, it here means lonely place; because neither in bad company nor in a crowded place do we find a tendency to meditation.

836. vīramātā

Mother of warriors. Vira is the name of Ganesha. Mata is a mother. In the Padma Purana, speaking about Vira, Shiva says, "This Vira, O Devi, is always dear to my heart, he is the teacher of wonderful feats, he is worshipped by multitudes of Ganeshas." After hearing this Devi replies, "I desire to have such a son, when shall I see such a bliss-conferring son?" Then Shiva says, "Let this man be thy son, who is pleasing in our eyes. Through you that son will become accomplished,"

Vīra also means warriors. Since, She Herself is a warrior, she is addressed here as mother of warriors.

837. viyatprasūḥ

Ambāl is the Mother of the ether or space.

Taittirīya Upaniṣad (II.1) says

तस्माद्वा एतस्मादात्मन आकाशः सम्भूतः

tasmādvā etasmād ātmana ākāśaḥ sambhūtaḥ

This means from the Self (the Brahman) originated space.

आकाशाद्वायुः।

वायोरग्निः। अग्नेरापः। अद्भ्यः पृथिवी।

पृथिव्या ओषधयः। ओषधीभ्योन्नम्। अन्नात्पुरुषः

Akashatvayuh, vāyoragniḥ. agnerāpaḥ. adbhyaḥ pṛthivī.

pṛthivyā oṣadhayaḥ. oṣadhībhyo annam. annātpuruṣaḥ.

The Upanishad continues to say that from space air, from air fire, from fire water, from water earth, from earth plants, from plants food and from food human beings originated.

Ambāl is the creator of space which in turn gave rise other elements

Chapter 17

The Glory of Lalithā Sahasranāmam

Sri Lalithā Sahasranāmam is both a Stotra and a mAlA mantra. Mahakavi Kālidas, in his Shyamala Dandaka, describes Sri Mata as *"Sarva mantratmike, sarva yantratmike, sarva tantratmike."* The namaas in Lalithā Sahasranāmam are not mere names but highly potent mantras.

The word "Mantra" comes from the roots "man" to think and 'tra' to protect. Manana Trayate iti Mantra: When recited with devotion in the mind, it protects the devotee.

Bhāskararāya quotes the Nitya Tantra that gives various names to Mantra such as *Pinda, Kartari, Bija, Mantra, Mala.* These are based on the number of syllables in the mantra.

"A monosyllable Mantra is named Pinda; a two-syllabled one Kartari; a Mantra having three to nine syllables is called Bija; one with ten to twenty-syllables is known as Mantra proper; and Mantras with more than twenty-syllables are called Malas; without any further distinction." The main mantra of Lalitāmbikā is Pañcadaśī (Panchadasi) which consists of fifteen bīja-s, and so rightly called a Mantra.

Lalithā Sahasranāmam is called Rahasya-Nama-Sahasra. The 1000 names form a big garland of Mantras, a mAlA mantra called Chintamani Mahavidyeshwari.

As Hayagriva said to Agastya Maharishi, Lalithā Sahasranāmam is a secret mantra. It is termed *'Guhyati Guhyam'* the secret of all secrets. Sage Agastya says that the Teacher may impart a secret to a student who is possessed of true Bhakti, to one who is thoroughly devoted to the Divine Mother; but it shall never be taught to one who has no Bhakti.

As the Sahasranāma also states – *nAmapArAyaNa prItA*, what better way to please Amba than by reciting the thousand names with a sense of overflowing love for the Supreme Mother of the universe? Every minute aspect of Srividya Upasana is covered in Sri Lalithā Sahasranāmam.

Every name recited should be a prostration at her feet, surrendering the self to her.

Lalithā Sahasranāmam is divided into four parts like in Brahmasutra -*Samanvayam, Avirodham,Saadhanam and Phalan.*

The first part talks about Brahman and is regarded as Samanvaya (Harmony), because it brings into a harmony diverse interpretation about Brahman.

The second part describes Avirodha (non-conflict, non-contradiction) and refutes the possible objections to Vedānta philosophy.

The third part talks about Sādhana, the means to spiritual knowledge, and the process by which ultimate emancipation can be achieved.

And finally, the fourth part describes Phala or the result, and the benefits of spiritual knowledge.

Like Brahma Sutra, Lalithā Sahasranāmam covers various aspects of spiritual knowledge. It includes several sastras. Let's see some examples of how it links with our dharmic Sastras:

1. Advaita Sastra: See naamas like *Ameya, Atmavidya, Ekakini, Antarmukha Samaradhya, Gunatheetah, Chinmayee, Chitshakti, Chetanaroopa, Brahamatmaikya Swarropini, Muktida* and so on. All these naamas point to one Supreme Being.

2. Mantra Sastra and Srividya connection: *Adishakti, Ichashakti, Jnanashakti, Kriyashakti Swaroopini, Odyanapeeta Nilaya, panchakritya parayana, gurumanadala rupini*...

3. Yoga connection: Naamas 101 to 110. *Muladharaika Nilaya, Brahmagranti Vibhedini*...It also talks about Kundalini Shakti. We explained it earlier.

4. Bhakti: *Bhaktigamya, Bhakti Vashya, Bhakti Priya, Bhakta Sowbhagya Dhayini, Dhyanagamya, Naama Parayana Prita,Kamapujita*...

5. Karmakandam: *Krutajnya, Shistapujita, Yajnarupa, Yajnapriya, Yajamanaswarupini*...

6. Other Naamas: *Mulaprakriti, Parapara, Viswarupa higlighting Brahmam as Shakti.*

With such a wide coverage, it serves as a "Maanav Dharma" or a teaching for all human beings.

In essence, Lalithā Sahasranāmam is a treatise, a great scripture that covers all aspects of our Sanatana Dharma and hence a boon to us. The more you chant it, the more you discover. In short, that is the Glory of Lalithā Sahasranāmam.

मुकुन्दा मुक्तिनिलया मूलविग्रहरूपिणी।

भावज्ञा भवरोगघ्नी भवचक्रप्रवर्तिनी॥१५७॥

mukundā, mukti nilayā, mūlavigraha rūpiṇī।

bhāvajñā, bhavarōgaghnī bhavachakra pravartinī॥157॥

838. mukundā

Muku means Moksham. As Ambāl gives Moksham, she is called Mukunda. She is the Giver of salvation.

Mukunda is also Vishnu. In the Bhagawatam, Shri Krishna is addressed numerous times as Bhagawati. In Lalithā Sahasranāmam, Ambāl is called Narayani. Lalithā Sahasranāmam (LS) and Bhagavad Gita (Gita) are closely connected.

There are a lot of similarities between them. Krishna gave upadesam to Arjuna in the battlefield; Lalithā Sahasranāmam was recited in the presence of Lalitha, sitting in her throne and surrounded by all Gods. In the Sahasranama, you will find naamas like Govinda rupini (267), Narayani (298), Vishnu rupini (893), and Vishnu Maya (339).

Gita Chapter XI Verse 12 says:

दिवि सूर्यसहस्रस्य भवेद्युगपदुत्थिता।

यदि भा: सदृशी सा स्याद्भासस्तस्य महात्मन:॥12॥

divi sūrya-sahasrasya bhaved yugapad utthitā

yadi bhāḥ sadṛishī sā syād bhāsas tasya mahātmanaḥ -12

If a thousand suns were to blaze forth together in the sky, they would not match the splendor of that great form.

Purusha suktham too says *'sahasra seersha purushaha'* meaning that Paramatma has thousands of heads. LS 282 says *"sahasra sirsha vadana"* meaning Lalithai has thousands of heads and faces.

Krishna says in Gita VII.14 'दैवी ह्येषा गुणमयी, मम माया दुरत्यया' *daivi hyesha gunamayi mama maaya duratyaya'.* He says it is difficult to cross His three types of his maya. LS. 339 says *vishnu maaya.*

These are some examples where Lord Vishnu and Lalithambigai are said to be one and the same.

Mukunda also means a precious stone.

839. mukti nilayā

Abode of liberation. She is the embodiment of mukti.

Bhagavadam describes five kinds of mukti: muktiś cha pañcadhā: — namely *sālokya, sārṣṭi, sārūpya, sāmīpya and sāyujya.*

Sālokya means SahaLoka, to have the same abode as Bhagavān.

Sārṣṭis: *tatraiva samāna Aiśvaryam api bhavatīti|* Sārṣṭi means to be there, while residing in His abode, have the same opulences as Bhagavan.

Sārūpya is SahaRupa, to have a form there like Him.

sārūpyaṁ tatraiva samāna-rūpatādi prāpyata iti|

Sāmīpya means Samipam, to be near and have the right to go into His presence.

sāmīpyaṁ samīpa-gamanādhikāritvam|

Sāyujyam, means to become identical with Bhagavan *sāyujyaṁ keṣāṁcit bhagavac-chrī-vigraha eva praveśo bhavatīti|.*

Ambāl offers Sayujyam- to merge yourself with Her.

Soundarya Lahari - Verse 22 says:

भवानि त्वं दासे मयि वितर दृष्टिं सकरुणां,

इति स्तोतुं वाञ्छन् कथयति भवानि त्वमिति यः।

तदैव त्वं तस्मै दिशसि निजसायुज्य-पदवीं,

मुकुन्द-ब्रम्हेन्द्र स्फुट मकुट नीराजितपदाम्

bhavāni tvaṃ dāsē mayi vitara dṛṣṭiṃ sakaruṇām

iti stōtuṃ vāñChan kathayati bhavāni tvamiti yaḥ|

tadaiva tvaṃ tasmai diśasi nijasāyujya-padavīṃ

mukunda-bramhēndra sphuṭa makuṭa

nīrājitapadām ||22||

Sankara Bhagavadpada says "O! Bhavāni! The moment a Bhakta begins his prayer with the words, Bhavaani tvam, seeking your compassion to bestow Your glance on him as 'Dasa' (servant), You offer liberation instantaneously, even before he could complete the word Bhavāni." The mercy of the mother is so great that the Ambika does not even wait till he completes his prayer but confers on him the saayujya padavi- the soul's merger with the Mother.

840. mūlavigraha rūpiṇī

Whose body is the root or basis. Which is the root?

Bhāskararāya says Mulavigraha refers to the Shakti of Rajarajesvari, which is the root of all other energies such as Bala, Bagala, etc.

There are ten Sutras in the Gaudapada-Sutras which treat this. Sutra 2 says: *"Saa Sambhavi Vidya Shyama Tat traya kriti: trivita Jaatha."*

It describes the threefold division of SriVidya Ambika -namely Sambhavi, Vidya and Shyama. The succeeding Sutras describe that each of these three produces many different energies. Lalitāmbikā is the root of all Shaktis.

841. bhāvajñā

Knower of thought. Bhāskararāya comments that Bhava has many meanings. Bhava means existence, nature, idea (for intention), action, Self, birth. It also means womb, sage, wealth, compassion, sport, dominion. So, different scriptures have attributed different interpretations to Bhāva. According to the Sutra, Bhava means Dharma; according to a passage in the Smrti, it means meditation. The root (Bhu) means the pure unconditioned one.

Nirukta is one of the six ancient Vedangas. Nir Ukta means "explained, expressed, or defined" It is the discipline of "etymology" (explanation of words). According to Yaska,, the author of Nirukta, every Vedic word has a meaning; and, denotes an appropriate sense. Yaaska says, Bhava means the six kinds of modifications called 'Shat Bhaavaas" namely being, birth, growth, etc. (Nirukta 1-1-3).

The six categories of logicians are also called Bhavas. Bhava also means those who are involved in earthly existence, or the followers of Bhava (Shiva).

The Glory of Lalithā Sahasranāmam

Ambāl is the knower of "Shat Bhaavaas" of all beings. She knows all the thoughts of people. So, we should always think about good things, keep our thoughts clean and be positive.

842. bhavarōgaghnī

Ambāl is the destroyer of pains of earthly existence.

Bhava is used here to mean saṃsāra or worldly life. Roga means disease. Saṃsāra is referred to as a disease. Ambāl relieves the pains of saṃsāra.

Bhava (root word is bhū) also means Shiva and his consort Shaktī. Both alleviate the pains of worldly life. What applies to Shiva is equally applicable to Shakti.

The Shiva Purana also says,

"vyadhinaam   bheshajam   yatvat   pratipakshasva bhaavata:l

tavat SamsaraRoganaam pratipaksha: Shivatava:ll

"Just as the medicine fights against diseases, Shiva is the enemy of the pains of Samsara."

843. bhavachakra pravartinī

Saṃsāra (life) is like a wheel that rotates births and deaths. Ambāl turns the wheel of Samsara like a wheel. She turns the wheel of earthly existence.

Bhāskararāya quotes the Manu Smriti (12-124) that says,

"Esha Sarvaani Bhutani Panchabir Vyapya Murthibhi: l

Janma vritti Kshayair Nityam Samasrayati Chakravat ll "

He, pervading all the beings by the five forms and constantly making them, by means of birth, growth and decay revolves like a chakra – a wheel."

Vishnu Purana says, chakra, means mind as "Vishnu bears in his hand, mind in the form of disc (cakra) which is constantly in motion, swifter than wind."

Bhava means Shiva, cakra means mind (as per Viṣṇu Purāṇa) and pravartini means guide. This means that Ambāl is the guiding factor of Shiva.

छन्दःसारा शास्त्रसारा मन्त्रसारा तलोदरी।

उदारकीर्तिरुद्दामवैभवा वर्णरूपिणी॥१५८॥

Chandassārā, śāstrasārā, mantrasārā, talōdarī।

udārakīrti, ruddāmavaibhavā, varṇarūpiṇī॥158॥

844. Chandassārā

Bhāskararāya calls it as the Prototype of the Chandas (metres). Ambāl is the (sāra- or saaram in Tamil) essence of Chandas. Ambāl is well-established in Chandas.

What is Chandas and what is its importance? Chandas has many meanings. It means meter, Vedic mantras, unrestrained conduct, desire and Sārā means strength, marrow, fixity, rule, water, Wealth, superiority.

In poetry, meter is the basic rhythmic structure of a verse or lines in verse. Like tala is to music, chandas is to poetry. Chandas has a rule of how many aksharas are there in a Chandas and how it is distributed into distinct parts /legs/ Paadams. Many traditional verse forms prescribe a specific verse metre, or a certain set of meters alternating in a particular order. The study and the actual use of meters and forms of versification are both known as prosody. For example, the foot of a stanza with eight syllables Anustubh. With nine syllables it is "Brhati" and with ten "Pankti". "Tristubh" has eleven syllables and "Jagati" twelve. *"Gāyatri", "Ushnik", "Anustubh", "Pankti", "Tristubh" and "Jagati"* are all Vedic metres.

During Sandhya Vandanam, we pray to the main seven Chandas as follows:

प्रणवस्य ऋषि ब्रह्मा, देवी गायत्री छंद:, परमात्मा देवता

भूराधि सप्त व्याहृतिनाम अत्री भृगु कुथस वशिष्ट गौतम कश्यप आंगिरस ऋषयः।

गायत्री उष्णिक अनुष्टुप बृहती पंक्ती त्तृष्टुप जगत्यः छन्दांसि।

अग्नि वायु अर्क वगीसा वरुणा इंद्रा विश्वे देवा देवताः।

"Gāyatri" is a maha-mantra, the king of mantras. The deity for Gāyatri is Savita. Gāyatri is the name of the meter also. Gāyatri, unlike most other mantras and slokas, has only three feet. Each foot has eight syllables and altogether there are 24 syllables. Because it has only three padas or feet it is called "Tripada-Gāyatri". There are other Gāyatris also. The first Vedic mantra in Rig Veda reads

ॐ अग्निमीळे पुरोहितं यज्ञस्य देवमृत्विजम्।

होतारं रत्नधातमम्

-Om Agnimeele purohitam Yajnasya devamrudivijam, Hotaram ratnadatamam- is in the Gāyatri meter.

All Vedic mantras in verse are Chandas. The Vedapurusha stands on Chandas. *"Chanda: paado Vedasya":* the Vedic mantras are supported by Chandas.

Each mantra has a deity (the deity it invokes), its own meter and its own saint (the seer who revealed it to the world). Mentioning the name of the rishi and touching our head with our hand have their own significance. It means holding the rishi's feet on our head. We first pay our respect to the sages because it is from them that we received the mantras. We then mention the chandas or meter of the hymn and touch our nose with our hand. Chandas protects the sound of a mantra and is like its vital breath. So, we place our hand on the nose, that part of our body with which we breathe. Without breath there is no life.

Bhāskararāya comments: Chandas is Gāyatri and other meters, Saara, her form is fixed. Among the meters Gāyatri is the essential one, the Panchadasi is its essence. In Bhāskararāya's Varivasya Rahasya (1-2 to 4), he describes: "For the sake of attaining that knowledge, fourteen methods are promulgated in the world as means. Among these the Vedas are the essential, in them the Gāyatri of which there are two forms, the first is the one which is chanted by all, the other is completely concealed in the four Vedas."

Sārā means strength or Maahatmyam. Ambāl's Mahatmyam is expressed through Chandas.

Chandas also means a way of conduct. The Vijnana bhairava bhattaraka says, *"Yatra yatra manas tustihi: manas tatraiva dharayet, tatra tatra parAnanda swarupam samprakashate"* "Wherever the mind finds pleasure in what it is directed, this supreme bliss becomes manifest."

So, according to this, whatever gives the perfect devotee delight that is dharma or righteousness, whatever displeases him is unrighteousness.

Bhāskararāya has written a book called "Chandobaskaram" on the Sastram of Chandas.

Kalidasa says in the prologue to Sakuntalam, "When in doubt, the opinion of the wise is the authority."

The Manu Smriti (2-6) says, *"shruti smriti sadaachaara: atmanas tusthireva cha"* "Righteousness means what is ordained in the Srutis and Smrtis, the custom of holy men as well as that in which the mind delights,"—that is the mind devoted to contemplation.

Sara is also rule or form. Chandas, desire. Devi is in the form of Icchasakti.

845. śāstrasārā:

Essence of the Sastras.

Sastra refers to Vedas, for it is explained in the Veda Sutra (1-1-8) 'From its being the source of Sastra.' That which lays down the rules (Vidhi) is Sastra" -which is the Vedas, the Smriti like Manusmriti.

846. mantrasārā- Essence of the mantras. Mantra may mean, Vedas, or the Mantras in the Tantras, or the sixty-four books about Mantras.

847. talōdarī

Talo refers to karatalam -palm of the hand. Like the soft and slender palm, Ambāl is Slender waisted. If the syllable A is added, the name becomes Atalodari. The Atala loka is her waist when she assumes the Virat Swarupam.

848. udārakīrti

Ambāl is of exalted fame. Bhāskararāya offers different interpretations:

ud, exalted, *ā,* all-pervading, *ara,* quickly obtained, *kirti,* fame. By worshipping Devi, one gets fame quickly.

Or āra, Mangala and other deities, ud, dispels, (what) the chanting of the name of Devi dispels the harmful influence of the deities such as Mangalā by means of "mangala dosha" ("mars defect").

Or ud, the golden Intelligence which resides in the disc of the Sun.

The Shruti (Chandogya Upanishad. 1-6-6) says "He that resides in the sun, the golden person... His name is Ud." Aras refers to certain kinds of weapon, 'i.e., Her fame is a weapon against the Person in the sun.

The meaning is by worshipping Her one obtains fame excelling the fame of that Person.

Or āra, the two lakes of nectar, ud, exalted, -i.e., Her fame is equal to that of the two lakes. This is explained in the Chandogya Upanishad (8-5-4): "ln the city of Brahman, called Aparajita (unconquerable) to be obtained by those who worship the qualified Brahman, there are two lakes of nectar resembling oceans by name Ara and Nya."

In English also, we say 'Aura of fame'

849. uddāmavaibhavā

Her glory is exalted. It is unlimited.

'Dama' means rope (*Thambu Kayir* in Tamil), that which limits, (Example: Damodaran-Name of Krishna who was tied

　The Glory of Lalithā Sahasranāmam

with a rope by Yashoda); ud, beyond. No limit to Her glory. Damodar is a very auspicious month for worshipers of Lord Krishna. It normally falls within the months of October and November.

850. varṇarūpiṇī

The letters make up her form. The Panini shiksha says, "According to the Sambhava school there are sixty-sixty-four aksharas or letters, these are promulgated by Svayambhu in the Prikrta or Samskrta Language." These sixty-four letters make up her form.

जन्ममृत्युजरातप्तजनविश्रान्तिदायिनी।

सर्वोपनिषदुद्घुष्टा शान्त्यतीतकलात्मिका॥१५९॥

janmamṛtyu jarātapta jana viśrānti dāyinī |

sarvōpaniṣa dudghuṣṭā, śāntyatīta kaḻātmikā || 159 ||

851. janmamṛtyu jarātapta jana viśrānti dāyinī

Janma means birth; Mrtyu means death; jaratapta refers to old age; vishranti means happiness in oneself, solace that retired people seek; dayini is giver. All the living beings go through the cycle of birth, old age and death. Ambāl provides peace to beings consumed by birth, death and old age.

852. sarvōpaniṣad udghuṣṭā

Sarva is all; Upanishad; udghusta is proclaimed. Udghusta: Ud, exalted, ghusta, according to the Kosa 'loudly proclaimed.

Ambāl's glory is loudly proclaimed by all the Upanishads. In our Sanatana Dharma, lot of importance is given to Upanishads.

The meaning of Upanishad as given by Acharya is: *Upa* is "Bringing the Self near to Brahman", and *Nishad* means "destroying ignorance" and hence it is called Upanishad."

Chandogya Upanishad 1-1-10 says:

नाना तु विद्या चा अविद्या च, यदेव विद्यया करोति, श्रद्धयोपनिषदा तदेव वीर्यवत्तरं भवतीति.

vidyā ca avidyā ca nānā tu means knowledge and ignorance are entirely different things; *yat eva*, anything; *vidyayā* karoti, one does with knowledge [about Om]; *śraddhayā*, with respect for one's teachers and the scriptures; *upaniṣadā*, as taught by the Upaniṣads; *tat eva,* that alone; *vīryavattaram bhavati*, is very powerful.

Whatever one does by knowledge, faith, by Upanishad, that alone becomes very powerful."

853. śāntyatīta kaḻātmikā

Ambāl is Kalā called Sāntyatīta. The Kalā in the ether is called Santyatita. Śantyatīta means transcending peace (Śhanti).

The Shaivagamas describe its nature as *Santyatitakala* that destroys duality and bestows bliss.

गम्भीरा गगनान्तस्था गर्विता गानलोलुपा।
कल्पनारहिता काष्ठाऽकान्ता कान्तार्धविग्रहा॥१६०॥

gambhīrā, gaganāntaḥsthā, garvitā, gānalōlupā।

kalpanārahitā, kāṣṭhā, akāntā, kāntārdha vigrahā॥160॥

854. gambhīrā

Fathomless. Gambhira is compared to a large deep tank (Mahahrada). Ambāl is in that roopam.

The Shiva Sutra (1-22) says, *"maha hrādanu samdhā nānan, mantra vīrya anubhavah"* - maha is great; hrada means a large or a deep piece of water, lake. Mahahrada means the supreme Divine energy. It also means Devi who pervades the universe and is beyond space and time.

"Meditation (Anusandhana) means the feeling of being merged in that. Mantravirya is the power of Mantra. Anubhava (experience), the clear manifestation, of the Self.

So, by meditating on Mahahrada, the great deep water, one experiences the power of the Mantra."

Or Gam, the Ganapatibija, bhi is fear, Ra drives out. She drives out fear.

855. gaganāntaḥsthā

Gagana is Akasa or ether. In Hindi too, Gagan means sky or heaven. *anta,* its end or destruction, *stha*, remains – meaning Ambāl stays even after the destruction of the ether.

The Shvetashvatara Upanishad. (3-9) says, "She is the one abiding like a firm tree in the sky." Ambāl resides in the ether. Permeates the sky.

The bīja for ākāś is ha. The bīja-s for other elements (air, fire, water and earth) are ya, ra, va, la. We say these during Pancha Puja. She is in the five elements. We worship them.

856. garvitā- Proud. Justifiably so as She created the universe. This naama should not be confused with ego that is associated with human mind.

857. gānalōlupā

Gāna means songs; In Hindi too Gāna means songs. Lolupa refers to enjoyment. There is a word 'Ganalola.'meaning a person who enjoys music. Ambāl is fond of music. Music and Ambāl are closely connected as in numerous kritis.

"*SaamaGaana Priye Sarvaloka Nayakiye Amba*– a song by Periyasami Thooran in Anandabharaivi. Shyāmala Dhandagam says *jaya saṅgīta rasike.*

858. kalpanārahitā

Kalpana, means imagination (Karpanai in Tamil); *Rahita* means free from. Ambāl is free from the attributes of imagination. She is not affected by the waves of the objective world, because they are only imagined. She is the endowment of Reality.

There is another interpretation by Bhāskararāya. This nāma is split into kalpa + nara + hita. Kalpa, even in the Pralaya, Nāra to men, hita, friend. The souls are called Nāras. As a saying goes, "*Nayaneethi Nara: Prokta: Paramatma Sanatana:*" that means as the living beings are led in the right path to Paramatma, the beings are called Nāras.

During Pralaya, the universal dissolution, Ambāl does good to souls by keeping them in her belly (hiraṇya garbha) in the form of Vasanas (tendencies). So, in the time of creation and preservation there is no need to question her compassion. The *Astāvakra gita* says, "In me is the infinite ocean of consciousness, the souls like waves naturally rise, beat, play and return."

Who was Aṣṭāvakra? There is an interesting story. Ashtavakra was a Vedic sage. His name literally means "eight deformities" as he was born with those defects. Sage Aruni, mentioned in the Chāndogya Upaniṣad, ran an Āśrama teaching the Vedas. Kahoḍa, one of his students, married his daughter Sujata. When Sujatha was pregnant, the fetus heard and learnt the correct chanting of the Vedas. Legend says that when the baby's father made mistakes in the intonation while chanting, the fetus spoke from the womb and corrected him. The father got angry and cursed him for being born with deformities, hence the name 'Ashtavakra'. Aṣṭāvakra Gīta (अष्टावक्रगीता) also known as Aṣṭāvakra saṃhitā is an Advaita Vedānta scripture which documents a dialogue between the Guru Aṣṭāvakra and Janaka, the King of Mithila. It is in the form of conversation between two enlightened souls.

859. kāṣṭhā

Means Goal. What goal?

Katha Upanishad 3-11 says:

पुरुषान्न परं किंचित्सा, काष्ठा सा परा गतिः ॥११॥

"beyond the Puruṣha there is nothing. That is the end, that is the final goal."

In this context "Ambāl is the goal, she is the supreme way."

One of the eight forms of Shiva is Bhīma, representing ether (element ākāś) and His wife is known as Kāṣṭhā. She is in the form of ten directions.

The Linga Purana says, "The divine Shiva called Bhima in the form of ether giving space for all things animate and inanimate."

The Vayu Purana also repeats the same.

Kashta also refers to a period consisting of eighteen minutes. Ambāl is the form of time too.

Bhagavad Gīta X.42 says

अथवा बहुनैतेन किं ज्ञातेन तवार्जुन।

विष्टभ्याहमिदं कृत्स्नमेकांशेन स्थितो जगत्॥42॥

atha vā bahunaitena, kim jñātena tavārjuna

viṣhṭabhyāham idam kritsnam, ekānśhena sthito jagat

What need is there for all this detailed knowledge, O Arjun? Simply know that by one fraction of My being, I pervade and support this entire creation.

860.akāntā-Aka, means sin and pain. Anta is end. Akanta is End of sin. Ambāl is the destroyer of sins. Nāma 167 *pāpa-nāśinī* and nāma *743 pāpāraṇya-davānalā* convey the same meaning. Some women have the name Kanta.

861. kāntārdha vigrahā

Having the half body of her husband. Kanta, supreme Shiva; ardha means half; vigraha refers to the body. Shiva is seen as Ardhanārīśvara.

Ka, the syllable ka, anta, the end of it means heaven, ardha, a division. The meaning is the heaven is a part of her body. Chāndogya Upanishad (3-12-6) says "All creatures constitute one quarter of Him. The remaining three immortal portions are in heaven."

कार्यकारणनिर्मुक्ता कामकेलितरङ्गिता।

कनत्कनकताटङ्का लीलाविग्रहधारिणी॥१६१॥

kāryakāraṇa nirmuktā, kāmakēḻi taraṅgitā।

kanat-kanakatāṭaṅkā, līlāvigraha dhāriṇī॥161॥

862. kāryakāraṇa nirmuktā

Karya means work or effect. Karana is the cause. Ambāl is free from cause and effect.

The Shiva Purana (Chapter 6-59) says: *na tasya vidyeta kāryaṃ, kāraṇaṃ cha na vidyate|* He has neither cause nor effect.

The Śvetāśvatara Upaniṣad (VI.8) also says: *na tasya kāryaṃ karaṇaṃ ca vidyate;* He has no body and no organs. *Karya*, the categories, Mahat, etc., karana, Mula—prakrti. Because in the Chaitanya (Brahman) these things do not exist. Ambāl and Brahman are not different.

Bhagavad Gita verse 3-22 says

न मे पार्थास्ति कर्तव्यं त्रिषु लोकेषु किञ्चन- *na me pārthāsti kartavyaṁ triṣu lokeṣu kiṁcana,*

O Partha, there is no duty for Me to do in all the three worlds.

But the law of cause-and-effect states that every cause has an effect. Then, how can we really comprehend Ambāl?

It is not easy as Bhagavad Gita (2.29) says:

आश्चर्यवत्पश्यति कश्चिदेन, आश्चर्यवद्वदति तथैव चान्य:|
आश्चर्यवच्चैनमन्य: शृणोति, श्रुत्वाप्येनं वेद न चैव
कश्चित्||29||

āśhcharya-vat paśhyati kaśhchid ena, āśhcharya-vad vadati tathaiva chānyaḥ, āśhcharya-vach chainam anyaḥ śhṛiṇoti, śhrutvāpyenaṁ veda na chaiva kaśhchit

Some look on the Self as a wonder; some speak of It as a wonder; some hear of It as a wonder; still others, though hearing, do not understand It at all.

The Self is incomprehensible because it is not known by the ordinary means of knowledge.

Although it is difficult to comprehend the idea of the Self, if one starts the practice of listening (sravanam), continuous reflection (mananam) and long contemplation (nidhidhyasan) it is possible to realize the Self in him.

863. kāmakēḷi taraṅgitā- kāma refers to Kameshwara or Shiva. Keli is joy; Tarangita flows like waves. In Hindi and Urdu also, Tarang means waves. kāmakēḷi taraṅgitā means Ambāl overflows with joy in the presence of Śiva.

864. kanat-kanaka tāṭaṅkā

Kanaka means gold; (remember Kanakadhara Storam). Tatanka means earrings. Ambāl wears shining gold earrings. Saundarya Lahari Verse 28 says:

करा

लं यत् क्ष्वेलं, कबलितवतः कालकलना

न शम्भोस्तन्मूलं, तव जननि ताटङ्क महिमा

karalam yat khsevalam kabalitavataha kalakalana

na sambhos tanmulam, tava janani tatanka mahima

Shiva becomes deathless, even after swallowing the terrible poison because of the power of Ambāl's tāṭaṅka (ear studs).

865. līlāvigrahadhāriṇī

Lila, *Līlā* means play or without effort, *Vigrahadhāriṇī*, wearing different incarnations. Ambāl takes different forms, just like child's play. A child loves to wear different dresses.

Līlā also refers to a Character in Yoga Vāsiṣṭha. Lila is the name of the queen of Padmaraja. She is mentioned in the Yogavasistha: "There was in this Royal family one named Padma... he had a beautiful Wife named Lila." By Her tapas, Goddess Sarasvatī appeared before Her and answered Līlā's questions on Realization.

In Bhagavad Gita Chapter 4- verse 8, Krishna says:

परित्राणाय साधूनां विनाशाय च दुष्कृताम्।
धर्मसंस्थापनार्थाय सम्भवामि युगे युगे॥8॥

paritrāṇāya sādhūnāṁ vināśhāya cha dushkṛitām

dharma-sansthāpanārthāya sambhavāmi yuge yuge

"To protect the virtuous, and to destroy the evil doers, and to establish Dharma on a firm footing, I am born from Yuga to Yuga."

Likewise, Ambāl takes different incarnations. She is known by many names right from Kanyakumari in the South to Vaishnavi in North, from Bhagavadi in Kerala, Bhavani in West to Mahakali or Durga in the East.

अजा क्षयविनिर्मुक्ता मुग्धा क्षिप्रप्रसादिनी।
अन्तर्मुखसमाराध्या बहिर्मुखसुदुर्लभा॥१६२॥

ajākṣaya vinirmuktā, mugdhā kṣipraprasādinī।

antarmukha samārādhyā, bahirmukha sudurlabhā॥162॥

866. ajā

Unborn. ja (ज). -born or descended from, produced or caused by. Jalaja is lotus, originating in the water. Jana means living being we say janangal in Tamil to mean common people. Janathipadhi is the president. You add 'a' to ja it means unborn.

Rg veda 1.81.5 says *na jAto na janishyate* - He was neither born nor will be born. Ambāl is unborn.

Bhāskararāya comments:

Śvetāśvatara Upaniṣad (IV.5) explains this state. अजामेकां लोहित शुक्ल कृष्णां,

ajām ekāṃ lohita śukla kṛṣṇāṃ,

There is one unborn prakriti - red, white and black - which gives birth to many creatures like itself-like an amoeba.

The Mahabharata also says, "I was not, am not, and will not be born at any time, I am the Ksetrajna of all beings, hence I am called Aja."

Prakṛti is described in the Upaniṣad as aja. Though it (prakṛti) changes its form, It is without birth and without beginning. Ambāl had no birth like humans. Lalithambike came from *Chitagni kundam*.

867. kṣhaya vinirmuktā:

Bhāskararāya comments:

Kshaya means house, Vinirmukta is freed. Generally, those who desire salvation abandon their houses out of fear of worldly objects. Many take 'sanyasam' running away to seek salvation. But for devotees of Devi, salvation is obtained even while they are in their houses. Those who obtain Salvation are seen while living as householders.

Bhāskararāya quotes Shiva Sthuti saying:

"yati paramichasi thaama, tyaja maa naama svakam thaama,

parapatha niyamana thaama, smara hrudi kamadvisho naama"

   The Glory of Lalithā Sahasranāmam

"If you desire the supreme abode do not abandon your own abode; remember in your heart the name of the foe of Kama, the way to the supreme abode."

Kshaya also means free from decay. Decay here means death.

When there is no birth, there is no death.

Brahman is beyond birth and death as everything originates from Him.

Kṛiṣhṇa says in Bhagavad Gīta (II.27),

जातस्य हि ध्रुवो मृत्युर्ध्रुवं जन्म मृतस्य च|
तस्मादपरिहार्येऽर्थे न त्वं शोचितुमर्हसि||27||

jātasya hi dhruvo mṛityur, dhruvaṁ janma mṛitasya cha

tasmād aparihāryer arthe, na tvaṁ śhochitum arhasi

"Death is certain for the born and rebirth is inevitable for the dead."

Since She is the Brahman, She is devoid of birth and death.

868. mugdhā- Beautiful. Mugdha means beautiful and innocent

869. kṣhipraprasādinī

Kshipra means quickly. Ambāl is quickly pleased by a few days' worship. Shiva is called Ashutoshi-one who gets quickly pleased. Ambāl is a part of him. Bhāskararāya comments from Saura Purana that says,

"O Dvijas, by worshipping other deities Salvation is gradually obtained, but by worshipping the Lord of Uma one is freed in the same incarnation."

He also quotes from the Tantraraja that says, "The prayers, oblations, worship, etc., performed without regularity make one fit (for salvation) in the next birth."

870. antarmukha samārādhyā- Worshipped internally. Antarmukha, introspection, i.e. worshipped by those capable of introspection

871. bahirmukha sudurlabhā

Difficult to attain by those devoted to external objects.

Saundarya Laharī (verse 95) says:

पुरारन्ते-रन्तः, पुरमसि तत-स्त्वचरणयोः

सपर्या-मर्यादा, तरलकरणाना-मसुलभा।

purA rantE-rantah:, puramasi tatastva charanayOh:

saparyA maryAdA tarala karaNAnAm asulabhA

You are the spouse of the destroyer of the three cities (Lord Shiva). Therefore, the privilege of coming near you and worshipping at your feet, is unattainable to the fickle-minded, who do not have control of their senses.

The shlokam means "It is difficult for those who have not controlled their senses to attain Devi."

त्रयी त्रिवर्गनिलया त्रिस्था त्रिपुरमालिनी।

निरामया निरालम्बा स्वात्मारामा सुधासुतिः॥१६३॥

trayī, trivarga nilayā, tristhā, tripuramālinī।

nirāmayā, nirālambā, svātmārāmā, sudhāsṛtiḥ॥ 163 ॥

872. trayī

(Similar to three) Triple revelation. Ambāl is in the form of three Vedas-Rig, Yajur and Saama. Generally, only three

Vedas are said to be the main scriptures. *'Striyaam rik saama yajushi, iti vedas trays trayee. "* Is the Kocha vachanam.

In the Kurma Purana Devi says to Himavan:

"Mamaiva anyaa parashakti: Vedasamjna puraatanee

Rik Yajus Sama Rupena, sarkathow sampravartate"

"I have another supreme ancient energy called Vedas, at the beginning of creation it appears as Rik, Yajur and Saman."

The Padma Purana also, "O Devi, you are called logic, the three Vedas and ethics."

The Devi Purana also says, "Since Devi is in the three divisions of the Vedas, namely, Rik, Yajur and Saman, she is called Trayi"

Devi Purana further says, "Rigveda begins with *Agni Meele* the syllable A, Samaveda begins with the syllable A *'Agne Ayahee'*, the Yajurveda begins with the syllabe I (ee)-*Ishe Tvorjevaa Tvaa*, by uniting these three A ee A, it becomes suchi (pure). Here the word suchi, means the bija of the Vagbhava (the first division of the Pancadashi). Therefore, Trayi also means the Vigbhavabija. So, Ambāl is known as trayi.

873. trivarga nilayā- Abode of the three objects of pursuit. *Trivargo Dharma Kamarthai* says the Kocha vachanam. Meaning Dharma, wealth, and desire

874. tristhā

Residing in the three. Which three? Tri, the three worlds, and others The Markendeya Purana says, "There are three worlds, three Vedas, three vidyas, three fires, three lights, three objects of desire, via, virtue, etc., three qualities, three sounds, three sins, three conditions of life, three times. three states of consciousness (Satvik, Tamas and Rajas), three Pitrus, day, night and twilight, three Matras, these 0 Devi, Saraswathi are thy form. hence, thou art called Tristha."

875.tripuramālinī-The ruling deity of the Antardasara chakra in Sri Chakram.

876. nirāmayā

Free from disease. Popular saying from the rig veda says:

ॐ सर्वे भवन्तु सुखिनः

सर्वे सन्तु निरामयाः।

सर्वे भद्राणि पश्यन्तु

मा कश्चिद्दुःखभाग्भवेत्।

ॐ शान्तिः शान्तिः शान्तिः॥

oṃ sarve bhavantu sukhinaḥ

sarve santu nirāmayāḥ

sarve bhadrāṇi paśyantu

mā kaścidduḥ khabhāgbhaveta।

oṃ śāntiḥ śāntiḥ śāntiḥ॥

"May all be happy, all be free from disease, be witness to all auspicious events and no one has to be a part of sorrow."

877. nirālamb- Alambanam means support. Ambāl herself is Sarvalambanam-support for everything. She is without any support.

878. svātmārāmā

Rejoicing in herself.

This name establishes her independence, since by it she is the destroyer of the root (i.e., matter.) The meaning of the

 The Glory of Lalithā Sahasranāmam

description is, she divides herself into two and these sport with each other.

The Brahadaranya Upanishad (1-4-3) says, "He was not happy, - therefore the lonely one is never happy. He desired a second, and he became thus. He made himself a pair and they embraced as man and woman. So, they became husband and Wife."

Or Sva, Her's, i.e., the Universe belongs to her, Atman, Brahman, ārāmā sports. She is in both Jagat and Atman. In these two she has the power of wandering at will. (Kerala temples are owned by Dewasvom- Belonging to the God"). The Markandeya Purana says, "Thou art the supreme and eternal Devi in whom all are established. Brahman is supreme and imperishable, and the Universe is perishable. Just as the fire is in the firestick and atoms in the earth, so remain Brahman. and the Whole Universe in thee."

879. sudhāsṛtiḥ

Stream of nectar.

In Nāma 106, Devi is described as 'Sudha dharabhi Varshini" Acharya says in Soundaryalahari, "Maheem Muladhare", and "Sudha Dhaara Saraihi" in Slokas 9 and 10. So, Ambāl is in the form of Amrudha dhaara- stream of nectar.

The nectar which is in the moon of the pericarp of the Sahasrara lotus flows through the Kundalini. The circles of the Dakini and other deities are watered by this stream whence the Kundalini becomes the energy of action.

संसारपङ्कनिर्मग्नसमुद्धरणपण्डिता।
यज्ञप्रिया यज्ञकर्त्री यजमानस्वरूपिणी॥१६४॥

samsārapaṅka nirmagna samuddharaṇa paṇḍitā |

yajñapriyā, yajñakartrī, yajamāna svarūpiṇī || 164 ||

880. saṃsārapaṅka nirmagna samuddharaṇa paṇḍitā

This is just one long word. samsara means family, panka means mire, swampy ground (pankajam-means lotus that grows in swampy waters), nirmagna is to sink. under, samuddharana is drawing out or up. panditha is skilled. The full word means Ambāl is skilled in pulling out those who are sunk in the mire of Samsara (life).

881. yajñapriyā- Fond of sacrifice. Yajna also refers to Vishnu. Ambāl is also affectionate to Vishnu.

882. yajñakartrī- Spouse of Yajnakarta- the Doer of Sacrifice. Yajnakarta is called yajamanan and he is considered Paramashiva.

883. yajamāna svarūpiṇī

This is a sequel to the earlier naama. In the eight murthi names of paramashiva, the last name is called yajamanan (master). Bhāskararāya quotes Linga Puranam that says:

Pancha Bhutani Chandrarkau, Atmethi Munipungavaha:l

Murthir-Ashtau shivasyahoo, devadevasya deematha:l

Atma tasya ashtami murthy: ejamaana havyaa paraa l

The five elements, the moon, Sun, and Self, the best of Munis say, are the eight forms of the Lord of Devas. The eighth form of him is self and the sacrifice (ejamaana).

Chapter 18

Devi - Supporter of Dharma

There is a lot of similarity between Lalithā Sahasranāmam and Bhagavad Gita. It covers the contents of the 10th chapter of Bhagavad Gita on Vibhuti Yoga, leading up to Chapter 18 of Moksha Sanyas Yoga. In Sanskrit, bhuti refers to aishwaryam (wealth or treasure). Vi expands it to something much larger or valuable beyond imagination. Like Nayaka and Vinayaka, Jaya and Vijaya. Vibhuti is a 'glorious form or manifestation' which is a great treasure. Vistaram is expansion. Vibhuti Vistara Yoga is explained in Bhagavad Gita Chapter 10 – 'The Infinite Glories of the Ultimate Truth.'

धर्माधारा धनाध्यक्षा धनधान्यविवर्धिनी।

विप्रप्रिया विप्ररूपा विश्वभ्रमणकारिणी॥१६५॥

dharmādhārā, dhanādhyakṣā, dhanadhānya vivardhinī|

viprapriyā, viprarūpā, viśvabhramaṇa kāriṇī || 165 ||

884. dharmādhārā

It means Devi is the Supporter of Dharma. The word dharma is known to all. It comes from the Sanskrit root word 'dhru' that means "to hold," or "to support" or "to maintain."

So, that which holds, keeps or maintains is dharma. Dharma maintains, or holds the very basis of this universe, the cosmic order. Dharma also means righteousness and a way of living since it enables one to be closer to the truth. If you split this naama into Dharma + A+ Dhaara, it means Dharma -the mode of life handed down by the ancient tradition and not contrary to the Vedas. A-in all places, Dhaara, flowing stream. Ambāl is a supporter of dharma in all places like a flowing stream.

Or Dharma is her support. Mahanarayana Upanishad 22.1 says "Everything is established in Dharma."

885. dhanādhyakṣā

Means Devi is the Ruler of wealth. Dhanadhyaksha refers Kubera - the Lord of wealth. Yakṣa-s are superhuman beings or demigods and generally considered as attendants of Kubera. Kubera is the chief of Yakṣa-s. Ravana's father was Visravas (son of Pulastya, one of the maanaseeka creations of Brhama or Prajapati) and Nikasa, a Raakshasi.

So, Ravana was the great grandson of Brahma. Kubera was the son of Visravas and Iladevi. So, Kubera was the half-brother of Ravana. Kubera was a great worshipper of Ambāl. Since there is no difference between the worshipper and the worshipped, Ambāl is said to be the Ruler of wealth.

886.dhanadhānya vivardhinī- One who increases Dhanam-Money, and Dhanyam - grain for devotees. Both are essential in life.

887. viprapriyā

Fond of Vipras, the wise people.

Vipra, the wise possessing a knowledge of the Vedas and other Sastras.

A Brahmana should be known by his birth. He is called Dvija, (twice born) on account of his purificatory ceremonies.

He becomes a Vipra by knowledge. One who possesses all these is called Shrotriya. She is fond of the learned and wise.

888. viprarūpā

Of whom the Vipras are her manifestations.

This is an extension of the previous nāma. After having said that She is fond of learned men, this nāma goes a step further and says that She is the embodiment of knowledge itself.

The Shruti says, "All the Devatas reside in the Brahmana who knows the Vedas." The Parasara Smriti also says, "The Brahmanas are known in the three worlds as sacred, for by the flow of their speech sinful people are purified." Brāhmana is a qualification based on the knowledge acquired; so known as vipra.

Or Vipra, Brahmanas, rupa, nourishes, -i.e., by the repetition of mantras (of Devi) and homas (oblation) etc. Brahmanas get nourished. They get Tejas.

The Apastamba Smriti says,

apamaanat tapovriddihi, sanmaanat tapasa kshaya:

archita: pujito vipro dugda gauriva seethati

"By disgrace, brahmana's penance is increased, by adulation their penance is destroyed. If the Brahmana is adored and worshipped, he becomes exhausted like a cow after milking. Just as the cow is nourished during the day by tender grass, so the Brahmana is nourished by repetition of the mantras and by homa."

889. viśvabhramaṇa kāriṇī

Causing the revolution of the Universes.

Viśva means the entirety of all universes; Ambāl is always referred as akhilāṇḍakoṭi brahmāṇḍa nāyakī अखिलाण्डकोटि ब्रह्माण्ड नायकी which means that She is the creator of number of universes. Bhrmana means revolution (their creation, preservation, and destruction); Bhramana also means going round, moving circularly. kāriṇī-one who causes.

The Shruti (Śvetāśvatara Upaniṣad) 6-1 says, "Some scholars think this world came into existence naturally. They call it nature. Some others are confused and call it time. They are wrong. That power by which the wheel of Brahman is revolved, is the glory of the Lord."

Or Visva, Vishnu; for the word Visva is explained thus when it occurs in the Vishnu Sahasranamam, (lst name). Viṣṇu Sahasranāma first nāma is 'Visvam Vishnur Vashatkaraha'- visvam refers to Vishnu- the one who has manifested as the universe and everything in it- the Viraat-Purusha. That which pervades everywhere is Vishnu. The Universe revolves.

Did Ambāl cause Bhramana or revolution of Vishnu?

There is a story in the Kaalika Purana.: "Vishnu once travelling through the sky, mounted on his vehicle Garuda, flew over the Devi named Kamakhya residing in the Nilachala in the Kamarupa country, without respecting her; then by the force of Devi's anger he fell into the ocean and there he remained swirling in the waters; after a long time Lakshmi (his spouse) began to look for him, and hearing of this event from Narada, she appeased Devi, by penance and rescued Vishnu. Afterwards he worshipped Devi and went to Vaikuntha.

                     The Glory of Lalithā Sahasranāmam

The Bhagavad Gita (18-61) also says,

ईश्वर: सर्वभूतानां हृद्देशेऽर्जुन तिष्ठति।

भ्रामयन्सर्वभूतानि यन्त्रारूढानि मायया॥61॥

īshvaraḥ sarva-bhūtānāṁ hṛid-deśhe 'rjuna tiṣhṭhati

bhrāmayan sarva-bhūtāni yantrārūḍhāni māyayā

"All beings which are fixed on the wheel of the Universe, he causes to revolve by his Maya."

विश्वग्रासा विद्रुमाभा वैष्णवी विष्णुरूपिणी।

अयोनिर्योनिनिलया कूटस्था कुलरूपिणी॥१६६॥

viśvagrāsā, vidrumābhā, vaiṣṇavī, viṣṇurūpiṇī।

ayōni, ryōninilayā, kūṭasthā, kularūpiṇī॥166॥

890. viśvagrāsā

Consumer of the universe.

Vishva, of all things animate and inanimate. grāsā has many meanings. Grāsa (ग्रास) refers to "one who consumes" (the destruction of the three abodes). grasa also means food.

The word Grass in English is an example of food for animals. Vishvagrasa refers to Ambāl's act of dissolution. This has been discussed in nāma 752 māhāgrāsā. The KathoUpanishad. (2-25) says,

यस्य ब्रह्म च क्षत्रं च उभे भवत ओदनः।

मृत्युर्यस्योपसेचनं क इत्था वेद यत्र सः॥२५॥

yasya brahma ca kṣhatram ca ubhe bhavata odanaḥ.

mṛtyur yasyopa sechanam ka itthā veda yatra saḥ. 25

"The Brahmana and Kshatriya are both His food, death is His condiment, who then knows Where he is." The Brahma Sutra (I-2-9) also confirms this: अत्ता चराचरग्रहणात् meaning "The eater (is God), on account of the appropriation of all that moves and does not move (as his food)."

891. vidrumābhā

Vidrumā means coral. The nine precious stones are

(1) Muktā or pearl, muthu (2) Māṇikya, (3) Vaidūrya, (4) Gomeda, (5) Vajra, (6) Vidrumā, (7) Padmarāga, (8) Marakata, and (9) Nīlam

Ambāl has the color of coral.

Or Vit, knowledge, druma, tree. Ambāl is the tree of knowledge. She is jnana rupini. Just as one tree creates many other trees, Ambāl spreads jnana.

892.vaiṣṇavī: "'Vaishnavi' means the one who is related to lord "Vishnu".

She is in the power of Vishnu.

Devi Mahatmiyam says

सर्वमङ्गलमाङ्गल्ये शिवे सर्वार्थसाधिके।

शरण्ये त्र्यम्बके गौरि नारायणि नमोऽस्तु ते।

शङ्खचक्रगदापद्म शार्ङ्गगृहीतपरमायुधे।

प्रसीद वैष्णवीरूपे नारायणि नमोऽस्तुते।

The Devi Purana. says, "Ambāl is sung as Vaishnavi for various reasons (1) because she hears the Shanku or conch, Chakram-disc and Gatha-club, (2) the mother of Vishnu, (3)

and the destroyer of foes (of Hari) or (4) Vishnu Himself. In
the above quotation four meanings are given.

893. viṣṇurūpiṇī

Ambāl is in the form of Vishnu

Bhāskararāya quotes extensively from Puranas and
Smritis.

In the Brahmānda Purana Lalitopakhyana, Devi says,
'Mamouva Pourusham Roopam Gopika Jana Mohanam' -
"My male form is attracting the Gopikas the milkmaids."

In the same place Vishnu says to Virabhadra,

Bhoge Bhavanirupa sa Durgarupa cha sankare

Gope cha Kalika rupa bhumrupa cha matatmika

'The ancient Shakti of the Lord is divided into four forms,
that Shakti becomes Bhavani in its Bhoga or ordinary form, in
battle she takes the form of Durga; in anger that of Kali; and
she is also my male form."

In the Kurma Purana, Himavan praises Devi as:

Sahasra Murthanam Ananta Shaktim

Sahasra Bahum Purusham Puranam

Shayanam abdow Lalithe Tavayva

Naraayanakyam Pranatosmi Rupam

"O Lalita, I do namaskarams to your form called Narayana,
which has a thousand heads, which is of infinite energy,
having a thousand arms, the ancient Person, reclining on the
waters."

In the same Kurma Purana when Shiva showed his universal
form to Mankanaka, Mankanaka asked:

kimetat bhagavtrupam sugoram vishvatomukam "

"What is this terrible form of thine, facing every side; who is she shining by your side?"

Shiva answers this question, after explaining the glory of his own nature, as "She is my supreme Maya and Prakrti of triple qualities. She is Narayana, supreme, unmanifested, in the form of Maya."

In the Sanatkumara Samhita. describing to king Prabhakara, the devotion to Vishnu, and describing to his wife, Padmini, the devotion to Parvati, it is said: *"Evam Devyatmana svena rupena cha janardana:"* - "Janardana is thus in the form of Devi as well as in his own form; the only one is worshipped in two forms Devi and Vishnu." The Brahad Parasara Smriti also says, "He who with delighted mind worships Durga, Katyayani, and Vagdevi, obtains the world of Vishnu."

The Padma Purana also says, "One who does abhishekam to the image of Chandika with sugarcane juice and places her on a golden vehicle, enjoys the presence of Vishnu (after death)."

The Aditya and Shiva Puranas., "She who dwells by his side is the young Parvati and Hari also is a part of him."

The Vamana Purana also says, "One who on the full-moon day of the month Magha worships Devi according to rule, he obtains the benefit of the Ashvamedha sacrifice and (after death) he shines in the world of Vishnu."

894. ayōni- One who is without origin.

Yoni, means origin, cause, or abode. A-yoni, having no abode or origin

 The Glory of Lalithā Sahasranāmam

895. yōninilayā

The place of origin for all

Yoni is Prakrti; for it is explained thus in the Muṇḍaka Upaniṣad (III.i.3) *rukmacarṇaṁ kartāramīsaṁ puruṣaṁ brahmayonim.* This means 'the Brahman, the luminous Creator is the cause of Brahma, the hiraṇyagarbha or the Supreme Being.'

Therefore, brahmayonim means the Nature or prakṛti. Prakṛti is the cause for creation, when it is associated with the soul.

Brahma Sūtra (I.iv.27) also says "Brahman is declared to be the *yoni* (source)."

Or Yoni is Maya. It is explained thus in the Śvetāśvatara Upaniṣad 4-11, "He who presides over the Yoni (Maya), Nilaya, limits, i.e. Ambāl limits the Maya.

Or Yoni, the causes of the Universe, viz, Brahma, etc., Nilaya in whom all these rest.

Or Yoni, the three-angled chakra, Nilaya, she dwells therein in the form of Bindu. In that triangle, there is a chakra in the form of Bindu, in it there is a holy thing (Brahman) which the Brahmavits perceive by their Self only. The meaning is they perceive Brahman separated neither from the Self nor from the Bindu.

In short, this nāma says that She is the Creator.

896. kūṭasthā

Kuta literally means cheating or deception. In Hindi too, Khota means Fake. But it has many other meanings too. Here kuta means ignorance as it hides one's own nature of atma (which is born out of anandam or bliss) and makes one fall into Samsara; Stha, is governing. So, kutastha refers to one who governs ignorance.

Devi Mahatmyam says:

या देवी सर्वभूतेषु भ्राँति रूपेण संस्थिता,

- ya devi sarvabhuteshu bhranti rupen sansthita

नमस्तस्यै नमस्तस्यै नमस्तस्यै नमो नमः

- namastasyai namastasyai namastasyai namo namah

Bhranti is delusion or ignorance. She hides our true form with ignorance. To that Devi who resides as delusion, I offer my namaskarams.

Bhagavad Gita, 12-3 says,

सर्वत्रगमचिन्त्यञ्च कूटस्थमचलन्ध्रुवम्

sarvatra-gam achintyañcha kūṭa-stham achalan dhruvam

Those who worship the all-pervading, the unthinkable, (kutastam) the unchanging, the eternal, and (achalan) the immoveable, attain me.

Bhāskararāya comments on other meanings of Kuta.

"Kuta means a machine, deception, zodiac, anvil, illusion, mountain peak, and summit, insignificance, part of a plough, vanity, gate of the city."

Or kuta, ignorance, stha, seat, 'i.e., the foundation of ignorance is in her.

Or kuta "mountain peak", stha, she remains motionless like a mountain peak.

Or kuta, the iron anvil which remains on the ground while iron instruments are fashioned on it: stha, she remains unchanged like this.

Or kuta, the multitude of Universes, stha, these reside in Her.

Or kuta, Vagbhava, etc. (the three divisions of Pancadasi Mantra) stha, she remains in them.

Or kuta the gate of the city. i.e. the three-angled cakra which is Within the Sricakra, stha- she remains in it.

897. kularūpiṇī

Kula means noble, eminent or race or chief. It means Ambāl is in the form of those devotees who follow the path of the Kaulas – the Sakthas who worship Shakti.

वीरगोष्ठीप्रिया वीरा नैष्कर्म्या नादरूपिणी।

विज्ञानकलना कल्या विदग्धा बैन्दवासना॥१६७॥

vīragōṣṭhīpriyā, vīrā, naiṣkarmyā, nādarūpiṇī।

vijñāna kalanā, kalyā vidagdhā, baindavāsanā॥167॥

898. vīragōṣṭhīpriyā- Fond of the assembly of warriors.

899. vīrā

Valorous. We know the great valor of Ambāl who fought with many asuras like Bhandasura, Chanda Munda and others as described in Devi Mahatmyam. Her spouse Śiva, and Her sons Gaṇeśa and Kārttikeya are warriors. They have proved their valor while destroying evil forces.

900. naiṣkarmyā

Abstaining from actions

The Shruti (Kaivalya Upanishad. 22) says, *"Na PunyaPape Mama"* - "I am neither sinful nor righteous." Bhagavad Gita 5-10 also says, "lipayate na sa papena" -He is free from the taint of action."

The Yoga Sutra (1-24), "lshvara is a person untainted by pain, action, the result of action and mental impression."

Thus ends the Bodhini Kala with the ninth hundred shloka in the Saubhagya Bhaskara composed by Bhāskararāya.

901. nādarūpiṇī

In the form of Nada.

In Naama 299, we have seen Ambāl is described as नाद-रूपा Nāda-rūpā. She is in the form Sound. Muṇḍaka Upaniṣad confirms it by saying (I.i.7), "aksharāt sambhavatīha viśvam" which means 'from akshara (Śabda Brahman) the universe originates.'

Amba Sthuti says, *"Ananda Lakshanam Anahata Namni Deshe, Naadatmana Parinatham Thava Rupam Eshe."* Nada is above the Pranava. The great ones say. "O Eshe, Queen, your blissful form, is manifested as Naada in the place called Anahata, experienced by the mind turned inwards; the blessed ones express it by tears in their eyes and by horripilation."

Nada-Brahma is known as the sound of God, essentially meaning that the whole universe was created from the energy of sound.

Or whose form is in Nada. The Svacchanda Tantram. says, "That which I described to you by the name of Rodhini, above that resides Nada... one should meditate on the supreme Shiva going upward sitting on the lap of that." (See name 296.)

902. vijñāna kalanā

Causing perception

Vijñāna means knowledge or perception that is required to realise the Brahman and kalanā means causing or effecting.

The Glory of Lalithā Sahasranāmam

So, Vijñāna kalana means causing the direct perception of Brahman.

According to the Kurma Purana, "Vijnana means retaining in the mind the fourteen Vidyas with their meanings." Knowledge of all the fourteen vidyā-s is known as vijñāna. And Ambāl causes that knowledge.

903. kalyā

Skilful

Kalya has many meanings. The Viswakosam says, "Kalya means creation, dawn, a person without disease, a smart person, auspicious speech etc." Ambāl is the embodiment of all these qualities.

904. vidagdhā- Meaning Ambāl is Artful or Shrewd.

905. baindavāsanā

Baindava refers to bindu or dot and āsana means seat. This nāma says that Ambāl is seated on Baindava- as Bindu Vasini.

The central point in the inner most triangle of Śrī Chakra is known as bindu. This bindu being the sarvānandamaya chakra, is called as baindava sthāna.

So, Baindava means Sarvanandamaya chakra (the 9th one).

The Baindava resembles the round spot above the brows. The Svacchanda Tantram says, *"Haakini Mandalath Urdwam Bindu Rupam tu Vardulam"* "Above the Hakini circle there is a disc called Bindu" Then, after describing the lotus, and Shiva, it says *""vaamabhage samaseena shantyateetha manonmani"* - there is Ambāl in the form of Manonmani, which is above the Hakini, on Shiva's left side"

Or Baindava, means the collection of Bindus, and Asana, her support. The Jnanarnava Tantra Shiva says, "I will explain to you the collection of Bindus which are in the form of Bija, know, 0 Parvati, Ha with Bindu as Brahma, Sa with Bindu and Sarga as Hari and myself, 0 Queen of Devas, the relation between Hari and Hara is that of inseparable association..." After describing Vama, etc., Iccha, etc., waking state, etc., all those are in the form of Bindus, thus it is concluded by explaining, "Evam Bindu Trayar Yogat Tripura Naama Rupini"- "Thus as (Devi) is joined to the three Bindus, she is named Tripura."

Or prefixing the A to the name like Abaindavasana: Ab, in the water, aindava, the multitude of moons, like the multiple images of moon on water, Asana, she remains, (the meaning is) Though Ambāl is one, she remains as multiple images in the multitude of Jivas, like the multiple reflections of one moon in different waters.

Brahadaranya Upanishad 12 says, "Ekatha Bahutha Chaiva Dhrusyate Jala Chandravat"- "Brahman is seen as one and as many like the moon in the water."

तत्त्वाधिका तत्त्वमयी तत्त्वमर्थस्वरूपिणी।

सामगानप्रिया सौम्या सदाशिवकुटुम्बिनी॥१६८॥ सौम्या

tattvādhikā, tattvamayī, tattvamartha svarūpiṇī।

sāmagānapriyā, saumyā, sadāśiva kuṭumbinī॥168॥

906. tattvādhikā

Transcending the categories.

She is beyond tattva-s or principles or philosophies.

Tattvas, are those which provide enjoyment to all beings and remain until the Pralaya or dissolution. Since Ambāl is unaffected by the destruction of Tattvas, Ambāl is called Tattvaddika- beyond Tattvas.

907. tattvamayī

This is a sequel to the previous nāma. This nāma says that She is the embodiment of tattva-s.

Bhāskararāya offers different interpretations.

In earlier naama, Tattvadhika (906), means Shiva tatvam; Tattvamayi is, Shiva himself. The meaning is, she is both Samprajnāta and Asampranjāta Samadhis. Samadhi is a state of enlightenment that one attains by concentration of the mind. Let me explain further.

There are two kinds of Samadhis as explained in the Jnānārnava;

"The Samprajnāta Samadhi arises by transcending Shiva. The Asampranjāta one arises with the Shiva-Tattva. " Each of these Samadhis produce different reactions as explained in this scripture.

The Samprajnāta is twofold quick, and very quick. The Asampranjata one is slow and very slow. The Samprajnāta Samadhi is indicated by laughing, crying, by horripilation, trembling, and perspiration, etc.

The Asamprajnāta Samadhi is indicated by the non-movement of the eye lids and stationary body."

Both these two samadhis are attained by concentration of the mind in a certain light or Tejas. That light must be perceived through a Guru alone.

Or Tattvamayi, the three Tattvas, viz, Atma Tattva, Vidya—Tattva and Shiva—Tattva. She is collectively in the form of these three Tattvas as well as transcending the three.

Or there are three Tattvas Sat, Chit and Ananda. From Shiva to earth there are thirty-six Tattvas born from Brahman. Of these Shiva and Shakti correspond to Ananda (literally, they are merged in Ananda).

Sadashiva, Ishvara and Suddhavidya correspond to Chit; and all the Tattvas from Maya to earth correspond to Sat. Of these three the Shivatattva includes the other two, the second Vidyitattva includes the second and third with a trace of the first. The third Atmatattva is the third with the traces of the other two. Of course, Shivatattva corresponds to Ananda because it is a blissful one, Vidya to Cit, and Atman to Sat, taking the meaning of mere existence. Thus is the secret of the three Tattvas.

908. tattvamartha svarūpiṇī- The meaning of the words 'That and Thou.'

Tat refers to Shiva, and twam to the Jivas as used in the Mahavakyas. Ambāl is in the form of both Shiva and the Jivas.

909. sāmagānapriyā

Fond of Sāma songs.

There is a popular song *"sAmagAna priye ambA, Sarvaloka nAyakiye ambA"* in Ananda Bhairavi Ragam, composed by Periaswamy Thooran. It addresses Ambāl as 'Sāma Gana Priye – One who is fond of Sāma Ganam (Songs).

Or Samaga, the singers of Samaveda, ana, life, priya, fond. She is fond of Sāma Veda singers.

Sāma Veda is rendered in musical notes. It is said thatShivais very fond of Sāma Veda. Rāvaṇa got boons fromShivaby singing Sāma Veda.

Kṛṣṇa says in Bhagavad Gītā (X.22)

वेदानां सामवेदोऽस्मि देवानामस्मि वासव:।

इन्द्रियाणां मनश्चास्मि भूतानामस्मि चेतना॥22॥

I am the Samaveda amongst the Vedas, and Indra amongst Devas.

910. saumyā:

Benign or harmless. Ambāl is adored in the Soma sacrifice.

Shiva gets the name Soman from Sa Uma, accompanied by Uma.

As Ambāl is part of him, she gets the name Saumya.

Or Moon is also called Soman. Monday is called Somavaaram. As per Kocha Vachanam,"Somaha Karpura Chandryoha:," What Ambāl provides is pleasing like the moon.

Saumya also means beautiful or one who is calm.

911.sadāśiva kuṭumbinī: The consort of Sadashiva; Belonging to the family of Sadāśiva. It means that she is in the form of Shyamala, Suddhavidya, Ashwaruda and others.

सव्यापसव्यमार्गस्था सर्वापद्विनिवारिणी।

स्वस्था स्वभावमधुरा धीरा धीरसमर्चिता॥१६९॥

savyāpasavya mārgasthā, sarvāpadvi nivāriṇī।

svasthā, svabhāvamadhurā, dhīrā, dhīra samarchitā ॥169॥

912. savyāpasavya mārgasthā: She is the ruler of the Savya and Apasavya paths (right and left paths). It is said,"Savyam, Dakshina Vamayoho"- meaning Right and Left Paths. This nāma says that She is worshipped by Her devotees by either of these paths.

These are also known as dakṣiṇā mārga and vāma mārga. They are described in many ways.

Bhāskararāya offers a variety of explanations:

It is said that there are three paths to Surya Mandala (A mandala, in Sanskrit means "circle" - Sūryamaṇḍala (सूर्यमण्डल) refers to the "circle or disc of the sun"). These three paths are described as Uttara (north), Dakshina (south)-and Madhyama (middle). The galaxy of stars is called Nakshatra Mandala. The nakshatra Mandala is described as the "Veethis" or Streets through which the Sun travels. The Sun is said to travel through Three Nakhsatras (constellations) beginning with Ashvini make one Veethi (line), and three Veethis make a Marga (path).

These are fully described in the Vayu Purana.;

"Ashvini, Krttikai, and Bharani form Nagaveethi. Rohini, Ardra and Mrgasiras, form the Gajaveethi. Pushya, Aslesha and Aditya (Punarvasu) form the Airavati veethi.

These three Veethis form Uttara path. The two Phalgunis and Makha form Rhsativeethi. Hasta, Chitra and Swati are named Govithi. Jyestha, Vishakha, Anuradha, is Jāradgaviveethi. These three Vithis form the Madhyama path or Middle Marga. Mula, Purva and Uttara-āsadha is Ajaveethi. Shravana and Dhanihstha and Satabhisak are called Mrgaveethi. The

 The Glory of Lalithā Sahasranāmam

two Bhadrapadas and Revati is Vaisvānaravithi. These three form the Dakshina path." Thus, there are three paths to Surya Mandala.

Or Marga, means the Uttara path, deriving the meaning from that which belong to Mrga, for the north path has relation with the Mrgasiras Nakshatra. Savya, means the middle path because it is on the left side of the south. Apasavya of course means the south path. This is one explanation.

savyāpasavya mārgasthā means Ambāl is the ruler of all the three paths.

Or Savya, the way of gods called the path of light only to be attained by renunciation; apasavya, the way of the Pitrs called the path of smoke, etc., attained by worldly men. The word Mārgastha means the world of Vishnu, the residing place of Dhruva. Dhruva is the polestar on which depends the established paths (mārga) of the sun and the planets; hence mārgastha means Dhruva. As there are three paths. Ambāl is called savyāpasavya mārgasthā.

The space to the North and above the Saptharishi (seven Rishis) mandala, where the star Dhruva resides, is called Vishnu Path. It is the abode of clean yatis, sanctified ascetics free of any vice. These are the yogis who identify themselves with Vishnu. This is the third path. Thus, Ambāl is said to be on all the three paths. This is another explanation.

Ambāl is in both Savya and Apasavya paths and may be worshipped in both paths. The reality is that Tripurasundari is not separate from the deities Tripura-Bhairavi and others who are worshipped only by the Vāma path, the Devatas Sharada and others who are worshipped only by the Dakshina path, and the deities such as Shivaduti etc., who are worshipped by either or both the above paths.

Or according to the Shiva-Sutra (III, 45). Savya means Idā-Nādi, apasavya, Pingala, marga, meaning Sushumna, Stha, she is to be reached (by restraining the breath-Yoga).

Bhāskararāya offers many more explanations. We are not covering all of them.

In conclusion, Bhāskararāya adds, those who do not strictly follow the above prescribed paths in their worship are subject to misfortunes.

As the Shruti says, (Chandogya Upanishad 6-2-16): "Those who do not recognise these two paths, (consequently) become worms, birds, etc." The next naama says that Ambāl removes such misfortunes through chanting her names and by her compassion.

913. sarvāpadvi nivāriṇī

Remover of all misfortunes. This name proceeds to show that Devi removes all misfortune, by compassion, by repeating her names, easily.

In the Kurma Purana, Devi says,

"Ye tu Sangan Parityajya Mamekam Charanam Gathaha:

Upasate Sada Bhaktya Yogam Aisarvaryam Ashritaha:" and so on...

"Those who, forsaking attachment, take refuge in me, and ever worship me with devotion, by the method of divine Yoga, having compassion on all beings, tranquil, self-controlled, free from envy, humble, wise, ascetic, of vows performed, with minds fixed on me, Whose lives are in me, delighting in narrating my wisdom, whether, Sanyasins, or Grhasthas, or Vanaprasthast or Brahmacarins, and even those who are devoid of these characteristics, if they repeat my name, ever devoted to me, I quickly destroy in the same birth even mountains of misfortune by the lamp of wisdom."

In the Harivamsa Vishnu says to Devi: "The bondage of men consists of death, difficulty, the death of sons, loss of wealth... in all these misfortunes, You alone protect; there is no doubt."

In the Varaha Purana also, in the stotrams that praise of Devi by Brahma and others, it is said: "0 Devi, for those who attain thy supreme refuge, no misfortunes or dangers arise."

What should be done in misfortune? One should remember the feet of the mother. What does that remembrance do? It makes even Brahma, etc. serve you."

914. svasthā

Independent

swa-stha, Swa means one's own. In Kerala, temples are called Devaswom meaning "Owned by the God" and Stha means stable, steady, thus Swastha denotes one's own natural independent state with a healthy body and mind.

Ambāl is independent on Her own. She is devoid of any agitation created by pain.

In Chaandogya Upanishad 7-24-1, Narada asks:

भगवः कस्मिन्प्रतिष्ठित इति स्वे महिम्नि
यदि वा न महिम्नीति.

bhagavaḥ kasminpratiṣṭhita iti sve mahimni

yadi vā na mahimnīti

Nārada asks, 'Sir, what does bhagavah: rest on?' Sanatkumāra replies, 'It rests on its own power—or not even on that power [i.e., it depends on nothing else]'.

Sva also denotes Swarga or heaven Stha, abiding therein as its ruler.

915. svabhāvamadhurā

One whose nature is sweet. Bhāskararāya offers different meanings.

Swabhavam means by one's own nature. Madhura means sweet. Ambāl is so sweet by Her own nature that everybody likes Her. (It applies to human beings too).

About being sweet, the Viswakosam says,

"Madhuram rasavat swaathu priyeshu madhuro anyawat,

Madhura Shatapushpaayaam mathuli nagaripito:"

"What is sweet, and things liked by all. It's a flower called Shatapushpa, Mathuli and a mountain."

Or Sva, her, Bhava, residence, Madhura refers to the city of Madurai. This means Ambāl who is the goddess Meenakshi in Madurai.

Or if you split the word into Sva-Bha- Avama-Dhura, it means Sva, her, Bha, light, Avama, the best, the best of the wise, Dhura, yoke. Like the yoke of the cart that bears the load, Ambāl bears the burden of her devotees. takes is the most important part, she is the leader of the wise.

Or Svabha, the knowledge of the Self, vama to create, i.e. those who inculcate the knowledge of the Self, Dhura, she is the leader (of them).

Or, Su, well, abhava, absence of desire, hatred, partiality, mercilessness, etc., Madhura. It is understood by the expression well (Su) those who possess the above qualities, via, desire, hatred, etc., are not good ones.

Or Sva, in her devotees, Bhava by remaining, Madhura sweet.

Or Sva, their own (devotees) Bhava, by devotion, Svabhava- By nature are Madhu, best fruit (knowledge) ra, gives.

916. dhīrā

Wise or one who is brave or strong.

Or Dhi, the knowledge of non-duality, ra, gives.

Avadutagita, 1ˢᵗ Shlokam says,

ईश्वरानुग्रहादेव पुंसामद्वैतवासना।

Eshwara anugrahaadeva Pumsam Advaitha Vaasana

"By the grace of the Bhagavan alone, one gets the desire to non-duality."

917. dhīra samarchitā

Adored or worshipped by the wise.

She is adored by scholars. If the word is split into Dhi-rasam-archita, it would mean Dhi, the Wisdom called Dhi, (In Gaytri Mantra, we say DHI-YO: Sanskrit for "intellect", this is the essence of this part of the Gāyatri Mantra.) Rasa, bliss, archita, worshipped. This nāma means that for the sake of obtaining bliss, one worships Devi.

चैतन्याघ्र्यसमाराध्या चैतन्यकुसुमप्रिया।

सदोदिता सदातुष्टा तरुणादित्यपाटला॥१७०॥

chaitanyārghya samārādhyā, chaitanya kusumapriyā।

sadōditā, sadātuṣṭā, taruṇāditya pāṭalā॥170॥

918. chaitanyārghya samārādhyā

Worshipped with (Chaitanya) consciousness as the offering.

Chaitanya चैतन्य refers variously to 'awareness', or 'consciousness', 'Conscious Self', or 'Pure Consciousness or the Chidrupa. The Siva-Sutra (I-1) says, "Chaitanya is the Self." Arghyam, is the water offered in worship. The Niradhara Puja, the worship without support, is in the mode of Chidrupa based on the non-duality of consciousness.

The Bhavopanishad says "It is called Jnanam arghyam or "Wisdom is Arghya." –The Suta samhita. (1-5-19) says: "One should worship with devotion, the Mahesvari, who becomes oneself by one's own spiritual experience. That worship alone confers salvation." "Soham Bhaavena Bhaavayet" is another saying.

Or, according to the Viswakosa, Arghya means Vidya. It is said generally that the mantras belonging to female deities are called Vidyas, and those belonging to male deities are called mantras. So, in this naama, a mantra Chaitanyaarghya refers to the Bhuvanesvari mantra. Samaaradhya is worshipped by means of the above mantra.

     The Glory of Lalithā Sahasranāmam

The Suta Samhita (4-42-52) says:

"Japitwa Dasa Saahasram Mantram Chaitanyavaachakam,

Mahapaathaka Sangaicha Muchyate Paathakaantharai:"

By repeating the Chaitanya mantra ten thousand times, one is released from the multitude of great sins as well as from other sins. Here the commentator explains that the Chaitanya mantra is the Bhuvanesvari mantra.

919. chaitanya kusumapriyā

Fond of Chaitanya flowers. Sowndarya Lahari Shlokam 3 says

अविद्यानामन्त-स्तिमिर-मिहिरद्वीपनगरी

जडानां चैतन्य-स्तबक-मकरन्द-सुतिझरी।

Avidyanam antas-timira-mihira-dweeppa-nagari

Jadanam chaitanya-stabaka-makaranda-sruti jhari

Avidhyaanaam-ignorant, devoid of knowledge, Antha-in their hearts

Thimira-with nothing but darkness,Dweepa-nagaree-you are the light

Mihira- of the rising sun,Jadaanaam- For the unfortunate,Sthabaka-you are a bunch of flowers, Makarantha-from which the nectar, Chaithanya- of life consciousness, Sruthijhare-flows forth

Oh great Goddess, To those who are not knowledgeable, you are the city of lights, removing the inner darkness

To the inert ones, you are like the nectar that flows from the bunch of flowers having a mind-elevating effect.

Chaitanya is compared to Kusuma flower as it produces the strongest result of the mind. Devi is the flow of honey in the flower of Chaitanya.

The kusuma flower mentioned here represents eight qualities that are the basic requirements for spiritual progress. Each such quality is referred as a flower in the following verse:

अहिम्सा प्रथमम् पुष्पम् पुष्पम् इन्द्रिय-निग्रह:

सर्व-भूत-दया पुष्पम् क्षमा पुष्पम् विसेशत:।

ज्नानम् पुष्पम् तप: पुष्पम् ध्यानम् पुष्पम् तथैव च

सत्यम् अश्टविधम् पुष्पम् विष्णो: प्रीतिकरम् भवेत्॥

ahimsā prathamam puṣpam puṣpam indriya-nigraha:

sarva-bhūta-dayā puṣpam kṣamā puṣpam viseśata:|

jnānam puṣpam tapa: puṣpam dhyānam puṣpam tathaiva ca

satyam aṣṭavidham puṣpam viṣṇo: prītikaram bhavet|

This verse says non-violence is the first flower, conquering the senses is the second flower, pity on living beings is the third, compassion is the fourth, wisdom is the fifth, penance is the sixth, truth is the seventh and meditation is the eighth flower.

Chaitanya is said to be the combination of eight qualities mentioned in the verse and these flowers together is referred as kusuma flower.

920. sadōditā- Devi is Ever sublime.

921. sadātuṣṭā- Devi is Ever contented. Always happy in the company of Sajjans (Sadhus).

922. taruṇādityapāṭalā

(Devi is) Rosy like the morning Sun

Devi assumes different colors according to the form under which she is contemplated. The Smrti also says, "When she confers salvation, she becomes peaceful (in appearance) and white in color. In her aspects as controlling women, as controlling kings, controlling men she becomes red in color. In her aspect of controlling wealth, she becomes the color of saffron. In the action of slaying, she becomes black. When creating enmity, she becomes tawny. In the Sringara, she becomes rosy colored. Devi, the supreme light is to be meditated upon as differently colored as according to her different activities."

Chapter 19

Devi -The Ruler of Five Elements

This chapter begins with Shlokam 171.

दक्षिणादक्षिणाराध्या दरस्मेरमुखाम्बुजा।

कौलिनीकेवलाऽनर्घ्यकैवल्यपददायिनी॥१७१॥

dakṣiṇā, dakṣiṇārādhyā, darasmēra mukhāmbujā।

kaulinī kēvalā,'narghyā kaivalya padadāyinī॥171॥

923. dakṣiṇādakṣiṇārādhyā

The Sanskrit word 'dakshina' means either 'south' or 'right'.
Adakshina is just the opposite meaning North or left. Aradhya
means worshipped. Devi is worshipped by right and left
hand. Dakshiṇa (दक्षिण) also refers to the "offering of a gift",
representing one of the various services (upacāra) of a pūjā
(ritualistic worship of a deity). First, we must understand
something about āchāra-the method of worship. It is the
way, custom and practice of a particular class of sādhakas or
worshippers. There are different kinds of worshippers. The
Kulārṇava-Tantra mentions seven, in their order of superiority,
the first being the lowest: Vedācāra, Vaiṣṇavācāra, Śaivācāra,
Dakṣiṇācāra, Vāmācāra, Siddhāntācāra, (or Yogācāra), and
Kaulācāra, the highest of all. Dakṣiṇācāra is of the pure kind,
hence called 'right-handed worship'- the left hand being

impure. The opposite kind is left hand worshippers called adakshinacara or vāmācāra.

There are specific methodologies of these two kinds of worship. We will not go into those details. Those who follow the Dakshinamarga mode of worship (the right-handed) are called 'Dakshinas' or Pandithas and those who follow the Vamamarga (the left-handed) are called Vamanan. (Ambāl is in the vamabagam of Shiva)

Devi is worshipped by both dakṣinācāra and vāmācāra methods as explained in nāma 912.

Dakshina has other meanings too. Dakshina also means wise men, Adakshina- means foolish men. Aradhya, worshipped. Ambāl is worshipped by both wise and foolish people. It is explained in Bhagavad Gita too.

The Bhagavad Gita (7-16) describes four kinds of worshippers:

चतुर्विधा भजन्ते मां जना: सुकृतिनोऽर्जुन|
आर्तो जिज्ञासुरर्थार्थी ज्ञानी च भरतर्षभ||16||

chatur-vidhā bhajante mām janāḥ sukṛitino 'rjuna

ārto jijñāsur arthārthī jñānī cha bharatarṣhabha

"Four kinds of good men worship me, O Arjuna- the distressed, the seekers of knowledge, the seekers of wealth, and jnanis the wise, 0 best of Bharatas."

In a nutshell, this nāma says that Devi is worshipped by all kinds of people.

924. darasmēra mukhāmbujā

Poets compare the face, hands and feet of deities to lotus. In this nāma, Ambāl's face is compared to lotus as mukhāmbujā. We all know what is mukham – it is face. Ambuja is lotus –

born from water. Dara (दर) means a conch-shell; Smera (स्मेर) means smiling. Darasmera Mukambuja means Devi whose lotus face is filled with smiles. Here, Devi's teeth are compared to shining white conch shell. Dara also means protecting (the devotees). Devi's face is always gracious to her devotees. Even during the times of the great deluge, Her face remains shining. When Shiva performs the cosmic dance causing annihilation, Devi remains as a witness without showing any signs of fear. Even during the terrible annihilation, She continues to smile. She is ever pleasant and smiling to devotees.

"mandasmita-prabhāpūra-majjatkāmeśa-mānasā" says the twenty eighth shlokam in Lalitha Sahasrnamam. Smita means smile and mandasmita means a gentle smile. Devi is always sporting a special soft smile.

There is a saying, "Face is the index of mind." If your mind is calm and peaceful, it shows up on the face. Chanting Lalithā Sahasranāmam is one way to keep your mind calm. We can get inspiration from these names of Ambāl to keep a smiling face. There is no cost involved in a gentle smile.

925. kauḻinī kēvalā

Pure and worshipped by the devotees of the Kula.

Kaulinī is the one who follows kaula mārga. We get the name in Shlokam 37 कुलाङ्गना कुलान्तस्था कौलिनी कुलयोगिनी.

There is also reference to Kaula Marga in Nāma 441. In shloka 125, क्लीङ्कारी, केवला, गुह्या, कैवल्य पददायिनी, we get the nāma Kevala (623). Kevala means devoid of all attributes (Kevalam also used in Tamil) or freed from pleasure and pain.

In the Shiva-Sutra (III, 35) Shiva is named as "Kevalin who is freed from those two." The word Kevala is used to signify 'jnanam.' This nāma indicates Kaulinis- those who follow Kaula Marga get established in jnana or the real self, freed from pleasure and pain.

Another interpretation is in Nāma 623 that says Kevalā means She is one without a second. She alone exists.

926. anarghyā kaivalya padadāyinī

Giving the abode of priceless salvation.

Anargha (priceless), unlimited, Kaivalyapada, is the fifth state of salvation.

Sage Patañjali in his yoga sūtra (IV.36) says, "kaivalyam dharma dharmiṇaḥ puruṣasya." The interpretation of this sūtra is 'The freedom of liberation is the very state of this substance or the being. It is not to be attained, not that you experience something new, that liberation is the very nature of the being." Kaivalya stage is already embedded in the soul, but efforts are not initiated to realize it. Yoga teaches the path on how to reach this stage of salvation.

स्तोत्रप्रिया स्तुतिमती श्रुतिसंस्तुतवैभवा।

मनस्विनी मानवती महेशी मङ्गलाकृतिः॥१७२॥

stōtrapriyā, stutimatī, śrutisaṃstuta vaibhavā।

manasvinī, mānavatī, mahēśī, maṅgalākṛtiḥ॥172॥

927. stōtrapriyā

Fond of praise.

Stotra means praise. Basically, Stotras fall into two categories

One is describing the qualities in the loukika way as worldly people say.

Namaskaras Tat Asicha Siddanthokti Parakramaha

Vibhuti Prartana Cheti Shatvidam Stotra Lakshanam

There are six kinds of worldly stotras or praises. The great men say, "Salutation (Namaskara), Blessings (Ashis), praising the attainments (Siddhantokti), praising exploits (Parakrama), rehearsing glory (Vibhuti), prayer for prosperity (Prarthana). These are the six characteristics of praises."

The other refers to the divine stotra namely, rehearsing the attributes and forms of the deities about whom mantras are chanted.

For example, there are many nāmas that describe the stotras on Devi like the names: Trijagad vandyā (627) meaning – She is truly revered and worshipped in all the three worlds; Mithyā-jagadadhiṣṭānā (735) meaning – She is the cause and refuge for this illusory universe (mithya-jagat) that speaks of Devi's glory; Icchashakthi-jnanashakthi-kriyashakthi-svarupini (658) and so on.

Ambāl is fond of praise by verses like in Devi Māhātmyam, or Vedic verses like Śrī sūkta, Durgā sūkta, etc.

Devi is pleased with both forms of Stotras.

Or stotrap, the waters which are to be praised, these (waters) mean here Devas, Pitrus, Men and Asuras. The Shruti says, "Apo va idam Sarvam." "All this indeed is water."

Therefore, it can be interpreted that Devi likes the Devas, Pitrus, Men and Asuras who praise her.

928. stutimatī

Recipient of praise. This is a sequel to the earlier Nāma. If Ambāl is worshipped with praise, one gets mati which means knowledge. In Tamil and Malayalam also, the word mati is used for intelligence or knowledge. It also means Stuti; by praising her, one gets Mati-knowledge and i-wealth. (Splitting up Mati into mati +i).

929. śrutisaṃstuta vaibhavā

Whose glory is celebrated in the Vedas. Śhruti means Vedas (as they were heard by the Rishis) and saṃstuta means experience. This nāma says that Devi's glory is celebrated through Vedas. Shareerapurusha:, Chanda:purusho, Vedapurusho, Mahapurusha:

The Kurma Purana says: "Devi has four Shaktis; they are declared to be her own nature, and she is the support of these four; These are Shanti (peace), Vidya (knowledge), Pratistha. (fixity), and Nivrtti (restraint). Hence, the Supreme Lord Shiva is said to be four-formed. By these four Shaktis, the supreme Lord enjoys his own bliss."

The following popular verse says that Shiva is the source of knowledge of Veda-s, Upanishads and epics.

श्रुति स्मृति पुराणाम् आलयम् करुनालयम्

नमामि भगवद्पादम् शङ्करं लोकशन्करं

śruti smriti purāṇām ālayam karunālayam

namāmi bhagavadpādam śaṅkaraṁ lokaśankaraṃ

Meaning of the above verse: I prostrate to Lord Śiva, who causes welfare to the universe, who is the repository of the divine Knowledge of Vedas, Upanishads and texts of mythology and who is the embodiment of mercy.

930. manasvinī- Intelligence. Manas is mind. Ambāl has an independent mind.

931. mānavatī- Gracious-minded. Devi has a mind of high moral values.

Māna means the elevation of mind, the expression indicating the forgiveness of sin.

932. mahēśī

The spouse of Mahesa (Shiva).

The Devi Purana says, "Mahesasya Vadhur Yasmat Mahesi Tena Saa Smruta" "As she originated from Mahadeva and worshipped by great men (Mahat), and as she is the wife of Mahesa she is called Mahesi." She is also addressed as Māheśvarī in nāma 208.

933. maṅgaḻākṛtiḥ

Devi is of auspicious appearance. (Mangal is auspicious.)

विश्वमाता जगद्धात्री विशालाक्षी विरागिणी।

प्रगल्भा परमोदारा परामोदा मनोमयी॥१७३॥

viśvamātā, jagaddhātrī, viśālākṣī, virāgiṇī।

pragalbhā, paramōdārā, parāmōdā, manōmayī॥173॥

934. viśvamāta- Mother of the Universe. Because of being Viśvamātā, She is Śrī Mātā (the very first nāma 1).

935. jagaddhātrī- Supporter of the world. The root Dha means to bear, sustain, like in Gangadhara, jadadhara. Hence, she is called by the wise the sustainer of the Universe.

936. viśālākṣī- Large-eyed. Padmapurana says "Varanasyaam Visalakshi.

"She is the deity worshipped in Kashi or Varanasi. Saundarya Laharī (verses 52 to 57) extol Her eyes.

937. virāgiṇī- Dispassionate. Vairāgya means freedom from all worldly desires.

938. pragalbhā- Brave, Strong. She is strong in the action of creation, etc.

939. paramōdārā- Supremely generous. parā means Supreme. Udāra means great. Devi is great in space and time. Or Para, supreme, Moda, bliss, ā, on all sides, ra. gives. She gives supreme bliss.

940. parāmōdā- Parā means supreme and modā means joy, delight, gladness, pleasure. Supremely delightful. This nāma says that She is the embodiment of supreme joy (bliss).

941. manōmayī

Devi is Mind. Because the pure Brahman is (to be) fixed in the mind. Or Manomayi: mind is the chief instrument.

A vedic verse says मनसैवानुद्रष्टवयं, नेह नानास्ति किंचन।

manasaivā anudraṣṭavyaṃ, neha nānāsti kiṃcana|

Through the mind alone (It) is to be realized. There is no difference whatsoever in It. "By mind alone it is to be seen." According to this, Manas is the chief instrument in creating self-knowledge.

व्योमकेशी विमानस्था वज्रिणी वामकेश्वरी।

पञ्चयज्ञप्रिया पञ्चप्रेतमञ्चाधिशायिनी॥१७४॥

vyōmakēśī, vimānasthā, vajriṇī, vāmakēśvarī।

pañchayajñapriyā, pañchaprēta mañchādhiśāyinī॥174॥

942. vyōmakēśī

One whose hair is the ether. In her Virat, (universal) form the ether becomes Devi's hair; or she is the wife of Vyomakesa, Shiva.

Or Vyomaka, small, Isi, ruler, she is the ruler of even atoms.

943. vimānasthā

Residing in the celestial chariot. Vimanastha refers to the Devas who remain in the celestial chariot, she is not different from them.

Bhāskararāya gives different interpretations:

Vi, much, māna, protection of her devotees, stha, engaged: such is her position.

Or Vi much Mā, light, Ana, chariot, Stha, residing. She remains in radiant chariots such as Kirihcakra and others.

Or Vi, without, life, limitation, i.e., unconditioned Brahman, Stha, residing in that; or she limits the Brahman, or she is without limitation.

Or Vi, much, Mā, measures, Vimāna-meaning establishes decision, i.e., Vimāna, scriptures, stha, remains, i.e., she is described in the Vedas. Vimāna, proof which are not opposed to the Vedas, Devi remains therein in the nature of Dharma. Or Vimāna, the fourteen Vidyas (Purana, Nyaya, Mimamsa, etc.)

The Glory of Lalithā Sahasranāmam

944. vajriṇī

Shiva is known as Vajrā and his consort is Vajriṇī. There is another interpretation to this nāma which says that She is in the form of Indrāṇī, wife of Lord Indra, the possessor of the Vajra, the thunderbolt; Indra has a powerful weapon called vajrāyudha (said to be created from the bones of the Rishi Dadhīchi), the thunder bolt. Rishi Dadhīchi gave up his body for Indra so that his bones could be used by Indra to make Vajrayudha, a strong weapon, for killing the evil Vritra.

Vajrini suggests that Lalithambā is bearing Vajrayudha in hand. Or adorned with jewels called Vajra.

945. vāmakēśvarī

Vāma has many meanings such as beautiful, splendid, Shiva. Vamakeshvara here means the name of a Tantra. Vāma are those who follow the Vama path. They do not follow Pancha yajnas. Vāmakeśvara tantra is said to be an important tantra for Śrī Vidyā worship. This tantra discusses on internal worship of Shakti called as Vāmakeśvari.

946. pañchayajñapriyā

Devi is fond of the five yajnas or sacrifices. According to the Vedas, the five sacrifices are: Agntihotra, Darśapūrṇamāsa, Chāturmāsya, Paśubandha and Soma. The smritis refer to five yajñas as Deva, Pitr, Brahman, Bhuta, and Manushya yajñas. They are called pañca mahāyajñas.

Deva yajña is meant to appeasing Devas, Brahma yajña for the knower of Vedas, Pitṛ yajña for ancestors, bhūta yajna for animals and living beings, and Manushya yajña for men and atithi (guests).

Also, in agnihotram, offerings (Ahuti) are made in five different homa kundams. This is also called Panchayajnam.

Chāndogya Upaniṣad (V.4 to 9) talks about five types of sacrifices that cause the birth of man. They are offered by Devas as oblations. First, Devas offered water as oblation from which appeared Soma (moon). They offered Soma as the second oblation from which appeared rain. They offered water as third oblation and there appeared food. They offered food as the fourth oblation and there appeared fluids of procreation. They offered fluids of procreation as the fifth oblation and there appeared the foetus.

947. pañchaprēta mañchādhiśāyinī

This nāma suggests that Devi is reclining on couch formed of corpses. Brahma and the other three gods Vishnu, Rudra and Eswara are the four legs of the couch and Sadashiva is the mattress. Brahma, Vishnu, Rudran, Eswaran and Sadashivan are termed as corpses as they are unable to do their respective functions.

Bhairavayāmala says in the Bahurupāstakaprastāra:

"Shivatmake Mahamanche Mahesanopa Barhane

Mrudakacha Chatushpaadaha kachiputcha Sadashivaha

Tatra Chete Mahesanee Mahatripurasundari"

"On that great and pleasant couch Whose pillow is Mahesana, of whose four legs are Brahma, etc., and whose mattress is Sadashiva, reclines the great Tripurasundari, the great Queen."

This nāma is discussed in Saundarya Laharī (verse 92). Verses 92 onwards are more akin to prayers:

गतास्ते मञ्चत्वं द्रुहिण हरि रुद्रेश्वर भृतः

शिवः स्वच्छ-च्छाया-घटित-कपट-प्रच्छदपटः।

त्वदीयानां भासां प्रतिफलन रागारुणतया

शरीरी शृङ्गारो रस इव दृशां दोग्धि कुतुकम्

gatāstē mañchatvaṃ druhiṇa hari rudrēśvara bhṛtaḥ

śivaḥ svachCha-chChāyā-ghaṭita-kapaṭa-prach

Chadapaṭaḥ|

tvadīyānāṃ bhāsāṃ pratiphalana rāgāruṇatayā

śarīrī śṛṅgārō rasa iva dṛśāṃ dōgdhi kutukam||92||

"Brahma, Vishnu,Rudra and Ishvara have taken the shape of the four legs of the couch in order to serve you very closely. And Sadashiva has formed Himself into the bedspread, reflecting your crimson glory in His lustrous whiteness, thereby causing amazement to you by presenting Himself as the very embodiment of erotic sentiment."

पञ्चमी पञ्चभूतेशी पञ्चसङ्ख्योपचारिणी।

शाश्वती शाश्वतैश्वर्या शर्मदा शम्भुमोहिनी॥१७५॥

pañchamī, pañchabhūtēśī, pañcha saṅkhyōpachāriṇī|

śāśvatī, śāśvataiśvaryā, śarmadā, śambhumōhinī||175||

948. pañchamī

Means the Fifth.

In the order of Brahma, Vishnu group of deities, Sadashiva is the fifth, His spouse is Panchami. The Suta Samhita says even Sadashiva the fifth, requires the help of the Mother: "Rudra is the best of the three, the supreme Shiva, the possessor of Maya. Sadashiva who is with the Mother and is possessed of permanence, is better than the omniscient Shiva, the possessor of Maya. Of this there is no need of discussion."

Vārāhi Devi is also known as Panchami. Pañchamī forms a part of one of Vārāhi mantra-s. She is one among the seven mātā-s known as sapta (seven) mātā-s and fifth in that order. Hence Pañchamī.

949. pañchabhūtēśī

Ruler of five elements called *'Panchabhutam.'*

Ambāl is the ruler of five elements. Taittirīya Upaniṣad (II.i.1) says, *satyaṁ jñānam anantaṁ brahman* which means truth, knowledge and infinite is the Brahman. The Upanishad further says, "From the Brahman comes space, from space air, from air fire, from fire water, from water earth and so on." Thus, Upanishad says that the five elements originated from the Brahman.

As Ambāl is the Brahman, this nāma says that She is the embodiment of the five elements.

Or Panchabuta, fivefold, because that is the garland called Vaijayanti formed of five elements and five gems.

The Vishnu Purana says, "The club-bearer's (Vishnu's) garland called Vaijayanti is five-formed as it consists of five elements, it is also called the element-garland,0 twice born one." Here 'five-formed,' means the five kinds of jewels namely pearl, Manikya, Marakata, sapphire, and diamond. These gems are said to represent the five elements.

The Vishnu-Rahasya also says, "From earth comes the blue-black gem, from water pearl, from fire the Kaustubha, from air Vaidurya, from other Pushparaga. Thus, the five form

the Vaijayanti garland of Vishnu." Vaijayanti means one who
is victorious.

950. pañcha saṅkhyōpachāriṇī

Worshipped with five services or courtesies called
'Panchopacharam.' These are *'gandha, pushpa, dhupa,
deepa naivedyam* which are generally offered in our daily
puja to any deity. Ambāl is worshipped by these five types of
reverent offerings such as gandham (sandal paste), puṣhpam
(flowers), dhūpam (incense), deepam (light) and naivedyam
(food). Each of them represents one of the five elements. They
are earth, ākāśa, air, fire and water.

951. śāśvatī

Eternal. In Tamil also, we use the word *'saswatham'* for
something permanent.

Ambāl is eternal. Saswat also means frequently. In this
context it means She is worshipped continuously by her
devotees.

Kaṭoupaniṣhad (5-12) says, "To them alone belong eternal
attainment, not to others."

952. śāśvataiśvaryā

Possessing eternal dominion.

Śāśvata is eternal + Aiśvarya is dominion referring to the
five corpses that form Her seat. "*Panchapretasanaruda*" is the
underlying meaning.

The other meaning is permanent wealth. She is the
embodiment of eternal wealth, the wealth of knowledge and
prosperity.

953. śarmadā

Giver of happiness

Śarman means Joy, bliss, comfort, delight, happiness. This nāma may be interpreted as Ambāl gives eternal happiness or bliss.

954. śambhumōhinī

Bewildering Shambu. Ambāl charms Shambu.

Who is Shambhu? Shiva as Dakshinamurthy was seated under the Banyan tree, he was called Shambhu. Sam means eternal bliss. Bhu refers to creation. The source for eternal bliss is Shambhu. That source of joy is Shambhu. This joyful source is stationed in one place. Totally silent with no movement. If he stays still, how can he impart knowledge to humanity? It requires moving around and speaking to people. So, Shambhu, the source for eternal joy decided to become the creator of the joy 'Sankara' and incarnated himself as Adi Sankara.

In Sri Rudram, we recite:

नमोहन्त्रेच हनीयसेच नमोवृक्षेभ्योहरिकेशेभ्यो

नमस्ताराय नमः शंभवेच मयोभवेच

नमः शंकराय च मयस्कराय च

नमः शिवाय च शिवतराय च॥८॥

Sri Rudram first pays obeisance to Shambhu, then secondly to Sankara, the teacher and subsequently, to Shiva Panchaksharam (the holy five letters Namasivaya) that are obtained from the teachings of the Guru in that order.

 The Glory of Lalithā Sahasranāmam

धराधरसुता धन्या धर्मिणी धर्मवर्धिनी।
लोकातीता गुणातीता सर्वातीता शमात्मिका॥१७६॥

dharā, dharasutā, dhanyā, dharmiṇī, dharmavardhinī|

lōkātītā, guṇātītā, sarvātītā, śamātmikā||176||

955. dharā

Ambāl is in the form of earth (Prithvi). She is the Goddess Earth, Prakṛti.

Or Supporter of the Universe as Dhara means bearing, supporting, or holding, like in Gangadhara, Jadadhara. The Jnanarnava says, "The Letter La is the goddess of earth, with mountains, forests and deserts, having fifty scared places and all the places of pilgrimage etc." The bīja akśara of earth is la ल and usage of la refers to prakṛti.

956. dharasutā- The daughter of Himavan.

957. dhanyā

Fortune - Dhanam means wealth. Or possessing wealth.

Bhāskararāya quotes from Bhavishyouttara Puranam:

"It is said that four kinds of thoughts arise in the last stage of one's life. These are Artha, Raudra, Dhanya, and Shukla.

Artha is that thought which arises through illusion, the desire to possess dominion, worldly pleasure, beds, seats, women, scents, garlands, jewels, cloths and ornaments.

Raudra is said by the wise to be that meditation in which arises desire and not indifference though he had experience from wounds, fire, beating, cruelty, bodily injury etc.

Dhanya is that in which arises a thought by following the Upanishads, and by the performance of great vows about the causes of bondage, and the tranquility of the five senses and compassion of all beings.

Shukla is that meditation in which by practice of Yoga, the inner Self is fixed on its unity with one reality Brahman.

The result of the above four is thus set forth in the same Purana. "The man who practises *Artha* becomes Tiryak, an animal (born as plants, animals or birds) or mineral; he of *Raudra*. descends lower; the one of *Dhanya* goes to the Devas and attains good results; and one of *Shukla* is freed from (future) births.

Therefore, in meditation. the wise man should cultivate the Shukla state which removes the pain of re-birth, beneficial, enables one to cross the ocean of existence and which calms passion."

Krishna says in Bhagavad Gītā (VIII.5 and 6).

अन्तकाले च मामेव स्मरन्मुक्त्वा कलेवरम्‌।

य: प्रयाति स मद्भावं याति नास्त्यत्र संशय:॥5॥

anta-kāle cha mām eva smaran muktvā kalevaram

yaḥ prayāti sa mad-bhāvaṁ yāti nāstyatra sanśhayaḥ

"Those who relinquish the body while remembering Me at the time of death will come to Me. There is certainly no doubt about this."

यं यं वापि स्मरन्भावं त्यजत्यन्ते कलेवरम्‌।

तं तमेवैति कौन्तेय सदा तद्भावभावित:॥6॥

The Glory of Lalithā Sahasranāmam

yaṁ yaṁ vāpi smaran bhāvaṁ tyajatyante kalevaram

taṁ tam evaiti kaunteya sadā tad-bhāva-bhāvitaḥ

"Whatever one remembers at the time of death, O son of Kunti, one attains that state, being always absorbed in such thoughts".

That is why, Sanatana Dharma encourages us to always develop the habit of praying and engage in divine thoughts.

958. dharmiṇī- Righteous. We say Sahadharmini when we refer to wife.

959. dharmavardhinī

Vruddi is to increase. Ambāl is one who increases dharma, righteousness in all devotees. So, She is called Dharmavardini.

Vamana Purana says, "Control of the senses, purity, and Wifehood with devotion refer respectively to Samkara, the Sun, and to Devi. Shiva and his spouse, meditated upon by men, increase in them these (three) qualities."

Vardha also means cutting or dividing and, in this sense, She cuts (removes) the deceptive nature of materialistic world for Her devotees.

960. lōkātītā

Transcending the worlds. Ambāl is beyond the worlds.

Lokas, from Indra to Vishnu loka, transcending these, she resides in the city of Parashiva called Mahakailasa.

The Shiva-Dharmottara says that the city of Parashiva transcends all worlds. Again, after describing the lower worlds, it says: "Above the abode of Vishnu, one should know the great divine, city of Shiva". This great city of Shiva is called

Apada, men devoted to works return from this world. After describing the city of Shiva which is to be attained by those devoted to good works, again proceeds, 'Above the city of Shiva there are three supreme seats, eternal, ever pure, resorted by Skanda, Uma and Shiva...' Those who attain this supreme seat, devoted to meditation, do not return to the terrible ocean of Samsara. They become merged in Mahesvara, possessed of the strength of Shiva, and attain the supreme city of Shiva."

Or Lokas, the Jivas, Atita transcending.

961. guṇātītā- Transcending Guna -quality or attributes. Ambāl is beyond attributes.

962. sarvātītā- Transcending all. Sarva, all words. The Jnanarnava says, "Know Para-Brahman, which transcends speech and is beyond counting, as ourselves."

963. śamātmikā

Tranquility. Ambāl is 'Shanta Swarupini' – Sama means tranquilizing – softening the activity of the world.

"Prapanchopa Samam Shivam Shantam Advaitam Chaturtham Manyante"

–says Nrusimhatapaneeyam

बन्धूककुसुमप्रख्या बाला लीलाविनोदिनी।

सुमङ्गली सुखकरी सुवेषाढ्या सुवासिनी॥ १७७॥

bandhūka kusuma prakhyā, bālā, līlāvinōdinī।

sumaṅgaḻī, sukhakarī, suvēṣāḍyā, suvāsinī॥ 177॥

964. bandhūka kusuma prakhyā- Resembling the Bandhuka flower. Bandhuka is a tree in Bengal, and its flower is very red. Ambāl is of that red color.

965. bālā

Little girl. The Tripura-Siddhanta says, *"Bala leela Vishastvaat Baleti Gatita Priye"* "0 beloved one, as you play like a child, you are called Bala."

Ambāl is called Balambika, as a nine-year-old girl. *'Yaa Sada Navavarshyva Sarvavidya Mahakani:"*

966. līlāvinōdinī

Taking pleasure in amusement. Lila, the play (of the activity) of the Universe. Lila is the name of the wife of Padmaraja, a king mentioned in the Yogavasistha. Vinodini, she leads that queen into right action. The story is given thus: Lila Devi worshipped Sarasvati and pleased her and received knowledge from Sarasvati and brought back her husband to life. If the word Lila is taken as a separate name, it means Lakshmi. The Devi Puranam explains it thus: "Lakshmi is called Lila because she plays (Lalana)."

967. sumaṅgaḻī

Very auspicious. Su, beautiful, Mangala, Brahman. The Vishnu Puranam says, "That, by remembering which, drives away misfortune from men and gives much benefit, that supreme Brahman they know as Mangala." Elders bless married women as 'Deera Sumangali Bhava'

The Atri Smriti says, "The performance of right action and avoiding wrong action is called Mangala by Rishis who speak of Brahman."

968. sukhakarī- Giving happiness. Ambāl always gives happiness to devotees.

969. suvēṣāḍyā- Decked with beautiful dresses and ornaments (Alankaram).

970. suvāsinī- Ever married. Suvasini, a woman whose husband is living

सुवासिन्यर्चनप्रीताssशोभना शुद्धमानसा।

बिन्दुतर्पणसन्तुष्टा पूर्वजा त्रिपुराम्बिका॥१७८॥

suvāsinyarchanaprītā, śōbhanā, śuddha mānasā।

bindu tarpaṇa santuṣṭā, pūrvajā, tripurāmbikā॥178॥

971. suvāsinyarchanaprītā

Pleased by the worship of married women. Lalithā Sahasranāmam is specially intended for suvasinis. suvāsini-s are highly revered and worshipped at the end of navāvaraṇa pūja.

You see nowadays in many temples and even homes, they have suvasini puja where the suvasinis themselves are considered an amsam (part) of Ambāl and worshipped. It shows how women are respected in Sanatana Dharma.

972. Aśōbhanā

Ever beautiful. Sobhana is also a feminine name.

Saundarya Laharī consists of two parts, Ānanda Lahari (1 to 41) and Saundarya Laharī (42 to 100). The first forty-one verses talk about bliss and the next fifty-nine verses talk about Her beauty.

973. śuddha mānasā

Pure minded. Ambāl can be realised only with pure mind focused on Her alone, devoid of other thoughts. When you chant Lalithā Sahasranāmam, your mind should not wander here and there- keep your cell phone away or switched off.

974. bindu tarpaṇa santuṣṭā

Pleased by offerings in the Bindu.

Bindu is the Sarvanandamayacakra; The central point of Śrī Cakra is called bindu. Offering argya on the bindu is called tarpaṇa. This Tarpana as argya on the bindu by the four Varnas are: Brahmanas with milk, by Ksatriyas with ghee, by Vaisyas with honey and by the fourth varna with mead.

Bindu means also the Wise men and she is pleased by their offerings.

975. pūrvajā- First born.

976. tripurāmbikā

Tripurāmbikā is the presiding deity of eighth āvaraṇa or covering of Śrī Chakra. This āvaraṇa is the innermost triangle of Śrī Chakra in the midst of which is the bindu, the central point of Śrī Chakra, is placed.

दशमुद्रासमाराध्या त्रिपुराश्रीवशङ्करी।

ज्ञानमुद्रा ज्ञानगम्या ज्ञानज्ञेयस्वरूपिणी॥१७९॥

daśamudrā samārādhyā, tripurā śrīvaśaṅkarī।

jñānamudrā, jñānagamyā, jñānajñēya svarūpiṇī॥179॥

977. daśamudrā samārādhyā

Worshipped by ten Mudras. What are mudras? Mudras are positions of fingers practised in worship. The ten Mudras are from Samksobhini to Trikhanda and they are the means by which she is regularly worshipped according to the manner laid down in the Nityahrdaya.

Śrī Chakra has nine coverings or āvaraṇa-s and each of them is ruled by a Shakti. Each of these Shakti-s has a mudra and this accounts for nine mudra-s. In the ninth āvaraṇa Lalitāmbikā is worshipped with yoni mudra.

978. tripurā śrīvaśaṅkarī

The ruler of Tripura. Tripurasundari is the name of the deity which presides over the fifth Chakra. In Thiruvottiyur near Chennai, we have a famous temple of Tyagaraja and Tripurasundari. Tyagaraja Swamigal composed five songs called Pancharatnam on Goddess Tripurasundari of the Thyagaraja Temple at Thiruvottiyur. These are inscribed on the walls of the temple. One of them is 'dārini telusukoṇṭi Tripurasundari ni' in Suddha saveri ragam.

979. jñānamudrā

This is formed by joining the tips of the thumb and fore finger (to make a circle and extending the other fingers), or Jnana, by knowledge, Mud, bliss, Ra she gives. This nāma describes Ambāl as jñānamudra as She is the symbol of knowledge.

980. jñānagamyā

Devi is to be attained by knowledge.

The Kurma Purana says, "My unconditioned nature is to be attained by wisdom alone and is bare absolute consciousness, benevolent. freed from all limitations, infinite, immortal, supreme, that supreme abode is to be attained through much difficulty. Those (wise men) thinking, knowledge is the best means, enter me."

   The Glory of Lalithā Sahasranāmam

981. jñānajñēya svarūpiṇī

Knowledge and knowing. The importance of knowledge is being repeatedly stressed in this Sahasranāma. This nāma says She is the knowledge and the knowing. The previous nāma said that She can be approached only through knowledge. Nāma 979 said that She is the symbol of knowledge.

योनिमुद्रा त्रिखण्डेशी त्रिगुणाम्बा त्रिकोणगा।

अनघाऽद्भुतचारित्रा वाञ्छितार्थप्रदायिनी॥१८०॥

yōnimudrā, trikhaṇḍēśī, triguṇāmbā, trikōṇagā |

anaghādbhuta chāritrā, vāñChitārtha pradāyinī || 180 ||

982. yōnimudrā- This is the ninth Mudra; or she gives happiness in the womb: or Yoni is the. veil which covers Bindu.

983. trikhaṇḍēśī- Ruler of Trikhanda. Trikhanda is the tenth Mudra.

Or Trikhanda means the three divisions of the Panchadasi Mantra.

984. triguṇa

Ambāl is endowed with three qualities. It means that the primordial matter Prakriti of the Samkhyas forms the basis of the three qualities, Sattva, Rajo and Tamas. The Vayu Purana says, "This Yogesvari creates as well as destroys forms; she has many forms, many functions, and many names, by function and by her sport she is threefold in the world, hence she is called Triguna." The Vishnu Purana also says, "I rever that eternal energy, which is thy energy which is in all beings and in all souls, the basis of the qualities."

The Devi Purana explains in another way: "As she has three steps, the three paths (of Ganga) the three qualities, etc,"; for it says, "Bali was bound by three steps, the Ganga came from three places, Svarga, by three qualities Sattva, Rajas and Tamas, she performs the functions of creation, preservation and destruction, hence she is called Triguna."

985. āmbā-Mother. She is the mother of all worlds. The very first name in Lalithā Sahasranāmam is Om Sri Matha.

986. trikōṇagā -Residing in the triangle. Trikona is Yonichakra.

987. anaghā- Agam means sin, pain misery. Anagha means sinless.

988. adbhuta chāritrā- Adbhuta means wonderful. Charitra refers to deeds or history. Devi whose deeds are wonderful.

989. vāñChitārtha pradāyinī- Bestowing the desired deeds.

Chapter 20

The Universal Mother

We begin this chapter with Shlokam 181.

अभ्यासातिशयज्ञाता षडध्वातीतरूपिणी।

अव्याजकरुणामूर्तिरज्ञानध्वान्तदीपिका॥१८१॥

abhyāsāti śayajñātā, ṣaḍadhvātīta rūpiṇī।

avyāja karuṇāmūrtir, ajñānadhvānta dīpikā ॥ 181 ॥

990. abhyāsāti śayajñātā

This naama can be split into Abhyās, Atiśaya and Jñāta. Abhyās means to concentrate one's attention upon, or to practice. In Marathi too, abhyas means to study or practice. In Tamil, we call it Abyasam.

Atiśaya means surprise, superior, or abundant. Don't we say Atisayam in Tamil? jñāta means to know or to comprehend. In Hindi, we ask *Jaanta Hai Aap,* do you know? You see the similarity between Sanskrit Jnata and Hindi Jaanta.

Ambāl is surprisingly realized only through Abyasam or constant worship. One should practice continuously to focus one's entire attention to know Her supreme qualities. The importance of the mind focus is emphasized here to know Her. The more you practice, the closer you get to know Ambāl.

As it is said, "Till sleep as well as till death one should employ himself in reflection on the Vedanta," she is known by

constant meditation upon the unity of Brahman and the Self."
Evil thoughts will disappear by meditation on Ambāl.

Bhāskararāya quotes Brahma Sūtra (IV.i.1) that says,

आवृत्तिः असकृदुपदेशात् ॐ ॥ ४.१.१ ॥ *Avritti: asakrid upadeshat*

Avrittih - repetition, practice of meditation on Brahman (is necessary);

Asakrit - not only once, many times, repeatedly.

Upadesat - because of instruction by the scriptures.

"Repetition is necessary, since Upanishads instruct repeatedly." It's called Avritti in Sanskrit. It is explained that such repeated instructions should be heard of, reflected on, and meditated upon.

The repeated instructions of the Upanishads is Aham Brahmasmi, "I am the Brahman" or Tatwamasi "I am That" or such mahā vācaka-s or the great sayings.

The Brahmānda Purana says: "She whose limbs are knowledge, whose body is science, and whose abode is heart, is to be seen by constant meditation. By constant practice in meditation, she becomes manifested through the union with the Self."

In Bhagavad Gīta (IX.22). Krishna says

अनन्याश्चिन्तयन्तो मां ये जना: पर्युपासते।

तेषां नित्याभियुक्तानां योगक्षेमं वहाम्यहम्॥22॥

ananyāsh chintayanto māṁ ye janāḥ paryupāsate

teshāṁ nityābhiyuktānāṁ yoga-kshemaṁ vahāmyaham

ananyāḥ—always; chintayantaḥ—think of; mām—Me; Krishna assures:

"Those who always think of Me and engage in exclusive devotion to Me. To them, whose minds are always absorbed in Me, I take care of their welfare, and provide security"

Likewise, by constant practice of meditation, Ambāl becomes manifested in us.

991. sadadhvātīta rūpinī

shad means six and adhva means path. There are six types of paths of worshipping Her - Varna, Pada, Mantra, Kalaa, Tatva, Bhuvana- and atīta means transcending. She transcends six methods of worship.

What are the six methods? Bhāskararāya provides detailed explanation quoting from various scriptures. The six methods are:

Varna -meaning Letters (also means outward appearance, exterior, form, figure, shape and this means idol worship. varna also means alphabet.

She is mātrukā varna rūpinī – nāma 577)

Padadhva -Words (Combination of alphabets)

Mantra -Prayer, Ambāl is mantra rupini

Kalā -Arts (-64 arts and also time)

Tattva -Categories (principles of Agama), and lastly

Bhuvana -Worlds (Ambāl is also known as Bhuvaneswari, Akilandeswari).

Of these six, three are the parts of Vimars'a and the other three of Prakasa.

The Virupaksha-Panchasika says, "The quality of-Vimarsa is attributed to three, viz" words, mantras and letters, of Prak'as'a, is worlds, categories, and parts."

About these the Jnānārnava says, "In this Chakra there are six methods, 0 Devi, adored by warriors. Thus one should meditate by six methods upon the pure Srichakra"

Or six methods, the six kinds of devotion, these are the means of attaining Devi. The Kularnava says, "To him, whose mind is purified by the mantras of Shiva, Vishnu, Durga, the Sun, Ganapati and Indra (or Indu), appears the knowledge of Kula (Devi)." The meaning is that those who in previous births were followers of any of the six kinds of devotion, attain in this birth the devotion to Devi.

992. avyāja karunāmūrti

Compassionate Without partiality.

Avyāja means not pretending. karunāmūrti means the embodiment of compassion. Like Karuna Nidhi means the treasure house of compassion. Ambāl is the Mother of Universe -Akhilandeswari. And Compassion is the quality of a mother. She being the Supreme Mother, the great ones say, "Glory to Devi the compassionate one." When a mother ties a child with a rope for some mischief that a child does (eating mud, getting hurt), the child thinks, Oh what kind of mother she is – she has no heart to tie me up?

At the time of Kumbhabhishekam of the temple in the Sringeri Mutt at R. A. Puram Chennai (2012), Sringeri Jagadguru Shankaracharya Sri Sri Bharati Tirtha Mahaswamiji spoke about the Compassion of Mother Sharadamba.

He said, "A mother has the same amount of love and affection towards all her children. Even for a child that doesn't show any liking for the mother, she only showers affection." Maternal love has no equal.

Sri Adi Shankaracharya said – कुपुत्रो जायेत क्वचिदपि कुमाता न भवति (A bad son may be born, but there can never be a bad mother). In our Dharma, the position offered to a mother is the greatest. The Shastras mention that a person should prostrate before his mother first, then the father, and then the Guru – मातृदेवो भव। पितृदेवो भव। आचार्यदेवो भव।

Such is the greatness of the Divine Mother that one of the names in the Lalithā Sahasranāmam is "सर्वापद्विनिवारिणी" – the one who saves you from all dangers. Every man in this world is faced with some problem or the other, irrespective of his stature in life. The only person who can protect us from these problems (dangers) is Jaganmatha (The Universal Mother) With Her blessings, all our problems will be removed.

The Devi Māhaatmyam explains the different ways in which the Jaganmata protects us from all problems.

She killed many personifications of evil like Mahishasura, Shumba, Nishumba, Raktha Bheeja, Chanda and Munda and protected the world.

In Soundaryalahari, Sri Adi Shankaracharya has said that even Shiva needs the Mother to create the world:

शिवः शक्त्या युक्तो यदि भवति शक्तः प्रभवितुं

न चेदेवं देवो न खलु कुशलः स्पन्दितुमपि।

The Svetashvatara Upanishad, also mentions describes the Lord along with Goddess Uma –

"उमासहायं परमेश्वरं प्रभुं त्रिलोचनं नीलकण्ठं प्रशान्तम्"

One cannot describe the extent of Her compassion. She is an ocean of compassion.

This is explained in another name in Lalithā Sahasranāmam – "करुणारससागरा".

Maternal compassion is seen abundantly in the animal kingdom too. Markata Nyayam and Marjara Nyayam. We should pray to Sharadamba that She bless us with the heart to follow the do's and don'ts mentioned in the Shastras. We should seek Her blessings with full heart so that we don't go in the wrong direction.

993. ajñānadhvānta dīpikā

She is the lamp that dispels the darkness of ignorance. The lamp here means the source of knowledge.

The Bhagavad Gita. (10-11) says:

तेषामेवानुकम्पार्थमहमज्ञानजं तम:।

नाशयाम्यात्मभावस्थो ज्ञानदीपेन भास्वता॥11॥

teṣhām evānukampārtham,aham ajñāna-jaṁ tamaḥ

nāśhayāmyātma-bhāva-stho, jñāna-dīpena bhāsvatā

"Out of compassion to them I, residing in their heart, dispel the darkness of ignorance by the lamp of knowledge."

Many of us know the most common prayer "Tamasomo Jyotirgamaya." तमसो मा ज्योतिर्गमय, meaning 'Lead us from darkness to light' from the Brihadaranyaka Upanishad. Ambāl leads us from darkness of ignorance to the light of knowledge.

आबालगोपविदिता सर्वानुल्लङ्घ्यशासना।

   The Glory of Lalithā Sahasranāmam

श्रीचक्रराजनिलया श्रीमत्त्रिपुरसुन्दरी॥१८२॥

ābālagōpa viditā, sarvānullaṅghya śāsanā ।

śrī chakrarājanilayā, śrīmattripura sundarī ॥ 182 ॥

994. ābālagōpa viditā

Ābālam means including children, gopa means cowherds (gopa also means a protector or a female guardian) and vidita means known, understood, perceived. Ambāl is known even to children and cowherds.

Bala, Brahma, etc., gopa, the protector, i.e. Sadashiva; or Balagopa, Krsna; the meaning is Ambāl is known to everyone from Sadas'iva, Vishnu down to children.

The nāma means that She is perceived by the highest level of divinity to the lowest level of human existence, children.

Śrī Rudram (I.8) says, *utainam gopā adrśan, adrśan udahāryah* which means 'keepers of cows and bearers of water have seen Him.'

995. sarvānullanghya śāsanā

Whose commands are never disobeyed. It's like in the army where none can disobey the command of a superior officer.

But Bhāskararāya questions, it may be asked, since 'familiarity breeds contempt,' when it is known to each person that he himself is Devi, will not her command be ignored?

The following verse name is the reply to the question. Sarva (all) referring to Brahma, Vishnu, etc. Acharya in Saundarya Lahari. (Verse 24), says

त्रयाणां देवानां त्रिगुणजनितानां तव शिवे

भवेत् पूजा पूजा तव चरणयोर्या विरचिता।

"Brahma creates the Universe, Vishnu protects it, and Rudra destroys it, I annihilate all these three as well as Shiva. And finally, under thy orders indicated by the movement of thy creeper-like brows, Sadasiva approves of the same."

996. śrī chakrarājanilayā

Abiding in the Royal Sri Chakra.

Sri Chakra, consisting of Bindu, triangle, etc. It is said, "Sri Chakra is the body of Shiva and Devi." The meaning is

just as the Jiva resides in the body so they reside in the Sri Chakra.

The Shri Chakram depicts the advaitic identity of Shiva and Shakti. That is why the two kinds of Chakras of Shiva and Shakti are intertwined. The (four) triangles with the apex upward are known as Shiva cakras and the (five) triangles with apex downward are known as Shakti Chakras. The angles at which these intersect, the lotus petals on the outer corridors, the circular lines, the square design at the outermost, all have specific prescriptions; these are given in Soundarya Lahari Shloka 11.

997. śrīmattripura sundarī

The divine Tripurasundari.

The wife of Tripurasundara, Paramasiva whose body has the three, BrahmaVishnu and Rudra.

The Kalika Purana says, "By the will of the Pradhana the body of Shiva became triple.

Then the upper part of Maheshvara became Brahma with five faces, four arms, and whose body had the color of the pericarp of the lotus. His middle part became Vishnu of the blue color, having one face, four arms, bearing the conch, disc. club and lotus. The lower part became Rudra having five faces, four arms and the color of a white cloud and the moon as a crest jewel. As these three Puras are in him, he is called Tripura."

श्रीशिवा शिवशक्त्यैक्यरूपिणी ललिताम्बिका।

एवं श्रीललिता देव्या नाम्नां साहस्रकं जगुः॥

śrī śivā, śivaśaktyaikya rūpiṇī, lalitāmbikā।

ēvaṃ śrīlalitādēvyā nāmnāṃ sāhasrakaṃ jaguḥ॥183॥

998. śrī śivā- The Divine Shiva, meaning auspicious

999. śivaśaktyaikya rūpinī

The union of Shiva and Shakti.

Ambāl's roopam (called Saamarasya Roopam) is the essence of Shiva and Shakti together. There are many comparisons to illustrate their unity- like Thailam tilathiva, sesame seeds and oil, Chandrasya Chandrikeveyam, moon and moonlight, Bhaskarasya Ushnatheyavam, sun and heat and so on. None of these can be separated from each other.

Again, coming back to the very first verse of Soundarya Lahari, Adi Sankara says:

शिवःशक्त्यायुक्तोयदिभवतिशक्तःप्रभवितुं

नचेदेवंदेवोनखलुकुशलःस्पन्दितुमपि।

अतस्त्वाम्आराध्यांहरि-हर-विरिन्चादिभिरपि

प्रणन्तुंस्तोतुंवाकथ-मक्रतपुण्यःप्रभवति॥

sivah saktya yukto yadi bhavati saktah prabhavitum

na ced evam devo nakhalu kusalah spanditum api

atastvam aradhyam hari hara virincadhibhir api

pranantum stotum va katham akrtapunyah Prabhavati

Only when Shiva is united with Shakti, He becomes able to manifest Himself.

Otherwise, He cannot even move. Nakhalu kushalah - is not capable indeed

Spanditumapi - even to move. How then could anyone who has no merit -Akritapunya- be able to bow to, or even praise One such as you, adored by Vishnu, Shiva and Brahma.

Adi Sankara combines the beauty of Shiva and Shakti to share with us in Soundarya Lahari - the "Waves of Beauty."

In this very first verse, He emphasizes the necessity of thinking of Shiva and Shakti as one and only unitive content which is called Absolute Beauty. They are not functioning separately but form one unified non-dual function here. When Shiva is not united with Shakti, he has no function at all.

Some commentators say if 'e' is taken out of Shiva, he becomes a shava - a dead body when he is not united with Shakti.

There is in this verse a reference to the three gods: *Harihara virinchadhibhir api*- Brahma, Vishnu and Shiva, who have three distinct functions to perform within the totality of the field in which Shiva and Shakti are together.

This verse adores the Supreme Mother, who is ever compassionate, carrying out all the activities to sustain the universe. Those who have good karmas accrued over past births alone become capable of seeking Her through various forms of Her worship.

When it is not easy for Brahmā, Vishnu and Purānic Shiva to worship Her, the kind of good karmas one needs to worship Her through Śrīvidyā Upāsana is subtly explained in this verse.

Bhāskararāya quotes the Vāyavīya-saṃhitā that says, "By the will of S'iva, the Supreme S'akti becomes one with the S'iva-Tattva. Again, she manifests at the beginning of creation like oil from the oil grain." Here 'Union' means the supreme equality, the being absolutely without difference, The Shaura Samhita. says, "The Shakti which is separate from Brahman is not different from Brahman itself. Such being the case it is only called Shakti (as separate) by the ignorant. It is impossible to distinguish the difference, O wise one, between the Shakti and the possessor of Shakti."

The Valmiki Ramayana, also says: "As there is only one movement of air, only one Odhyana-Pitha (in the world), and only one manifested Cit Shakti, also, there is only one Union (of Shiva and Shakti)."

Or Shiva, the Shivachakras, Shakti, the Shaktichakras, Aikya, Union. Brahmānda. Purana says, "In the triangle Bindu must be united, the eight-angled one is to be united with the eight-petalled lotus...He who knows the necessary relation between the parts belonging to Shiva and the parts belonging to Shakti in the Srichakra is the real knower of the chakra." We will talk a little more about SriChakra as it is symbolic of Shiva Shakti Ikyam. (based on Deivathin Kural of Kanchi Mahaperiyava).

In Sri Chakra, there are nine chakras, triangles- Four of them pointing upwards called Shiva Chakras, And Five of them pointing downwards called Shakti Chakras. Soundarya lahari Verse 11 starting with चतुर्भिः श्रीकण्ठैः शिव युवतिभिः पञ्चभिपि describes them fully.

In this sloka (# 11), the Shri Chakram (also called the Shri Yantram) is described. The very mention of 'Shri Vidyā Pujā' implies the Pujā' of Shri Chakram. Every deity has a Yantram exclusively associated with it. But those who do Shiva Pujā' and or Vishnu Pujā' do not usually keep the corresponding Yantrams in the Pujā'. Maybe in temples under the various altars of the deities the corresponding Yantrams would have been formally installed. But in households where Shiva or Vishnu Pujā' is done only the Bana lingam or the Salagramam is kept, but not the Yantram. In the panchayatana Pujā' which includes worship of Ambāl one keeps the stone called 'svarNa-rekhā'-Shilā". But when you worship Ambāl alone, you don't keep that 'Shilā' but only the Shri Chakram is kept.

In some places along with the Chakram, an image with hands and feet may also be kept.

The regimen of worship for any deity has both 'mantra' and 'Yantra' associated with it. A certain sequence of sounds repeated often and often gets the beatification of the presence of that devatā (divinity) prescribed by it. Just as each devatā has a physical form with limbs, so also each devatā has a form

                    The Glory of Lalithā Sahasranāmam

in a stringed sequence of sounds. It is called the sound-form, just as the recitation of mantras aims at the mantra-form.

In addition, there is the Yantra-form for each devatā'. The form has lines, triangles, enclosures, circular or otherwise; these are not just geometrical figures. Each of them has a meaning and significance.

They have extraordinary power. Each Yantram is set to absorb and bring into focus the paramātmā in the form of that devatā. In addition to the repeated mental recitation of the mantra, one does Puja to the Yantram also. Within the triangles of the Yantras and other enclosures, the seed-syllables (bIja-aksharas) corresponding to the mantra pertaining to the devata would be inscribed. The very devatā that is the life of an idol with arms and feet is also considered to be brought alive in the corresponding Yantram,

In fact, the Yantram is even more comprehensive; for it includes the native residence of the devatā and all its accessory deities within itself.

The Mother Goddess, whom we call ambaal, has many forms like Meenakshi, durgā, Bhuvaneshvari, Shāradāmbikā etc. Each of these has its own Yantram. But it is very common that even the worshippers of these forms do only the Shri Chakra Puja, rather than the Puja of the murti (form). This is so not only in houses, but in temples also. Famous durgā temples have only Shri Chakra installed therein. Sringeri has Shāradāmbikā as the main Murti; however, the Yantra Puja is for Shri Chakram. All this goes to show the importance of the Shri Chakram.

Lines, circles, squares, figures formed by these – all these configured into a Chakra along with a centre point (madhya-bindu), is called a Yantram. Only such a design has the power to bring into focus the power of the particular devatā – in fact it is an infinite power –and so may be called a 'Divine Design'. (This is Mahaperiyava's own word). These designs collect and absorb divine energy and have the power to radiate that energy.

In the Shri Chakra, the central portion is circular. There are nine triangles there. They criss cross one another, thus producing forty-three triangles. The central dot is also considered to be one triangle. Together the triangles number forty-four. These forty-four triangles are classified into six Avaranas. The straightforward meaning of this word 'Avaranas' is 'what hides.

Here it should be taken to mean track, corridor, row, or prakara in Sanskrit. If several people crowd around one individual, the latter is naturally 'hidden'. So, they form an Avaranam around him. The central dot is also taken as one Avaranam just as it is taken also as a triangle. In fact, around it the other forty-three triangles constitute five Avaranas. Together with it we talk of six Avaranas. Outside of these six Avaranas and forty-four triangles, there are three rounds or corridors. They constitute three more Avaranas and thus we have nine Avaranas in all.

Muthuswami Dikshidar's 'nava-Avarana' compositions in music are well-known.

The Shastras describe and enunciate who lives in what Avarana, what is the principle involved, who is the adhi-devata, what kind of anugraha (Grace) they can bestow, what mudra is to be shown to them and so on. The compositions of Dikshidar go through all this in brief.

Out of the outermost three Avaranas (rounds) of the total nine, the two inners are made up of lotus petals arranged in two circles. The ninth Avarana is a design looking like three compound walls; but now it is not a circular structure but of square design. The whole thing is a unique design with an infinite divine potential.

Her five triangles represent the Pancha bhutas (five elements). She holds five flowery arrows, noose, goad and bow. The noose or Paasam is attachment, the goad or Angusam is revulsion, the bow is the mind, and the flowery arrows are the five sense objects. Their union is harmony or samarasa.

The nine interlocking triangles form forty-three small triangles each housing a presiding deity associated with aspects of existence. Its 43 triangles are surrounded by a circle of eight petals that, in turn, is surrounded by a 16-petalled circle. The Sri Chakra is also known as Sri Yantra or the nav chakra because it can also be seen as having nine levels. The yantra represents the union of masculine and feminine divine. It is worshipped since thousands of years though its origin is unknown.

But one must be careful.

A Yantra means that every bit of it, whether a line or a circle or an angle, has to be of the right size and proportion as prescribed. It cannot err even a little this way or that way. Just as a mantra, with a wrong incantation, produces contrary effects, so also a small mistake in the design of the Yantra can cause havoc. In the Shri yantra again, if the apex of the central triangle faces west instead of east, as it should, results can just be the opposite. So, when you sit opposite to it for worship, the apex should be on the side nearer to you and not on the farther side. One has to be really more careful with the Puja of a Yantram than that of an idol (vigraha), in terms of the ritualistic do's and don'ts

It is not enough to just wish for great observances. We should be able to observe the shastric injunctions correctly.

Only then we will reap the right benefits. Certainly, Shri Chakra has been eulogized in the Shastras to the sky. But the very same Shastras have also prescribed a certain regimen for such Puja.

A Yantra is not just the residing seat of a devatā; it is the devatā itself. It is not just a representation, or a copy. It is the presentation of the devatā and not a re-presentation. More so in the case of Ambāl. For, Her Divine Presence is very special in Her Yantra. It is because of this that Ambāl Puja is mostly done to Her Yantra than to Her most beautiful physical form.

Kanchi Mahaperiva says that The Shri Chakra is not just Her residence. The Shri Chakra is Ambāl Herself!

When She is in the Meru peak, the Avaranas are piled up peak upon peak in a three-dimensional manner. It will be in the form of an upright cone. Such a three-dimensional configuration of Shri Chakra is called 'Meru-prastāram'.

People call it just 'Maha Meru' colloquially. When the Chakra is two dimensional it is said to be 'Bhu-prastāram'.

A mixture of the two, where the beginning Avaranas rise higher and higher, but later the latter AvaraNas are all in the same plane, is called 'ardha-Meru' (ardha means 'semi'). A Purna-Meru is that which has all the Avaranas in the Meru-prastara style.

In Sringeri, Sharadamba is seated on the Meru of the Sriyantra, on a golden throne, inside the garbha-griha. In Kanchipuram and in Tiruvidaimarudur MukAmbāl sannadhi, what you find is Purna-Meru. In Mangadu, it is ardha-meru. In the Kamakoshtam at Kanchipuram it is Bhu-prastāram.

The Shri Chakra, Shri Vidya, Shri Mata, Shri Puram all pertain to the Devi, the Mother Goddess, Lalita Tripurasundari. The prefix ShrI is the prefix usually given for respect and has no extra connotation of Lakshmi, the Goddess of Prosperity and Wealth.

The Chakras and the mantras associated with other devatās are distinguished by their name itself carrying the name of the devatā – as in, Shiva-Chakram, Sudarshana-Yantram, etc. Only in the case of Lalita Tripurasundari, the Chakram, the Yantram are known as The Chakram, The Yantram, The Mantram.

All this is not to be read or studied like reading fiction or for academic interest. They must be seriously learnt straight from a Guru.

We all worship Sri Sharadālmbāl installed in Sringeri. What is the meaning of Sharada?

Kanchi Mahaperiva explains. Shloka 15 of Ananda Lahari starts with the word Sharat-jyotsnāl-shuddham: who is as pure and white as the autumnal moonlight. The word 'sharad' becomes very apt when one refers to Goddess Sarasvati. It is in sharad-ritu (the autumnal season) that we do Puja to Sarasvati. So, She is called Shārada.

Adi Sankaracharya had a special affinity to the Shārada. name. Sarasvati was very important to him because we know he reached the peak of excellence in scholarship. In North India there is the custom of referring to Shārada. as Sārada. It means the One who graces you with the essence (sāram) of Knowledge. This may be another reason why the Acharya had an affinity toward the name and so the name of the deity he installed in Sringeri is Shāradāmbāl.

We started the Lalithā Sahasranāmam with Om SriMaata, Sri Maharajni, Srimat Simhasaneswari - representing Creation, Sustenance and Destruction, the naama Shivashakti Ikya Rupini represents Tirodanam and Anugraham thus meaning Panchakritya Parayana - the doer of five functions. ('srushtikarthri – brahmaroopa; goptri – govindaroopini; samhaarini – rudraroopa; tirodaanakari – eswari; sadaasivaa – anugrhatha; pancha krutya paraayanaa').

The Sahasranamam ends with the most appropriate and unique Naama in the next one. Now we come to the last Naama -the thousandth one in Lalithā Sahasranāmam - which itself is the name of Lalithāmbā.

1000. lalitāmbikā

Mother Lalitha.

Thus by the first three names the goddess is indicated as the creator, preserver, and destroyer of the Universe, by the next two names, she is indicated as possessing two other functions, vis., annihilation and re—manifestation which belong to no other deity, from the sixth name to the last the same deity Who-possesses these five functions was described in different ways and is indicated by the name Lalita which is her Special name and belongs to no other deity.

Lalithāmbikā: Lalita as well as Mother. She is called *Sakala Loka Janani.* She is also called Lalithā as she does 'lalanam' playing softly as we do with a baby or child. The meaning is given in the Padma Purana: "Transcending all worlds she sports (Lalate) hence she is called Lalita." 'Worlds 'means her surrounding lights or deities. 'Transcending being above their abodes in the Bindu-place. 'Sports' shines brilliantly.

The Wise say, "The word Lalithā has eight meanings, vim, brilliancy, manifestation, sweetness, depth, fixity, energy, grace, and generosity; these are the eight human qualities."

The Kama-Shastra says: Lalithā means erotic actions and tenderness; as she has all the above-mentioned qualities, she is called Lalithā.

It is also said that "You are rightly called Lalithā as you have nine divine attendants (in the Srichakra), and your bow is made of sugarcane, your arrows are flowers, and everything connected with you is lovely (Laliti)." The word Lalitha also means beautiful.

This deity according to the Padma Purana is the deity worshipped at Prayag.

॥ इति श्रीब्रह्माण्डपुराणे उत्तरखण्डे श्रीहयग्रीवागस्त्यसंवादे श्रीललिता सहस्रनाम स्तोत्र कथनं सम्पूर्णम्॥

॥ iti śrī brahmāṇḍapurāṇē, uttarakhaṇḍē, śrī hayagrīvāgastya saṃvādē, śrīlalitā sāhasranāma stōtra kathanaṃ sampurnam ॥

Thus, Hayagrīva completed the recitation of one thousand nāma-s to sage Agasthya. In this Lalitha Sahasranāma there are exactly one thousand nāma-s.

May Sri Lalithambā shower all with Her divine blessings.

While every effort has been made to ensure the accuracy of this book, some errors may have gone unnoticed. If you come across any inaccuracies or have suggestions for improvement, please don't hesitate to reach out. Your feedback is invaluable and will help enhance future editions.

Thank you for your understanding and support!